ABOUT THE AUTHOR

Dr. Belson was born and educated in Australia. After serving in the R.A.A.F. in North Africa and Europe, he took his Bachelor degree at the University of Sydney. In 1950 he joined the Audience Research Department of the B.B.C., where he was responsible for a wide range of audience research. This included the development of research techniques for assessing program efficiency, studies of the impact of television, and studies of projected audiences as a basis for program planning. His Ph.D. (University of London) was completed while he was at the B.B.C. and was based primarily on mass media research.

In 1958 he left the B.B.C. to join the London School of Economics and Political Science. There, as Head of the Survey Research Centre, he is responsible for testing and developing methods of social and business research, and for a major series of studies of juvenile delinquency.

Dr. Belson has lectured and published widely about television and the other mass media and about the methods of research. His book "Studies in Readership" was awarded Book of the Year by the European Society for Opinion Surveys and Market Research. He holds the first Gold Medal of the Market Research Society in Britain and the Thomson Gold Medal for Media Research (1963).

THE IMPACT OF TELEVISION

The Impact of Television

METHODS AND FINDINGS
IN PROGRAM RESEARCH

By

WILLIAM A. BELSON, B.A., Ph.D.

ARCHON BOOKS
HAMDEN, CONNECTICUT

© 1967 *by W. A. Belson*

First published in the United States of America 1967
Reprinted 1968

Archon Books
The Shoe String Press Inc.
60 Connolly Parkway
Hamden, Connecticut 06514

Made and Printed in Great Britain by
Fletcher & Son Ltd, Norwich

Preface

Subject matter and presentation

This book is presented in five sections. The first section deals with the use of research to provide information about the population's interests, attitudes, values, state of knowledge, and availability for viewing. With this information, broadcasters may more efficiently gear their programs to people. Such enquiries are referred to here as *planning* studies. The second section of the book is concerned with the degree to which informative programs can be understood by the people for whom they are prepared. This is often referred to as program *comprehensibility*. Section III deals with the *effects* of specific programs or series of programs and Section IV, which is quite large, is about television's *social impact*. Section V presents the case for making greater use of television research, and suggests ways of doing this. At the end of the book, there is a substantial list of reports and texts relevant to one or another of Sections I—IV.

In each of Sections I—IV, the pattern of presentation is the same. The first chapter in a section is a statement of the case for doing work of the kind featured in it. The chapter immediately after it gives a detailed description of a recommended technique for doing such work. Then come several chapters, each of which is a report of an enquiry based upon that technique. These reports are meant to illustrate the use of the technique as well as to present research findings of value and interest in their own right.

Those for whom the book was prepared

I have prepared this book for readers of different backgrounds. For students and teachers of mass communication, I hope that it will provide useful information about the efficiency and the impact of television, and that it will encourage some to conduct research of the kind I have described. It is meant also for those program directors and producers whose difficult task it is to provide broadcasting services which are entertaining and interesting and which are nonetheless in conformity with the long term welfare of the viewing and listening public. I had also in mind, social and government administrators interested in the efficiency and the standards of broadcasting services, educationists who want to reach the many and *be understood* by them, teachers who want to know what

v

television is doing to people. Parts of the book are, I believe, particularly relevant to the needs of manufacturers, market researchers and members of advertising agencies, all of whom are professionally interested in the efficiency of television as an advertising medium. Above all, I wanted to reach the general reader interested in knowing about the nature of television's impact upon society and about the different ways in which this impact can be measured and controlled. Finally, I hope very much that the book will come to the notice of those whose job it is to do research for broadcasting, because I believe that the techniques described and illustrated here will be of value to them.

The origin of the studies reported in the book

Many of the reports presented herein are based upon research conducted under my direction when I was a member of the Audience Research Department of the British Broadcasting Corporation. One of the others, the study of audience availability, was a BBC project in which I had no part. Another, the one dealing with television's effects on the interests and initiative of viewers, I conducted as an academic project with part of the financial support coming from the BBC and the Central Research Fund of the University of London. The report dealing with the impact of television upon the reading and buying of newspapers and magazines was conducted in a business setting, and was financed fully by the London Press Exchange Limited.

Where and when the research was done
and the number of people taking part

Much of the research was conducted in the broad area of Greater London with its population of over eight million people. However, several of the enquiries were carried out in additional population centres in England, and the availability study was based on a national sample. In all, over 21,000 members of the public took part in the reported enquiries, along with a great many interviewing personnel. The first of the reported enquiries was completed in 1952, and the last of them in 1963. The value to the reader of the earlier reports is, in my opinion, no less for the passing of time. This is partly because they are presented as examples of certain research techniques in action, and partly because they provide information of a fairly basic kind. Moreover, very little of what is in this book has had anything more than limited release. Quite a lot of it has not previously been published at all.

The choice of reports for presentation

All but one of the enquiries presented was conducted under the writer's direction and all were selected as illustrative of one or another of the techniques featured in the book. The bibliography at the end provides an extended list of research publications by many different people, all such publications having at least some bearing upon the subject matter of the book. Some are reports to which reference has been made directly in the text itself, some provide reading on related issues, and a few are further examples of work based upon one or another of the four research procedures which I have highlighted.

Acknowledgments

Both in the research enquiries around which this book is written and in bringing the book to publication, I had help of many different kinds from many people. I am very glad to record my indebtedness and my gratitude:

to Mr. R. J. E. Silvey, Head of the Audience Research Department of the British Broadcasting Corporation, for giving me the opportunity to work in British television research in the first place, and for his permission to base various of my chapters on work which was done within his department;

to my former colleagues in the BBC, Mrs. Mary Adams, Mr. S. W. Bonarjee, Mr. B. P. Emmett, Mrs. G. Wyndham Goldie, Mr. Andrew Miller Jones, Mr. Asher Lee, Mr. F. H. Littman, Mr. J. Scupham, Miss M. S. Withers;

to social scientists serving on advisory and supervisory committees of the BBC, Baroness Wootton of Abinger, Emeritus Professor Sir Cyril Burt, Professor D. W. Harding, Dr. M. G. Kendall, the late Professor Rex Knight, Emeritus Professor C. A. Mace, Emeritus Professor T. H. Pear, Professor A. Rodger, Professor W. J. H. Sprott, Dr. R. H. Thouless, Professor P. E. Vernon;

to Dr. M. Abrams, Mr. J. R. Bittleston, Dr. Leo Bogart, Mr. A. Bristow, Dr. T. E. Coffin, Dr. J. Eliasberg, Sir Harold Evans, Mr. B. Groombridge, Mr. C. Golby, Mr. Harry Henry, Dr. J. D. Hundleby, Dr. J. T. Klapper, Mr. C. Mayhew, M. P., Mr. P. Smulian, Mr. E. Whitley, Miss J. Morton Williams, Mr. Aubrey Wilson;

to the London Press Exchange Limited for the generous sponsorship of one of the enquiries reported herein; to the Central Research Fund of the University of London for financial help in another enquiry; to the members of the Reference Library of the BBC; to the editors of academic and business journals for permission to present material of mine which they have published;

to Miss E. P. Briaris, Miss L. E. Heggie, Miss J. Mason, Miss S. R. Merchant, Miss H. M. Skordis, Miss P. M. Winser for help of many different kinds in the preparation of the book.

I would like to thank the many people, in London and elsewhere, who have provided or gathered or analysed the information on which the book is based: over 21,000 members of the adult public, many interviewers, and many analysts. It is exciting to design research and to see the results: but in between these two stages comes a great deal of work and of care by many people, and without this nothing worthwhile is achieved. For my own labours, the book is enough, but how shall I ever thank properly the thousands who went through the survey interviews, or the thousands who came specially into town and there helpfully and cheerfully went through questions and tests to assist in the work being done? I am deeply grateful to them.

Finally, I want to say that this book would not have been written without the help of my wife, Peg. She worked with me, through long-late evenings, in the course of project planning, the development of measuring instruments, and the writing of the book.

Responsibility for the views expressed

In the reports of *research*, I have done all I can to keep out statements of opinion. This applies also to my descriptions of research techniques. However, opinion certainly does enter into the four chapters in which I have tried to describe the case for doing certain kinds of work. These are chapters 2, 12, 16 and parts of chapter 20. Opinions are also present in the last chapter ("Television Research: Past and Future") in which I have tried to identify the reasons for present day under-use of research in relation to television and to suggest ways in which this situation might be changed. All opinions expressed in the book are my own and for them I take full responsibility.

W. A. BELSON

Contents

SECTION III: MEASURING THE EFFECTS OF PARTICULAR
PROGRAMS

SECTION IV: THE SOCIAL IMPACT OF TELEVISION

SECTION V: TELEVISION RESEARCH: PAST AND FUTURE

[1]

Research in the service of television

The proper management of television calls for a considerable knowledge of the viewing public and of the impact of programs upon that public. Occasionally, a decision based largely upon guesswork will succeed, perhaps even brilliantly. However, in the long term, decision making by those in television, whatever their roles, will be good and successful only if it is based upon the relevant facts: facts about the values, the interests and the knowledge of viewers; facts about the sizes of audiences and about audience opinion of programs seen; facts about success in communicating information and ideas; facts about the way programs affect people. From one situation to another, the nature and the number of the facts that are needed will vary, but to act without them is to invite at least some degree of failure.

In television, the importance of having the relevant facts is emphasized by the pervasiveness of the medium, its social and industrial potential, the time the public gives it and the high cost of running it. Re-starting after the war, television was by the end of 1964, in about 90% of the homes of Britain and its programs were available to 99% of the people of the whole of the United Kingdom wherever they might be. The amount of time given to television by viewers has risen steadily from a weekly average of 13 hours per adult viewer in 1953 to over 18 hours a week at the present time. At peak hours it has become common for audiences of many millions to be watching the one program at the one time. Mass audiences enjoy television, relax with it, become tense with it. To millions, it presents not only the world's classics, nature studies, advertisements, thoughtful discussions, programs about health, economics, politics, but also the details of crime and numerous portrayals of violence. Its programs are watched by the young as well as the old and often the young watch it well into the night. In 1964 over eighty million pounds[a] was spent on television advertising, and the cost of running the television service that year was over seventy million pounds.[b] In America, the pattern of growth and of penetration was the same, though it occurred more

[a] This amount includes television advertisement duty.
[b] For both BBC and the Independent Television Companies.

rapidly, and the expenditure of money on the medium was enormous. Clearly decisions about how this medium is run and about what is shown on it are of considerable importance to the whole nation. Accordingly it is most desirable that every reasonable effort be made to provide those in television with the information necessary for making good decisions.

A form of information which is necessary for decision making in television, and which in fact is provided in plenty, is the *size of audience* for the different programs. Such information can tell the broadcaster if he is reaching the proportion and the sector of the viewing public he is aiming at and whether or not the program is successfully competing with its opposition for audience size. On the basis of this information it may well be that the broadcaster will take the program off the air or leave it on. Audience size also influences the amount charged for television advertisements. In the live theatre and in the cinema, a measure of audience size is readily available through box office records. In television however, the audience is quite unseen and special research has to be undertaken to determine the number of people viewing any particular program. This type of information is gathered by research organisations throughout the world and is in widespread use.

However, size of audience, alone, is not enough if the broadcaster is to be efficient and is to make responsible decisions. He must also have information about *audience reaction* to his own and to opposition programs. He must know whether or not, and to what degree, the viewers like a program, find it interesting, approve of it. Such information, collected systematically, may well make clear to a broadcaster why it is that a particular program failed to attract a large audience in the first place or why it has begun to lose its audience. It may alert him to public dissatisfaction with certain parts or aspects of a program which otherwise has a fairly high degree of audience appeal. It may tell him that people are growing tired of an old favourite and that they go on watching it now only because the alternative program is worse. With this sort of information, the planner can make decisions which are both responsible and competitive, about *what* to change or remove. Moreover he will be in a position to learn from his mistakes, rather than guessing wrongly about what went wrong and making the same mistake all over again later on. Though this type of information has been collected and used by some for many years, this is by no means the universal position of those who plan and design programs. Many try to make do without it and their decisions are likely to be the worse for this.

Admirable and important as they are, both these classes of information represent a form of 'wisdom after the event'. In television in particular, it is highly desirable to avoid unnecessary mistakes in the first place. One research procedure which can do much towards this is what has been called the 'planning' or the 'charting' enquiry. Thus surveys may be carried out to chart those of the characteristics of viewers which are relevant to good program planning — for example, their interests, their values, their tastes. It is hard to see how broadcasters can properly plan in the absence of such information, though some certainly appear to try to do so. Planning studies can also make a great deal of difference to the design of specific programs, for they can be made to reveal what people know already about the program's proposed subject matter, the main areas of their ignorance, their present attitudes in relation to that subject, and so on. This sort of research is certainly feasible but relatively little of it is done. In its absence mistakes in terms of content and design can be made all too easily.

There is another form of information which is very much under-supplied. This concerns the degree to which viewers *understand* what is presented to them through television. People of differing abilities and backgrounds are offered, through television, the same pictures and the same statements. It is hard to see how all of them can be expected to understand equally well, and there is evidence that some fare quite badly. Commercial material is no exception. Failures of this kind, whether for commercial or non-commercial material, are wasteful. They spring partly from the fact that many broadcasters do not speak or think in the terms of their viewers. But over and above this, communication through the mass media is a process more difficult and more failure-prone than many users of these media seem to think. The special value of studies of program understanding is that these can alert broadcasters to the occurrence of failures. If such studies are properly conducted, they can also tell broadcasters a great deal about the *causes* of failures — things such as the use of over-technical language, too great a concentration of unfamiliar words, complex statements, statements that are confused. Long term efficiency is dependent upon an alertness to the possibility of communication failure, and upon a build-up of a body of knowledge about the causes of such failure.

Another important form of enquiry — and one which is fundamental to responsible broadcasting — involves the measurement of the social and other effects of particular programs or of series of programs. People frequently postulate, in public or in private, what they think these effects may be, and the views that different people express are not necessarily in agreement. Thus a crime series featuring tough police action may well be said by some to be making people less well disposed towards the police, whereas others may say that it helps to teach young people that crime does not pay. A series of programs described by its producer as social satire may be praised by some as sharpening public thinking about accepted values and condemned by others as corrupting those values. Such opinions are frequently expressed in the absence of meaningful evidence either way. Though it is quite possible to conduct research to find out what a program is in fact doing to its viewers, this step is rarely taken. Instead, it may well be that a program is removed or retained on the basis of the amount and the nature of influential comment that is made.

Until recently, the effects of television on family life, on the use of leisure, on health, and so on, were frequently talked about at the same speculative level. It was said that television was killing sport and that it was reducing such things as attendance at the cinema, the buying of newspapers, the taking of holidays, attendance at adult evening classes, and a great many other things. Indeed, wherever changes seemed to be taking place, television viewing was quite likely to be named as the culprit. It is highly desirable that speculation about these and other matters should be given publicity and a good hearing. However, it is also desirable that this speculative phase be followed as quickly as possible by technically competent research to find out what television is in fact doing. Both viewers and responsible broadcasters would be better off with *knowledge* about such matters.

There is no dearth at all of *size of audience* information or of the will to use it. Whereas information about *audience appreciation* of programs is by no means universally employed in program planning and design, it seems that the case for collecting it and for using it in making decisions is becoming more widely recognised. By contrast, *'charting'* studies for broad planning purposes are not often made, and those for the development of specific programs are rare indeed. Nor has much been done over recent years by way of measuring the *effects of individual programs* or of assessing program *comprehensibility*: In fact there is a considerable imbalance in the distribution of program research.

There are various reasons for this neglect of planning studies, of comprehension testing and of enquiries into the effects of exposure to program material. One of the reasons is that the usefulness of the neglected forms of research has not been properly presented and promoted to the television industry. One must remember too, that the *size of audience* measure has long dominated management thinking. Nor have many academic researchers, in Britain at least, become sufficiently involved in television research to have any interest in conducting these particular kinds of enquiries. But perhaps the most important reason of all for the present situation is that the techniques for conducting any of these three kinds of research have not yet been sufficiently documented and demonstrated for them to be understood and brought into general practice.

In presenting *The Impact of Television*, it was my hope that I might contribute at least a little towards remedying present deficiencies. To this end, I have tried to set out the case for conducting research of the neglected kind, have described techniques for carrying it out and have presented reports of a number of enquiries which demonstrate the techniques in action. I hope too, that these reports will be of interest in their own right, for all of them are about the *impact of television*.

CONDUCTING RESEARCH FOR PROGRAM PLANNING

An Introductory Note

Chapter 2 presents the case for conducting 'planning' studies of different kinds, and points to the ways in which they can serve the program planner and production staff. Chapter 3 describes, in working detail, various techniques for conducting such studies. Chapters 4 to 11 consist of reports of various 'planning' studies which were carried out through one or another of the research techniques described in Chapter 3. Each is meant to illustrate a 'planning' study in action and so to provide practical help to others aiming to do similar work. Chapters 4 to 11 are also meant to provide research findings likely to be of interest in their own right.

Of the eight illustrative chapters, Chapters 4 to 6 describe enquiries meant to provide information for *general* planning purposes, whereas the enquiries reported in in Chapters 7 to 11 were conducted to help in the development of particular programs or series of programs. References in this section to articles and books will be found in alphabetical order on pages 370–375.

[2]

The place and the function of the planning study

For a television broadcasting service to operate efficiently, a great deal must be known about its audience. Television broadcasting occurs within a social setting in which there are, at any one time, differing patterns of behaviour, a wide range of values and interests, sectional differences in morality, a great range both in knowledge and in abilities. Those who determine program policy and program content cannot afford to be for long out of step with the complexities of this setting. To a marked degree they constitute the framework against which the program service must work out its relative success or its relative failure.

Detailed information about the viewing population may be required for the development of single programs or for general programming tactics. A planning study, as I use the term, is nothing more than a research inquiry designed to provide this kind of information. If broadcasters knew all about the people for whom they were preparing programs, then planning studies would not be necessary. But in fact they do not have anything like this sort of knowledge and they could hardly be expected to have it. Many broadcasters are drawn from some special sector of society; all too often, a specialized education has separated them even further from the general population. Moreover they are for the most part extremely busy people and with the best will in the world they could not gather and carry within themselves that great store of knowledge about the habits, the attitudes, the wants and the state of knowledge of the public which is so necessary for efficient programming. This special and difficult position of the broadcaster is a central point in this book and to it I shall be returning again and again. It constitutes much of the reason for carrying out research for broadcasting and it is a particularly important reason for conducting 'planning studies'.

Different kinds of planning studies can be carried out and a description of these is given in this chapter. The description starts with those kinds of 'planning' studies which are meant to serve broadcasting in the broader sense and it then goes on to those which are meant to be of assistance in the detailed preparation of specific programs.

RESEARCH FOR THE OVERALL PLANNING OF STATION OUTPUT

The availability of people for listening or viewing
Information about the availability of people for watching or listening
to programs is fairly basic to the broad planning of a program service.
Availability is not a simple matter of whether people of specified backgrounds are at home: it is also a matter of what these people ordinarily do
at home at different times of the day or evening and what this implies
about their mental availability and their receptivity to different forms of
program output.

At what times are people retiring or wanting to retire? What proportion
of household heads in different occupational groups are home by 6 p.m.
or 6.30 p.m. or 7 p.m.? Is 8 p.m. about right for entertainment material of
a particular kind to be presented on television? Are household chores
sufficiently finished by some particular time in the evening for the period
immediately after this to be regarded as peak hour for advertising purposes? In this particular connection, we must bear in mind the fact that
advertising breaks are at present frequently used by housewives to get back
to unfinished chores, or to put the kettle on, or to do some other short
household job. What time or times in the morning would be best for presenting radio material requiring careful attention? At what times during
the day are housewives 'putting their feet up' and what kinds of program
would best match their moods and wants at this time? Are rather young
children still up and about at the time when essentially adult programs are
put on? These are just a few of the questions about physical and mental
availability which must be answered if programs are to be properly timed.
It is not enough to go by the figures for program sizes in the past because
these figures don't tell us enough about the satisfactoriness of timing with
respect to such things as attention level and efficient communication. Nor
do they tell us enough about the number of people who did not watch or
listen because the timing was wrong.

It is obvious that competition between services will bring new factors
into the situation. Thus a planner may feel that a program best suited to
presentation at 9.30 p.m. will have to go on at 7.25 p.m. because it is his
best counter to a rival's program starting at 7.30 p.m. Nonetheless a regard
for efficiency and for public service makes it essential that broadcasting as
a whole be guided by an awareness of the basic facts of the public's availability.

Serving people's interests
If broadcasters aim to cater for the existing interests of a population,
they need to know the kinds of things that poeple are in fact interested in.
The range of these interests is considerable, though the number of people
who follow one as distinct from another varies from the tens of millions to
the relatively few, as illustrated in Table 1.

This sort of information has not been generally available and yet decisions have constantly to be made as to what should be the subject matter

TABLE 1

*The 'followings' for some selected interests**

	QUITE or VERY Interested
Interior decoration of the home	54%
Keeping a pet	37%
Football (following or going or playing)	31%
Dancing (going or watching)	23%
Photography	12%
Sailing	7%
Sculpture (going to see it or doing it)	4%

* Figures drawn from the full array for London adults (Summer) as presented in Chapter 4.

of a program and as to how much time should be given to one interest as distinct from another. For instance, how should time be apportioned between cricket, rugby, soccer, motor-racing, show-jumping, athletics? How should it be apportioned between Shakespearian drama, opera, popular records, adventure, wild life in Britain, the way of life abroad? There are a great many of these different interests. A programmer who does not have access to empirically derived data concerning the forms these interests take and the size of the following of each is in danger of making quite a lot of unsound judgments. The specialized background of many broadcasters seems to the writer to increase the likelihood of this happening, and to strengthen the case for providing planners with systematic information about what the public's interests actually are.

In no way would the provision of such information preclude an attempt by a broadcaster to increase the following of some interest. In fact an awareness of the proportion of the population so far following it and of the different main forms which that interest tends to take could help him to do his proselytising job better and in a more responsible way than might otherwise be the case. If for instance this interest had a very small following, the broadcaster would, presumably, keep a reasonable curb upon his allocation of time to it and choose a suitable time of day for it. If the people he aimed to influence were found not to have even a rudimentary knowledge about the interest, then his approach would have to be very different from that suitable for those who were knowledgeable about it.

The advertiser is likely to be specially concerned with getting this sort of information, for through his agents he must make use of appropriate carriers or backgrounds or contexts for his advertisements. Thus he is likely to want his advertisements presented in settings which will catch the interest and attention and goodwill of the people to whom he hopes to sell his products. But is he really in a position to have this done? Does the advertiser or his agent know enough about the interests of the intended buyers for the advertisements to be constructed in this way? In many cases the answer is "no".

Charting the public's tastes in entertainment and humour

Broadly, the same sort of argument applies to the presentation of entertainment programs and of humour in particular. Does the producer know enough about the values and the laugh potential of his audience to stay 'on target' most of the time? In this regard, the producer may well get an indication from a studio audience that his outside audience is laughing too, but how will he ever know if he has really tapped the richness and the variety of the entertainment potential of his society? Could it be instead that he is only dishing out well tried mediocrity? In any case, reliance entirely upon trial and error can be a rather expensive process.

People in the entertainment profession seem to me to be in a very difficult position when it comes to performing through, or even controlling, the *television medium*. Consider the position. The *theatre* performer who has had the good fortune to play to full houses and to receive the applause of his audience will assume, quite rightly, that the performance is appreciated. Moreover he will quickly come to recognise that there are parts of the performance, especially items of humour, which are particularly liked by the theatre audience. The danger, however, is that the tastes of his *theatre* audience will not necessarily be those of the *mass audience* to which he suddenly gets access when he performs on television or radio. In a large city, a theatre can be filled night after night by people whose sum total is but a small proportion of a television audience. Moreover the theatre audience is self-selected—these people come, presumably, because what is offered seems to be to *their* particular liking.

If the successful performer is brought into a television program and acts on the assumption that the tastes and the humour of the mass audience are the same as those of his own self-selected audience, he may go seriously wrong. Nor, for obvious reasons, should he regard the reactions of a small studio audience as a safe sort of guide to mass reactions, because the studio audience too is made up of self-selected people who, moreover, may in some cases be specially encouraged to give applause.

Yet the live theatre is a major source of talent for television entertainment. What would happen, we might ask, if an entertainer had developed his ideas of what people like from his variety experience or, say, from beginnings at the Windmill theatre? The reader may care to follow this line of thinking further, relating his thoughts to some current trends in entertainment in British television.

A body of information about the public's tastes in relation to entertainment and to humour would be of considerable value to those who control entertainment programs on television or radio. Whether to try to lead taste or simply to satisfy it would be for the planners to decide, but here again the availability of relevant facts about audiences would allow broadcasters to plan and to act with that audience properly in mind. Efficiency and responsibility both demand this.

Charting the values and the moral codes of society

The broadcaster needs information also about the values and the moral codes of all parts of society — and not just that part of it from which he himself comes. How can he treat the public's values and moral codes with due respect if he does not know what they really are? It is not hard to find, in broadcasting fare, marked and frequent violation of these codes based, it would seem, either on ignorance or on a failure to care.

It is well established that a large proportion of the population sees programs with violence and sexiness in them, and it is reasonably clear that many of these people are moved by what they see and that many enjoy it. But just because people are gripped or entertained by this kind of material, it does not follow that it fits in with or nourishes the values they are trying to uphold in themselves or to develop in their children. Obviously many broadcasters care about such matters. Many are dedicated people. But have broadcasters got enough information to prevent themselves or those working for them from making wrong assumptions about the values and the moral codes of society? Indeed, has the Independent Television Authority in Britain yet got enough of this kind of information to be able properly to discharge that part of its function which is concerned with such matters[a]? Has the B.B.C. got enough of this kind of information? Have control bodies abroad got it?

Let me take this argument a step beyond that of rights and wrongs to the question of efficiency in conveying ideas to people. If a message is broadcast in the context of something which runs counter to the values and the social codes of an audience, there is a very real risk that people in the audience will reject or distort or select from it in accordance with what they feel or believe[b]. The public relations of the broadcasting organisation are also deeply involved.

The public's level of knowledge

Perhaps the greatest need of planners and of production staff is information about the basic knowledge of audiences and about those of their abilities which are called upon in understanding and storing the information presented to them. Be it in television or in radio, the *words* of a communicator convey meaning to the extent that the audience knows them too. A person's existing *level of general knowledge* determines to a marked

---

[a]   Section 3 of the Television Act of 1954 requires, amongst other things, that nothing be included in the programme "which offends against good taste or decency or is likely to encourage or to incite to crime or to lead to disorder or to be offensive to public feeling".

[b]   The literature of psychology testifies strongly to the occurrence of selecting and distorting processes [6, 31, 38, 47, 68, 98]

degree whether or not he can understand what is being said—that is, whether or not the broadcaster is talking above his head or beyond him.

Obviously such barriers to understanding are matters of degree, because people vary considerably in their general knowledge and in their word knowledge. Nonetheless, for any projected audience there is some most appropriate level at which to pitch the message and the broadcaster who is properly aware of that audience's state of knowledge has a better chance of success than the one who is without it. Unfortunately, information of this specialized kind tends not to be available, so far, in any collected and usable form.

RESEARCH FOR THE SHAPING OF SPECIFIC PROGRAMS

While a broad knowledge about the interests and the abilities and the values of society is necessary for efficient program planning on the broad front, it is rarely enough for the design of particular programs or series of programs. For these, detailed and specific information about the public's knowledge and state of mind is needed. For instance, if a producer was preparing an informative program about the way of life in India, it would pay him to find out first what people do and don't know about the subject. This would tell him where the main gaps in knowledge were, whether or not he could safely assume certain things to be known, upon what background knowledge he could hope to build. For instance, does his target audience know anything about the caste system or would this have to be explained right from the beginning before going on to the present social situation? Does his target audience know anything about the religions of India and the bearing of religion on the origins of Pakistan? Are people in the target audience—particularly the younger ones— much aware of Britain's past in India? Information about audience awareness would have to be collected especially for this particular program.

Take another example. Suppose a broadcaster was preparing for a series of programs on mental illness. If is was his intention to try to make people more tolerant towards ex-mental patients, the producer would do well, first of all, to find out if people are in fact lacking in such tolerance. If not, then he would have to think again about the whole point of trying to increase tolerance. If people *were* found to be intolerant, then he would certainly do well to find out the reasons for this so that he might avoid trying to 'sell' tolerance on the basis of something that most people would not accept.

Here is a third example. If the proposed program was intended to deal with the attitudes of the British towards Americans, then it would be essential to start by finding out what these attitudes actually are.

RESEARCH FOR PLANNING AT EITHER THE GENERAL OR THE SPECIFIC LEVEL

Program staff are most unlikely to have collected, in any incidental way, or as part of their education, information either of this general or of this specific kind. Their only dependable way of getting it is through systematic research — research for program planning.

One point about this recommendation needs to be made clear however. I am not suggesting in any way at all that research should be made to interfere unduly with the creative processes of a broadcasting service. Research should be offered and must be used simply as an *aid* in making good decisions and in avoiding bad ones. Nor do I imagine that there will ever be all the information needed at any given time, and in its absence judgements will nonetheless have to be made. Let me say too that I am not trying to enter into a controversy about whether broadcasting should attempt to serve the status quo in society or whether it should seek to lead and change people. Whichever the purpose of the system, information about the viewing and the listening public is essential. One more point about the function of 'planning' studies: they are but part of the information service which I think is needed; its other necessary facets I have referred to in Chapter 1 and in Sections II, III and IV of this volume.

[3]

The techniques for carrying out planning studies

Planning studies can be carried out through a number of different research methods. Prominent among these is the standard sample survey [93] in which people constituting a representative sample of a population are asked questions, usually in the context of a face-to-face interview. The interview ordinarily takes place in the respondent's own home or in the street, through it may on occasions be conducted elsewhere. This method is used mainly for getting people's opinions and attitudes and/or for getting information about recent behaviour of some specified kind. Another research procedure available for the *planning* study is the *large group testing* technique. With this technique, people come by invitation to some centre and there are put through various tests and/or other controlled procedures. The method is closely geared to a technique aimed at eliminating the effects of such unrepresentativeness as arises from the participants being, in a sense, volunteers. It is best used (as a tool of program planning) when standardized tests of ability or of attitude have to be carried out, and where the necessary control over the respondent would not normally be available in the respondent's own home.[a] A third method available to the planner is that in which a series of group discussions (five to eight people in a single group) is employed for the derivation of leads or ideas which may perhaps be sufficient in themselves but which are best regarded as providing guide lines for sample survey work or possibly for large group testing. Apart from such sources, the planner may derive limited but useful data about the population from official statistics.

What follows in this chapter is a selective descriptive of these sources, brief and general where the method is already well documented in other texts and detailed where it is not.

OFFICIAL SOURCES

Official and semi-official publications presenting United Kingdom statistics are numerous, and there are available very useful descriptive classifi-

[a] 'Large group testing' has another major application in the testing of reaction to program material to which group members are first exposed under controlled conditions.

cations of these[b, c]. By no means all of these statistics are likely to be of direct relevance to the program planner, but some certainly are. Thus through publications based upon censuses of the population[d], it is possible to read off population distributions in terms of characteristics such as: age; sex; marital status; nationality; age at which full-time education ceased; occupation; industry in which employed; number of rooms in the accomodation occupied; certain household amenities; area in which residing. The departments responsible for the census are also responsible for quarterly and yearly statements which include population estimates.[e] Also of possible interest to the program planner are the distributions given, under another head, in terms of personal income and expenditure[f].

Such sources of information about the general population certainly can help the planner, but they cannot possibly be expected to provide anything like all the information he needs. For efficient planning he will need to know about people's interests, their values and their moral codes, their tastes for different kinds of program material, their mental and physical availability at different times of the day and evening and other information specially related to the purposes and policies of broadcasting. For information of this kind to become available, special enquiries would have to be carried out. The appropriate method for making such enquiries would in some cases be the sample survey method; in others it would be the *large group testing* method.

THE SAMPLE SURVEY AS A TOOL OF PLANNING

In the more usual form of the sample survey, interviewers meet and question people who, taken altogether, are intended to constitute a representative cross-section of some specified population. This representative cross-section may be arrived at through what is often called random sampl-

---

[b]   See, for example, "The Sources and Nature of the Statistics of the United Kingsdom", edited by M.G. Kendall [65].

[c]   The following classes of statistics are described in "Statistical Sources For Market Research", published by the Market Research Society of Great Britain [69]: Population and Vital Statistics; Labour and Employment; Raw Materials; Industry; Building, Housing and Dwellings; Transport and Communications; Retail Trade and Distribution; National Income and Expenditure; Local Government; Imports and Exports; Advertising and Readership.

[d]   See, for example: *Census 1961, England and Wales: Preliminary Report. Census 1961, England and Wales: Age, Mental Conditon and General Tables. Census 1961, England and Wales: Country Reports.*

[e]   See, for example: The Registrar-General's Quarterly Returns for England and Wales; The Registrar-General's Annual Statistical Review. For additional population data, see Annual Abstract of Statistics and "Monthly Digest of Statistics" (Central Statistical Office).

[f]   See "National Income and Expenditure", a publication of the Central Statistical Office.

ing or it may be arrived at through quota sampling. The interviewer usually asks a series of questions as set out on a questionnaire, though on some occasions she may be more free in her choice of questions, as for instance in what is called *free interviewing*. In such work she would nonetheless have been instructed to secure certain kinds of information and her questioning would be focused accordingly. Several varieties of free interviewing are from time to time used, under such names as *motivation, depth, focused, intensive.*

The methods of the sample survey are well documented in technical publications and the reader interested at the highly technical level will no doubt pursue them there [13, 19, 36, 57, 58, 61, 62, 64, 67, 79, 83, 93]. Even in the present rather general context, however, some elaboration of the method is necessary, particularly in terms of its several variants listed above. This is necessary because these different variants can serve somewhat different functions for the planner.

The first of these elaborations to be dealt with here concerns the method used for securing a properly representative sample of informants—that is, the method of sampling.

The Method of Sampling[g]

In conducting a sample survey, it is essential to control interviewers with respect to *which* people they interview. In most cases the aim of such control is to ensure that the people interviewed are representative of the population about which the researcher is seeking information. These people must be, as it were, a cross-section of it. In Britain, there are two systems for doing this and they are usually referred to as *random* sampling and *quota* sampling respectively. The term *sample* is used to denote the cross-section to be interviewed. Once the sample has been determined, the interviewers go to work with questioning as directed.

Random sampling [2, 78, 79, 93]

Two closely related features of the random system applied to individuals are that (i) the final identification of sample elements (that is, of areas and of people) has to it an essential random character and (ii) the people to be interviewed are *named* in the interviewer's instructions, so that the latter has no choice as to whom she interviews. As an immediate consequence of this second feature, the interviewer is required to call on a number of occasions in order to meet and to interview particular persons named on her list. Many organizations require that at least three call-backs, spread over several days, be made before the interview concerned is abandoned. Some organizations specify more than three call-backs. An important consequence of the call-back requirement is that the random types system

(g)   This very brief reference to sampling is to procedures frequently used in Britain. There is available a number of texts which deal with survey sampling both in excellent detail and on a broad base. See, for example: Leslie Kish (1965), *Survey Sampling*, John Wiley & Sons Inc.

does not lend itself to the completion of a survey in a single day (as, for example, would be required in a series of *daily* surveys of listening and viewing)[h]. It is also more costly.

Quota sampling [76, 77, 93]

The derivation of sampling subareas for the quota system may well be on the same lines as for the random system. However, when it comes to the actual *people* to be interviewed, the method for selecting them is quite different. The interviewer is given a description, in terms of certain variables, of the kinds of people to be interviewed. Thus she may be told to interview so many in each of several different age groups, so many men and so many women, so many from each of several different social groups. This description of her target is referred to as her quota. Within the confines of this quota she is free to choose the individuals she interviews. She may (according to her instructions) make her interviews at homes or in the street or both, but the necessity to make any call-backs does not ordinarily arise.

The uses of the two systems

Let me turn now to the possible uses of these two systems for conducting *planning studies*. The quota system is thought of in many quarters (though not all) as being specially open to bias through the freedom of interviewers to select their respondents. In principle at least (and in the absence of adequate evidence about bias potential) there seems to be little case for running this risk if there is time for the call-back system to be operated and if the necessary funds are available. Accordingly, the random rather than the quota system should, in the writer's opinion, be employed where the information required is to be used for the long-term planning of a program service. Where separate surveys have to be conducted day by day, there may be no alternative to using the quota system. The same possibly applies where low-cost information may be required for the development of a single program and where it seems to the broadcaster that the information will not be needed again.

The random sample system is, I consider, the appropriate tool for ascertaining the *availability* of people for listening to or watching broadcasts. It is also appropriate, with certain modifications, for studies of the population's interests, values, leisure-time activities and goals. Also with modifications, it can provide information about the functions which the public considers broadcasting to be usefully fulfilling and ways in which it is considered wasteful or in some way inconvenient or unsatisfactory.

The same method can be used to provide the advertiser with information about the conditions of viewing available in different sections of the popu-

[h] With a *continuing* daily survey, it might be possible to include an equal number of first, second, third, etc. call-back interviews each day. However the proper maintenance of such a system could be involved and demanding, and may in any case lead to bias.

lation, about prevailing attitudes towards television advertisements and about the level of attention ordinarily given to them. Such items of information bear upon the character of the presentation he should use and upon the limits of complexity and of subtlety that may be employed if he is to get his message across.

There are, however, limitations to the use that may be made of the random system as an aid to planning. These are mainly that it can be expensive and time-consuming, so that it tends not be to suitable for solving problems related to specific programs where a producer wants an answer very quickly and cheaply. Here, the quota system (where callbacks are not usually made) is likely to be the more serviceable.

Questioning Methods [36, 71, 83, 93]

Another important aspect of the survey interview on which some special comments are required is the way in which information (needed for planning purposes) is elicited from people once an interview has been secured. There are different ways of doing this and these include: the traditional *structured* interview in which the respondent is asked a series of quite specific questions to which the answers are written down or otherwise recorded by the interviewer[i]; the *self-completion* technique in which the respondent completes a diary or a questionnaire which is introduced by the interviewer but completed in her absence; *specialized* interviewing of the kind *free* or *depth* or *focused* or *intensive*. These different eliciting methods can serve different kinds of planning purposes.

The structured survey interview.

This is by far the most frequently used method and it is one which is quite often administered by housewife interviewers working on a part-time basis. It is relatively inexpensive to administer and it may be used for gathering information about a wide variety of opinions and of behavior. Examples are: opinions about specific programs and specific aspects of programs; occupational and educational background; aspects of viewing behaviour. Its value to the program planner as a general purpose tool must not be under-estimated.

The Diary [75] and the Self-Completion Questionnaire [9] techniques

These two methods, already in general use in various branches of social and market research, are particularly useful in certain kinds of planning studies. For instance the *diary technique* has been used by the BBC in 'availability' studies. In these, it was used to provide a half-hourly record, for each day of a week, of whether or not the respondent was at home and of the different things that the respondent was doing. The diary technique obviously depends upon the informant being conscientious enough to enter her records carefully and before she forgets what she was doing at different times of the day. It depends too upon her having and keeping

[i]   See references 14, 17, 33, 34, 36, 43, 55, 73, 80, 82, 83, 86, 87, 90, 92.

in mind the type of information which the researcher is seeking without allowing this awareness to affect her behavior or to influence the accuracy of her replies. Some individual researchers may well regard it as a method which they would not use if a suitable alternative was feasible: but for *availability studies* extending over several days, it is hard to see what the suitable alternative might be.

The *self-completion questionnaire* can serve a different function. The respondent is usually set going by the interviewer in filling in the questionnaire, but is left to complete it in the interviewer's absence. Ordinarily, the interviewer later collects it by appointment. This method has been used by the writer in gathering information about a very long list of the public's interests[j] and certainly it could be used in studies of a similar kind. It should never be used where the respondent's collaboration with others in the family could reduce the accuracy of the information given and it should never be used in studies of respondent knowledge or abilities. Its use should be limited to situations where the respondent needs time and thought to provide the information, where she is better off without the possibly oppressive and hustling presence of an interviewer (as when respondant memory is involved), and also when the length of the eliciting procedure would make it too expensive for the interviewer to work with the respondent all the way through the questionnaire. At the same time, the very fact that the questionnaire must be completed by the respondent in the absence of the interviewer means that the questionnaire has to be extremely well explained, very simple to complete and that it must be made distinctly interesting and attractive. A questionnaire of this kind is described in Chapter 23. Inexpensiveness in gathering large quantities of information is one of its features.

Specialized interviewing[k]

Quite often the information required may not be of the kind that can be secured through direct questioning, but is yet available through specialized interviewing of some kind, variously called free, [l] depth, [m] focused, [n]

[j]   See Chapters 4 and 23.
[k]   See references: [14, 42, 50, 52, 58, 63, 72, 84]
[l]   Free interviewing usually refers to an interview in which an interviewer is free to choose her own wording and in which she has at least some freedom concerning the order and the general strategy of her questions. *Free interviewing* is really a generic term which could include aspects of depth, focused and intensive interviewing.
[m]   Depth interviewing usually refers to interviewing designed to go deeper than direct questioning allows. It may be designed to get information about private matters not readily admitted or about matters of which the respondent is not ordinarily aware [58].
[n]   Focused interviewing usually refers to a process in which the interviewer focuses her questions on some limited number of points, possibly just one. She may range quite widely round a point but this would be done only as a means of getting the required information on that particular point [63, 72].

intensive[o]. It is not difficult to think of information in this category. Thus a planner who is keen to maximise his audiences, may want to know what motivates switching between programs at certain times and precisely why it is that many people don't try certain programs at all. He may want to understand what it is that constitutes the special appeal of a very successful performer on a rival channel, or the relative failure of his own new protégé. He may need information as to why a new service of educational programs is failing to draw its expected volume of viewers.

Interviewing techniques for getting elusive information of the kind referred to in the preceding paragraph are almost sure to be expensive in that they must be administered by interviewers selected for high intelligence and trained specially to do such work. This may well mean that the size of the sample used will not be as large as that used in ordinary surveys. Nonetheless such enquiries can have considerable value to the planner in providing him with insight into the dynamics of the television medium and of his own station in particular.

A word of warning is in order here. The essential feature of some of the specialized techniques referred to here is a *detection process* of a distinctly objective kind, with every effort being made to reduce the ambiguity of the information collected. What must be avoided at all costs is the imposing of some dogma or pet theory upon ambiguous data. A great deal of this sort of interpretative activity goes on under the guise of psychological expertise. It can be disastrously misleading and it can be no substitute for an objective approach.

The Limitations of the Survey Interview

The survey interview, in one or another of the forms referred to above, can be a highly versatile procedure and it can be used to provide information of many different kinds. Nonetheless, it has its limitations. In particular, it cannot give the researcher that degree of control over respondent behavior which is really necessary for the quantitative assessment of things like: general or specific *knowledge* of relevance to program planning or to program development; extensive attitude testing, some of it of the more subtle kind; awareness of issues; abilities, including such things as word knowledge and capacity for understanding abstractions or arguments. For work of this kind, a different research tool is necessary, namely the *group testing* technique.

GROUP TESTING AS A TOOL FOR PLANNING

With the *group testing* technique, groups of people of up to 40 at a time are put through controlled questioning procedures, numbers being built up through additional groups to the level required. Group members are

[o] Intensive interviewing usually refers to a process in which the interviewer works intensively over some small area of enquiry (e.g. an hour to ascertain a single item of information). The techniques of familiarization, aided recall, probing, checking, challenging and cross-examination may all be used. It is in principle a process of interrogation [14].

drawn from the general public and, *provided certain difficulties concerning their representativeness can be overcome*, the group testing technique may be used both for general charting purposes and for gathering advance information of a detailed and perhaps delicate kind about the people for whom a particular program is to be prepared. These are *not* discussion groups. Group members write down answers to questions, working without discussion. With a reasonably skilled administrator, these conditions can be established and a high degree of co-operation ensured. People are usually most helpful once they understand and respect what is being done. When the subject is television or radio, co-operation is practically guaranteed.

People coming to these groups are recruited through written invitation to the general public. Certain measures, described below, are taken to ensure that those who come are as representative as possible of the population from which they are drawn. The letter of invitation, a standard one for this kind of work, invites attendance at a meeting of viewers or listeners. The invitee is asked to bring a friend if he or she wishes and to indicate intentions (about coming and about bringing a friend) on a reply-paid card. The letter does not specify a testing procedure but simply states that the evening will include the showing and judging of new TV material and the discussion of good and bad aspects of the television service. Properly handled, this system leads to the attendance of 20–30 % of those asked to evening meetings, and practically everyone brings a friend. The method is inexpensive and it provides results rapidly.

The Problem of Representativeness [12, 60, 70, 85, 97]

The value of this method as a tool of program development rests upon a solution to the problem of how to make sure that the people who come are representative of those invited. After all, when only about a quarter of those asked actually come, there is room for a lot of self-selection and unrepresentativeness.

What do we know about the extent of their representativeness? What sort of people are they who come? Quite a lot of research has been done in order to answer this question. One of these enquiries [12] was based upon information about 5,225 persons who were invited to attend group meetings at the BBC. As it happened, certain information had been gathered about all these people in another and quite independent survey. This other survey had provided details such as occupational background, social class, age, sex, marital state, level of satisfaction with TV and radio programs, the amount of their viewing and listening. Accordingly it became possible to compare, in these terms, the people who came to the meeting and those who did not.

The main source of unrepresentativeness was in fact in terms of the occupational background of the invitee[p]. Of invitees with professional

---

[p] 'Occupational background' was based upon respondent's job or, if he or she was not in a job, upon the job of the respondent's head of household.

background, 35% came; 43% of the semi-professional group came; 33% of the highly skilled; 31% of the skilled; 22% of the moderately skilled; 16% of the unskilled. People over 60 years of age came much less than those below 60. For the sample as a whole, there was little difference in terms of marital state. Those listening to or seeing a great many programs came more often than those listening to or seeing only a few, though between these extremes (and this range accounted for the great majority of people) there was no appreciable variation in turn-out in terms of the number of programs seen or heard. There was some tendency for those who were highly satisfied and those who were dissatisfied with BBC *sound* programs to come more than those who were 'moderately satisfied', but this tendency or any other tendency did not appear when it came to level of satisfaction with *television* (BBC) programs.

Other studies of this kind have been carried out [16] but whenever possible in terms of different characteristics, so that to-date comparisons have been made in terms of about 200 different questions. Between them these comparisons have indicated that the people who come as a result of an invitation of the kind described here are somewhat more likely than the others: to be interested in 'organizing' activities or in meeting people and going to see things; to be readers of what are often called the 'quality' papers; to have read papers and magazines fairly regularly without being the ones to buy them; to have left school aged 16 or later. In addition, they had among them somewhat more of: those who owned durable goods of various kinds and/or had a telephone in the home; the unmarried; those who had possessed a TV set for a long time. Those who did *not* come tended somewhat more than the others: to have lived in their district for a long time, to have 'Mum' living nearby, and to have gone to school in the district where they live now. In other words, they appear to have been somewhat more 'dug in' than were the people who came. In the course of this work, these and other differences have emerged and they make it clear enough that the people who come tend somewhat to be different in some ways from those who don't come.

However, it is essential that we see these differences in proper perspective. The main source of difference is in fact 'occupational level or background'. It is possible to reweight or re-balance the people who come so that they resemble closely the total public in terms of occupational level. This is simply a matter of multiplying the results of the unskilled by 'x', those of the skilled by 'y' and so on, *according to their relative frequencies in the population*. Once this is done, most of the differences found to exist between those who came and those who did not tend to become rather small. Some disappear altogether and the final comparison is marked much more by similarities than by differences.

This does not mean that *all* differences disappear when the 'volunteers' are equated to the population in this way. We know that some of the differences don't disappear, namely those that happen to be *in*dependent of a person's occupational level — his age, marital state, tendency to

Conducting research for program planning

read papers without buying them, and possibly others. The general body of evidence does indicate, however, that the representativeness of invited groups is in fact something which is subject to control within practical limits and to this I shall now turn.

In practice, what can be done to secure representativeness?

It is doubtful that *full* representativeness in the groups can be achieved. But something approximating to this is certainly feasible, if the following method of control be used in recruiting members and in handling results. This method involves two phases.

Stage 1 of the control system.

The first phase of control occurs at the time the invitations are issued. Research of the kind described here has made it possible to build-up precise information about the rates of turn-out of people of different occupational background and of different ages. Table 1, which is based on London, gives details of one such set of information.

TABLE 1

Turn-out rate by age and occupational level

Occupational level in last job held	Age of Invitee			
	16–19 %	20–29 %	30–49 %	50–60 %
Professional and Semi-professional	*	40	48	34
Highly Skilled	34	35	33	31
Skilled	30	37	29	27
Moderately Skilled	20	24	28	20
Semi-Skilled	14	24	22	20
Unskilled	12	12	20	19

* *Not applicable*

From this table, it can be seen that people aged 30–49 and of highly skilled occupational background have a 33% turnout rate, whereas those aged 20–29 and of unskilled background have a turnout rate of only 12%.

Provided information about the age and occupation of invitees is available, the above data make it possible to exercise a lot of control over the composition of those coming. Thus if we know the number from a particular occupational/age group we want in the final sample, we can rapidly work out how many should be invited. Though men and women accept such invitations at about the same rate, sex composition of the final sample ought also to be controlled against chance unrepresentativeness. The necessary contact with and information about invitees (i.e. age and occupational level) may well be available from recent surveys conducted for other purposes. If not, a special survey may have to be made to make contact with potential invitees and to secure the necessary information about them. The interview in such a survey would be of a very brief kind and the quota system of sampling would probably be used.

This system of control is of course only partial. In the first place, the planned proportions may be only approximately secured, and this is increasingly likely to be so when the total number to be secured becomes small (e.g. below two hundred). Secondly, even if those who do come are exactly as planned in terms of age, sex and occupational level, it is still quite possible that they are yet insufficiently representative in terms of one or more other characteristics of importance to the inquiry. Accordingly a second stage of control is necessary.

Stage 2 of the control system.

This second stage of control involves reweighting the results when carrying out the analysis, though the information necessary for the reweighting must be gathered during the testing procedure. Thus if it turns out that the final sample is under-represented in terms of a characteristic of importance to the inquiry[q], then the results from the people *with* this characteristic should be given extra weight — the effect of which would be to ensure that such people contribute in proper proportion to the total result.

But in terms of which characteristics should this reweighting be done? There should at least be a reweighting or trimming of the age, sex and occupational composition of the aggregated groups once these are known precisely. In many studies this will be enough to control 'unrepresentativeness through volunteering' in its more important forms. But in principle and in fact it is certainly possible that further unrepresentativeness may exist *within* specific age-sex-occupational subgroups. Accordingly certain further steps are desirable. The writer's practice has been (i) to build into the group testing procedure questions in terms of several variables which may conceivably be related to the topic under study, (ii) to analyse the results to find out which of these variables are in fact associated with test score (i.e. the dependent variable), and then (iii) to introduce such variables, wherever possible, into the trimming or reweighting process[r].

[q]   That is, it is correlated with the variable being studied (sometimes referred to as the 'dependent variable').

[r]   Obviously one can only achieve this reweighting where the population distribution for the variables concerned is known. This is in fact the case for many of the variables which have emerged as associated with 'unrepresentativeness through volunteering' and in due course cross-tabulations in terms of all these variables should become available. In the meantime, however, there are gaps in this kind of information and we can never expect to find, ready-made, population figures for some of the variables which a researcher may think of as possibly associated with the issue under study. It is always possible to gather and develop such information through the recruiting survey, but doing this can raise problems of various kinds.
Another point of importance − though an obvious one − is that it is pointless to use as controls (for reweighting purposes) variables with respect

How groups are handled

So far there has been only brief reference to what one can expect to get from test-room groups of this kind and to the techniques necessary for administering test sessions. It is necessary to take each of these matters a little further.

An essential requirement for group testing is the imposition of tight control over the group—not an oppressive, school room control, but one which is firm, friendly, and respected. In London, the best starting time for group meetings is early evening. It is usual and effective for those taking part to receive light refreshment on arrival and for the test administrator to start by outlining to group members what they will be doing during the evening and asking for their co-operation. It is essential that they learn at this early stage of certain interesting things that will happen later in the evening, such as the allocation of tickets to television shows, the judging of new entertainment films, arrangements for general discussion of TV programs at the *end* of the session. After this introduction, group members are told of three important rules:

1. There can be no discussion or collaboration of any kind once the questioning has started;
2. Absolute frankness is essential (all respondents remain anonymous throughout these evenings);
3. Real effort is essential.

These three rules are stressed as being of great importance, and are repeated as necessary. They must be maintained throughout the session and it is clear that the test administrator must have a strong though pleasant personality. At least one assistant is needed in the test room for the distribution of test materials, for helping individual group members if necessary and for helping to maintain the proper testing conditions.

The session is best conducted at long conference tables and it is preferable to have three of these in parallel, with the test administrator standing back from the centre one. It is usually best to have as few breaks as possible in the testing procedure, for it is very hard to get group members started again on serious thinking once they have relaxed for any length of time. The best way to provide needed rest is to introduce a three to four minute break during which the respondents simply relax or talk as

---

to which there is no difference between the test room sample and the population which the latter is meant to represent — no matter how highly correlated these be with test score. In other words, for a variable to qualify as a control (for reweighting purposes) it must be both statistically associated with the issue under study *and* a source of difference between the test room sample and the population represented by the latter.

There is one other technicality which must be mentioned. The methods ordinarily used for selecting these controls yield a small composite of variables, to be applied as a composite, and not a series of separate variables. Full details of this technique are available. [11]

they wish. Groups of up to 80 people can be tested in this way, but it is extremely tiring for the administrator to have as many as that and experience suggests that 40 is just about right.

The writer has used test room groups in quantitative studies of various kinds. Groups have, for example, completed tests of knowledge about topics of widely different kinds. Group members will readily complete attitude tests (some on prepared lists and others requiring free responses) on practically any topic. Nor is it necessarily difficult to administer standardized tests, including even timed tests of intelligence. Under conditions of assured anonymity people will make statements of a remarkably candid or self-revealing kind. Controlled experiments with two groups seeing different things can readily be carried out. This system also lends itself-well to the initial (written) collection of ideas and images for development into highly relevant questions, and into attitude inventories for use in subsequent group work or in surveys. In fact this was done in preparation for several of the studies reported in this section.

It is rare indeed to find anyone seeming disgruntled or being difficult at these meetings. The overwhelming reaction of group members is that they find the evening interesting — something different from anything they have done in a very long time.

SMALL GROUP DISCUSSION AS A TOOL FOR PLANNING

There is another technique which is based upon groups and which is often used for the derivation of ideas and leads relating to some problem or issue. With this techique, a series of small groups each engages in discussion of a topic defined by a discussion leader. Ordinarily there are five to eight people in a single group, all of them drawn from some relevant sector of the population. Further groups of about the same size go on meeting one after the other until such time as no new ideas are emerging. The role of the discussion leader, who is a member of the research team, is to keep his group talking on the topic, to see that all its members contribute and to press for elaboration of points of seeming importance raised by one or another member of the group. He is non-directive in the sense that he does not try to impose ideas on group members. [84]

Group members are usually paid a small fee for taking part and their fares are refunded. They receive light refreshments on arrival or during the discussion. They may be asked to talk about a specified social issue or some proposed new program or product or marketing idea or, indeed, concerning anything about which program staff or others may want to sound out people's ideas. Groups so engaged usually talk vigorously, and members appear to stimulate each other in the process.

It is most important that this method be seen solely as a source of ideas and not as providing quantitative results of the kind that are derivable from the sample survey technique or from group testing. It is simply a source of ideas which may perhaps enrich or stimulate thinking but which is best regarded as setting quantitative follow-up research onto relevant and promising lines.

The value of the method as a source of ideas is that it can give fairly quick results. Its disadvantages ought, however, to be carefully noted. In the first place, the participants must not be regarded as simply expressing ideas that they brought with them to the discussion room: other people's comments can produce in members thoughts that they never had before. This means that we must think very carefully in interpreting discussion results. Secondly, some members appear to impose their ideas on less forceful members and some don't say very much. Another difficulty is that the discussion, which has to be fully tape recorded, and which may include much useless material, has subsequently to be analysed — and this can take quite a lot of time.

On balance, my own inclination is to use the group discussion method only if the aim of the operation is to stir up ideas that people don't ordinarily have in mind or which they may find it too difficult to express on paper. Otherwise it seems advisable to use the *large group* technique with its written response system, with its greater economy per head in terms of analysis and group-leader costs, and with the opportunity it provides for holding a discussion on a specified issue once the paper and pencil work has been finished.   .

[4]

Charting the interests of a population[a]

One of the kinds of information which in Chapter 2 was recommended to program staff and to the program planner concerned the *interests* of the public. By interests I mean things like home decorating, watching ballet, watching or playing football, following motor racing, seeing places of historic importance, learning about people in other countries, photography, keeping pets, modern science, and so on. The public's interests are in fact many and varied and the followings of the different interests range from many millions to relatively few. Detailed information about these interests seems to the writer to be essential to those whose job it is to plan programs for the public. Without it, the planner constantly faces the danger that he will allocate to topics amounts of program time which are out of step with the numbers in the population to whom they are in fact of interest. To the extent that the program planner is concerned with catering for the public's interests, he must know what these interests are and the relative sizes of their followings.

The results presented in this chapter are offered as information of this kind. Though they deal with only London and Birmingham, it is hoped that their presentation will be useful in its own right and will also encourage others to develop similar information for other regions.

THE METHODS OF RESEARCH

The derivation of a list of interests for study

The results presented here are in terms of 120 different areas of interest which were selected in the following manner. In preparation for an earlier study [232] a compilation had been made, tending towards exhaustiveness, of the kinds of topics and activities which members of the London public regarded as their interests. To achieve this, approximately 350 London adults were asked to write down, over a period of a week, what their interests were, adding more as they thought of them. The 85% who

[b] Based upon information gathered by the writer in the course of a major enquiry in Britain conducted in 1955–6 and published by the B.B.C. as "Television and the Family" [231]

did this were fairly representative of Londoners in terms of occupation level, education, age and sex. The final list consisted of over 400 areas of interest which, for present purposes, was subsequently generalized down to 111(b). Since many of the items in the 400⁺ were similar to each other and since some were really only different aspects of a somewhat broader interest, this amount of reduction was possible without appreciable loss or selectivity. The full list of 111 categories is given in the context of Table 1.

The questionnaire and the survey

Subsequently the list was built into a questionnaire which was administered in each of four separate surveys. Though the primary purpose of these four surveys was not related to the measurement of interests at all, they did provide large representative samples for the derivation of the population data presented in Tables 1 and 2.

The questionnaire into which the list of 111 interests was built was of the self completion kind: the interviewer took the questionnaire, which was in the form of a booklet, to the respondent, got the respondent started on it, made an appointment to collect it in approximately a week, and called for it then (and if necessary several more times). As a unit in this booklet-questionnaire, the list of interests was presented on two sides of a coloured page. It was preceded in the questionnaire by pre-tested instructions and the list itself was presented in the following form.

YOUR PRESENT-DAY INTERESTS

Tick(s)   X = NOT interested in it (or actually dislike it)
or cross   √ = MILDLY interested
here   √√ = QUITE interested or VERY interested

... Interior decoration of the home.
... Home crafts (e.g. rug making, weaving, embroidery, and so on).
... Furniture (e.g. modern, antique, and so on).
... Pottery or chinaware.
... Doing odd jobs about the home.
... Reading books of fiction.
... Reading books of a serious or informative kind.
... Keeping a pet (e.g. cage bird, dog, cat and so on).
... Keeping or breeding fish.
... Shopping or window shopping.
... Attending auction sales.
... Having visitors or going visiting.

(The list was continued in this form for the rest of the 111 items)

(b)   The 400⁺ items were also used as a source of a 50-item cross-section of the public's interests, as part of another enquiry. See Chapter 23 and reference 232.

The part of the questionnaire used for getting the respondent started was in fact this list of interests. Before taking the questionnaire back from the respondent, all parts of it (including the list of intersts) were checked for completeness.

The booklet questionnaire was used in each of four separate surveys, each based upon representative samples of viewers and non-viewers. Two of these surveys were conducted in Greater London, one in the winter (2440 cases) and the other in the summer (2320 cases). The third was in Birmingham in the winter (2340 cases) and the fourth in Wakefield in the summer (1130 cases). The two winter surveys were made in 1955 and the two summer surveys in 1956. In drawing the samples there was stratification in terms of geographic area and economic level. For the purposes of the main enquiry[c], these samples excluded: people living in the more economically depressed 15% of the polling districts in the region; those aged over 65 years; the small number who at that time had owned TV sets for more than 5 years. For all four surveys, taken together, about 5% of those listed for interview were not contacted after 3 calls and approximately 2% refused to co-operate. Of the 8,230 booklets which were left, 6% were not completed to at least some degree.

All viewers in the initial sample were asked to complete the booklet. For reasons connected with the design of the enquiry for which the rest of the booklet was prepared, only every *second* non-viewer was asked to complete it. This made it necessary, in analysing the interests section of the booklet, to double-weight the records of the non-viewers.

THE FINDINGS

The results for London and for Birmingham[d] are presented in Tables 1 and 2. In each of them the interests are set out in order according to the number of people (in the London summer survey) claiming to be "quite or very interested" in them.

One noteworthy feature of Table 1 is that there is very little difference between the three sets of distributions. This is even more noteworthy in view of some of the basic differences between the two towns concerned. On the other hand there are major differences in the number of people who profess any substantial degree of interest in the different topics and activities in the list and it is this kind of difference which is likely to be of relevance to the work of production staff and program planners.

In Table 2 a comparison is made of the distribution of interests in different population sectors. This has been done only for the London-summer data because to present the differences for all surveys would be both cumbersome and highly repetitive. The results from the London summer survey are in fact very similar to those from the other surveys. Another

[c]   That is, the effects of TV upon aspects of family life and sociability [231].
[d]   The results for Wakefield, which are not included here, were not appreciably different from those for the other two areas.

TABLE 1.

The percentage distributions of interests from three surveys in two towns

Areas of Interest	London Summer			London Winter			Birmingham Winter		
	How Interested			How Interested			How Interested		
	Quite or very	Mildly	Not	Quite or very	Mildly	Not	Quite or very	Mildly	Not
	%	%	%	%	%	%	%	%	%
Going away for holidays (e.g. seaside, country, abroad and so on)	71	25	4	68	27	5	68	27	5
Family celebrations (e.g. birthdays, Christmas, and so on)	54	39	7	53	40	7	51	43	6
Interior decoration of the home	54	37	9	54	36	10	54	38	8
The English country-side (e.g. reading about it, hearing about it, going to see it, and so on)	53	39	8	45	43	12	48	42	10
Listening to the radio	47	50	3	52	45	3	52	46	2
Having a good talk with a friend or acquaintance (e.g. while shopping, while visiting, over a cup of tea, and so on)	47	42	11	46	42	12	43	43	14
Doing odd jobs about the home	46	43	11	45	44	11	48	45	7
Watching television	45	37	18	45	37	18	52	33	15
Gardens and gardening (including flower shows and window boxes)	44	44	12	39	41	20	40	44	16
Having visitors or going visiting	44	46	10	43	46	11	36	48	16
Day outings	44	45	11	42	45	13	36	49	15
Going to the theatre	43	46	11	43	46	11	36	49	15
Travel abroad	40	37	23	39	36	25	33	35	32
Labour saving gadgets and ideas	39	47	14	40	49	11	37	51	12

(Continued Table 1)

Areas of Interest	London Summer How Interested			London Winter How Interested			Birmingham Winter How Interested		
	Quite or very	Mildly	Not	Quite or very	Mildly	Not	Quite or very	Mildly	Not
	%	%	%	%	%	%	%	%	%
Places and people in Britain and in different parts of the world.	39	47	14	34	51	15	33	49	18
Keeping a pet (e.g. cage bird, dog, cat, and so on)	37	35	28	38	34	28	39	38	23
Reading books of fiction	37	41	22	38	40	22	30	39	31
Generally relaxing	36	53	11	34	53	13	32	56	12
Reading books of a serious or informative kind	36	42	22	34	41	25	26	42	32
Taking part in (or listening to) arguments, debates or discussions.	35	39	26	37	39	24	31	38	31
Having acquaintances or friends just 'drop in'	35	49	16	35	50	15	30	55	15
Variety or vaudeville shows	35	44	21	38	43	19	41	44	15
Shopping or window shopping	33	40	27	34	38	28	34	36	30
Giving parties or attending them	32	46	22	33	48	19	30	48	22
The royal family	32	52	16	35	49	16	38	46	16
Football	32	32	36	32	32	36	36	33	31
Exchanging letters or presents or cards	31	49	20	30	50	20	30	48	22
Light music (vocal or instrumental) *other than* swing or jazz	30	55	15	26	57	17	23	56	21
Clothes generally (e.g. fashions today, dress design, and so on)	30	40	30	30	41	29	31	39	30

(Continued Table 1)

Areas of Interest	London Summer How Interested			London Winter How Interested			Birmingham Winter How Interested		
	Quite or very	Mildly	Not	Quite or very	Mildly	Not	Quite or very	Mildly	Not
	%	%	%	%	%	%	%	%	%
Strolling in the park or strolling about generally	30	48	22	26	50	24	25	51	24
Talking about the past as you used to know it	30	34	36	30	52	18	33	51	16
Boxing	29	31	40	30	33	37	31	34	35
Having a meal 'out' somewhere	29	51	20	27	49	24	25	50	25
Going to see cathedrals, and places of historic importance	29	44	27	29	44	27	29	47	24
Watching horse jumping	28	40	32	30	39	31	31	42	27
Cooking	27	34	39	25	36	39	26	35	39
Playing gramophone records	27	47	26	31	45	24	26	46	28
Providing visitors with entertainment	27	49	24	26	51	23	23	52	25
Furniture (e.g. modern, antique, and so on)	26	44	30	25	46	29	24	47	29
Going to the cinema	26	54	20	28	54	8 I	25	52	23
International and world affairs	26	52	22	22	56	22	18	55	27
Athletics	25	44	31	28	41	31	25	44	31
Swimming	25	50	25	25	46	29	23	46	31
The customs of past generations and of other peoples	25	41	34	20	45	35	15	45	40
Politics and affairs of government generally	24	49	27	23	52	25	20	50	30

(Continued Table 1)

Areas of Interest	London Summer How Interested			London Winter How Interested			Birmingham Winter How Interested		
	Quite or very	Mildly	Not	Quite or very	Mildly	Not	Quite or very	Mildly	Not
	%	%	%	%	%	%	%	%	%
Cricket	23	34	43	22	32	46	21	31	48
Dancing (e.g. going to dances, ballroom dancing, folk dancing, and so on)	23	33	44	21	35	44	23	32	45
Getting to know more people	23	56	21	22	56	22	24	56	20
Playing cards (e.g. cribbage, poker, whist, solo and so on)	23	43	34	23	42	35	20	41	39
Home crafts (e.g. rug making, weaving, embroidery and so on)	23	36	41	25	36	39	25	36	39
History (e.g. ancient, modern, Roman, 19th Century. English. American and so on)	23	37	40	20	38	42	15	39	46
Hearing about well known people	22	54	24	21	55	24	21	55	24
Serious or classical music (vocal or instrumental)	22	39	39	23	35	42	16	32	52
Mechanical things generally	21	33	46	20	36	44	23	35	42
Musical evenings	20	41	39	20	43	37	18	43	39
Crossword puzzles	19	41	40	19	38	43	15	37	48
Military band music	19	49	32	19	46	35	24	48	28
Playing board games (e.g. dominoes, monopoly, draughts, shovehalfpenny, darts, chess, and so on)	19	49	32	20	48	32	21	46	33
Hair styles	18	31	51	18	32	50	19	34	47

Conducting research for program planning

(Continued Table 1)

Areas of Interest	London Summer How Interested			London Winter How Interested			Birmingham Winter How Interested		
	Quite or very	Mildly	Not	Quite or very	Mildly	Not	Quite or very	Mildly	Not
	%	%	%	%	%	%	%	%	%
Ice or roller skating	17	42	41	18	42	40	17	40	43
Matters connected with your church or chapel (e.g. church work, prayer, hymns, attendance at church, and so on)	17	39	44	15	39	46	19	47	34
The pools	17	36	47	21	38	41	18	41	41
Social gatherings (e.g. whist drives, weddings, jumble sales, and so on)	17	44	39	18	44	38	17	45	38
Making your own clothes	16	19	65	13	21	66	12	20	68
Modern science	16	42	42	16	41	43	12	40	48
Motor or cycle racing	16	29	55	20	29	51	19	32	49
Snooker or billiards	16	27	57	13	27	60	15	29	56
Tennis	16	35	49	15	35	50	12	29	59
Cosmetics and make-up	15	29	56	16	29	55	15	33	52
Going to the local (i.e. pub, inn or hotel)	15	36	49	13	38	49	16	36	48
Carpentry or woodwork	14	24	62	14	25	61	12	25	63
Local affairs	14	63	23	12	60	28	16	61	23
Paintings	14	39	47	12	37	51	8	34	58
Ballet	13	27	60	14	30	56	9	22	69
Table tennis	13	40	47	13	40	47	12	34	54

(Continued Table 1)

Areas of Interest	London Summer How Interested			London Winter How Interested			Birmingham Winter How Interested		
	Quite or very	Mildly	Not	Quite or very	Mildly	Not	Quite or very	Mildly	Not
	%	%	%	%	%	%	%	%	%
Film stars	13	40	47	12	42	46	11	44	45
Keeping a collection of something (e.g. stamps, gramophone records, etc.)	13	27	60	12	27	61	10	27	63
Membership of clubs and associations	13	36	51	13	37	50	13	37	50
Amateur dramatics	12	39	49	12	33	55	13	34	53
Drinking beer, wine or spirits	12	39	49	11	52	37	12	49	39
Having friends in to watch television	12	34	54	13	30	57	12	36	52
Photography	12	42	46	8	41	51	10	39	51
Planning and organising (e.g. administrative activity, committee work, etc.)	12	24	64	10	23	67	10	24	66
Pottery or chinaware	12	34	54	13	32	55	14	35	51
Swing or jazz music	12	42	64	12	27	61	11	26	63
Wrestling or Judo	12	23	65	10	25	65	12	25	63
Parlour games (e.g. conjuring or card tricks, paper and pencil games, practical jokes, and so on)	12	40	48	12	44	44	13	44	43
Attending lectures or talks	10	36	54	11	34	55	10	29	61
Naval and military history	11	31	58	11	32	57	9	33	58
Physical culture	11	38	51	11	40	49	12	42	46
Attending auction sales	11	21	68	8	25	67	9	25	66

Areas of Interest	London Summer How Interested			London Winter How Interested			Birmingham Winter How Interested		
	Quite or very	Mildly	Not	Quite or very	Mildly	Not	Quite or very	Mildly	Not
	%	%	%	%	%	%	%	%	%
Any gambling or betting, not counting the Pools, (e.g. cards, on dogs, on horses, etc.)	10	26	64	7	23	70	6	24	70
Playing a musical instrument of some kind	10	29	61	10	26	64	9	27	64
Trade unionism	10	29	61	9	28	63	9	26	65
Fun Fairs	9	30	61	8	31	61	10	35	55
Voluntary social and welfare work (e.g. W.V.S.)	9	34	57	8	34	58	8	34	58
Rowing	9	36	55	8	32	60	7	32	61
Philosophy	8	35	57	8	31	61	8	27	65
Stock car racing	8	20	72	8	21	71	9	24	67
Shooting	7	17	76	7	15	78	8	18	74
Fishing	7	22	71	6	14	80	8	18	74
Golf	7	17	76	4	17	79	4	14	82
Model making or toy making	7	21	72	8	22	70	6	21	73
Poetry	7	22	71	6	22	72	5	25	70
Sailing	7	29	64	6	28	66	6	27	67
Writing, other than letters (e.g. stories, essays, reports, etc.)	7	17	76	5	17	78	3	16	81
Hockey	6	19	75	4	20	76	4	18	78

(Continued Table 1)

Areas of Interest	London Summer How Interested			London Winter How Interested			Birmingham Winter How Interested		
	Quite or very	Mildly	Not	Quite or very	Mildly	Not	Quite or very	Mildly	Not
	%	%	%	%	%	%	%	%	%
Keeping or breeding fish	5	14	81	5	11	84	4	16	80
Amateur radio transmission or engineering	4	10	86	4	10	86	5	11	84
Sculpture	4	19	77	3	16	81	2	12	86
Civil defence	4	30	66	3	33	64	5	32	63

feature of Table 2 is that it presents information only about the number of people who were "Quite or Very Interested" and excludes the "Mildly interested" and the "Not interested" ratings. This has been done mainly for brevity and also because the differences between population sub-groups are more discernible at this particular level of intensity of interest. .

Though some of these interests are held fairly equally through all age, sex and class sectors of the population sampled, for most of them there is at least some degree of noteworthy variation in going from one age group to another or from men to women or from one social class to another. Many of these differences are large and a planner cannot afford to be unaware of them.

TABLE 2.

Adult interests in London (summer survey) By age, sex and occupation

Percentage Quite or Very Interested

Areas of Interest	Age			Sex		Occupational Level*			House-wife		All
	21–30	31–50	51–65	Male	Female	1+2	3+4	5+6+7	Working	Not working	
	%	%	%	% %		%	%	%	%	%	%
Going away for holidays e.g. seaside, country, abroad, and so on)	81	72	64	68	74	70	72	70	76	70	71
Family celebrations (e.g. birthdays, Christmas, and so on)	61	55	49	53	55	38	53	59	61	65	54
Interior decoration of the home	50	57	53	53	55	59	56	52	60	59	54
The English countryside (e.g. reading about it, hearing about it, going to see it, and so on)	51	54	53	51	56	57	53	52	54	55	53
Listening to the radio	51	45	48	43	51	29	47	51	53	48	47
Having a good talk with a friend or acquaintance (e.g. while shopping, while visiting, over a cup of tea, and so on)	54	48	42	37	56	42	48	4 7	57	56	47
Doing odd jobs about the home	33	48	51	53	39	45	43	49	40	41	46
Watching television	47	47	42	45	45	28	40	53	50	45	45
Gardens and gardening (including flower shows and window boxes)	32	46	50	43	46	39	45	45	49	49	44
Having visitors or going visiting	51	46	37	34	54	42	46	43	54	58	44
Day outings	49	45	38	41	46	34	39	50	50	44	44
Going to the theatre	56	42	37	32	53	47	44	41	58	46	43
Travel abroad	56	40	31	39	41	53	47	31	40	35	40

* In terms of skill and training required for the job.

(Continued Table 2)

Percentage Quite or Very Interested

Areas of Interest	Age			Sex		Occupational Level*			House-wife		All
	21–30	31–50	51–65	Male	Female	1+2	3+4	5+6+7	Working	Not working	
	%	%	%	%	%	%	%	%	%	%	%
Labour saving gadgets and ideas	47	42	30	35	43	35	39	40	46	46	39
Places and people in Britain and in different parts of the world	46	41	33	39	40	56	44	32	36	38	93
Keeping a pet (e.g. cage bird, dog, cat, and so on)	40	39	33	32	41	32	34	41	48	36	37
Reading books of fiction	48	38	29	30	44	44	40	33	43	41	37
Generally relaxing	46	36	30	36	35	25	34	39	38	33	36
Reading books of a serious or informative kind	41	37	31	42	30	61	42	26	26	26	36
Taking part in (or listening to) arguments, debates or discussions	35	37	33	40	31	50	38	30	30	30	35
Having acquaintances or friends just 'drop in'	39	35	34	29	41	25	37	36	40	42	35
Variety or vaudeville shows	26	36	40	39	32	12	27	45	40	33	35
Shopping or window shopping	42	34	25	13	53	14	33	36	59	49	33
Giving parties or attending them	48	32	22	24	40	24	33	33	44	37	32
The royal family	25	32	38	24	40	19	32	34	41	43	32
Football	29	35	28	50	13	24	31	34	21	9	32
Exchanging letters or presents or cards	38	29	31	16	45	22	31	33	44	45	31

* In terms of skill and training required for the job.

(Continued Table 2)

Percentage Quite or Very Interested

Areas of Interest	Age			Sex		Occupational Level*			House-wife		All
	21-30	31-50	51-65	Male	Female	1+2	4+4	5+6+7	Working	Not working	
	%	%	%	%	%	%	%	%	%	%	%
Light music (vocal or instrumental) other than swing or jazz	35	30	27	28	33	32	36	24	34	30	30
Clothes generally (e.g. fashions today, dress design, and so on)	48	30	19	12	48	22	31	31	53	44	30
Strolling in the park or strolling about generally	36	31	25	29	31	20	28	34	38	25	30
Talking about the past as you used to know it	24	28	38	26	34	12	26	38	34	36	30
Boxing	26	33	25	45	13	18	27	33	18	14	29
Having a meal 'out' somewhere	39	30	22	20	38	35	31	26	41	37	29
Going to see cathedrals, and places of historic importance	26	31	28	24	34	42	31	25	35	32	29
Watching horse jumping	21	30	29	28	29	18	26	32	41	25	28
Cooking	3ò	28	23	35	18	24	26	29	21	16	27
Playing gramophone records	50	25	16	25	28	20	25	29	35	21	27
Providing visitors with entertainment	34	26	24	24	30	29	26	28	33	30	27
Furniture (e.g. modern, antique, and so on)	31	27	20	19	33	30	25	25	37	32	26
Going to the cinema	41	26	18	21	31	12	25	30	36	26	26
International and world affairs	27	26	26	34	19	49	27	20	17	18	26
Athletics	29	27	19	36	14	26	25	26	19	10	25
Swimming	32	29	15	28	22	20	25	26	28	18	25

* In terms of skill and training required for the job.

(Continued Table 2)

Percentage Quite or Very Interested

Areas of Interest	Age			Sex		Occupational Level*			House-wife		All
	21-30	31-50	51-65	Male	Female	1+2	3+4	5+6+7	Working	Not working	
	%	%	%	%	%	%	%	%	%	%	%
The customs of past generations and of other peoples	23	26	25	25	25	34	25	24	21	26	25
Politics and affairs of government generally	22	24	26	32	16	38	26	20	15	15	24
Cricket	24	24	20	35	12	38	25	18	13	10	23
Dancing (e.g. going to dances, ballroom dancing, folk dancing, and so on)	38	22	16	14	33	15	25	23	33	27	23
Getting to know more people	34	23	17	19	27	24	25	21	31	23	23
Playing cards (e.g. cribbage, poker, whist, solo and so on)	31	24	18	28	18	19	23	25	17	20	23
Home crafts (e.g. rug making, weaving, embroidery, and so on)	23	23	22	7	38	18	25	22	36	39	23
History (e.g. ancient, modern, Roman, 19th Century English, American, and so on)	25	23	20	23	21	37	24	19	19	19	23
Hearing about well known people	20	21	24	17	27	15	21	24	24	26	22
Serious or classical music (vocal or instrumental)	32	20	18	21	23	39	28	13	19	20	22
Mechanical things generally	20	24	16	35	6	23	23	18	7	5	21
Musical evenings	24	19	19	16	23	20	19	20	26	19	20
Crossword puzzles	20	20	18	18	20	19	19	20	20	20	19
Military band music	10	17	27	20	18	13	18	22	17	19	19

* In terms of skill and training required for the job.

(Continued Table 2)

Percentage Quite or Very Interested

Areas of Interest	Age			Sex		Occupational Level*			House-wife		All
	21-30	31-50	51-65	Male	Female	1+2	3+4	5+6+7	Working	Not working	
	%	%	%	%	%	%	%	%	%	%	%
Playing board games (e.g. dominoes, monopoly, draughts, shove-halfpenny, darts, chess and so on)	26	21	11	24	14	9	19	23	15	14	19
Hair styles	30	18	9	3	32	7	17	20	36	30	18
Ice or roller skating	21	18	12	16	17	10	15	20	25	14	17
Matters connected with your church or chapel (e.g. church work, prayer, hymns, attendance at church, and so on)	13	16	20	11	22	17	17	16	17	22	17
The pools	13	18	19	23	11	4	14	23	17	10	17
Social gatherings (e.g. whist drives, weddings, jumble sales, and so on)	19	18	15	11	23	7	16	20	27	23	17
Making your own clothes	20	17	11	2	29	8	17	16	24	32	16
Modern science	19	18	12	21	11	24	18	12	13	9	16
Motor or cycle racing	20	19	9	23	9	13	15	18	14	7	16
Snooker or billiards	13	18	15	27	4	12	14	19	8	6	16
Tennis	26	16	10	15	18	27	19	11	16	15	16
Cosmetics and make up	29	15	6	3	27	6	15	17	33	25	15
Going to the local (i.e. pub, inn or hotel)	16	15	12	20	9	14	11	18	12	7	15
Carpentry or woodwork	13	16	12	25	3	18	15	12	3	3	14
Local affairs	10	15	14	17	10	15	14	13	14	9	14

* In terms of skill and training required for the job.

Percentage Quite or Very Interested

Areas of Interest	Age			Sex		Occupational Level*			House-wife		All
	21–30	31–50	51–65	Male	Female	1+2	3+4	5+6+7	Working	Not working	
	%	%	%	% %		%	%	%	% %		%
Paintings	16	14	12	12	15	23	16	10	10	15	14
Ballet	17	13	11	8	18	22	15	10	15	16	13
Table tennis	22	13	6	16	10	15	15	10	10	8	13
Film stars	18	12	11	8	17	2	8	20	22	15	13
Keeping a collection of something (e.g. stamps, gramophone records, etc.)	27	12	7	13	13	14	14	11	18	8	13
Membership of clubs and associations	12	15	10	17	8	18	14	11	8	7	13
Amateur dramatics	16	11	12	9	16	11	13	11	19	12	12
Drinking beer, wine or spirits	15	14	8	17	8	13	11	13	10	5	12
Having friends in to watch television	13	13	11	10	15	8	10	14	21	12	12
Photography	17	12	10	17	8	22	12	11	8	6	12
Planning and organising (e.g. administrative activity, committee work, etc.)	8	14	11	16	8	27	14	7	7	8	12
Pottery or chinaware	12	13	11	5	20	15	12	12	20	19	12
Swing or jazz music	27	12	2	12	12	4	12	13	17	9	12
Wrestling or Judo	17	13	8	19	4	4	11	15	7	5	12
Parlour games (e.g. conjuring or card tricks, paper and pencil games, practical jokes, and so on)	12	13	9	12	11	7	9	15	11	11	12

* In terms of skill and training required for the job.

Areas of Interest	Age			Sex		Occupational Level*			House-wife		All
	21–30	31–50	51–65	Male	Female	1+2	3+4	5+6+7	Working	Not working	
	%	%	%	%	%	%	%	%	%	%	%
Attending lectures or talks	12	11	11	11	11	27	12	6	11	8	11
Naval and military history	11	13	9	17	6	10	12	11	8	6	11
Physical culture	11	13	7	16	6	7	12	10	8	6	11
Attending auction sales	6	12	10	9	12	10	9	12	14	13	10
Any gambling or betting, not counting the Pools, (e.g. cards, on dogs, on horses, etc.)	9	10	10	14	6	4	8	13	8	5	10
Playing a musical instrument of some kind	13	10	8	10	10	17	11	8	8	9	10
Trade unionism	8	11	10	16	4	7	9	12	7	2	10
Fun Fairs	9	9	9	8	10	2	5	15	12	10	9
Voluntary social and welfare work (e.g. W.V.S.)	8	9	10	6	12	13	10	7	6	14	9
Rowing	12	9	6	14	4	10	9	8	6	6	9
Philosophy	9	9	7	9	7	12	9	6	5	5	8
Stock car racing	10	10	4	10	6	0	6	12	9	6	8
Shooting	9	8	5	14	1	8	8	7	2	1	7
Fishing	8	8	5	11	3	7	8	6	6	2	7
Golf	5	8	7	10	5	16	7	6	4	4	7
Model making or toy making	6	9	5	11	3	11	7	6	5	2	7
Poetry	10	7	6	5	8	17	8	4	6	5	7
Sailing	14	7	4	8	7	11	7	6	7	5	7

* In terms of skill and training required for the job.

Percentage Quite or Very Interested

Areas of Interest	Age 21–30	Age 31–50	Age 51–65	Sex Male	Sex Female	Occupational Level* 1+2	Occupational Level* 3+4	Occupational Level* 5+6+7	House-wife Working	House-wife Not working	All
	%	%	%	%	%	%	%	%	%	%	%
Writing, other than letters (e.g. stories, essays, reports, etc.)	8	7	6	8	6	12	9	4	5	4	7
Hockey	8	6	4	5	6	8	5	6	7	6	6
Keeping or breeding fish	4	6	3	5	4	6	5	4	4	4	5
Amateur radio transmission or engineering	4	5	3	7	2	7	4	3	5	0	4
Sculpture	3	3	6	4	3	11	4	2	3	3	4
Civil defence	2	4	4	4	4	1	4	4	4	3	4

* In terms of skill and training required for the job.

[5]

Charting the availability of people for watching programs[a]

Another kind of study referred to in Chapter 2 was the *availability* enquiry. Such a study is usually designed to tell the program planner how many and what kinds of people are at home and free to view at different times of the day. Its results can indicate which of several time slots is the most promising one for reaching a particular audience.

One of the BBC's availability studies was carried out several years ago [26]. The BBC's full report of findings is a large and detailed one and what is presented here consists only of data which I have selected or summarized to illustrate what can be derived from this class of enquiry.

THE METHODS OF ENQUIRY

This particular 'availability' enquiry was conducted through the *diary technique*. A diary was left[b] with 2981 members of a national sample (United Kingdom) and was fully completed by 2365 of them. Ages of diarists ranged from 15 years upwards.

The method for completing the diary was explained to the respondent. In addition, the diary carried instructions about how to fill it in and a filled-in page as an example. The diary was designed to receive entries for each half-hour of the day from 6.30 a.m. till 12.00 midnight, for the seven days of a week. For each half-hour, the information wanted was: whether or not the respondent was at home; what the respondent was doing during that half-hour; whether he was viewing or listening to the radio (and if so, to what programs). Personal details concerning the respondent had been recorded by the interviewer. The diary was collected by the interviewer (by appointment) shortly after the end of the diary period.

---

[a] Based upon a BBC enquiry [26]
[b] The diary was introduced at the end of an interview conducted by the BBC in the course of a separate and different enquiry.

FINDINGS

Table 1 gives the percentage at home (columns 1, 3 and 5) for each of Saturday, Sunday, and Monday to Friday. It also gives the percentage of informants who were at home and up (columns 2, 4 and 6). The table indicates the existence of considerable variability in the percentage at home (and up) by time of day and, of course, by day of week.

Table 2 deals with weekdays only. It shows the difference in the percentage at home according to sex, age, class and number of children. Whereas there are many periods when approximately the same proportion of different sub-groups are at home, there are also periods when the proportions are different to an appreciable degree — a matter of importance to the program planner.

The BBC's analysis also gives the percentage viewing and listening in each half-hour and various of the activities of those not viewing. Figure 1, taken from the BBC's report, presents such details in a composite diagram for the 15–24 year olds.

Some Comments on the Study of Availability

The small body of findings presented here is a selected one intended only to illustrate the type of data which the method can yield. Nor is the present application of the method the only possible application of it. It should, for instance, be possible to achieve an empirically based classification of at-home activities in terms of the amount of attention which could, at best, be given to television while these activities are going on. A half hourly record of such at-home activities, in these terms, might be particularly useful. Its usefulness could be increased by combining it with information about the interests of viewers, for in this way the program planner would know what were the interests of the people in a position to attend to TV at any particular time of the day. With the aid of an adequate system for storing data he could readily supplement this information with other evidence collected in the availability survey (e.g. age, sex, educational background).

Charting the availability of people for watching programs

TABLE 1.

Percentage at home by day of week

(April 1961)

	Saturday		Sunday		Monday to Friday*	
	At home	At home and up	At home	At home and up	At home	At home and up
	(1)	(2)	(3)	(4)	(5)	(6)
Morning	%	%	%	%	%	%
6.30 – 7.00	86	7	96	3	90	13
7.00 – 7.30	85	17	94	4	85	28
7.30 – 8.00	80	31	94	12	72	38
8.00 – 8.30	74	44	91	26	61	47
8.30 – 9.00	66	51	90	43	48	41
9.00 – 9.30	61	54	87	61	42	39
9.30 – 10.00	55	51	86	72	40	37
10.00 – 10.30	47	44	83	75	35	33
10.30 – 11.00	41	39	77	72	33	31
11.00 – 11.30	39	38	73	70	33	31
11.30 – 12.00	42	41	72	70	33	31
Afternoon						
12.00 – 12.30	50	49	76	75	38	37
12.30 – 1.00	59	58	80	79	44	43
1.00 – 1.30	66	65	82	81	48	47
1.30 – 2.00	63	62	80	79	44	43
2.00 – 2.30	53	52	75	74	34	33
2.30 – 3.00	49	48	72	71	31	30
3.00 – 3.30	46	45	70	69	30	29
3.30 – 4.00	47	46	66	64	29	28
4.00 – 4.30	49	48	66	64	32	31
4.30 – 5.00	54	53	70	69	39	38
5.00 – 5.30	63	62	71	70	48	47
5.30 – 6.00	67	66	73	72	61	60
Evening						
6.00 – 6.30	72	71	68	67	74	73
6.30 – 7.00	72	72	65	64	76	75
7.00 – 7.30	68	67	64	64	73	73
7.30 – 8.00	64	63	68	68	72	72
8.00 – 8.30	63	62	71	71	71	70
8.30 – 9.00	63	62	72	72	72	71
9.00 – 9.30	63	61	73	72	73	71
9.30 – 10.00	63	60	77	72	74	67
10.00 – 10.30	68	56	84	64	79	59
10.30 – 11.00	75	45	89	48	87	42
11.00 – 11.30	82	29	94	24	90	20
11.30 – 12.00	86	12	95	11	92	9

* Averages for the five days are for all informants.

TABLE 2

Percentage at home on Monday to Friday*, According to age, sex, class and number of children

	Sex		Age				Class			Age of Children		All Cases
	Men	Women	15– 24	25– 44	45– 64	65+	A	B	C	Und-er 5	5– 14	
Morning												
6.30– 7.00	84	95	92	90	88	94	95	97	87	89	88	90
7.00– 7.30	74	93	86	83	81	92	95	92	79	86	79	85
7.30– 8.00	56	88	69	73	66	90	87	85	65	77	70	72
8.00– 8.30	40	81	47	62	57	88	79	70	56	66	64	61
8.30– 9.00	27	69	26	49	48	82	55	52	46	58	51	48
9.00– 9.30	22	60	20	42	39	81	41	44	40	54	41	42
9.30–10.00	21	56	17	41	36	77	35	41	40	52	39	40
10.00–10.30	18	51	15	36	32	70	32	37	35	47	35	35
10.30–11.00	16	47	12	33	30	64	28	35	32	45	33	33
11.00–11.30	16	46	12	32	29	62	26	34	32	42	33	33
11.30–12.00	18	49	13	34	30	64	24	33	34	44	36	33
Afternoon												
12.00–12.30	22	54	21	41	36	70	29	37	41	52	43	38
12.30– 1.00	28	62	28	46	41	73	36	44	47	58	48	44
1.00– 1.30	31	63	29	48	45	80	46	49	48	56	50	48
1.30– 2.00	26	60	22	43	39	79	42	47	42	51	46	44
2.00– 2.30	17	48	13	35	31	68	28	35	34	42	34	34
2.30– 3.00	15	44	12	33	30	64	27	33	32	38	32	31
3.00– 3.30	17	41	9	29	28	61	26	28	30	35	30	30
3.30– 4.00	18	40	12	28	28	59	25	29	30	33	31	29
4.00– 4.30	19	46	12	34	31	61	24	32	34	40	36	32
4.30– 5.00	22	51	17	40	37	66	32	37	38	47	43	39
5.00– 5.30	32	62	29	48	48	74	35	47	50	55	52	48
5.30– 6.00	50	73	45	61	62	80	45	58	62	67	66	61
Evening												
6.00– 6.30	64	79	66	72	72	83	62	74	75	73	76	74
6.30– 7.00	69	82	65	74	77	82	69	75	76	74	76	76
7.00– 7.30	68	77	61	73	77	81	67	75	74	77	74	73
7.30– 8.00	67	76	58	73	75	81	68	72	73	76	76	72
8.00– 8.30	68	76	55	71	73	80	67	71	72	77	74	71
8.30– 9.00	68	76	56	74	74	80	67	73	71	78	75	72
9.00– 9.30	68	77	57	75	76	82	68	73	72	77	78	73
9.30–10.00	71	80	59	77	78	86	71	78	76	78	81	74
10.00–10.30	75	85	69	81	81	88	75	81	82	85	85	79
10.30–11.00	83	90	80	86	87	92	81	86	87	88	89	87
11.00–11.30	88	93	88	92	92	94	87	92	92	91	93	90
11.30–12.00	90	94	92	92	92	94	88	93	91	91	94	92

* Averages for all five days.

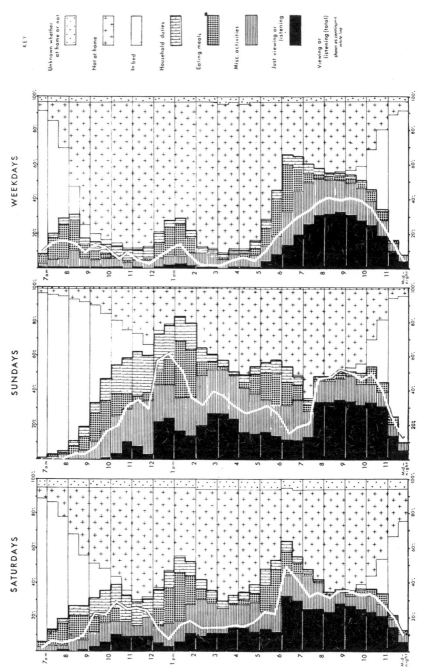

Figure 1

[6]

First steps in charting the public's general word knowledge[a]

Two major enquiries into the public's understanding of sound broadcasts [105, 154] had produced firm evidence that certain programs frequently were not understood to some serious degree by the general public to whom they were presented. Moreover, this failure was closely associated with the fact that the public was unfamiliar with many of the words which were used in these programs. A recommendation stemming from one of these enquiries [105] was that lists should be prepared, for the use of production staff, which were illustrative of the public's general word knowledge. The present enquiry was a first step towards this goal.

American researchers in education and communication have had available to them frequency counts of large numbers of words, the frequency count tendency to be offered as an index of their relative familiarity. The work of Davis [116] and of Kirkpatrick and Cureton [127] indicates, however, that the correlation between frequency count and measured difficulty can be relatively low[b]. Over and above this, however, these counts were based upon American usage. Comparable lists based upon English counts did not exist.

One American document provides evidence of an empirical kind about actual word difficulty. This presents 3,000 words which were known by at least 80% of American fourth grade students [113]. Its value in Britain is limited, however, by the fact that it refers to the American scene and to children. Vernon [153], faced by the absence of obviously relevant material relating to British adults, sought to develop a general guide to word difficulty. He tested 380 regular recruits to the Royal Navy on 100 words which were then set in order according to the frequency with which they were known by the recruits.[c] The study reported in this chapter was an

---

[a] Based upon a 1956 enquiry by Jean Morton-Williams (then of the BBC's Audience Research Department) in association with the author.
[b] Kirkpatrick reported correlations ranging from $+0.47$ to $+0.56$.
[c] From these data Vernon [153] derived groups of words which ranged from easy to hard and which were to be used for rating the difficulty of words other than the tested 100.

attempt to establish information of a broadly similar kind about the general listening and viewing population.

THE METHODS USED

The selection of the words and of the people tested

The words tested were drawn from talks which already had been broadcast by the BBC in one of its three sound broadcasting services. The 100 words drawn were selected, so far as could be judged selectively, to provide a wide range in level of difficulty. Vernon's scale of word difficulty [153] was used to guide this selection.

The people tested for their knowledge of the selected 100 words were approximately 500 members of the general adult population of London. They had come by invitation to Broadcasting House where they underwent a series of word knowledge tests and where numerous personal details were also recorded. Certain matching techniques (described under Analysis) [d] were used to try to eliminate unrepresentativeness amongst the accepting invitees who were, in fact, some 25 % of those invited.

The methods of testing

The people taking part in the enquiry did not know beforehand that tests of any kind would occur. They came in groups of about 40 at a time, had light refreshment on arrival, were introduced to what would be done, and then proceeded through testing under the usual conditions of silence and of anonymity [d]. All tests were of the paper and pencil kind [d].

The choice of an appropriate test of word knowledge had been made on the basis of experimental work [e] conducted some weeks before the present enquiry. The method so chosen was what is called the Creative Response method. This is the method in which the respondent is given the test word and writes down its meaning. Marking was deliberately 'very lenient' because the preliminary work had indicated that this was the appropriate marking system [e].

[d] See also the detailed description of these techniques in Chapter 3.

[e] There are at least two traditional methods for measuring word knowledge. One method is to give the respondent the true meaning of the test word *hidden* amongst some incorrect 'meanings'. There are usually about five of these incorrect 'meanings'. The respondent is asked to pick out the correct meaning. This method is called Multiple Choice. The other method is simply to ask people to write down the meaning of the test word. This method is called Creative Response. Multiple Choice and Creative Response testing usually give different results, the former being the easier one for the respondent. The question which the researcher must ask, therefore, is which to use. In the present case, *the one to use is that which is the more closely associated with (i.e. predictive of) whether or not a word conveys its intended meaning when presented in its normal context.* In other words, the test we need is the one which tells us if a word is well enough known for it to convey its intended meaning. The work undertaken to answer this question indi-

Matching the people tested to the general population

The test room records of the 500 respondents were used for the development of an estimate of the word knowledge of the adult population of London. In various stages [g], these respondents had been matched to the general population in terms of three highly relevant variables. These were: the level (in terms of skill and training) of the respondent's present job or last job; the type of newspaper read by the respondent; the type of school which respondent had attended. The relevance of these three variables lay in the fact that each had a substantial numerical association with word knowledge (as tested in this enquiry)[h].

cated that the Creative Response method was better than Multiple Choice in this respect. In technical terms, its correlation with 'communication of intended meaning' was higher than was the correlation for Multiple Choice for the majority of the tests made [f]. A problem still remained however. Should the reply on the Creative Response test be marked leniently or hard? Here again the answer must depend upon which method of marking gives the higher correlation 'with whether or not the test word communicated its intended meaning when presented in normal context'. On this criterion, *creative response marked leniently* emerged as the better measure to use (because its correlation was more often the higher of the two).

[f]   Twenty separate tests were made, each based upon a separate word.

[g]   The original invitations to members of the public had been controlled so that, of those who came, there was a wide distribution in terms of each of five different sectors of the population. These sectors had been defined in terms of the occupational level (present job or of last job) and they were: the professional, semi-professional, administrative and executive who were estimated at that time as making up 4.5% of the London population; the highly skilled(10.0%); the skilled (22.8%); the moderately skilled (27.3%); the semi skilled and the unskilled (35.4%). In the original enquiry, the point of this five-way split was to allow the development of separate estimates of the word knowledge of each of these sectors, because previous research has indicated that there were major differences between them in terms of word knowledge. To render the test room sample more representative of the general population, each of the tested sectors was separately matched to its equivalent sector in the general population. This matching was in terms of type of school attended and type of newspaper read, each of which had been shown by the present enquiry to have a substantial numerical association with word knowledge as tested ($+0.61$ and $+0.66$ respectively). Subsequently, and for the development of estimates of the word knowledge of the total adult population of London, the results from the five occupational sectors were combined, *each with due weight*. Thus Group I's score on the word 'decade' was given a weight of 4.5 (since 4.5% of the population were at that time estimated as being in this group), that of Group II a weight of 10.0 and those of Groups III, IV and V weights of 22.8, 27.3 and 35.4 respectively. A new average could then be computed. This was done separately for each of the 100 tested words.

[h]   These were, respectively $+0.64$, $+0.66$ and $+0.61$. Other correlates of word knowledge are given in Table 3. The three used for matching had a multiple correlation with word knowledge of $+0.75$.

The effect of such matching was virtually to eliminate those *known* differences between the tested 500 and the general adult population of London which were correlated with level of word knowledge[i, j].

THE FINDINGS

Table 1 gives the percentage correct for each of the 100 words tested. It gives this information for the adult population (of London) as a whole.

From this table it appears that 35 of the 100 words tested were known at test level to fewer than 50% of the general population. Indeed, some known to much fewer — the hardest 10 of them to fewer than 8%. Since all of the words tested were taken from broadcast material, it would seem that some re-levelling of the broadcaster's sights was necessary. At least as important is the fact that only 9 of the 100 words were known (to test level) by as many as 90% of the population.

The test of word knowledge which produced these results did not involve putting these words into normal broadcast context and it may therefore seem to some that the state of word knowledge indicated in Table 1 may in fact be less a barrier to communication than it seems. Thus it is often argued that context suggests or gives the meaning of a word. There is in fact some evidence available on this point. A study conducted in collaboration with the author [40] involved a comparison, for 20 words, of word knowledge scores *in* and *out* of context. There was in fact a tendency for a higher score to emerge when words were presented in context than when presented alone. However the average difference was quite small (an increase of 2% per word). Moreover, whereas context did in some specific comparisons increase appreciably the number able to get the word *right*, there were other specific comparisons where context led to appreciably *fewer* getting it right. Apparently context *can* be misleading too.

The other question which is bound to be asked is whether or not it is possible for a sentence to convey its intended meaning in spite of one of its words being unfamiliar to the listener. There are several sources of evidence on this point. The work of Vernon [154] and Belson [105] indicated a high degree of correlation between word knowledge and comprehension

[i] Even though the matched sample was fairly similar to the general adult population in terms of age and sex, these two variables were not included as explicit matching criteria because they were not correlated with word knowledge (see Table 3) — so that deliberate matching for them could in fact make no difference to the final estimate of the public's word knowledge.

[j] This system of matching does not necessarily make the final estimate of the public's word knowledge fully trustworthy because it is always conceivable that a correlate of word knowledge which is largely independent of those used for matching has been left out altogether. That there is such a variable and that it would make much difference to the results must not be put too high, but it does remain feasible.

TABLE 1.

Estimates of percentages knowing words at test levels

Word Tested	Percent*	Word Tested	Percent	Word Tested	Percent
nexus	0.4	proximity	49	complicated	80
burgeon	1	intermediate	49	exaggerated	80
polemics	1	discrepancy	50	annual	81
empirical	1	hazardous	53	guard	81
stultified	4	pillaged	54	decide	81
calumnies	4	environment	56	omission	81
intrinsic	4	shrewd	58	city	82
autonomous	4	amicable	59	recurrence	83
peripheral	7	vigilant	59	aroma	83
salubrious	7	gradient	60	subscriber	83
obsequious	9	collaborate	65	forthcoming	83
paradox	12	menacing	67	modest	84
chronological	13	destiny	68	vigorous	84
ambiguous	15	sequel	68	dispute	85
hypothetical	17	anticipation	68	preserved	85
decade	17	eliminated	68	betray	86
credence	22	minority	70	postpone	86
bigoted	23	clients	70	exports	86
piety	23	inferior	70	entry	87
ratification	23	inevitable	71	abolish	87
vehement	27	simultaneous	71	requested	88
itinerary	27	feasible	71	climb	88
subtle	34	curtail	72	thaw	88
tenacious	37	celebration	72	expanded	89
nutrient	37	efficient	73	escape	92
opinionated	39	deliberate	73	foreigner	92
vulnerable	40	melancholy	74	tale	94
prudent	42	coincide	74	isolated	94
fundamental	44	threaten	74	mistake	94
meticulous	45	notorious	74	sufficient	95
incentive	45	flexible	76	to profit	96
flair	48	important	76	halted	96
incapacitated	49	capacity	77	purchase	98
		fact	77		

* Rounded to nearest whole percent (with exception of 'Nexus').

of the talks in which these words occurred. Another study*, conducted in collaboration with the BBC, indicated that the presence of a difficult word in a sentence not only reduced substantially the listener's understanding of the passage in which it occurred, but interfered also with (i) grasp of the next passage and (ii) retention of the preceding passage. Finally, preliminary work done in preparation for the present study indicated that

---

* "The effect on comprehension and recall of introducing difficult words into a talk", D. Harvey, University of Aberdeen.

though listeners did at times grasp the meaning of a passage in spite of unfamiliarity with some important constituent word, this tended to be a minority occurrence.

There is one last point bearing on Table 1 which I think ought to be made. Matching volunteers to the public is not yet an exact process, and it does remain possible that complete matching would have altered somewhat the percentages in Table 1. However, the evidence available about representativeness of test-room groups strongly suggests that any such alteration would lead to a reduction rather than to an increase in the size of these percentages.

The Creative Response method allows one to see the kinds of errors made by respondents. Worth noting amongst these are the following: 'ratified' was confused by several with 'rectified'; 'empirical' was occasionally taken to have some connection with 'the empire'; one respondent defined 'bigoted' as 'to be born' (i.e. "Abraham bigoted Isaac").

Word knowledge in different sections of the population
Information was available from the enquiry about word knowledge in different sections of the London population. Table 2, which relates word knowledge to occupational level, illustrates how in this study word knowledge fell with each step down the occupational scale.

TABLE 2.

Word knowledge scores by occupational level

	%Correct
Professional, semi-professional, executive	87.3
Highly skilled	75.3
Skilled	64.0
Moderately skilled	53.1
Semi-skilled and unskilled	49.8

The difference between the professional group and the semi-skilled was very great indeed and even the highly skilled and the moderately skilled were substantially different in terms of the words they knew. Such differences are of prime importance to the broadcaster, and his awareness of them can make a lot of difference to whether he is understood by the many or by the few.

Table 3 illustrates some of the other ways in which word knowledge varies within the London population. It relates different characteristics to word knowledge through correlation indices[k]. These characteristics include occupational level.

[k] A correlation of +1.0 would indicate a 100% relationship, one of +0.7 indicates a 49% relationship and one of 0.0 a complete absence of relationship.

TABLE 3.

The correlates of word knowledge

Variable	Correlation	Variable	Correlation
Occupational level	+ 0,64	Type of school attended*	+ 0.61
Anyone under his/her		Whether 'quality' or	
authority in last job (yes		'popular' newspaper	
or no)	+ 0.32	taken	+ 0.66
Intelligence	+ 0.57	Types of books read**	+ 0.37
Age finished full-time		Library member	
education	+ 0.54	(yes or no)	+ 0.32
Any exams passed		Ever hear Third Program	
(yes or no)	+ 0.58	(yes or no)	+ 0.18
Further education since		TV owner (yes or no)	+ 0.06
finishing full-time		Age	+ 0.03
education (yes or no)	+ 0.31	Sex	+ 0.02

* Whether (a) primary or elementary or secondary modern or central or (b) technical, or grammar or university or teachers training college.
** e.g., reads history or biography or plays or poetry.

For most of these relationships there is little that is surprising. Thus they indicate substantially higher word knowledge amongst those in the upper occupational and educational levels, and amongst the readers of papers like The Times, The Observer, The Sunday Times, The Daily Telegraph. People who claimed that they read history or biographies or plays or poetry had higher word knowledge than the others. This applied also to those who said they sometimes listened to the Third Program, and to those who said they were members of a library. However, the size of the difference in each of these three cases was much smaller than some of the others indicated in Table 3. Interestingly, neither age nor sex nor TV ownership was associated meaningfully with word knowledge score.

[7]

A planning study for the television series "Britain in decline?"[a]

A pre-broadcast study dealing with the public's awareness and evaluation of changes in Britain, both in the way of life at home and in her position abroad.

AIMS

The enquiry reported here was carried out at the end of 1955 in preparation for a series of television programs about Britain's position at home and abroad. This series was to consist of six programs in which 'Britain of 50 years ago' was to be compared with 'Britain today'. It was hoped that in this way those seeing programs in the series would be led to think more about the changes that had taken place and also about the import of such changes to present-day Britain. However, for the proper preparation of a program intended to inform and to educate, certain information was needed about the existing attitudes and knowledge of the intended or target audience. It was to provide such information that the present study was made. The study was focused on the following questions.

Do English people think that Britain has 'declined' or 'improved' over the last half century?
In what particular ways, if any, do they think she has declined? What evidence do they cite, and what do they claim to be the causes?
In what particular ways, if any, do they think she has improved?
Who or what has, in their opinion, caused these improvements?

Information of this kind would make it possible to make a more informed selection of subject matter for the program, to avoid wrongly concentrating upon evidence already known to and considered by viewers at the expense of evidence but little known or considered.

It would allow the broadcasters to focus attention upon those ideas about causes which did not happen to be in line with the facts. Certainly

[a] This report is based upon work conducted by the writer and reported in the BBC document VR/56/1. [24]

it would be wasteful to concentrate upon producing awareness of certain kinds of changes when that awareness existed already. Equally it is well to know just *how* people think on a particular issue before attempting to modify that thinking: the psychology of selection and distortion in line with one's beliefs is too well established to be ignored,[b] and able communicators ordinarily start by making an assessment of what they are up against.

METHODS

The sample

The sample of people taking part in this study consisted of 416 adult viewers who came by invitation to local centres. Most of those invited had been interviewed in the recent past in the course of the BBC's Survey of Listening and Viewing so that name, address, age and sex were known in advance and could be used in the manner already described in Chapter 3 to secure a sample representative of the target audience in terms of age, sex and social class. The tests were made in six different regions in England, well scattered geographically. Where, as in two regions, advance information about age and class was not available in sufficient quantity, the electoral registers for the area were used to supplement the number required, though inevitably this reduced control over the ultimate *composition* of the group and made more necessary a process of later matching described below.

The rate of turn-out for all invited was 26%, and the 416 who came consisted of these people plus a friend in most cases. Because of the controls built into the invitation system for the majority of the invitees, the 416 who came proved to be approximately representative of the target audience in terms of age, sex and social class, though there was clearly room for improvement in this respect. Accordingly, after testing had been completed and results entered on punch cards, an adjustment of sample composition was made by replicating record cards within under-represented sub-sections. The cards replicated were selected randomly within the sub-groups concerned. There was no discarding of cases in this process of matching the sample to the target audience because all matching was done by weighting *up*. In the final analysis of data it emerged, as indeed it should, that this process had rendered the adjusted sample fairly closely representative of the target audience in terms of educational background as well as age, sex and class[c]

---

[b]   See references 6, 31, 38, 47, 68, 98.

[c]   As explained in Chapter 3, this system of matching the total sample to the target audience in terms of age, sex and class, and possibly in terms of other variables as well, does not in itself ensure that matching is complete or sufficient. The experimental evidence available strongly suggests that matching for these things plus educational level is in fact sufficient for tests of the kind being made here, but a certain wariness against over-confidence in this respect is necessary and desirable.

Prior to their starting tests in the test-room, no indication whatever had been given to these people of the purpose of the meeting, though it was clear from the outset that the evening would end with general discussion of the good and the bad features of the television broadcasting service.

Testing procedures

After light refreshment on arrival, respondents were told enough — but no more — about the purpose of the meeting to prepare them for what was to come. Their preparation included a period devoted to establishing the three rules of procedure for this sort of work: that they should work without discussion and without mutual assistance of any kind; that they should be completely frank in what they put down; that they should give their full effort to getting down whatever was asked for. They worked under conditions of assured anonymity and their replies were entered by them in small booklets.

The period of preparation took up to half an hour and after this they went through the following procedures, sitting throughout at long tables.

(1) They used a graduated verbal scale to indicate whether they thought Britain had 'gone *up*' or '*down*' over the last 50 years or so, it being made clear that the question was a *general* one and that it referred both to the way of life 'here in Britain' *and* to her 'position in the world'; there were seven points on the scale which ranged from 'gone *down* VERY MUCH', through 'just about the same' to 'gone *up* VERY MUCH'.

(2) After this they were asked to write down exactly what they had in mind in making the latter judgment, that is, to explain this judgment or rating.

(3) In the next stage they used specially prepared sheets to indicate any ways in which they thought Britain had '*gone down*', and then to say, for each way mentioned (i) what made them think she had 'gone down' (the evidence) and (ii) who or what they thought had caused this decline. Then, on the same kinds of sheets, they entered any way(s) in which they thought Britain had improved and who or what had caused such improvement(s).

(4) The fourth step was a voting process in which the whole group voted (using a form of private ballot) on statements offered by group members about various ways in which Britain had changed. This occurred only after the completion of steps (1)–(3) above.

(5) Finally, group members filled in a personal detail sheet which asked for information about age, education, job, interests, program preferances, whether a viewer or not (as a check on their being viewers) and various other items of information.

Group members were assured of their anonymity and knew that their answers were strictly confidential. The full session took 2 hours, was carefully supervised and resulted in a rich yield of statements and comments. At the end of it, but only then, there was general discussion of what was right or wrong with TV programs.

<h3 style="text-align:center">FINDINGS</h3>

<h4 style="text-align:center">GENERAL OPINION ABOUT THE DIRECTION OF BRITAIN'S CHANGE</h4>

As shown in Table 1 below, 40% took the view that Britain had 'gone down' over the last half century and 52% that she had 'gone up'.

TABLE 1.

Opinions about the direction of change

Britain has gone *down* VERY MUCH	5% ⎫	
Britain has gone *down* A FAIR AMOUNT	19% ⎬	40%
Britain has gone *down* A LITTLE	16% ⎭	
Britain has STAYED JUST ABOUT THE SAME	3%	3%
Britain has gone *up* A LITTLE	14% ⎫	
Britain has gone *up* A FAIR AMOUNT	23% ⎬	52%
Britain has gone *up* VERY MUCH	15% ⎭	
NO OPINION or impossible to say	5%	5%
	100%	100%

As might perhaps be expected, those claiming that Britain had 'gone up' were dwelling upon a different aspect of the matter from those claiming that she has 'gone down'. Thus, as indicated by Table 2, those who believed that Britain had 'gone up' appraised the situation mainly in terms of matters *within* Britain. In the other hand, those who thought she had 'gone down' tended to have made that appraisal in terms of Britain's *position in the world*. This does not necessarily mean that those for whom domestic issues were the deciding factor didn't know about Britain's position abroad, or vice versa. It only means that different sections of the population dwelt upon (or considered important) different aspects of Britain's position and that they made their general evaluation in terms of these.

TABLE 2.

Respondent pre-occupation in making a general rating

Generalized rating		In making the rating, respondent is putting greater weight upon		
Britain rated as going		*Matters abroad*	*Matters at home*	*Uncertain/ Equal weight*
Up	(52%)	8%	34%	10%
Down	(40%)	26%	7%	7%
Other	(8%)	0%	2%	6%

WAYS IN WHICH BRITAIN IS GOING 'DOWN' OR 'UP'

The third stage in the test procedure was aimed at charting public aware-ness of particular ways in which Britain had (i) declined and (ii) improved, each individual being required to write down, his or her own list of 'ways'. This, let me emphasize, is quite different from asking people to signify agreement or disagreement concerning a statement actually put before them. *Volunteered* ideas are thought to provide an indication of the degree to which issues are in the forefront of the respondent's thinking and as such are 'living issues' likely to interest viewers. Quite a lot of time was allowed for this enumeration and respondents were encouraged to go on writing. As in all other parts of the testing period, collaboration between group members was very much discouraged (and in fact there was little sign of it occurring).

The details so collected were then collated and classified under those heads which their own content seemed to suggest as most suitable. This is the form of analysis known as content analysis and a full description of it is given in Chapter 13.

The resulting classifications are set out in Table 3 and against them are: (i) the percentages nominating them as areas of decline, (ii) the percentages nominating them as areas of improvement, (iii) the percentages nominat-ing them irrespective of whether they were thought to be areas of decline or improvement (i.e. totals of the entries in columns 1 and 2).

Two rather general observations should be made about Table 3. In the first place, the figures in the 'totals' column may be taken as an indication of the kinds of things which are likely to be in the forefront of people's minds when they consider 'change in Britain' (whether it be for better or worse). Thus there appears to be a big difference in the public's concern about changes with respect to 'the arts' (3%) and concern about changes relating to 'industry' (95%). Accordingly a program focused upon changes in industry would seem to be much more likely to meet with in-terest (and to be considered relevant) than one dealing with changes in the arts.

The second point to be made about Table 3 is that those claiming that Britain had 'gone *up*' with respect to some activity or condition were not necessarily disagreeing with those who said that Britain has 'gone *down*' in that respect: they were very often talking about different aspects of the one broad issue. Thus the 48% who said that Britain was 'going up' with respect to industry were referring to things like full and secure employment, working conditions, wage rates, hours of work and so on, while the 47% nominating industry as an area of *decline* were referring to things like in-dustrial output, will to work, pride in workmanship, industrial unrest. Again, the 46% claiming a decline in international relations were thinking mainly in terms of world *power* while the 17% who thought Britain was 'going up' were thinking more in terms of 'influence on the moral plane'. Finally, the 39% who thought there was a decline in 'our way of life' were

TABLE 3.

Types of 'decline' and 'improvement' volunteered

Area of reference	Percentage volunteering it		
	As area of decline	*As area of improvement*	*Total*
	%	%	%
Industry	47	48	95
(e.g. level of output; willingness to work; management − labour relations; full employment; wage rates).			
Health (including health services)	4	65	69
International relations	46	17	63
(e.g. as a world power; as a colonial power; in prestige and respect; in foreign relations; in moral influence)			
Way of life	39	23	62
(e.g. level of responsibility and independence; seriousness of purpose; civil liberties; level of materialism; community spirit; fullness of life; opportunity; breadth of horizons).			
Education	8	44	52
(e.g. standard of education; educational facilities).			
Standard of living	0	43	43
Economics abroad	28	10	38
(e.g. position in world economics; world markets; export trade; standard of goods; specific exports).			
Housing	4	28	32
(e.g. number available; quality and design).			
Social services and general welfare (excluding health service − see above)	2	28	30
(e.g. care of aged and infirm; family allowances; child welfare).			
Science and new developments	0	30	30
Transport	11	9	20
(e.g. efficiency; disaster rate; condition of rolling stock).			
Crime	17	1	18
Cost of living	17	0	17
Leisure and entertainment	3	13	16
Character, manners, morals	13	1	14
Sport	7	5	12
The Church and religion	11	0	11
Family life	5	2	7
Government	4	3	7
'The arts'	1	2	3
The press	1	0	1

thinking in terms of individual responsibility and initiative, seriousness of purpose, growth of materialism, etc., while those saying there was improvement (23 %) had in mind ideas of the kind: 'broadening horizons', 'a fuller way of life', 'increased social equality' and 'improvements in material welfare'. This is not to deny the occurrence of direct conflict or of confused views, but it does serve to emphasize a point made earlier, namely that people, in appraising a situation rather differently, are often only looking at it from different points of view. The material in Table 5 shows where there tends to be *real* conflict of opinion.

Turning to the actual 'changes' enumerated (see from Table 3) the main areas of alleged *decline* were: industry, namely industrial output and industrial relations; international relations, particularly in terms of world power; some aspects of 'way of life' including reduced responsibility and reduced seriousness of purpose, less individualism, undisciplined youth, loss of civil liberties; economics abroad (mainly trade and quality of goods); crime (i.e. an increase); cost of living; character, manners and morals; the Church and religion. The main areas of *improvement* were: health; industrial *conditions* (i.e. for employees) and production methods; education; standard of living; science; housing (i.e. better houses and more of them); social services and general welfare; some aspects of 'way of life' (e.g. fuller life, more opportunity, more equality).

'CAUSES' OF DECLINE

It will be recalled that when respondents were giving 'ways in which Britain had declined', they were asked to follow this up by stating the nature of the evidence for their opinions and the cause(s) to which they attributed the decline.[d]

Generally speaking, the *evidence* cited was scanty and not very useful, whereas *causes* were numerous and at times illuminating. Details are set out below under the headings already used in Table 3. When setting out 'causes', the practice is adopted hereunder of (i) giving the percentage, among those nominating a decline, who gave a cause and (ii) stating the more frequently named 'causes'.

Industry: Output; Industrial Relations
(47 % say 'decline' versus 48 % 'improvement')

The *evidence* more frequently cited for 'a decline' included: poor workmanship, shoddy goods; personal observations and hearsay concerning laziness in industry; comparisons by old hands of 'past and present' willingness to work; the number of 'frivolous strikes'; cases of technicians or skilled men who went abroad (for better pay and conditions).

[d] The reason for seeking such information was to find out if the evidence on which they were going and the causes they had in mind might possibly be broadened or otherwise be made more adequate — and if so, in what way this might be done. All the 'ways' were written down before any request was made for 'evidence' and 'causes'.

'*Causes*'. Some 93% of those claiming a decline offered 'causes'. Of these, by far the most frequently given was 'the unions', some of the references being 'too much power', 'abuse of power', 'restrictive practices'. Others were: no pride or interest in the job; the destructive nature of mass production (i.e. it destroys craftsmanship and both pride and interest in the job); taxation (which kills the urge for extra earnings and reduces business initiative); full employment (which makes jobs 'too safe'); a general unwillingness to work hard, laziness, an exaggerated sense of well-being, relaxation of effort after the war; too much wanted for too little (by the working man); obsolete equipment; insufficient skilled labour (due to emigration, poor training facilities, etc.); insufficient incentive; ineffective control by management.

International Relations
(46% say 'decline' versus 17% 'improvement')

The *evidence* given for the claim was of the following kind: trouble spots throughout British territories; the fact that "every little nation seems to think it can cock a snook at us"; the fact that "we seem to fall in with the policy of other governments, waiting for them to take the lead"; the loss of territory from time to time; "less respect seems to be given to English people abroad".

'*Causes*' were offered 73% of the claimants, the more frequent being: the passing of the "John Bull attitude", weakness, the absence of any great or forceful leader; lack of statesmanship, foreign policy; a tendency to play second to the U.S.A.; the rise of two other great powers (U.S.A. and Russia); the giving up of possessions abroad, the "rise of the colonies", the loss of empire; the development of the atomic phase in warfare, inadequate military strength; the "use of force and repression" in Kenya and other possessions, the maintenance of troops where they are not wanted; "exploitation of underprivileged people", too much interference with others.

Way of Life

(39% say 'decline' versus 23% 'improvement'. Note that this notion refers to personal responsibility and independence, seriousness of purpose, level of materialism, amount of dedication and of "pulling together", civil liberties).

Evidence: day-to-day cases of selfishness; attitudes of trade unionists to their leaders; the attitudes of children and teenagers; the size of cinema crowds; monopolies in industry; the retaining of emergency powers by Government; use of troops to break strikes; length of military service; the fact that "anything different is frowned on"; the way that people "expect things to be done for them"; overcrowding; traffic chaos.

Causes. Approximately 60% gave causes, the more frequent of which were: too much welfare and state care (which makes people do less for themselves); the quantity of mass entertainment readily available; American films and comics; insufficient discipline and training of youth; growth of state controls and red tape.

Economics Abroad
(28% say 'decline' versus 10% 'improvement')

Evidence: loss of overseas orders and reduction in exports; the rising cost of exports; adverse comparisons of advertisements in American and British trade journals; Britain's dependence upon American dollars.

Causes. Approximately 95% of those nominating a decline gave a reason for so claiming, the more frequently given being: the trade unions, strikes and disputes; unwillingness of employees to 'do a fair day's work'; high production costs associated with wages being too high for the work done; the production of shoddy goods; poor marketing techniques; increased competition in a buyers' market; the low price of competing goods; "inability of Britain to keep her trade commitments"; too slow in filling orders; collapse of the colonial system of economy; heavy commitments abroad and heavy defence costs; the last two wars (involving a heavy drain on assets and loss of markets).

Crime
(17% say 'decline' versus 1% 'improvement')

Evidence: most of the evidence consisted of: 'newspaper reports of robbery and other crimes'.

Causes. Approximately 95% of the claimants gave a cause, the more recurrent being: not enough control or discipline of children by parents; mothers are too often out at work, leaving children alone; the housing shortage; broken homes; punishment for crime is not severe enough; not enough police; a growing desire for material things and 'to take life easily'; the war and national service.

Cost of Living
(17% say 'decline' versus 0% 'improvement')

Evidence: daily experience of high prices; fluctuating prices; tax taken from pay; the number of married women going to work; comparisons of costs before and since the war.

Causes. Some 93% of these gave 'causes', the more frequent ones being: heavy taxation, cost of armaments, the 'abuse of Purchase Tax' (which "was intended to stop *luxury* buying"); trade unions; restrictive practices of trade unions, strikes; constant wage rises, "war-time habit of high wages"; the Government, the Government's abolition of price controls; a general unwillingness of people to work hard; the Welfare State; nationalization; "the middle'man (who fleeces us)".

Character, Manners and Morals
(13% say 'decline' versus 1% 'improvement')

Evidence: petty pilfering, crime, sex crimes; the number of divorces, amount of adultery; cases of malingering to avoid work and of lazy working habits; incidence of "fiddling and faredodging"; "pushing and shoving"; "no respect for anyone or anything"; the growth of the Pools; sexy advertisements.

Causes. Some 88% of these claimants gave causes, the more frequent of which were: lack of parental control of children, bad home life; the decline of Church and religion; the war and National Service (producing moral laxity); 'education and other broad-view influences' (e.g. 'too much broad-mindedness'); the 'modern habit of tolerance'; mothers going out to work; too much money in the hands of youth; the 'modern get-rich-quick' attitude; the levelling of society so that there are no "betters" left to be looked up to.

Transport
(11% say 'decline' versus 9% 'improvement')

Evidence: number of road accidents; experience as a driver; dirty railway stations and premises; out-of-date railway equipment.

Causes. About 95% of those claiming decline gave causes and these included: not enough good roads, too many cars, increased traffic; bad driving, too much hurry; not enough police; dirty stations and railway facilities; not enough money put up by the government; shortages of railway manpower; the government's increase of controls.

The Church and Religion
(11% say 'decline' versus 0% 'improvement')

Evidence: half empty churches; full cinemas and the amount of time spent in pleasurable activities; the belief that Christianity is not necessary; the prevalence of swearing and blasphemy; increased juvenile crime.

Causes. Approximately 95% of these claimants gave causes, the more recurrent of which were: the absence of "real spiritual leadership" from the Church; clergymen are of the wrong type; an absence of religious example on the part of parents; too much Sunday entertainment available (including TV); people are too busy and are becoming "more materialistic"; education.

Education
(8% say 'decline' versus 44% 'improvement')

Evidence: reduced standards compared with the past, increased failure rates, children of 7–8 unable to read or write; juvenile delinquency; the remarks of school children.

Causes. Causes were given by 27 of the 32 people claiming the decline. The main ones given were: shortage of teachers, inadequate salaries for teachers; lack of discipline in schools; over-crowded classrooms; too much entertainment available to the children; poor study methods; "amateurs and theorists in control" of the system; Government policy.

Sport
(7% say 'decline' versus 5% 'improvement')

Evidence: Britain's being beaten at most sports, frequently by her "continental pupils" and frequently in fields originally dominated by her; she "now holds honours in no field but cricket"; an absence of local playing fields.

Causes. Some 20 of the 28 claimants gave causes, and these included: insufficient facilities for training; those responsible for control and selection in sport are inefficient, too old, out-of-date; not enough interest is taken in youngsters; the war.

Family Life
(5% say 'decline' versus 2% 'improvement')

Evidence: divorce rates; mothers going out to work; small families; undisciplined children; prevalence of family rows; cruelty to children.

Causes. Sixteen of the twenty claimants gave causes, the more recurrent of which were: mothers are out at work while children have lunch at school; insufficient disciplining of children, no real home life; lack of family entertainment; small families; cost of living; lax morality; the war.

Housing
(4% say 'decline' versus 28% 'improvement')

Evidence: obvious overcrowding; divorce cases.

Causes. There were approximately 10 causes given by the 16 persons claiming decline and these causes included: too many people coming here from abroad; too many building controls; the war (destruction of buildings); poverty; poor building materials.

Government
(4% say 'decline' versus 3% 'improvement')

Evidence: "too much politics and not enough get-together in Parliament", "jobs for the boys", security leaks, evidence of Government waste, apathy in local government affairs, the "hushing-up of mistakes".

Causes. Six of the sixteen claimants gave causes which included: general laxity and apathy of M.P.s.; not enough young men in Parliament; the Cold War, the arms race.

Health
(4% say 'decline' versus 65% 'improvement')

Evidence: increasing amount of disease (e.g. cancer and TB); more food poisoning, dirty streets, dirty cafes; pollution of the atmosphere; "people are now more tense and nervy".

Causes. Between them, the 16 people claiming the decline gave 12 causes, which included: dirty handling of food; apathy or lack of interest in matters of public health; reduction of Government spending on the Health Scheme; the pace of modern life; the National Health Scheme.

Leisure and Entertainment
(3 % say 'decline' versus 13 % 'improvement')

Evidence: 'people don't seem to make their own entertainment now'; 'very few people take an active part in entertainment now'; poor TV and radio shows.

Causes. The 5 causes coming from the 12 claimants included: "too much laid-on (canned) entertainment"; TV ("killing other activities"); not enough use of "lesser" material.

'CAUSES' OF IMPROVEMENT

The investigation of ideas about 'causes' of *improvement* was less detailed than that into ideas about 'causes' of *decline*, because it was intended that the program should concentrate more upon decline. Accordingly, the

TABLE 4.

Claimed causes of 'going up'

	% Naming it
Better education	16
The Welfare State	11
The National Health Service	11
The government	10
The war	10
Enthusiasm and hard work	8
Improved production methods and plant	8
Broadcasting	8
'Our statesmen' (Churchill named frequently)	7
Medical research	7
Scientific research	7
The trade unions	6
The Socialist government	6
Higher wages and more money generally	6
The character and opinions of the average man	6
International co-operation	5
Full employment	5
Greater educational facilities	4
Better houses	4
Improvements in housing conditions	3
International competition in trade	3
Better medical care	3
British sportsmen	3
State aid in education	2
The co-operation and support of the "colonies"	2

groups' enumerations of 'causes of going up' were geared simply to improvement in *general*, rather than to improvements in *specific fields*. In Table 4 is a list of the more frequently given causes and against them the percentage of the sample putting them forward.

VOTING ON PARTICULAR STATEMENTS

In the fourth stage of the testing procedure, group members voted, using paper and pencil, upon statements put forward by their own members. There was a special way of going about this. The Chairman asked group members to call out (without any discussion) what they thought were causes of decline or of improvement in Britain. They were told that their statements had to be brief and that each statement should be about a single cause. The Chairman wrote these down, stopping the process when he had several on which votes might be taken. He had, if necessary, to reduce double statements to single ones and to rephrase statements in simple, unambiguous forms. He usually did this aloud, checking his interpretation and modification with the author of the statement. Next, each of these statements, possibly modified, was read out to the group with the instruction that members indicate, on a special form, whether or not they agreed with it or simply had no opinion about it. When this was done, further statements were elicited by the Chairman and treated in the same way.

Because groups tended not to be larger than 40 in size and because 40 is an insufficient base for a meaningful statement about distribution, it was necessary for the Chairman to have with him at each session the statements voted on by previous groups. This was to ensure that a new statement which happened to be the same in meaning as one voted on in another session was given precisely the same wording as it had on that previous voting occasion [e]. During the series of sessions, new statements continued to come up and these had to be treated as fresh statements. Nonetheless, the number of distinct statements that came from the groups with any frequency was not all that great and provided that equivalent statements were given the same wording, meaningful quantitative bases could be built up. For some matters of special interest to program staff, the Chairman saw to it that an appropriate statement *did* come up and was put to the vote at every session. One consequence of this voting system was that the numerical base for calculating the percentage agreeing or disagreeing varied from over 400 to about 40, though those with a base of less than 100 are not included in this report.

For voting, each respondent had a sheet laid out as follows for up to fifty different statements.

1.	agree	disagree	no opinion
2.	agree	disagree	no opinion
3.	agree	disagree	no opinion

[e] With sessions around the country sometimes being held simultaneously, this partially broke down; however, telephone checks between the three Chairmen allowed the system to operate to a workable degree.

The Chairman gave a number to each statement as it was put to the vote (i.e. 1, 2, 3, 4, 5, and so on in order of vote) and the respondent simply circled his or her vote against whatever the number of the statement was.

The main results of this census are set out in Table 5. However, they must be interpreted very cautiously. Since people were *asked* to vote on each proposition, the total of the votes cast for and against a given proposition does *not* nevessarily represent the public's *preoccupation* with it. (For instance, 2 out of 3 agreed to a particular statement about 'the arts', but only 3% had spontaneously mentioned 'the arts' as an area in which Britain had either 'gone up' or 'gone down'). What it *does* do is to indicate the extent to which people will agree or disagree with the statement *once it has been brought to their attention.*

TABLE 5.

Agreement or disagreement with statements

Statements put to the vote	Percentages who		
	Agreed	Disagreed	Had no opinion
	%	%	%
1. *Relating to Industry*			
People are no longer prepared to do a fair day's work.	65	27	8
There is a growing amount of inefficiency in industry.	61	21	18
There is not enough firmness in dealing with strikes and other forms of unrest.	79	14	7
People have more of a "don't care" attitude about their work now than they used to.	74	25	1
There has been a decline in productivity.	51	36	13
The quality and workmanship of our goods is going down.	81	15	4
Working conditions are better now.	91	4	5
There are too many foreigners coming to work in this country.	48	34	18
2. *Relating to Health*			
The general standard of health has gone up.	95	2	3
Britain has gone up in the way of health service.	96	0	4
3. *Relating to International Relations*			
Our importance in world politics and international affairs has gone down.	71	20	9
From the point of view of the armed forces, we are less important than we used to be.	58	32	10
We are spending too much on armaments and the armed forces.	48	39	13
Britain has declined in her prestige abroad.	66	23	11
We now have better relations with our colonies and the countries of the Commonwealth.	62	22	16

Statements put to the vote	Percentages who		
	Agreed	Disagreed	Had no opinion
	%	%	%
4. Relating to Way of Life			
There is less reward now for hard work and initiative.	68	29	3
People don't do things so much for themselves now.	67	23	10
We are not as enterprising as we used to be.	60	27	13
The money you save now is not worth much because of the way prices are rising.	89	10	1
As a country we are less united than we used to be.	64	27	9
Hire purchase is creating a false way of life.	67	26	7
5. Relating to Education			
There is greater opportunity for education now.	95	1	4
We've gone up as far as education is concerned.	77	10	13
6. Relating to Standard of Living			
The standard of living has gone up.	87	4	9
7. Relating to Economics Abroad			
We are exporting more now.	56	25	19
Britain has gone down as far as foreign trade is concerned.	60	17	23
In her dealings with other countries Britain's financial position is not so strong as it used to be.	86	4	10
8. Relating to Housing			
There is a better standard of housing nowadays.	84	9	7
9. Relating to Social Service and Welfare			
There is much more care and thought for elderly folk.	76	12	12
Britain has gone up in the field of child welfare.	90	1	9
10. Relating to Crime			
There is more crime now.	73	20	7
We have become too soft in dealing with crime.	82	14	4
11. Relating to Leisure			
People now spend less time doing things in connection with spare time interests.	64	25	11
12. Relating to Character, Manners, Morals			
The general level of morals in the country has declined.	70	23	7
Britain has declined in manners and general courtesy.	76	16	8

(*Continued Table 5*)

Statements put to the vote	Percentages who		
	Agreed	Disagreed	Had no. opinion
	%	%	%
13. *Relating to Sport*			
We've gone down as far as sport is concerned.	44	43	13
14. *Relating to Church and Religion*			
We've gone down as far as religion is concerned.	73	12	15
15. *Relating to Family Life*			
People do more for their children now than they used to do.	66	22	12
Britain has declined because there is less family life than there used to be.	64	23	13
There is a lack of parental control nowadays.	72	20	8
16. *Relating to Government*			
Britain has declined because people are less interested in the way they are governed than they used to be.	48	38	14
17. *Relating to 'the Arts'*			
As far as the arts are concerned we've gone down.	32	35	33
The theatre is not what it used to be.	47	40	13
18. *Relating to Science*			
In the field of science we don't compare as well as we used to with other countries.	23	67	10
In the matter of *using* scientific findings we don't compare as well as we used to with countries.	26	61	13

Some differences according to viewer characteristics

There was no appreciable difference in the ideas and the assessments of people above and below 30 years of age, but differences in terms of both sex and educational background were quite marked. Thus men were more pessimistic than women and those members of the sample with higher educational qualifications were more pessimistic than those with lower. And as might be expected from this, it is the male section of the sample and the 'better educated' who tend to judge in terms of Britain's 'position in the world' rather than in terms of 'matters at home'.

SUMMARY[f]

The evidence indicates that rather more people thought that Britain had 'gone up' over the last half century than thought that she has 'gone down'.

[f] It must be remembered that this enquiry was conducted in 1955. Its findings will not necessarily apply in a later period.

But those claiming improvements and those claiming decline were for the most part thinking of *different* aspects of Britain's changes during that period: the ones claiming decline were thinking mainly of Britain's position in relation to the rest of the world, while those claiming improvement were thinking mainly of things 'at home'.

In the enumeration of different ways in which Britain had *improved* or *declined*, the main areas (or categories) of claimed decline were, in order of frequency of mention: (1) industry (from the point of view of output and of attitude towards work); (2) international relations (from the point of view of world power and influence); (3) general way of life (from the point of view of personal responsibility, initiative, discipline of youth); (4) economics abroad; (5) economics at home (from the point of view of the cost of living); (6) crime (in terms of its prevalence); (7) character, manners and morals; (8) Church and religion; (9) transport. On the other hand, the main categories of claimed *improvement* were, in order of frequency of mention: (1) health; (2) industry (from the point of view of the conditions for the worker); (3) education; (4) economics at home (from the point of view of standard of living, wage levels, availability of goods); (5) science and new developments; (6) housing; (7) social services and general welfare; (8) general way of life (in terms of a fuller way of life, greater opportunity and equality, more kindness and friendliness); (9) international relations (from the point of view of Britain being a force for good in the world and from the point of view of her colonial relations).

The preceding paragraph also indicates that people who postulated *improvement* with respect to a particular category (e.g. industry or international relations or general way of life or economics at home) tended to be thinking of rather different things from those postulating *decline* in relation to the very same category. This applies not only to each of the above four categories, but to most of the others as well, and it appears to be something which went on to a major degree. In other words, differences in evaluating Britain's position appear to have sprung more from a major difference in the viewer's focus or perspective or pre-occupation than from differences of opinion on specific points.

This tendency of viewers to have been thinking of different things (in evaluating Britain's situation) does seem to offer a fruitful approach to the producer's stated task of getting people to think in a balanced way about Britain's position, for the study clearly indicates the particular things they tended to overlook.

The evidence also indicates the broad issues that were likely to be in the forefront of people's thinking — irrespective of the aspects focused upon — when they judged Britain's position. Thus nearly all of them (95%) referred either optimistically or pessimistically to industry, 69% referred to health, and 63% to international relations, whereas only 3% referred to 'the arts', 7% to family life, 11% to Church and religion, and 12% to sport. This information offers fairly clear pointers to issues of interest to viewers — though equally it may indicate that one or another broad issue, judged by expert opinion to be important (but so far figuring but little in the viewer's active thinking), should be brought more to the viewer's attention.

Viewers' agreement or disagreement with particular statements when directly presented with them (Table 5) indicated the degree to which points of view of possible importance to the producer's argument or thesis are likely to be accepted or rejected (irrespective of the degree to which the respondent is *pre-occupied* with them). Table 5 thus indicates some of the things a producer can take for granted in viewers and some that he cannot.

[8]

"Mental health"[a]

A planning study for the television series "The Hurt Mind",
dealing with the ideas and the attitudes of the public concerning
mental illness.

This enquiry was undertaken in 1956 in preparation for a series of television programs dealing with mental health and bearing the general
title of "The Hurt Mind". There were to be six programmes in this series
and in them it was intended to deal with different aspects of mental illness,
particularly its apparent causes and the different ways of treating it. This
preparatory enquiry was intended to answer the following questions.

1. What do viewers think is meant by mental illness?
2. How sympathetic or otherwise are people towards the mentally ill?
3. What do viewers think are the main kinds of mental illness and what do
   they think are its causes?
4. What do viewers think are the main ways of treating mental illness and
   how do they rate the effectiveness of these methods?
5. What impressions do they have of mental hospitals and of the conditions
   there?
6. Was there anything about a mental hospital that viewers felt they could
   not bear being shown?

It was expected that answers to these and to several other questions
would serve the following purposes: (i) they should indicate whether or
not it was necessary to spend program time in correcting images and in
softening attitudes; (ii) they should identify the kinds of information that
people most lacked (with respect to type, causes and treatment of mental
illness) so that the effort to inform them might be most efficiently focused;
(iii) they should help the producer to avoid showing things especially up-
setting to the viewer.

[a]   This report is based upon research conducted by the writer as a member of
      the Audience Research Department of the BBC and later published as "The
      Ideas of Viewers About the Mentally Ill" in *Mental Health*, Vol. 16, No. 3,
      1957 [8].

METHODS

The research method used was the group testing technique already described in some detail in Chapter 3. What follows is an essentially abbreviated description of it.

Viewers, broadly representative of Londoners in terms of age, sex and social class, came by controlled invitation to a central meeting place. These viewers did not know on arrival what the nature of the meeting would be, though they were aware that the evening would end with a general discussion of programs. There were approximately 180 viewers in all, meeting in four groups of about 45 each.

Once in the test room, group members were told of the purpose of the first half of the session. Their anonymity was heavily stressed and the dependence of both the B.B.C. and the public upon the frankness of their answers was put clearly before them. The test administrator or chairman called out the various questions and group members entered their opinions in small booklets. Conditions of silence and of non-discussion were maintained. Far from being a difficult topic on which to get answers, it was at times difficult to stop people from writing and the general yield of information was large.

In the subsequent analysis, special matching methods (see Chapter 3) were used to reduce such residual bias as occurred through the invitation system. The outcome of this was that the final group was quite closely representative of the viewing public in terms of social and occupational level, age and educational background[b] — variables which were empirically established as associated with attitudes and ideas of the kind being studied. This process does not ensure full representativeness[c], but it provides a considerable movement towards it. For safety however, and because this sample was a small one, the results are being regarded as giving answers accurate only within about 10%; accordingly the various quantifications set out under FINDINGS take the following form: one person in five; a large majority; about a third. The results don't necessarily apply beyond London.

FINDINGS
What do Viewers Think is Meant by Mental Illness?

A distinction between mental illness and insanity

About three-quarters of the group made a distinction between mental illness and insanity. While many thought that the difference was a matter of degree (the insane being the more advanced or acute cases), the main reason for making the distinction was that the insane were thought of as

[b] In other words, the 180 person sample taking part (and their results with them) was reweighted to resemble the public in terms of these variables.
[c] This is because volunteers may conceivably differ from others in terms of variables additional to (but independent of) the four named. See Chapter 3.

more or less incurable and the mentally ill as curable. Some respondents made the distinction on the ground that mental illness is caused by the environment while insanity is hereditary.

The different kinds of mental illness

Group members were asked to name as many as they could of the different mental illnesses. While their responses only rarely yielded the technical name for an illness, they did include a large number of *symptoms* of one kind or another. Of these, by far the most frequently given were those implying something akin to the anxiety neuroses (frequently described by viewers as 'nervous breakdowns' and sometimes as 'anxiety'). There were other references however: thus about one in five seemed to be referring to a form of paranoia, (e.g. 'they imagine people are talking/acting against them'). Other viewers referred to symptoms which seemed to imply one or another of the following: manic or depressive tendencies (one person in five); schizophrenia (about 1 in 4); obsessions, fixations or phobias (1 in 5); psychopathic personality (some used the terms 'cries easily', 'no conscience') (1 in 10); mental deficiency (1 in 10). Others references, given by about one person in twenty, included: 'epilepsy', 'brain injury', 'tumour', 'amnesia'/'lapse of memory', 'sex perversion', 'inferiority complex'. Between one and two people in ten included in their replies some general references of the kind: 'insanity', 'brain illness', 'brain fever', 'demented'. There was very little reference to senility. Here and there were single, odd, expressions like: 'sleeping sickness', 'egoism', 'polio', 'loss of personal habits', 'bed wetting' and 'without Christian beliefs'.

Things the mentally ill do which make them different from other people.

Asked about this, the most frequently mentioned differences given by the viewers were in terms of social behaviour. Half the group mentioned this in one form or another. Examples are: 'the mentally ill are irresponsible'/'have no moral sense'; they steal'; 'they are dirty'; 'they may be a danger to others'. Slightly fewer (two persons in five) referred to differences in terms of physical behaviour and mannerisms, such as: 'inadequate speech'; 'gaze past you into space'; 'odd movements of limbs and odd postures'; 'peculiar or neglected clothing'. A third of the group referred to confusion and lack of reason in their behavior (for example: 'can't think properly', 'can't recognise people', chronically 'absent minded') and about the same number thought that they were emotionally unstable. One person in four said that the mentally ill had delusions or hallucinations, the most common of those mentioned being 'delusions about persecution'. About a tenth of them referred to fear and withdrawal on the part of the mentally ill.

Some possible sources of viewers' opinions

Over half of the people in these groups claimed that they personally knew someone who was mentally ill and about three-quarters of them said that they have *at some time* known a person who was mentally ill. In addition, about two in five of them claimed that they have, at some time or other, seen a film on mental illness: in many cases this was "Snake Pit". (These may seem high proportions. Be that as it may, there was absolutely no reference in the form of invitation which could have suggested that mental illness would be discussed).

Attitudes of Viewers Towards the Mentally Ill

Group members were also asked how they felt towards the mentally ill. A few expressed their feelings as 'impatience with them', a small number openly rejected them, and about one person in five admitted fear of the mentally ill. *The great majority, however, expressed sympathy towards them*, most people making a direct statement to the effect that they were sorry for them, were sympathetic towards them, or would like to help them. Some of these (1 in 4) also urged treatment or care or kindness. One small group, while definitely sympathetic, had a feeling of frustration about trying to get across to them or trying to deal with them. About one person in ten, while sympathetic in attitude, had reservations to the effect that the mentally ill are very difficult to handle, and that it requires a lot of patience to do anything for them.

Asked how they would feel if a mental hospital was opened up near to where they live, one in five either said they would not really like it or expressed definite apprehension about it.

Causes of Mental Illness

The groups were asked to give as many as they could of the *causes* of mental illness. The causes so enumerated were predominantly *environmental* in kind, only one in four of the respondents mentioning or implying heredity. Moreover, relatively few of the environmental causes were of a blameworthy nature and respondents were very largely of the opinion that mental illness could happen to anyone.

Of the environmental causes: about eight persons in ten referred to strain or worry or shock; four in ten blamed surrounding conditions of the kind 'frustration', 'conflict', 'housing conditions', 'family troubles', and 'loneliness'; two in ten referred to childhood or past experiences such as 'ill treatment or rejection as a child', 'shock', 'nervous strain'; half of them gave injury or illness or disease as a cause, the majority of these implying injury to the brain. About one person in ten named one or another form of 'bad living' (e.g. 'too much drink', 'drugs'), and approximately the same number referred to 'sex problems'. A few named post-natal conditions and menopause.

Of the quarter mentioning hereditary causes, very few referred to inherited characteristics of a predisposing kind, most of the references being simply to 'heredity'.

The Treatment and Cure of the Mentally Ill

The chances of cure

Asked about the success of present-day medicine in curing mental illness, there was a considerable amount of confidence in the likelihood of cure, about three-quarters saying that a cure is effected very often and most of the rest that cure is effected occasionally. This contrasts very sharply with their views on the chances of cure 50 or more years ago, only about 1 % thinking that cure was, at that time, effected often and the majority that it occurred hardly ever or not at all.

Type of treatment available

Ideas about what treatment was provided in present-day mental hospitals varied quite a lot though there was a slight tendency for psychological-type treatment to be mentioned more often than purely physiological treatment, seven persons in ten referring to the first and six in ten to the latter.

Amongst the psychological-type treatments mentioned or referred to were: analytical methods, the main references being to psychoanalysis (four in ten gave this); rest and relaxation (two in ten); occupational therapy (1 in 10); kindness (1 in 10); humanist treatment such as outings, visits from friends, bright surrounding (1 in 10). Of the physiological-type treatments, the main emphasis was on shock treatment (4 in 10) and the use of drugs (3 in 10). About two persons in ten mentioned surgery and a few references were made to 'tracing the trouble to its physical cause'.

This view of present-day treatment contrasts very sharply with views about what it was like 50 or more years ago — where the main references were to isolation and punishment and discipline.

What mental hospitals are like

On being questioned, the great majority could name at least one mental hospital in Great Britain and three-quarters of the group could name two or more. It so happened that there had been considerable press publicity, some little time before these tests, about at least one mental hospital. It is possible that this affected the high yield on this question. Moreover, about four persons in ten claimed that they had already been on a visit to what they regarded as a mental hospital. Asked about mental institutions other than mental hospitals, the main references were to rest homes and to clinics. Throughout the test session, however, there seemed to be very little conscious distinction between primarily custodian institutions and other kinds of mental hospitals. Indeed, with quite a lot of viewers, there seemed to be little awareness of the existence of the former.

It is, presumably, against this general background that viewers answered when asked to say what they thought it was like for patients in mental hospitals and, later, when asked what was wrong with present-day facilities in mental hospitals.

About two persons in ten either held that there was nothing wrong or knew of nothing wrong with such facilities. The most frequent complaint was that there was insufficient trained staff (four persons in ten claimed this). About a third said that accommodation was inadequate, mostly to the effect that there were too few hospitals or that the present buildings were out-of-date. The same proportion held that treatment and medical knowledge were inadequate, mostly on the following grounds: there is not enough individual treatment; not enough is known about the nature of mental illnesses; patients are not sufficiently occupied; there is not enough freedom of movement for the patients; patients are too much isolated from every-day life; the mild and the advanced cases are mixed.

But views about conditions were not predominantly unpleasant ones. In saying what they thought it was like for patients, the most frequent single reference from viewers was to the provision of jobs and hobbies as part of occupational therapy (three persons in ten said this). Two in ten referred to cheerful surroundings, and about the same number commented that patients were treated kindly. There was also approving reference to: amenities such as television and radio (one in ten), methods of medical treatment (one in ten), quality of staff (one in ten) and the provision of outside contacts for patients.

Here again the picture contrasts sharply with that of the mental hospitals of the past, where practically every reference was of a negative kind and where some of the more frequently given views were: too much force, restraint or ill-treatment; like a gaol; bad living conditions; buildings were insanitary, grim, gloomy; they functioned as dumping grounds and not as hospitals; patients were treated as incurable; no individual treatment; staff were untrained and unsuited by temperament; they were the worst possible places.

Action likely to be taken by respondent over mental illness

Group members were asked what they would do if someone in their own circle appeared to be developing a mental illness. Three out of ten of them indicated that the action they would take would be of a non-professional kind, namely, attending to the treatment themselves at home. The majority, however, claimed that they would seek professional advice or treatment — though only one person in ten specified that he or she would take *immediate* action.

What is it Like in a Mental Hospital?

Viewers were asked how they would feel about being shown over a mental hospital and seeing the patients there. Here again answers must be presumed to be against a background in which (i) four out of ten of them had already visited at least some part of what they think of as a mental hospital and (ii) the majority of them at present know, personally, at least someone who is mentally ill.

Two-thirds of them appear to have been favourably disposed towards such a visit, mostly on the grounds that it would be 'interesting' or 'educational'. Of those not so disposed, some said that it would upset them and others that they would be nervous or fearful.

Asked if there was anything which they would prefer not to see on such a visit, a third of them said either that they would be willing to see all or that they felt that they *ought* to see all. Of the remainder, about half wanted to avoid the extreme and the violent cases and others preferred not to see 'shock treatment' or 'patients in extreme pain or in fits'. A few referred to 'the grotesque', to 'screaming' and to 'their moans and groans'.

About four persons in ten had, it will be recalled, seen at least one film on mental illness. About a third of these said that the film had upset or shocked them and that their reactions were unpleasant. Of the others, some said it 'interested' them and others that it made them feel pity or sorrow for the mentally ill.

Should the Series be Broadcast?

Asked if they thought the series should be put on, a majority said it should. This was, however, a very hypothetical question and its real purpose was to bring out viewers' reasons for supporting or opposing the broadcast of such a series. Amongst those saying 'put it on', about half gave as a reason that it would improve their knowledge on an important matter. Others said that it might help those afflicted at home, or it might show us how fortunate we are. Amongst those opposing it, some argued that: it might itself produce mental illness (1 in 10) and others that it would be too depressing or morbid (1 in 10).

SUMMARY OF FINDINGS

Several points emerged fairly clearly from this enquiry.

(1) A large majority of the viewers tested expressed sympathetic and kindly feelings towards the mentally ill. In this, however, many of the viewers tend to be excluding from the category of 'mental illness' a group which they would call 'the insane' and to be thinking largely, though by no means exclusively, in terms of something akin to the anxiety neuroses. These viewers also tended to feel that the causes of mental illness are largely enviromental, are not blameworthy, and that mental illness 'can happen to any of us'. Precisely how viewers feel towards the group they exclude from 'the mentally ill' (that is, the people they call 'the insane') does not emerge from this analysis.

(2) There was a general feeling of confidence in the possibility of curing the mentally ill, and viewers' ideas about facilities and conditions in mental hospitals did not tend to be unpleasant ones. While they are not without criticism, these viewers seemed sharply aware, on both these counts, of major progress over the last 50 years or so.

(3) In answering questions about treatment available for mental illness, viewers referred almost equally to psychological and to physiological methods. In this and in many of their other references, they appeared to have a lot of ideas to put forward and to be generally more knowledgeable than on many other topics, apparently because many people have had at least some personal contact with a mentally ill person at some time in their lives.

[9]

A planning study for the series of programs "Talking of America"[a]

Dealing with the Londoner's knowledge of an attitude towards America and Americans.

BACKGROUND AND AIMS

One of the very early planning studies based upon the 'group testing' method was concerned with the knowledge, opinions and attitudes of certain sections of the London population in relation to America. This information was required by the producer of a forthcoming series of six sound broadcasts under the general title "Talking of America".

The audience for whom the series was to be prepared had been defined by the producer as 'adults under 45 years of age', of middle and upper middle class background[b] and equally composed of men and women.

In this series it was proposed that American and English speakers should discuss the attitudes of the English towards America. Accordingly, it was necessary to know beforehand just what these attitudes were. In addition, the series was intended to inform the audience about America and the American way of life and for this to be done efficiently, it was essential to be aware of what people already knew and of what they did not know.

[a] This report is based upon an enquiry conducted by the writer in 1952 as a member of the Audience Research Department of the BBC and reported in the Department's LR/52/1959 [21]. Because the sample used was relatively small (a total of 203 cases), the study is presented here only as an example of the use of the 'group testing' method for the planning of a program.

[b] This specialization may seem strange when one is using a mass medium like radio. However, a growing body of evidence had made it clear enough that there were major differences in the abilities of people of different educational backgrounds to understand radio talks and discussions.[c] Accordingly some producers prepared such material with a restricted and fairly homogeneous audience in mind, being aware that many outside of this group would also hear it, but being prepared for only partial understanding on their part.

[c] See references [105, 114, 133, 146, 154, 156]

To meet these and other requirements of program production, a limited enquiry was carried out. Its several aims included the following:

1. to develop information about the target audience's level of knowledge about America;
2. to ascertain the attitudes and opinions of this audience with respect to each of the six aspects of America with which the series was to be concerned, namely: education; foreign affairs; home life; amount of crime; democracy and government; materialism.

THE METHODS OF RESEARCH

The research method used was that of 'group testing', conducted along the lines already described in Chapter 3. The study was based upon a total of 203 Londoners who came by controlled invitation to the BBC and who, because of this initial control over invitation, resembled the target audience fairly closely in terms of age, sex and social background. They met in groups of 15–20 at a time and first of all underwent the standard orienting procedure (described in Chapter 3) with its explanation of the purpose of the meeting, with its setting up of incentives to co-operate, and with its teaching of the three rules of procedure. Stated briefly, these three rules called for: absolute frankness; no discussion until the end of the session; real effort with the questions.

After this, each member of the group performed the following written tasks: (i) wrote down his/her opinion of Americans and of the American way of life; (ii) worked through a carefully prepared list of statements about Americans, saying for each of them whether he agreed or disagreed (or had no opinion); (iii) indicated the degree of his willingness to listen to the six proposed programs in the series and named any other aspect of American life he would like to hear about; (iv) gave various personal details, including occupation,[d] educational background, age and sex[e]; (v) indicated whether or not he had ever listened to "American Commentary" or "Letter from America". In addition, alternate groups were asked a series of questions to assess their knowledge of certain facts about America and the American way of life. Group members worked quite separately and these essential steps were all completed *before there was any discussion at all.*

One point of special interest about this testing procedure concerns the derivation of the list of statements about Americans. Approximately 40 listeners (of appropriate age and social background) had been asked in *preliminary* test sessions to write down all they could of their opinions of Americans and of the American way of life. They did in fact write very

[d] Present job for those in full-time employment; previous job for those retired; pre-marriage job for housewife or husband's job if she did not work before marriage.
[e] The personal details under (iv) were gathered mainly for the further matching of the sample of volunteers to the target audience.

fully and the results were then sorted to yield a large number of fairly specific statements. To this list were added some others of a possibly relevant kind and the total list, consisting of 56 statements, was administered as a sub-test in the present study. The test room group is in fact a very good source of such statements, for group members readily and frankly cooperate in giving their opinions.

<h2 style="text-align:center">FINDINGS</h2>

Before reporting the findings, several things must be made quite clear. In the first place, this study was made in 1952, since when America's position and influence in the world have greatly changed as have certain aspects of her internal affairs. Secondly, these findings refer to people aged 45 years and over, drawn from the upper half of the social strata. Thirdly, and most important, the sample is quite small and it consists solely of Londoners. These limitations must not be overlooked.

<h3 style="text-align:center">Opinions about Americans</h3>

There were two measures of opinion about Americans. One of these is what is called an 'open response' reply: respondents just wrote down what their opinions were and they did so without the aid of any list of statements. The other measure involved the presentation of specific statements, the respondents being required to indicate agreement or disagreement with them and the extent of this agreement or disagreement. We do not yet know properly the relationship of results from these two methods, though we *do* know that they yield results markedly different in some respects[f]. It seems, though it cannot yet be proved, that the open response method brings out opinions that are relatively predominant in the respondent's awareness. They are, as it were, dominant and immediate reactions. At the same time, these reactions may, because of their immediacy, be somewhat superficial and it seems unlikely that the picture they offer us will be a *total* picture of the respondent's various attitudes—in this case, of his or her attitudes towards Americans.

In Table 1 is set out the distribution of opinions freely volunteered.

The striking thing about this table is that nearly half the group volunteered an opinion to the effect that 'Americans are boastful or swaggering.' Next in frequency of reference, but well below it, came: they are friendly; they live at too high a pressure; they are unfit to be a world power; they work hard; they are generous; they are materialistic. These and other of the references seem to present an image of the American as brash, hard working, materialistic, patriotic but at the same time friendly and generous.

---

[f] A statement may be volunteered by only 10% but be endorsed by 30% or more when people are asked if they agree with it or not.

TABLE 1

Opinions of Americans, as volunteered by Londoners

	%*
They are boastful/swaggering	45
They are friendly	28
They live at too high a pressure (i.e. they hustle too much, they compete too hard)	24
They are unfit to be a world power (in the United Nations sense)	22
They work hard	20
They are generous	19
They place too much importance on material things	16
They are immature	15
They are ostentatious (dress the ordinary thing up as the extra-ordinary)	14
They are go-ahead and ambitious	14
They are good company/cheerful/like fun	14
They think that America is the only country in the world	11
They are politically immature	10
Films give us a false impression of American life	9
The American way of life is very much like our own	8
They treat negroes badly	7
They are courteous	7
There is a lot of crime and corruption in America	7
Money is far too important to them	6
Their clothing is loud/spivish/in poor taste	6
American children are ill-mannered and uncontrolled	6
They are home loving	5
Politics in America are undignified (mass hysteria)	5
The standard of living is higher there than here	5
Their politics are corrupt	5
They are noisy in speech	5

* On average, each group member offered about 3 opinions. Accordingly the above list will add to much more than 100%. Further, opinions offered by less than 5% are not given here.

Agreement or Disagreement with Opinions Actually Presented to Them

Subsequently, group members also voted on 59 statements about Americans and their institutions. The 59 statements referred between them to six different aspects of American life: education; foreign affairs and relations with Britain; home life; crime; democracy and government; materialism; the personal characteristics of Americans.

Because of the smallness of the sample, the device is used here of referring to the number of people agreeing or disagreeing with a statement as 'so many in ten'. This properly indicates the approximate nature of the results. In evaluating such figures, it may be taken that approximately 1 in 10 had no opinion on the average statement. Hence when 6 in 10 are said to agree with a statement, this usually means that about 3 in 10 *dis*agreed with it.

Personal characteristics of Americans

Votes in terms of the personal characteristics of Americans were very much in line with those suggested by the volunteering of opinions (though characteristically the percentage agreeing with a presented statement was higher than the percentage freely volunteering it).

Approximately three-quarters endorsed the view that Americans are boastful, over-patriotic ('they think America is the only country in the world'), 'enthusiastic', 'too impulsive', 'self-reliant'. About the same proportion voted them 'friendly', 'courteous and likeable'. Though some rated them 'immoral', rather more denied this. Finally, about 6 in 10 regarded them as 'immature'.

Education in America

It seems that the American standard of education was not one of the things that these people became spontaneously aware of when they thought about America, for rarely were opinions *volunteered* about it (see Table 1). When asked to *vote* on specific statements about American education, it emerged that the majority thought of the American education system more as a preparation for a job than as a preparation for living and that the American system was not as good or as thorough as the English system. About half disagreed with the statement that 'the American people as a whole are well informed'. At the same time, and perhaps paradoxically, there was a majority belief that Americans 'spend a lot of time and money seeking knowledge'. Presumably being 'well informed' suggests something more than does 'seeking knowledge'.

Foreign affairs and relations with Britain.

Somewhat over 6 in 10 agreed that 'the Americans have been most generous to Britain and other European countries', that they 'have a great sense of responsibility' and that 'Americans generally believe that they must take their part in world affairs'. On the other hand, a majority (of between 6 and 7 in 10) felt that they were 'immature' and 'impulsive', regarded American statesmen as 'not really very experienced in world affairs' and considered that American 'influence in world affairs is often dangerous'. Opinion about their being 'war makers' was equally split between 'yes' and 'no'.

About half took the view that 'Americans are really a danger to the British way of life' and about half disagreed. Some disagreed because they felt that the American influence was in fact *good* for the British and some because they thought the British could withstand any possible ill-effects of American influence.

Two other views that got endorsement from about three-quarters of the group, and which possibly bore on relationships with Britain, were: 'they think America is the only country in the world' and 'their servicemen have far too much money'.

Democracy and government

Seven in ten of these people endorsed the statement that the American election system 'is based on mass hysteria'. In addition, six in ten agreed that 'there is a lot of corruption and dishonesty in the American government' and that 'the big bosses control everything in America'. There was a fair balance of opinion for and against the proposition that 'the Americans are not really democratic at all' and between a third and a half took the view that 'there is no real freedom of speech in America'. As another facet of opinion about American democracy and government, group members were asked about the way Negroes were treated in America: about three in four felt that they were treated 'very badly'.[g]

Crime in America

Six in ten endorsed the view that 'there is a great deal of crime in America' and that 'the authorities don't seem to be able to stop it'.

American values

Some of the statements on which a vote was taken bore fairly directly upon American systems of values. Six to seven out of ten endorsed the proposition that 'money is far too important to them', that 'they don't have enough tradition' and that 'they read far too many comics'. This went along with a rejection, by over seven in ten, of the proposition that 'they have excellent taste'. While seven in ten agreed that 'they are hardworking', just about as many regarded their output as of poorer quality than the British article.

To this body of opinion, with its suggestion of materialism, must be added two complicating elements. One of these was that the vote went slightly *against* the proposition that 'Americans are uncultured and don't appreciate the fine arts'. This does not necessarily mean that some members of the test-room groups were contradicting themselves. Clearly an interest in money making and an absence of traditionalism do not prevent one from appreciating 'the fine arts': indeed, the opposite may be the case. The other complication was that group members were equally divided over acceptance and rejection of the statement that Americans 'have every bit as much depth of character as the Englishman'. This may mean that some group members regarded the Englishman also as materialistic, though equally well it may be that there were some respondents at least who felt that an element of materialism does not necessarily imply shallowness of character.

Home life

A majority of about six in ten believed that the Americans 'lead good home lives', and 'place a lot of importance on the family and home'. On

[g] This view, does, of course, pre-date the influx into Britain of West Indian and Asian migrants as well as developments in America over recent years, and it would be rather surprising if opinion on this matter had not now changed in some way.

the other hand, group members tended to believe that 'there is a much higher rate of divorce in America' (eight in ten thought this) and that 'American teenagers are uncontrolled' (six in ten). They tended to deny the propositions that 'American children are well behaved' (seven in ten denied this) and that 'young people in America are growing up with a fine set of values' (six in ten denied this). A majority of seven in ten believed that 'American women get out of the house quite a lot' and about half of the group members considered that 'in America, women rule the roost'. In view of some of these opinions, it is perhaps not surprising that a majority rejected the view that 'the American way of life is very much like o ur own'

The Level of General Knowledge About America

A series of questions about America was delivered to approximately half the respondents (i.e. first group, third group, fifth group, etc., in order of testing). These questions were aimed at testing the respondent's factual knowledge on the following range of subjects: geography and size of population; racial composition of the American population; the American system of government; domestic and social conditions; education; some aspects of American history and international relationships. The questions were read out (twice each) and group members had to write down their answers without discussion of any kind.

The responses set out below are based upon only about half the total number of respondents. Although these people were closely similar to the target audience in terms of age, sex and social class, the smallness of their number means that any results obtained from them must be interpreted only as approximations or pointers to the general level of the target audience's knowledge about America.

Geography and size of population
The majority answered correctly the questions under this head. Eight out of ten of those tested knew which oceans border the U.S.A. on east and west. Six in ten knew how many states there are altogether and about the same proportion could *name* four of them. The approximate relationship between areas of the United States and England was known by about half of these people while some three quarters had a general idea of the relative population sizes of the two countries.

Racial constitution of Americans in 1952. About a fifth of the people tested knew that about one American in ten was coloured but for the total tested there was a considerable overestimate of the size of the coloured population, nearly half thinking that at least one American in three was coloured. Less than a third had a roughly correct idea of the proportion of Americans who came from British stock, one in four had no idea at all and among the rest there was a tendency to underestimate.

American government and politics. Asked about Congress and the Senate, four in ten said they believed that the Senate is equivalent to the British

House of Lords and two in ten that Congress is equivalent to the British Parliament. Very few indeed appear to have realised that one is included within the other or to have a reasonable idea of the roles of *both* the Senate and Congress. About half were unable to discriminate in any way between the Republicans and the Democrats. One fifth of them identified the Republicans with isolationism and about the same number thought the two American parties were respectively equivalent to the Conservative and the Liberal/Labour parties in Great Britain. Less than a quarter knew that the President is Commander-in-Chief of the American armed forces.

For six in ten, the term 'the Solid South' had nothing like its true meaning. A few of the others thought it referred to the 'Negro homeland', about a quarter thought it was a general reference to the southern states, while only one in twenty knew anything like the full significance of the term. Only one third could name any of the 'minority' groups of America: 'groups' which were named with any significant frequency were Negroes, Jews, Communists, Isolationists and American Indians. Other minority groups occasionally nominated included "the Ku Klux Klan", "the really poor", the "Plymouth Brethren", "the immigrants", the "various religious groups", "the Republicans" and "the middle class"!

Domestic and social conditions. About one third knew that very few American families had a domestic servant, the tendency being to overestimate the proportion, some thinking the figure was about half or more. There was also serious overestimation of the number of American homes with a telephone. About two in ten thought that there were either more than 50, or less than 35 hours in the American working week, although the great majority gave a reasonably accurate estimate.

Education. Relatively few (one in ten) could name four universities or technological institutes in America, although three quarters could name at least one. Harvard or Yale, spelt in various ways, were frequently among the nominations. On the question of minimum school leaving age, there was a slight tendency to overestimate.

Historical and international

About three-quarters could not name the first president (the great majority of these thinking that he was Lincoln), and one third did not know which side won the American Civil War. A large majority could not say who Woodrow Wilson was or what he did. About one in ten could give a reasonably accurate estimate of the amount of money received by Great Britain in unconditional grants from Marshall Aid.

Seeing These Results in Perspective

It is most important that these findings be seen in proper perspective. They refer to the period 1952. The came from a small sample and the sample itself is restricted (deliberately) to London and to middle and upper middle-class adults aged 44 and under. The sample size alone means that the findings from the study can provide only a *general indication* of the level of knowledge of the target audience. It is for this reason that distributions of responses have been expressed in such general terms. Seen in retrospect, it is obvious enough that the sample in this pioneering study should have been made much larger. On the other hand, the results as they stand are useful in offering the producer considerably more than the estimates of, say, himself and his associates.

Finally, this enquiry is reported here, not as an example in quantification, but as a pioneering study employing a relatively new procedure.

[10]

A planning study for the television series "Facts and figures"[a]

Dealing with viewers' knowledge of economic concepts, words and events.

BACKGROUND AND AIMS

"Facts and Figures" was a ten-minute television program broadcast monthly and it was intended to provide information about economic trends and about national facts and figures. It relied upon diagrammatic presentation, supported by a semi-technical commentary.

The present study had two purposes.

(a) It was intended to reveal how well or badly the program's target[b] audience understood the technical words and concepts which were frequently introduced into the program and upon which its comprehension partly depended. It was meant also to reveal any major misunderstandings of these terms.

(b) It was intended to examine the target audience's understanding of certain past events (e.g. devaluation, wage freeze), the significance of which could also have been important for the comprehension of some parts of the program and which were common background to the series as a whole.

The program's target audience had been but partly defined at the time the enquiry was carried out. Thus the lower 25% in terms of occupational level had been excluded from the outset but it remained possible that there would be some further narrowing of the target if the basic words and concepts were *too* far beyond some sectors of it. Accordingly,

---

[a] This report is based on research conducted in 1954 by the writer as a member of the Audience Research Department of the BBC and reported in VR/54/498 [22]

[b] By 'target audience' is meant the viewers for whom "Facts and Figures" was designed.

93

provision was made for expressing the results separately for each of the four occupational groups contained within the maximum target audience. Occupational level, it should be added, is a descriptive category which has been found to be highly associated with the distribution of abilities of the kind being studied. The four groups were as follows:

		% of the viewing population at that time [c]
Group		
(I)	Professional, semi-professional, executive and administrative	top 7%
(II)	'Highly skilled' (e.g. tool maker, legal clerk, private secretary, shorthand-typist with qualifications)	next 13%
(III)	'Skilled' (e.g. fitter and turner, carpenter, cashier, superior shop assistant, insurance salesman)	next 30%
(IV)	'Moderately skilled' (e.g. bricklayer, housepainter, plumber, railway signalman, barber, dispatch clerk	next 27%

THE METHODS OF RESEARCH

Viewers taking part in this study came by invitation to Broadcasting House, meeting in groups of between twenty and thirty at a time. Details of the standard invitation system are given in Chapter 3. All of those invited were viewers who previously had been interviewed in the Audience Research Department's Survey of Listening and Viewing. From this survey there were available the details of name, address, age, sex and social class necessary for operating the invitation system. Of the 298 who came, approximately 50 proved to be classifiable as 'professional or lower professional' (Group I above) and approximately 80 came from each of the other three occupational groups. Within each of these four groups, the distribution in terms of age, and sex was similar to that in the general population[d].

Full details are given in Chapter 3 of the way in which test sessions of this kind were conducted, including information about the three standard rules of testing procedure, namely: no discussion; frankness; hard work. At each of the test-sessions of this project, the essential steps in the testing procedure were as follows. (i) Viewers were tested for their grasp of the meaning of each of 28 technical words and concepts which either were being used in the series already or were regarded by the program's economic adviser as being basic to it. Each such word was presented and tested in a verbal context. (ii) An assessment was made of viewers' general familiarity with, and understanding of, various events of significance to

[c] Percentages for viewers as estimated at that time.
[d] The invitation system allows for the control of age and sex distributions in the sample attending (see Chapter 3).

trends dealt with in the series (e.g. devaluation, rearmament, the post-war gold and dollar reserve crises). (iii) A record was also made of each respondent's occupational background and educational level, age and sex.

THE FINDINGS

Knowledge of Technical Terms and Concepts

The twenty-eight words tested are set out in Table 1, their order in that table depending upon their general level of difficulty as established in

TABLE 1

Viewers' knowledge of technical words

Terms (in order of difficulty)	Percentage of viewers knowing these words:				
	Group I %	Group II %	Group III %	Group IV %	All* groups %
Commodity prices	17	8	3	5	6[a]
Terms of trade	21	4	5	5	6
Primary producers	49	5	7	3	9
Index number	41	13	10	3	11
A point	34	16	10	6	12
At a slackening rate	51	40	13	11	20
Invisible exports	74	37	23	10	25
Sterling area	79	27	34	8	28
Dollar reserves	92	57	47	19	43
Provisional figure	87	74	46	19	45
Devaluation	89	53	54	29	48
Wage rates	81	57	55	30	49
Percent	94	73	51	35	53
Estimated	83	81	55	37	56
Average	87	66	60	40	56
A less rapid rise	89	68	56	41	56
Retail prices	89	78	74	44	66
Underwent a rapid rise	96	81	70	52	69
Fell	96	82	74	52	70
Volume	96	87	77	52	72
Stable	96	81	75	57	72
Earnings	85	85	83	55	74
Manufactured goods	96	84	83	54	74
Short time	89	87	82	59	75
Value	96	87	79	63	76
Imports	100	95	85	60	79
Exports	100	90	87	68	82
Overtime	96	96	88	67	83

* These averages are based upon the percentages shown in the other columns, *each one of them being weighted* according to the percentage of the viewing population falling into the occupational group concerned.

this study. (The 'easy' ones appear at the bottom of the list and the 'hard' ones at the top). The percentage of viewers getting each word approximately correct is shown alongside it.

The percentage of the complete target audience getting any particular term approximately correct is shown in the column headed 'ALL'. From this it will be seen that terms like 'overtime', 'exports', 'imports', 'value', and 'short time' (shown at the 'easy' end of the scale) are known by about three quarters of the full target audience. This target audience included the four occupational groups listed above and thus covered 77% of the full viewing population. This column also shows, however, that less than half knew the meaning of terms like 'devaluation', 'provisional figure', 'dollar reserves', and that less than one fifth could give the meaning of terms like 'commodity price', 'terms of trade', 'primary producers', 'index number', 'a point'.

As might be expected, however, the performance of the viewer was closely related to his occupational background. In Group I (estimated at that time to be the top 7% of the viewing population in terms of occupation level), the majority of the words tested were known by 80% or more and only five of them by less than half. In Group IV (the 'moderately skilled') on the other hand, only 67% could get the easiest word right and one third of the words were known by less than 20%. Groups II and III (the 'highly skilled' and the 'skilled' respectively) fell between these two positions.

This means, of course, that if the target audience were restricted to the top 7% of the viewing population (that is, professional and semi-professional people) it could reasonably be said that technical terms of the kind tested here would be familiar to most of that target audience. But if the target audience is extended beyond the top 7%, such familiarity cannot be counted on. If it be extended to include the whole of the top 75% of the viewing public, the fact must be faced that a large proportion of this target audience would be unfamiliar with many of the terms given in Table 1.

At all levels, female viewers were less familiar with these technical terms than were males. The differences were appreciable in all groups but were specially marked in Group IV — the 'moderately skilled'.

It should be noted that these words were tested *in verbal context* — that is, each word was presented to the viewer in a sentence and the viewer was required to write down the meaning of that word. While these contexts were designed to rule out known meanings or shades of meaning other than the correct one (e.g. to rule out the possibility that in the phrase 'volume of exports', 'volume' could mean 'book'), care was taken to avoid contexts which themselves virtually or partially defined the word being tested. This was done because the whole purpose of the study was to find out whether the tested words were sufficiently well-known for them to play their full part in communications in which they were used. (It is, of course, possible to increase the likelihood that a difficult word will be understood by *deliberately* bolstering it up with a context *designed* to make its meaning clearer, and if there is no alternative to using that word, this practice is desirable[(e)].)

Misconceptions about these terms

For relatively few of these terms was there evidence of some predominant form (or forms) of misunderstanding. There were, however, a few of these. Thus 'primary producers' (which only 9% got right) was thought by 27% to mean 'main manufacturers' or '*chief producers*' and there were many who thought it meant either 'manufacturers using raw materials' or 'producers of essentials'. 'Terms of trade', which the economist might define as 'amounts of imports that can be exchanged for each unit of our exports', was variously interpreted by about 20% as 'transactions' or as 'competition' or as 'bargaining', while about 15% thought it meant 'price paid or offered for goods' and almost as many defined it as 'terms agreed on between countries or between firms'. 'Commodity price', meaning price of raw materials, was defined as 'price of goods in general' by about 20% and there were many who thought it meant 'retail prices' or 'prices of consumer goods'.

Understanding of certain past events and of basic economic facts

Quite often the proper understanding of a communication depends upon the viewer knowing certain facts which are not given in the communication itself. For instance, in one edition of "Facts and Figures", a comparison was made of trends in British, American and German shares of the world export trade in cars. To the person who knew something of the conditions determining the volume of British exports during the period concerned, these comparative trends would have appeared reasonable and meaningful; *without* such knowledge, they must have seemed arbitrary and to the undiscerning they may well have suggested parallel changes in production. Obviously there is a strict limit to the amount of background information which a 10-minute broadcast can supply. Nonetheless, past research has shown that background knowledge of this kind has a lot to do with the level of comprehension achieved [105].

Accordingly, a test was made of viewers' knowledge about certain past events and economic facts which were expected to be of significance to some of the trends presented in "Facts and Figures". The test consisted of sixteen questions about economic and other aspects of the following events: devaluation of the pound sterling (1949); the wage freeze; the Korean war; the cotton slump of 1952; British rearmament; the gold and dollar reserve crises.

[(e)] At the same time, the results of a study by Delight [40] make it clear that the type of context *ordinarily* used by broadcasters may do little to help a word convey its intended meaning and may even do the opposite. Context *can* help and can be made to help, but merely to provide a context is not necessarily enough.

These events, the questions asked, and the answers which were regarded as adequate, were worked out in close liaison with the program's economic adviser. The majority of the questions dealt with the nature and the effects of these six events, though dates and causes were included where relevant.

It was found that knowledge varied markedly from question to question but, on the average, approximately 60% of the full target audience could give no reply or were quite wrong on any given question, about 10% had some very vague idea of the answer and the remainder (about 30%) gave a fair to good reply. This means that where facts and trends based in part upon these events are being presented, a certain amount of explanation would be necessary if anything more than a minority of the target audience was to understand them. It seems to suggest also that the target audience's background knowledge about *other* relevant events is likely to be similarly scanty.

Here again, performance and occupational level were closely related. About half of the professional and semi-professional group gave a fair to good reply to the average question, 40% being quite wrong or saying they did not know. As might be expected, the performance was worse with each step down the occupational scale. Thus, in the 'highly skilled' group, 50% were quite wrong on the average question; in the 'skilled' group, 60% were quite wrong on the average question, and in the 'moderately skilled' group, this figure rose to 70% (with about 25% giving a fair to good answer).

The target audience's knowledge also varied widely from question to question. For instance, 70% or more of the full target audience could give fair answers to questions about who was paying for British rearmament; could give reasons for British rearmament; could give the date of the commencement of the Korean war. About half had a fair idea of the effects of rearmament and of measures taken to meet the gold and dollar reserve crises. On the other hand, relatively few of the target audience had a fair to good knowledge of the following points; the names of the five major combatant countries in the Korean war; the effects of devaluation on either imports or exports; the results of stock piling during the Korean war; the effect of devaluation upon Britain's gold and dollar reserves; agreements involved in the wage freeze; the causes of the 1952 cotton slump. Indeed, with several questions, the percentage correct was 3% or less. While the top occupational group did better on each question than did the other groups, its knowledge about them was, nonetheless, often quite poor.

[11]

A planning study for the television series "Race relations in Africa"[a]

A pre-broadcast study dealing with viewers' knowledge and attitudes concerning Africa, its people and race relations.

BACKGROUND AND AIMS

The purpose of this enquiry was to provide the producer of the forthcoming television series "Race Relations in Africa" with information about the opinions and the knowledge of the audience for whom the series was intended. More specifically, the enquiry dealt with the following questions.

(a) To what extent is the television public *aware* of the problems of race relations in Africa?
(b) To what extent is the proposed audience hostile towards the subject as such?
(c) Is there a prejudice for or against seeing coloured people on television expressing their own points of view?
(d) What are the attitudes of the proposed audience towards:
   (i) alleged innate differences between black people and white people?
   (ii) existing black-white issues in British Africa[b]?
(e) What is the state of this audience's general knowledge of Africa and of the facts around which African race relation issues revolve?

An answer to question (a) would tell the producer to what extent he had to increase such awareness as distinct from taking it for granted. Answers to questions (b), (c) and (d) would tell the producer what kinds of attitudes he would be up against or have in his favour in presenting the program, and this information should indicate the manner of his approach, particularly on the more touchy issues. Further, detailed knowledge of the view-

---

[a] This report is based upon work conducted by the writer in 1952 as a member of the Audience Research Department of the BBC and reported in the BBC document VR/52/458 [20]
[b] At the time of the enquiry, no British territory had become independent.

71729

ers' attitudes should alert the producer to the existence of any widely held attitude that appeared to run counter to the facts: presumably there would then be some priority put upon the presentation of such facts. Answers to question (e) should provide a guide to the general level of viewer knowledge about Africa and black-white relations there, but should also indicate which facts the producer could or could not count upon his audience having already. Putting it another way, this information should tell him what basic facts he would have to provide and what he could take for granted.

THE METHODS OF RESEARCH

The target audience had been described as the general adult population. The 230 people actually tested approximated to a cross-section of this target, though as a sample they tended to be biassed slightly upwards in terms of intelligence and occupational level. The people initially invited had all been interviewed in the Audience Research Department's survey of listening and viewing so that the necessary details were available for using the system of controlled invitation described in Chapter 3.

As usual in such work, these people did not know beforehand that the subject of Africa or of race relations would be raised in any way at all in the course of the evening, though they knew that the meeting "would end with general discussion of TV programmes". These viewers came to Broadcasting House on various evenings, meeting in groups of 15–20 at a time. Also as usual, a certain amount of time was devoted to developing cooperation in group members and to teaching them the basic rules of procedure, namely: no discussion till the end of the meeting; real effort; complete frankness (group members were reminded that they were anonymous).

After this preparation, each group went through most of the following steps: (1) They wrote down, still without any indication of the researcher's interest in race relations, what they considered to be the main problems in British territories in Africa and in South Africa "these days". (2) They were then each given a typed list of 'problems' and asked to indicate each and every one of them which they considered to be a problem in British territories in Africa or in South Africa. (Naturally the list included a number of references to aspects of race relations, but these were set amid many other problems of a different kind.) (3) They had next to give written answers to questions which were meant to elicit evidence of hostility or otherwise to the idea of presenting the subject of race relations on television. (4) They were given tests of attitudes towards black people, and of opinion concerning a wide range of black-white issues in Africa. (5) They were tested for their knowledge of various facts about Africa and about the relationship of the black and the white people there. (6) They gave personal details about themselves (age, sex, occupational level, educational background).

Throughout, viewers entered their replies on paper and the three rules of procedure appeared to be operating effectively. Respondents were not hustled, care being taken to see that they had finished one question before going on to the next.

The full procedure was too long for any one person or group. Hence the practice was adopted of omitting, in orderly rotation, either question 3 or question 4 or question 5 from the procedure for any one group. As a result, there were samples of between 140 and 150 for each of these three questions and 230 for each of the others.

THE FINDINGS

Awareness of Race Relations as a Problem (230 cases)

Group members were informed (*after* arrival at the test centre and during the introduction to the evening's procedure) that the first half of the evening would be a special enquiry into viewers' ideas about Africa.

However, it was essential, in testing viewers' awareness of 'race relations as a problem in Africa', that no mention of this purpose be made until after the awareness test had been finished. Accordingly, group members were told that for the first two questions it would not be possible to give any further details than were included in the questions themselves: after this, the details would be given. The element of mystery in this situation appeared to have heightened the interest in the proceedings and no objections were noted. They were then asked to write—in *silence*—what they thought were the main problems "these days" in the parts of Africa controlled by Britain and in South Africa. They were asked to name as many as they could of these problems. They had two minutes for this and were required to keep on thinking and writing during that period. The point of this procedure was of course to find out how many of them freely volunteered one or another aspect of relationships between black and white people.

The constant danger in this operation was that someone in the group would *call out* his or her ideas. Because of this danger, the question had been preceded by some rather heavy stress on the need for utter silence, the chairman making it clear that if anyone called anything out it would ruin the hard work of everyone else. In fact, nobody called anything out.

An analysis of volunteered 'problems' gave the following results.

TABLE 1

Active awareness of problems of race relations

No response at all	23%
No mention or reference to 'bad race relations'	7%
Direct mention of 'bad race relations'	54%
Implied* mention of 'bad race relations'	16%

* These included such statements as "In Africa, blacks and whites should be equal, but this is not so"; "Segregation of black and white people"; "Dr. Malan wants to keep the black people down"; "The ban on the black man"; "Why shouldn't blacks be entitled to vote along with whites — we are all God's children?"

In the *second* part of the awareness[b] test, a list of problems was handed to each member. Group members were asked to go through the list, ticking any problems which they thought were present in British Africa or in South Africa. After this they were asked to put a second tick against any they thought were 'very important'. There were twenty-nine items in the list and three of them referred to aspects of race relations: 'bad race relations'; 'the colour bar'; 'racial disturbances'. The percentages endorsing these three items are shown in Table 2 below.

TABLE 2

Secondary awareness of race relations as a problem

Key Items	Item Endorsed As		At Least One of the Three Endorsed As	
	A Problem	A Very Important Problem	A Problem	A Very Important Problem
	%	%	%	%
Bad race relations	86	55		
The colour bar	87	71	97	84
Racial disturbances	73	53		

Table 1 indicates that about seven in ten were *actively* aware of some aspect of poor race relations as a problem in Africa. Further, 97% selected it as a problem when given the opportunity, 84% regarding it as a 'very important' problem. In other words, the program director could fairly safely assume that viewers knew already that there were problems of bad race relations in Africa and that the great majority regarded these problems as important.

Attitudes Towards Seeing Programs About Race Relations and Towards Seeing Coloured People on Television

To assess attitudes on the above matters, various statements were presented to group members who were required to indicate, on a verbal scale, the extent of their agreement or disagreement with them (or the fact that they had no opinion).

Over 90% claimed that they were interested in the general subject of the relation of the black and the white people in Africa, 60% professing a strong interest. At the same time, there was evidence that this attitude sprang partly out of a certain sense of duty towards Africa and coloured people, and that it was tinged in a large number of cases with an undercurrent feeling that to examine the subject would be somewhat unpleasant. In fact, only half of the viewers denied a statement to this effect (i.e. that the subject was a 'little bit unpleasant'), and only a tenth denied this strongly.

[b] This was administered only after the results of the first test had been collected

About three-quarters of the viewers said that they didn't mind seeing coloured people on television giving their own point of view and about a third strongly denied any antagonism towards the idea.

Vievers were also asked about their interest in hearing about economic, political and social aspects of race relations in Africa. They rated these subjects in the following order: social ('the way the black and white people mix in everyday life in Africa'); economic ('black-white relations as far as pay, living conditions and land owning are concerned'); political ('the black man's position in Africa as far as voting and politics are concerned').

Some Personal Attitudes towards Black People

Here, too, viewers were presented with statements (15 in all) involving black people. These dealt, between them with such things as innate differences between black and white people, willingnes to associate with them in various ways, personal attitudes towards them. Viewers were required to indicate, for each statement, whether they agreed, disagreed or had no opinion about it. In these 15 statements, there was no reference to African but only to black people: the purpose of this was to gauge general attitudes to black people in their own right.

There was a general rejection of the idea that black people are innately inferior to whites, only about one in ten endorsing the statement to that effect. The statements presented took the forms: 'the black man is born less intelligent than the white man' (seven in ten rejected this); 'black men will never be capable of doing really skilled jobs or of taking a leading part in world affairs' (eight in ten rejected this). In line with this position, eight in ten supported the statement: 'given a fair chance, the black man can become equal to the white in all things'.

The existence of innate *differences* (whatever their implications for inferiority or otherwise) between black and white people was also rejected by the majority: thus seven in ten rejected statements such as: 'black and white people have a different kind of blood'; 'the black man will always remain a savage under the skin'. Further, many of these viewers claimed that they would be willing to have black people living in their streets (6–7 out of 10), or to have educated black people meet them in their own homes (8 in 10).

In appraising views of this kind it must be kept in mind that about one in ten of the viewers tested *agreed* that black people were innately inferior, that about the same proportion personally disliked black people and that the same proportion again rejected the idea of having black people living in *their* street. In addition, up to two in ten were undecided on various of these matters.

Nonetheless and on balance the evidence does seem to point to a certain liberal feeling with respect to black people. However, when it come to the question of marriage between black people and whites, liberalism and permissiveness largely disappeared, with seven in ten rejecting the idea of inter-marriage, two in ten being undecided, and only one in ten supporting it.

A programmer might deduce from this evidence that if he wants to promote more liberal attitudes towards black people, he should especially avoid any undue concentration upon black-white marriages. He may also decide that for the whole area of black-white relationships, the present distribution of attitudes would call for a very careful presentation of any related facts.[c]

Attitudes on Black-White Issues in Africa

The same techniques were used to assess viewer attitudes on particular issues concerning black-white relations in Africa. Thirty statements dealing between them with the following issues were presented: land ownership, equality, inter-marriage, segregaton, education, government.

Land issues

Somewhat more people rejected than accepted (5 : 3) the proposition that the 'black people in Africa have their fair share of land'. Along with some 7 in 10 took the view that it was unfair of the whites 'to take the land from the black people', though only about half felt that the land should be given *back* to the black people. About half felt that the black people were not capable of looking after their land properly, and 7 in 10 claimed they were lazy in this respect. About 8 in 10 felt the whites in Africa should teach the black people *how* to look after the land properly.

Equality

About 8 in 10 rejected the suggestion that the black men in Africa can never be given equality with the whites there. Moreover, 8 in 10 supported the ideas that 'black people in Africa should have the same right to vote as the white man', 'should get the same pay for the same job', and that the law should be the same for the blacks and whites in Africa. The same large majority (8 in 10) *disagreed* with the view that 'the whites in Africa should not have to mix with the black people in cafes and buses'. The size of the majority taking a liberal view fell somewhat when it came to an immediate granting of full equality to the black man in Africa: six in 10 supported this suggestion, 2 in 10 rejected it and 2 in 10 were undecided.

Inter-marriage and segregation

A large majority (8 in 10) rejected the idea of complete geographical segregation of black and white people as a solution to African racial problems, but a similar majority rejected the proposition that it would help to solve the racial problems in Africa if marriages between blacks and whites were encouraged.

[c] A person's dedication to one view or another ordinarily tends to interfere with his intake of facts which don't happen to support his opinions or ideas.

Education and other aids

Eight to nine in every 10 felt that the white people should put a lot of effort into educating black people in Africa and a similar majority supported the view that as this work is carried forward, the black people should be treated more as the equals of the whites. Very few of the viewers tested availed themselves of the opportunity to argue that 'it is a mistake to help the blacks in Africa when there are so many poor people in Britain'.

Government

A majority (7 in 10) disagreed with 'what the Malan government is doing to the black people in South Africa' and felt that it was in South Africa that the real damage to black-white relations was being done. On the other hand, about 6 in 10 took the view that the treatment of Africans in the British colonies was 'generally good', though they did not go so far as to agree that Britain was in Africa solely for the good of the black people there (7 in 10 rejected this idea). Finally, there was a large measure of agreement that 'Britain should give the black people of the African colonies self-government as soon as they were ready for it' (8 in 10 agreed).

Summing up on Attitudes

These attitudes suggest that a sizeable majority — about 7 in 10 — has a fairly liberal or permissive view of race relations in Africa and that they support the idea that the whites in Africa have a duty to raise the level of the native people. On the other hand, between 1 and 2 in 10 were not liberal in this sense on many of the issues put to them and some were undecided. For the majority (7 in 10) liberalism did not extend to encouraging marriage between black and white people.

Knowledge of Facts About Africa
and About Race Relations There

Each of a large number of questions was read out by the test room administrator[d]. Prior to this the need for working alone had been re-stressed, as had the requirement that nobody should call out an answer of any kind. All answers were written in a small booklet. A fresh page was started for each new question and there was a stressed rule about 'not going back' to a question once the page was turned. This rule was necessary because sometimes it was essential to give the answer to an earlier question in order to phrase a later one. Several assistants helped in group control.

Group behaviour with respect to the above procedure and its rules appeared to be very satisfactory and in particular there was little to suggest the occurrence of cheating.

Knowledge about Africa's geography and population

While about half of the viewers realised that Africa is very large, there was a considerable under-estimate of its size, with practically nobody know-

[d] Each question was repeated before respondent began writing an answer to it.

ing the approximate area. About a third of the viewers were able to indicate the approximate position of the equator. Only about one in ten knew the approximate size of Africa's population although a third were able to say that it is larger than Britain's population.

European powers in Africa and regional divisions

Two-thirds of the viewers could correctly name two or more of the *European* countries with territories in Africa. Apart from Britain, which was given to them anyhow, half of them could name France, about the same number named Belgium and a small group (15%) could name Portugal. However, nearly a third named Holland or the Netherlands and there was a large collection of other quite erroneous answers including Russia, India, Canada and Egypt.

In general, there was only a slight tendency to over-estimate how many years ago Britain came into possession of most of her territories in Africa, and over half made an approximately correct statement. Half the group could name at least one of the nineteen British territories in Africa, a third named two or more, 10% named five or more, but no one could name more than eight. Darwin, Tasmania, and Colombo were included amongst the incorrect responses.

A map of Africa showing individual countries without names was given to each viewer. With the exception of the Union of South Africa very few were able to indicate correctly the position of individual territories in Africa. On the average, Rhodesia, Tanganyika, Uganda, the Gold Coast and Bechuanaland[e] were correctly indicated by about 10% and approximately correctly by about one third. Very few indeed got three right or approximately right, and for each territory about half were quite hopelessly out or simply could not offer an answer at all. The Union of South Africa was, however, relatively well-known, about two thirds locating it correctly and only a quarter being quite wrong. Incidently, one person worked with the map upside down and another marked South Africa in the Sahara Desert!

Indirect rule in Africa

About one-tenth had a rough idea of the meaning of 'indirect rule', although the majority of even these were hazy. There was another group, of between 1 and 2 in 10 who believed that it meant 'rule of blacks by whites'. Some of the remaining notions were: 'rule without authority'; 'people who rule themselves'; 'segregation of blacks'.

South Africa

About two-thirds of the viewers knew the approximate proportion of whites in the Union of South Africa, though there was a fairly marked tendency to under-estimate. A little more than a half could name both the

(e) As they were known then.

Dutch and the British as the main European stock in the Union, a further tenth named the Dutch (but not British) and nearly a fifth the British (but not the Dutch). Hence about three-quarters named one or both of them. Other European races named included Germans (12%), French (11%), and Portuguese. Nearly a quarter named Afrikaans and English as the main European languages in the Union and another quarter named them as Dutch and English. In all, two-thirds could name one or other of the main European languages.

No one was able to name all the main non-white groups in the Union (i.e. native Africans, Cape Coloured, Indians), although a tenth were able to name *both* Indians and Africans. The Indians were named by a third of the viewers; the Cape Coloured were almost completely omitted. Moreover when later asked what was meant by 'the Cape Coloured people', only à little more than a tenth were anywhere near the mark. The large volume of inaccurate responses included 'true black', 'whites permanently settled in the Cape', and the 'better class'.

A little less than a third had an approximate idea of the meaning of apartheid', the main answer being 'racial segregation' (22%). When it came to the Separate Representation of Voters Act, there was very little understanding indeed. Practically nobody (4%) knew the particular section of the population with which the act was concerned; only about a tenth could say what kind of thing it was intended to do (all of this tenth referring it to the 'black people' rather than to the Cape Coloured).

Nearly two-thirds could name Malan as Prime Minister of the Union, although less than a tenth could name the opposition party in the South African Parliament, some of the inaccurate responses being Torch Party (also called 'The Torch'), Democrats and Mau-Mau.

There was general agreement that there was, outside Parliament, white opposition to the policy of the Malan government (86%), although only about a fifth of the viewers could approximately name the Torch Commando as a group from which this opposition came. Further, when later asked the purpose of the Torch Commando, half had no idea, 40% thought it stood for anti-segregation or for racial equality, 10% gave other wrong answers, and only 3% connected it with the constitutional issue. On the question of black or coloured opposition to the policy of the Malan Government, about two-thirds agreed that there *was* such opposition, although only a third were approximately correct in describing its character (e.g. passive resistance, civil disobedience). Some of the incorrect responses were 'rioting', 'striking', 'emigrating', 'holding meetings by torchlight', 'forming a union'.

Kenya

There was only limited appreciation of the racial composition of the Kenya population. Although about half of the viewers were able to volunteer that there were whites in Kenya, only one tenth of them gave evidence that they knew there were Indians there too. Arabs were named only a few times. When *told* the names of the different races at present in Kenya, the Africans were judged to be in the majority and the whites incorrectly thought to be a larger group than the Indians.

When asked about the main activities of the whites in Kenya, half the viewers could say that the white population there was engaged primarily in agriculture, a few thought that its main activity was government and administration and the rest either did not know, or were rather wide of the mark, naming such things as big game hunting, or diamond mining, or teaching, or building as the main activity.

On the question of the attitude of Kenya whites to the black population, less than a tenth showed any awareness of a difference in attitude between the settlers and the government officials. About a third could correctly name troubles in Kenya related to race relations, but very few of these showed any real insight into the causes of these troubles.

Central Africa[e]

Practically no one (2%) could name all three of the territories referred to as Central Africa, although about a quarter were able to name at least one of them. After being *given* the names of the three territories concerned, and the information that a 'plan had recently been put forward concerning them', a fifth of the viewers correctly said or implied that this plan was for federation. Seventeen out of twenty had little or no idea why the proposal was supported by whites, and a small group (9%) said it was because federation would mean economic unity or something to that effect; a slightly smaller group said that it was because federation would give the whites greater control over the blacks. Ignorance about why the black people in Central Africa opposed federation was just as common, but a fifth thought it was because it would lead to deterioration of black status relative to the whites ('loss of equality', 'same as in South Africa', 'colour bar').

Viewers were almost totally ignorant of the names of prominent whites in Central Africa. Huggins was the only one mentioned and he was named by only 2%.

Sudan

Slightly more than a third knew that it was with Egypt that Britain had been associated in the administration of the Sudan. Subsequently asked why Egypt sought control over the Sudan, very few indeed (6%) said it had anything to do with the River Nile, a large group thinking that it would be a financial asset to Egypt ('minerals and crops', 'trade', 'more fertile than Egypt') and some that it would be a military asset; no less than a fifth thought that it would give Egypt control of the Suez Canal.

Nearly 90% had no notion of any important economic development in Sudan in which Britain had helped, nobody named the Gezira cotton scheme, although about one in ten named either 'cotton industry', 'irrigation' or 'agriculture'.

The Gold Coast[e]

The majority had no idea at all of any 'recent important developments' in the Gold Coast. Less than a fifth were aware that the Gold Coast had recently been granted self-government, and a small group answered in terms of 'Mau-Mau', 'Malan gains power', 'abdication of Seretse Khama'.

About three-quarters had a fair idea of the effects on white people of the climate of the Gold Coast, and slightly over half that there are relatively few whites in the Gold Coast. About half believed that the whites stay in the area only a short time and practically none that whites settle there permanently.

African exports

Asked about exports from certain areas, a fifth of the viewers named gold as exported from South Africa, one in ten named copper as coming from Northern Rhodesia, and less than one in ten named cocoa as coming from the Gold Coast.

Miscellaneous points

About a quarter realised that Britain had in the past had a hand in slave trade in Africa. Other countries named as being involved in the slave trade were France (19%), Spain (15%), Holland (9%), Portugal (2%). About two thirds of the viewers could name none of the countries thus concerned. When asked to name the main diseases to which Africans were subject, most viewers gave at least one. Those mentioned most frequently were malaria, sleeping sickness, dysentery and leprosy in that order.

SUMMING UP.

Although, as was noted earlier, the attitudes of these viewers towards the various problems of Africa tend to be liberal, their knowledge of the essential facts behind these problems is, on the whole, scanty. Clearly there is considerable need for the presentation of such facts. The present outline of existing knowledge should indicate where the need for facts is the more pressing.

CONDUCTING RESEARCH INTO THE AUDIENCE'S ABILITY TO UNDERSTAND PROGRAM MATERIAL

An introductory note

The whole of Section I was concerned with *'Planning' Studies*. Section II deals solely with the question of how well program material which is meant to inform can be understood by the people for whom it is intended. This has been referred to throughout the section as the *Comprehensibility* of program material. Planning studies conducted for the development of particular programs can help the broadcaster determine program content and the level of difficulty beyond which he must try not to go. On the other hand, the making of such a study cannot *guarantee* that a program will be as efficient as it might be in conveying its facts and ideas. The planning study can provide very useful guide lines, but it cannot possibly spell out the detail of presentation and should never be envisaged as doing so. Efficiency at this level depends upon the personal expertise of the broadcaster as a communicator.

A test of program comprehensibility can provide evidence of the broadcaster's success as a communicator. The evidence so far collected through enquiries of this kind indicates that there is a strong case for making more of them. When, as is usually the case, production is not preceded by any form of planning study, the case for testing program comprehensibility can be a very strong one.

Chapter 12 sets out the case for conducting tests of programme comprehensibility, Chapter 13 describes the methods available for making such tests, and Chapters 14 and 15 each presents an example of such a test. The examples are meant to provide information of value in its own right as well as to illustrate the methods of testing to those interested in doing this sort of work.

References in this section to articles and books will be found in alphabetical order an pages 375–377.

[12]

The place and function of studies of the comprehensibility of programs

What is a comprehensibility test, and
when should tests be carried out?

A test of a program's comprehensibility is simply a test to find out if that program can be understood as intended when people give it their full attention under optimum viewing or listening conditions. In such tests, members of the program's target audience are exposed to the program under controlled conditions, usually in a large test-room. They are instructed to attend to it carefully and they know that a test will follow. The test follows straight away and it is designed to find out how well or how badly the program communicated its intended meaning.

If a program cannot be understood under these optimum conditions, there is little chance of it communicating its message under ordinary viewing or listening conditions, when distractions and other causes of inattention will almost certainly be operative.

Comprehensibility tests can be used not only to identify those parts within them which are particularly at fault. The tests can be made to reveal the different kinds of misunderstanding which the program is likely to produce.

Comprehensibility tests should be carried out whenever there is any case at all for suspecting that a program or some part of it may prove difficult to understand. Comprehensibility tests should also be carried out, at least occasionally, as part of a checking routine. The point of conducting them on a routine basis is that program staff may be unaware that comprehension problems actually exist in the general run of the material which is broadcast.

Why should the comprehensibility of some
programs be questioned?

In Chapter 2, I referred briefly to several reasons for some informative programs being hard to inderstand. The main reason is that broadcasters of informative programs tend to be drawn from an upper-educated section of the community and hence tend to think and to speak in a manner different from that of the millions to whom they are broadcasting. For the correct meaning to occur in the non-stop context of a television or radio program, the audience has to be really quite familiar with the verbal and visual symbols presented. Otherwise the occurrence of meaning, in the audience, is not sufficiently automatic and that audience misses out here and there, slips behind, and eventually may stop even trying to understand. When the gap between broadcaster and audience is really large, as often it is, the extent of communication failure may be considerable.

Then again, the visual elements in an informative program may not be synchronised properly with the verbal explanation, so that visual and verbal elements take away from each˙other rather than combining. Synchronisation of vision and of words in an informative program is a highly skilled process and not one to be taken lightly. Even granted good timing, the visual elements may be relatively unmeaningful in their own right—as for instance in a visual illustration of some property of matter, or of a scientific concept, or of some newly discovered element in a human cell or, for that matter, of some part of a motor car engine or of the way a new headache remedy is supposed to work. It is generally accepted that visual symbols can create meaning more readily than can words; however, just like words, visual symbols can vary enormously in their power to convey what is intended of them.

The problem facing the broadcaster who wants to adapt his presentation to his audience is complicated by the fact that the mass audience is itself very mixed in its use of speech, in its familiar concepts, and in its ability to convert verbal and visual symbols into personal meaning. From the point of view of mass communication, the mass audience is really a number of different audiences. So to which or to how many of these should the conscientious broadcaster try to adapt his exposition? He may well feel that whatever he does, he cannot possibly cater for all. In that event, which audience sector will he decide to give up? Indeed, will he be encouraged, by this very difficulty, to drop altogether the idea of adapting his presentation to his audience?

Whereas the use of language and of visual elements familiar to the audience is vital to successful communication, it is not enough in itself. If the broadcaster wrongly assumes that viewers have a certain elementary knowledge of his particular subject, and so takes this as his starting point, he will be 'talking over people's heads'. He will be assuming that they know certain fundamentals which they don't, and this will be to invite communication failure. The reader's own experience of learned broadcasts should illustrate this point well enough, and it should allow him to consider how tough the going might sometimes be for the great many people who left school at fourteen or fifteen years of age.

On top of these difficulties are the problems of selective perception and of distortion. People are not like blotting paper when it comes to message intake. They can spend time pooh-poohing some of the ideas presented to them, accepting some and disagreeing with others, and even shutting their minds to some ideas altogether. They can engage in an unconscious process of converting or of distorting them. On many topics viewers are not the passive recorders of someone else's ideas.

These are by no means the only difficulties besetting mass communication. Some of the others are brought out by the studies reported in this section. The literature of psychology presents still others[a]. Indeed, the difficulties are such that even the highly skilled and conscientious broadcaster must expect some degree of failure to communicate his facts and his ideas to his audience.

What sorts of programs should be tested for comprehensibility?

Obviously comprehension testing is not equally relevant to all types of programs. Its special relevance is for informational programs; talks; documentaries; discussions; educational material. This is not to deny its relevance to some general entertainment programs, for certainly we need to know if jokes or funny subtleties are being seen. However, the problem of comprehensibility seems to be at its most serious with informational programs, and it is in this context that the comprehensibility of programs is dealt with here.

Are program staff aware of a problem?

Some broadcasters of informational programs appear to be less aware of comprehension problems than are others. Indeed, there are some who appear to regard their broadcasting activities as a sort of self-fulfilment — as an opportunity to express themselves — and who appear to have no particular pre-occupation with whether they are understood or not. Probably all broadcasters are guilty of this to some degree at least, forgetting the audience from time to time, taking pleasure in using subtle wording for its own sake, giving up the attempt to present things simply when it is hard to do so, failing to synchronise verbal and visual elements, lapsing into technical language. There are other broadcasters whose constant *purpose* is to be understood, but who seem to be insufficiently aware of the gap, educational or intellectual or technical, between themselves and the audience to have much chance of bridging it effectively and continuously. That gap can be enormous, taking the form of word-usage differences (especially with respect to technical language), concept differences, differences in ability to take meaning from a string of words and pictures put together in some complex way. To be able to do anything about the gap between himself and his audience, the broadcaster has to be vividly aware of that gap. Moreover, I think it helps if the broadcaster sees this gap as representing, not ignorance on the part of an audience, but a deficiency in himself as a broadcaster. Only this sort of interpretation of the difference can make

[a] See references: [6, 31, 38, 47, 68, 98, 158].

him sufficiently humble and sincere about bridging the gap for him to be able to do so in an acceptable way.

To be unaware of the problems of communicating to the mass audience is to invite at least some degree of failure. Comprehension studies are one means, and an important one, of developing such awareness.

The Importance of detecting incomprehensibility

Communication failure is costly in terms of money and in terms of wasted opportunity. The first of these is obvious enough, and it applies both to commercial and to non-commercial broadcasting. Something must be said, however, about loss of a particular opportunity.

The broadcasting medium, particularly television, has been regarded by many people as a means of providing the population not only with entertainment but also with information and with further education. Indeed, the B.B.C. has interpreted its Charter as laying upon it "the duty of carrying on the broadcasting service as a means of 'disseminating information, education and entertainment',[b] and, like the Charter itself, it has listed these functions in that particular order. The case for using the television medium to provide information and to educate is not hard to make. The great majority of people in Britain left school at 15 years of age or less and for most of these the further intake of knowledge has tended to be incidental to the purposes and processes of living. The mass media, particularly broadcasting, provide opportunity for giving people a long term and continuous service of an informative kind, whether it be in the context of entertainment programs or in a more direct form.

There can be no doubt that broadcasting in Britain has in fact contributed a major input of this sort. Nonetheless there seems to be a strong case for asking if its controllers have done all that they might have done in this respect. If messages cannot be fully understood, they become, for the people concerned, partly a waste of words and a partial waste of the talents of broadcasters. *Moreover if a failure to understand becomes usual, it is almost certain that many of the people so affected will eventually turn away from broadcasts purporting to be informative or educational.* In the writer's experience, people want useful information about the world they live in and, given a reasonable chance, will seek it out and absorb it. If that interest is frustrated, however, through the information provided being expressed in terms too technical, or too abstract, too clever or too muddled, they will eventually turn away from it. To the extent that this is happening — and it is submitted here that it is a very common occurrence — it can only be regarded as a great opportunity lost. Studies of the comprehensibility of informative programs, coupled of course with checks on their interestingness and their usefulness, are most important as part of an insurance against the loss of this opportunity.

[b] See page 10, B.B.C. Handbook, 1956.

In commercial broadcasting, incomprehensibility in the message can be very costly indeed. Certain facts have to be communicated in a very short space of time. These facts usually represent special qualities of the advertised product — qualities that are, in the long run, intended to stimulate buying activities. If a message about these qualities cannot be understood in the way intended, then some at least of the point of the advertisement is thrown away.

*When should comprehensibility tests be made
and how can the results be used?*

Testing a particular program before it is due for broadcast may well provide opportunity to modify it with respect to its main points of failure. That is the ideal situation. If, as in advertising, a lot of money is to be invested in the attempt to communicate a particular message, then it would seem essential to carry out a pre-broadcast check of this kind, in order to be able to modify if necessary, or even to discard, the advertisement concerned. With many television advertisements and with some other kinds of filmed material, the combination of pre-test and modification certainly is feasible. However, not all TV program material lends itself readily to this combined operation. Some may not be available even for pre-test, let alone modification. The most difficult of all is probably the TV 'talk' or discussion. With a 'talk' or discussion, program staff may not know what the speakers will say or how they will formulate messages till very close to the time of broadcast, or, quite possibly, till the broadcast goes out. If, as may well be, the talk has been recorded prior to broadcast, the clarification of parts of it which are found to be incomprehensible would probably require that the speakers concerned should reformulate what they have said. Even granted an ability on their part to modify what they have said in the direction of common language, the whole process of change would be a most difficult and chancy one: generally speaking, one would not attempt post-test modification of a TV 'talk' or discussion.

Programs of a less impromptu kind usually present fewer difficulties, particularly where the commentary and the other verbal elements of the program are the responsibilities of permanent staff. Even here, however, the practical difficulties of getting changes made should not be underestimated. With sound programs, it is likely to be easier than with television material, but in either case one of the more substantial barriers is the understandable resistance of creative staff to changing what they have carefully created.

The value of testing a program's comprehensibility does not, however, rest upon having the test carried out prior to the broadcast. Indeed, comprehension tests can be extremely useful when carried out just *after* the broadcast. Thus when a series of informational programs is being produced, comprehensibility tests of those of them already produced can help the broadcaster to adjust his ideas about the appropriate level at which to pitch *subsequent* programs in the series[b]. Establishing appropriate levels will, as various studies indicate [105, 154], raise issues such as: word difficulty and familiarity; sentence complexity; requirements in terms of background knowledge of the topic; speed of presentation; the simplicity or otherwise of the visual illustrations; the linking of verbal and visual elements. Indeed, the more that such studies can tell the producer about the relative importance of factors which determine comprehensibility, the greater will be his control over the efficiency of his *later* programs. The gradual development of such information through comprehension tests would, of course, provide a body of knowledge highly relevant to the techniques of communication and, we may assume, to the training of new program staff.

New concepts, new words

Finally, one further point is worth making. Some broadcasters argue quite feelingly against the systematic simplification of broadcasts. Some do so on the grounds that this process will leave the viewer unaware of new words and of concepts more subtle than or different from those the viewer already uses or knows. Naturally, one must sympathise with this view. Unfortunately, however, the use of a new or unfamiliar word tends to reduce the meaningfulness of the passage in which it occurs and to interfere with the intake and the retention of surrounding passages. It has the additional effect of discouraging people from watching such programs. The point of the matter is that the communication of specific facts does not lend itself to the incidental teaching of new words: the introduction of new and unfamiliar words impairs the communication process. Words are simply the symbols we use in getting a message to someone and the message won't get across unless it is couched in symbols common to speaker and to hearer.

This situation does not entirely rule out as pointless the sub-aim of teaching certain words and concepts in the course of a program. But when this *is* a legitimate aim of a program, it is essential that adequate teaching techniques be used. It is not enough simply to mouth the new words. Nor is it enough to set the new words in appropriate visual and verbal contexts. Nor can we expect the visual part of the program to make clear what the new word means. The least that must be done is to explain and

---

[b] Obviously programs tested in this way must not already have been broadcast to an audience from which the people involved in the test are drawn. Usually this requirement means that a recording must be made of the program either prior to its broadcast or during its broadcast and that the test be made on this recording more or less at the same time as the broadcast itself. When tests *after* the broadcast are necessary, they may have to be carried out in another region. Another device is to ask all invitees to watch a program broadcast at the same time on the other service and then to focus the comprehensibility test upon the program which will *not* have been seen before.

to illustrate what the new word means. Skilfully done, this can be made to *seem* incidental.

A broadcaster's case for having a sub-aim of this kind might be that a particular concept (or technical term) is necessary as a base for the further explanation of some point or issue. However, it is very doubtful that new concepts are what people most need for understanding the broadcast. So many seemingly profound things can be said in simple words. Moreover, people want and will readily absorb knowledge and wisdom phrased in their own familiar terms. On the other hand, they turn away in frustration from potentially interesting things when the broadcaster makes the mistake of using unfamiliar language and subtle concepts. All too often the man who argues for the use of new words and for developing new concepts in the audience is really just too lazy or too unskilled to convert his own ideas into the language of his audience. And of course he pays the obvious and wasteful price of this: he is not understood and eventually he is ignored. What is needed very much more than new words is real effort on the part of broadcasters to couch their ideas in the language of the audience. Comprehensibility testing can be a considerable aid to this process.

[13]

The techniques for testing
the comprehensibility of programs

Actual Understanding and Basic Comprehensibility

It is necessary to distinguish between assessment of the extent of understanding of a program under normal conditions of reception and assessments of the extent to which people are *capable* of understanding it if they really try to do so. The first of these two assessments provides a measure of understanding of the program as broadcast, that is, of *actual* understanding. The second provides a measure of the program's *basic comprehensibility*. Each measure is discussed in this chapter. However, it is worth saying at this point that *basic comprehensibility* is much the more relevant to program planning, and that it is much the easier to measure. It is for this reason that most of Section II is concerned with the *basic comprehensibility* of programs.

Understanding of programs as broadcast

A realistic assessment of a person's actual understanding of a broadcast would be in terms of what got through to him under ordinary conditions of reception. However, it is virtually impossible to determine this at a reasonable level of cost. The difficulty is that comprehension testing depends upon the availability of certain evidence which itself is likely to be lost through fading memory. Thus after several days, a point in the program which was understood or taken in quite well at the time of the broadcast may well have faded sufficiently from memory for the person concerned to be unable to recall the necessary detail or argument when asked to do so. In that case we could not know if the failure to recall should be attributed to an initial failure to understand or to *subsequent forgetting* of what was in fact understood at the time of the broadcast. In fact, the onset of forgetting and the rate at which it proceeds are such as to require that the testing of understanding should occur straight after exposure to the program material concerned. There is in fact a considerable body of information supporting this point of view [158].

However, if testing is to occur immediately after exposure, either we must have a special force of high grade interviewers poised to test people straight after they view at home *or* we must deliberately (and under controlled conditions) expose people to the program and follow this exposure with comprehension testing. The second of these conditions departs from those of normal reception and so is not usable in studies of understanding of programs as broadcast (that is, of *actual* understanding). On the other hand, 'home testing' immediately after the broadcast would be uneconomical because it would demand the employment of a very large force of special interviewers who could be used just once in any single program test. The use of such a method also raises the problems: (i) of how to get adequate testing conditions in respondent homes; (ii) of how to keep down the proportion of refusals to co-operate at such short notice. In the writer's view, the assessment of *actual* understanding (that is, of such understanding as was actually achieved at the time of the broadcast) is impractical.

This is not to say that the assessment of actual understanding is not at times desirable, for it could provide a broadcaster with an overall evaluation of how well he is getting across to people — their inattention being what it was. However, when he *does* have this information, he will not know how much of his failure is due to audience inattention and how much of it springs from the broadcaster's inability to present his material simply. For remedial purposes, research data of a less ambiguous kind are required.

The basic comprehensibility of programs

Basic comprehensibility testing can tell the broadcaster in a relatively unambiguous way whether or not he is pitching his message at a suitable level of difficulty and it can indicate to him the points of communication failure. With this information he will be in a position to take appropriate remedial steps (in relation to program material) and in this sense 'basic comprehensibility' testing is a very useful tool of program development.

For this particular measure, controlled exposure of respondents to the program being tested is the appropriate procedure and this is a relatively simple thing to arrange. Testing can occur immediately after all or part of the program has been presented. The methods used for conducting 'basic comprehensibility' tests are described in this chapter.

An Index of Comprehensibility

Before beginning the description of this method, there is one approach to comprehensibility measurement which is well worth mentioning. This approach is to develop an *index* of program comprehensibility along lines similar to that used by Flesch [119] in his development of an index of *readability*. Using empirical methods, Flesch identified various features of written material which were *correlated* with its measured readability (e.g. features such as average number of words per sentence; number of affixes per 100 words). He combined certain of these to give him an index of the readability of printed material. The index of readability for any passage could thereby be derived from a desk analysis of the material concerned. The index so derived would then indicate to the analyst how well or how badly the analysed passage compared with other items.

The idea of assessing comprehensibility from a desk analysis of program material is a distinctly attractive one. However, an index of this kind would be useful only to the degree that it did in fact predict comprehensibility. It would do this only in so far as the analyses made were based upon features of the material which had been established *empirically* as associated with measured comprehensibility[b]. Moreover, the joint correlation of these with measured comprehensibility would have to be quite high. There is no good reason for assuming such features of program material cannot be discovered and used in this way. Indeed, that would be no more than the systematic use of such information as is gained from comprehensibility tests of the kind described in this section. An index of comprehensibility is one obvious and desirable goal of comprehensibility research. Its application by program staff would, moreover, be a very effective way of impressing upon them what it is that makes a program hard or easy to understand. There could hardly be a better way of bringing to their attention, as production staff, the accumulated evidence on this vital matter. However, the derivation of any such system in relation to program comprehensibility must depend upon the existence of considerably more research evidence than is yet available. The techniques of research described in this section are, I think, sufficient to provide such information, but up till now not enough of this sort of research has been done.

At the same time, it is fairly clear that even a well developed *index* could not be a complete substitute for a direct measure of comprehensibility. It could not give us the details of the specific misunderstandings that had occurred nor could it *extend* our knowledge of the causes of success and failure. For these, a direct measure of comprehensibility would be needed.

Measuring the Basic Comprehensibility of Program Material

The main purpose of measuring program comprehensibility is to find out if some specified program is capable of conveying to its target audience the ideas and information which it contains. As stated earlier, comprehensibility studies are meant also to discover the kinds of misunderstandings that occur and to indicate the possible causes of misunderstanding. There are several ways in which to expose people to programs under optimum conditions and perhaps several ways of measuring the comprehension achieved.

[b] That is, they must have been established as *correlated* with measured comprehensibility.

Ways of exposing people to the material to be tested

One technique for exposing people to program material is to go to the home of each respondent, to present the program there with instructions to attend carefully to it, and then to test the exposee for grasp of program content. One very useful exposure device for this sort of work is a portable projector which is built into a container resembling a small television set. The image is projected onto a screen in this container. It can be used to show program material or advertisements. For material intended for broadcast solely for radio reception, a tape recording may be brought into the home in the same way.

The showing of this material in the home is best done by appointment, and it is a sufficiently novel and attractive technique to get a high rate of acceptance among those asked for an appointment to do it. At the same time, the method has disadvantages. One is that the home may be unsuitable for the sort of rigorous questioning which is necessary for comprehension testing; another is that the high skills necessary in the interviewers doing this work are such that there won't be many of them working at any one time and because of this the questioning of a sufficient sample may well take more time than the hurrying broadcasting industry can allow.

The other situation to which I have referred is what may be called the test room. Just as with the planning studies described in Section I, people who can be regarded as members of the program's 'intended audience' come by invitation to a meeting at some centre. In the invitation, the purpose of this meeting is not stated beyond the fact that the meeting will end with general discussion of programs. After standard preparation, group members are shown the program which is to be tested. This may be on film with normal sound accompaniment or it may be recorded material for radio broadcast. The presentation of filmed material may. be on a large screen or it may be on a television set in the test room. If the group is larger than half a dozen, and this is usually the case, projection onto a large screen is used.

A vital part of the instruction to the group is that they must attend to the program presented to them because they will be asked various questions about it after presentation. Over and above this, there is the standard preparation for test work (see Chapter 3) including the stressing of three rules: no discussion (until the discussion period at the end); real effort in writing down answers; absolute frankness in the knowledge that all members are anonymous. After the presentation of the program comes the testing of group members' comprehension of it.

This method, too, has its difficulties and these must not be under-estimated. One is that with a large-screen presentation of filmed material, there may be an accentuation of the degree to which various points in it are noticed. Another difficulty is that the system of recruitment used means that only about one in four of those invited comes. This difficulty has been discussed in detail in Chapter 3, where it was made clear that a considerable re-weighting of the test room sample to the characteristics of the total target audience can be carried out, and that in practice this is sufficient to reduce unrepresentativeness to a marked degree.

The different measures of comprehensibility that have been used

Quite a range of different methods have been used for assessing the ability of people to understand information presented to them through the printed or the spoken word. Some studies have included, but not necessarily relied upon, the ratings of respondents themselves as to how well they understood what was read or said to them [111, 112, 132]. Chall and Dial reported in 1948 [112] that they had found a high degree of association between listeners' ratings of their own understanding of a script and the performance of these people in answering questions about what was said in that script. On the other hand, Vernon's report of 1952 [155] indicated no such relationship. Even without Vernon's finding, it would seem unrealistic to assume such an association both to apply *generally* and to be appreciable, for it is common experience in research that people may be quite unaware of their own failure to understand either minor or major points and also that they are sometimes unwilling to admit the failures they *do* know about.

Another of the techniques used is what has been called by some the Essay method [111, 145, 154]: the respondent is required to write down what the test material was about. In some cases the experimenter's request is for all the *major points* in the talk and in others the request is for *everything* that was said. A panel of judges may perhaps be called in to assess the degree to which individuals' essays indicate that the test material has been understood. Another method, the Specific Questions technique, has involved the use of a series of narrowly oriented questions, each focussed upon a specific point in the test material. The form of these questions has varied. Thus subjects may be asked to finish each of a series of sentences [111] or to choose an answer to a question from some limited number of 'answers' offered to them [112, 114, 151]. These are called, respectively, the 'Sentence Completion' and the 'Multiple Choice' methods. Then again, subjects questioned about specific points in the message may be asked to formulate their own short replies to the questions asked — perhaps a single word or perhaps a sentence [105, 111, 113, 151].

The disconcerting fact about the Essay method and the Specific Question method is that they do not necessarily give anything like the same results. Thus Vernon found only a 23% agreement (i.e., +0.48 correlation) between score on an Essay type test and score on a test where the subject was given a choice of answers (the Multiple Choice method) (154). In his own research, the writer found only a 25% agreement between scores based on the Essay method on the one hand and the Specific Question method on the other [105]. Findings of this kind must alert us to the likelihood that either one or both of these techniques gives a misleading result, at least as far as the individual respondent is concerned, though it is still possible that the two methods will produce the same averages.

Reasons for choosing the method of specific questioning

In the absence of firm and fairly extensive evidence, it is very difficult to make a safe decision about which method to use, and probably some doubt must always remain about any indirectly based conclusion we may reach on the matter. This must be remembered when the reader considers the following arguments for choosing, as a measure of comprehension, a particular form of Specific Questioning. This is the form of Specific Questioning which requires the use of tightly formulated questions about particular points in the test material, with the respondent then formulating his own reply, usually a short one.

The choice of this method involved the rejection of the Essay method and of that form of Specific Questioning which presents the respondent with a limited number of replies from which he is to select that one which he considers correct (i.e. the Multiple Choice method).

Of the Essay method, a certain amount can be plausibly speculated for a start. (1) In the first place, the method seems particularly dependent upon the literary fluency of the respondent and also upon whether or not the respondent feels he ought to be producing a lot or a little. Certainly some respondents performing this task are content to stop after a little while and need a lot of urging to go on writing. Others write a lot with little or no urging. Writing a lot or a little might not be so important if people were highly systematic in setting down what they had taken in, but in fact there is a tendency for respondents using the Essay type method to put down a string of associated ideas, one triggering off the other, to the detriment of the recall of material that did not fall into that sequence. (2) When a person writes freely, it may be extremely difficult to judge from what he has written whether or not he has understood a particular point: his reference may be only fleeting and partial and it may be ambiguous. The professional gatherer of evidence seeking to dispel ambiguity (for example, the courtroom questioner) usually finds it necessary to ask rather specific questions (perhaps even a series of them) and to insist upon people answering to the point. A free or uncontrolled statement can leave us guessing about so much. This can be markedly so when the test material contains a good many different elements or ideas.

Much of the argument I have just set forth suggests that a more reliable procedure would be to focus questions upon those particular points in the test material with respect to which we want to test the respondent's understanding. This is a very demanding task for the question designer, but if he does his job properly he can examine and extract from the respondent's mind with a fairly high degree of direction and control.

The other technique which I ruled out in my earlier statement is the Multiple Choice method. It is true that with this method the questions asked can be highly specific. However, the respondent chooses his answer from the several which are offered, and the trouble with this method is that it can be extremely difficult to pose really adequate alternatives. All too easily, some of them are less plausible than others, even for the person who has not heard the test material at all. The design of answers for use in multiple choice questions is in fact a highly skilled process, and one for which there is hardly likely to be time in a research department geared to program production. Over and above the problem of getting equally plausible alternatives, respondents tested on this method stand to gain through pure guesswork. The dangers from guessing are at a maximum when the alternatives offered are simply 'true' versus 'false' (that is, in response to a statement that the test material 'said' such and such).

The alternative to a multiple choice answer is some form of free response answer of a very brief kind and it is this method which I have advocated be used. The respondent is asked a highly specific question and he must formulate his own brief answer to it. The method has the advantage of allowing the tester to pinpoint any item in the program that he wants to test for its comprehensibility. Obviously any form of open response system has weaknesses which have to be countered and to these I shall turn in later parts of this chapter.

My preference for the Specific Question method rather than the Essay method is supported also by a certain amount of research. In a BBC study conducted as part of my preparation for work on program comprehensibility, a sample of approximately 100 adults heard a recording of certain program material and then went through two separate tests of their comprehension of it. The first test was the Essay type and the second was the Specific Question type (creative response). There were major differences in the two scores and there was evidence that this did not spring out of any effect of the first test on the second[d]. Their correlation was in fact only $+0.5$ (indicating a 25% agreement between them). A comparison of the detail of the two sets of results showed that subjects were failing, in their essay type reply, to volunteer data which came out when the Specific Question technique was used: the opposite tendency did not occur. The comparisons also showed that the use of the Essay type test led to the examiners frequently, but often wrongly, giving the respondent the benefit of the doubt. Another source of inadequacy of the Essay method lay in the tendency of some people to give *opinions* of the program material rather than their understanding of the facts presented.

More work of this kind, ranged over varied programs, is necessary to resolve the issue quite firmly, but there is enough, between the small amount of research done and the logical consideration of the matter, to support the Specific Question method rather than the Essay method.

Working Details of the Specific Question Method

The nature of facts presented in programme material varies somewhat. The range of them includes: single facts such as the number of District

---

[d] A second group, matched to the first in terms of a number of variables, heard the same recording and then were tested on the Specific Question method only. Their score was much the same as that of the other group with respect to the Specific Question test.

Heating Systems in Britain at present, or the amount of money Britain spends yearly on certain services; groups of facts such as the different raw materials to be discussed at a specified conference; what some Cabinet Minister suggested on a particular occasion; the one or more reasons given for a decision or conclusion of some kind; statements about differences or similarities; statements of the advantage of one thing over another. Sometimes differences, similarities and advantages are directly stated but at other times they are only implied. Further, an item of information or an argument which is presented may in some cases be of major importance to the presentation — perhaps even its final conclusion — though in other cases it may be no more than an incidental or supporting fact. All of these forms of information are potentially of interest to the person testing comprehensibility. The advantage of the Specific Question method is that the tester can focus a question on any item of information according to his wishes. The formulation of the necessary questions for testing these points does, however, call for quite a lot of skill and care on the part of the question designer. Some of the difficulties he faces are common to all the questions he has to ask but others are more pronounced for certain kinds of question. These difficulties, and ways of dealing with them, are formulated in the next section. Just after the latter is a further section dealing with the marking or evaluation of the answers given by respondents.

Designing questions

(1) It is necessary right at the start to develop a clear idea about what the program material is supposed to be telling people. It is not unfair to say that at times this can be difficult to ascertain even with the script available for careful study. With lengthy or complex material it may be necessary for the question designer to check with the writer himself in order to ensure that his interpretation of the message is what the broadcaster intended.

(2) Another requirement, and a most important one, is that any questions asked must be written in the simplest language possible. Any difficulty in the wording of the questions themselves could wrongly reduce the respondent's opportunity to show what he really had understood of the program material. At the worst, he could have a really good grasp of what was said and yet fail to show this because he couldn't understand the questions being asked about it. The rule is that a question should *never* have in it a word or element more difficult than those in the passage being tested. And it is better if the difficulty level of questions is far below that of the test material. It is certainly possible to write such questions, but this requires determined care.

(3) Questions should be formulated in such a way that they test the respondent's comprehension of the points concerned rather than mere ability to repeat what the speaker said. However, I do not want to make too much of this difficulty, because in my experience the likelihood of a passage being repeated by the respondent after just one hearing is related

appreciably to his understanding of it — to the degree to which he relates it in a meaningful way to his existing knowledge and concepts.However, to the extent that there is a danger of mere repetition wrongly passing for comprehension, the danger would seem to be at its greatest with respect to facts directly presented and at its least with conclusions or implications which are not directly presented in so many words and which may in fact have been only implied. The main defence against this danger lies in the fact that the framing of a highly specific question requires the respondent to bring from his total reserve of memories about the program just that one memory which is appropriate to the question asked. Of course, it is still possible that an appropriate answer in the form of a repetition of a phrase from the program hides the fact that some key word in that answer is not really understood. If, at the time of framing the questions, this is suspected as a possible difficulty, it can be good policy to follow the question concerned with a request to the respondents to write down what they think that word means.

(4) In designing specific questions, it is often necessary to give the respondent a certain amount of information. Thus in asking the respondent *why* (according to the speaker) it had been impossible to avoid 'the present meat glut', it was necessary for the tester to reveal that the speaker had in fact referred to a meat glut and also that the speaker regarded this glut as unavoidable. Accordingly, any questions checking on either of these points would have to be completed *before* the answers to them were revealed through the setting up of a later question. Because of this, questions ordinarily run in a sequence such that one leads on to the next, with frequent revealing of answers to earlier questions. This maximises the respondent's chances of giving evidence of such understanding as he actually achieved. He never gets so 'lost' that he gives up and he doesn't have to know the previous answers to deal with the next questions. It will of course be obvious from this that the system of getting answers has to be such that people can't go back to an earlier answer and change it because they have just learned what it should have been. In fact, a small booklet is used, and the respondent turns to a fresh page for each new question; he is reminded throughout that there is no going back once the next question is asked. The questions are called out by the test administrator, one at a time and this means that a respondent cannot get help in answering a question by looking forward to a *later* question.

(5) Since questions have to be called out, it is essential that their wording should be in short sentences (as well as being of utmost simplicity).

(6) Other important features of the Specific Question method are as follows:—

   (i) The questions asked should be 'answerable' through a short reply, so that there is a minimum dependence upon literary fluency or upon a respondent's desire to write a lot or a little[e].

[e] From this point of view, the technique known as Sentence Completion may at times be useful, for it can be highly specific in framing a question and it allows

(ii) Single questions should not call for a whole string of unrelated facts; wherever possible, the rule should be that one fact requires one question.

The delivery of the questions.

Questions should be delivered under group testing conditions as already described in Chapter 3 and as partly indicated in the preceding paragraphs. Briefly, this involves careful preparation of the respondent, particularly with reference to two of the rules for group testing, namely: 'no discussion' and 'hard work'. All respondents know they are anonymous. The questions are read out and repeated and the answers are written in small booklets, one answer per page.

Methods of marking and analysis.

If a person has misunderstood a particular point in a program, it becomes most important to ascertain just what sort of misunderstanding has occurred. In ordinary circumstances, analysis of the results should be directed towards finding out both if particular points have been understood *and* the nature of any misunderstandings.

The percentage of people fully correct on individual questions can be ascertained fairly readily. A small panel of judges of relevant background can if necessary be brought in on cases posing special problems. Beyond this comes the study of misunderstandings and this is best done through a form of content analysis, some details of which follow, with more in a footnote[f]. Very briefly, the form of content analysis which I recommend is as follows. It is done separately for each question.

---

little scope for a voluminous reply. One of its weaknesses however is that it can at times be very difficult to make an incomplete sentence tell the respondent just what the question really is. Another is that the reply may also be ambiguous. Now and then it is possible to make a question of this kind overcome both difficulties, but for the most part a full sentence will be necessary for adequately framing the question.

[f] The sorting process is a demanding one. Its first object is to build up markedly homogeneous sub-groups. To do this, we must be ready to put aside any items (i.e. statements on strips) which are somewhat different from those in the developing categories. We can come back to these later, *after* rather pure sub-groups have shown up; above all, we must not dilute the latter before they can take form. Ambiguous statements are also put to one side for the time being, either for clarification by going back to the full record of the respondent concerned or for other treatment as indicated below. Once all statements have been dealt with in this way, the developing groups of statements are scrutinized to ensure that they really are homogeneous. Items that are spoiling homogeneity are taken out and reconsidered, some of them possibly going into the ambiguous heap. Ambiguous items are next dealt with to find out if they should in fact be in any of the present categories, or be returned to the ambiguous group or be put into the general heap yet to be sorted.

This total process will have familiarized the analyst with the statements as a whole. He now takes the remaining *un*ambiguous items and deals with them

(1) First of all, each separate misunderstanding is typed out, with a number against it to identify the respondent from whom it came. For some respondents there would be no such entry because they had properly understood what was being said. For others there would be a single statement or perhaps two. Occasionally there might be more. A hundred respondents might yield anything up to 200 such entries, and it is these entries which are content analysed. Each entry must be stated as nearly as is practicable in the language of the respondent.

(2) The sheets of statements are then cut up into strips, so that one statement appears on each strip.

(3) These strips are then sorted so that statements which say virtually the same thing are brought together. Through this process, relevant categories (of misunderstandings) show themselves or take form. Under no circumstances are category headings to be set up before the analysis begins, for this would be to impose upon the facts our preconceptions about the kinds of misunderstandings that have occurred, and typically it would result in squeezing statements into categories where they should not really be. Content analysis as I have described it here means that the categories come from the data itself, as is necessary in any process of discovery. Here, the process of discovery involves *finding out what misunderstandings did in fact occur*[f]. This is vital because it is only by seeing clearly the nature of the misunderstandings that occur that we put ourselves in a position to correct failures either in the present case or in the future. It is not enough simply to know we have gone wrong. We need to know how we have gone wrong. Guessing is no substitute

---

as follows. Some will lead to the development of a fresh category. Some will be variants of existing groups and will be placed near to these on the sorting table, but not mixed up with them. Those that still present problems (i.e. we can't decide where they go) are simply put to one side for later treatment and are not to be 'squeezed in somewhere'. By this time, we will have a small heap of items which are difficult to place and these now get our full attention. Some of them may finish up in small categories of their own (e.g. two or three items only in the group). Others will emerge as near-relatives of existing groups and will be placed near them on the sorting table. Some will finish up in the 'miscellaneous' group. Each grouping other than the miscellaneous items is then given a name *which describes its content as closely as possible*. This is a dangerous phase because even here any desires on the part of analysts to foist their own ideas upon the data can undo the empirical character of the process I have described. After this, the named categories are gummed onto paper (one category per sheet) and these sheets are then sorted into groups of categories according to their similarity. This process may now suggest that *several* of the named categories may with advantage be given a general description as well as the more individual titles already given to them. The process stops here . The data are in fact now in ideal form of the preparation of a truly empirical and graphic report about *the nature of such failures as have occurred*

for knowing—particularly when the necessary data are so readily available.

This method of analysis was not used in the studies reported in this section, namely those dealing with "Topic for Tonight" and "Facts and Figures". This is simply because I had not at that stage developed the method as described here. I think that the two studies referred to are the poorer for this. Full content analysis has been used in later studies. It is a particularly productive operation and it can contribute richly to any study of program comprehensibility.

[14]

The comprehensibility of "Topic for tonight"[a]

A series of short talks presenting the background to some event currently in the news.

BACKGROUND AND AIMS

This enquiry falls within the broad field of the effectiveness of broadcasting as a means of communication, and it was concerned mainly with finding out how well talks in the 'Topic for Tonight' series could be understood by the people for whom they were designed. The study had been preceded in 1950 by Vernon's work on the intelligibility of Forces Educational Broadcasts [154]. His investigation necessarily dealt with members of the forces. The present enquiry was concerned with the ordinary civilian population.

"Topic for Tonight" was a five-minute program which followed the ten o'clock news in the Light Programme each night, except Saturdays and Sundays. It had an average audience of 11 %. It was intended to provide background information on some item of news in a way that would add interest to it or would clear up some point which many people had forgotten or did not know. The talks were given by members of a panel of speakers, some of whom were specially qualified in the economic, political and industrial fields, and in foreign affairs, while the remainder were competent journalists.

The enquiry had four aims:

(1) The main aim was to find out how well talks in the "Topic for Tonight" series could be understood by the people for whom they were designed, that is, by their 'target' audience. In other words, their *comprehensibility* for the target audience was to be assessed. This target audience. was provisionally defined as that part of the general population which remains after excluding the bottom 30% and the top 15% on an occupa-

[a] This report is based upon work conducted by the writer in 1951–2 as a member of the Audience Research Department of the BBC and reported in the BBC document LR/52/1080: *An Equiry Into the Comprehensibility of 'Topic for Tonight'* [105].

tional basis. Similar assessments were to be carried out for the people who ordinarily listen to 'Topic for Tonight' (whether they be in the target audience or not) and for the general adult population.

(2) The second aim was closely related to the first. Level of comprehensibility was to be analysed according to the listener's educational background, intelligence, occupational level, age and sex.

(3) Thirdly it was intended that those talks which had been tested for comprehensibility should be analysed to establish some of the characteristics of talks which make for better understanding by the people listening to them.

(4) The fourth and simplest aim was to determine the following things: the frequency with which "Topic for Tonight" talks were heard and the percentage of people reached by them in a given period; the nature of the existing audience in terms of occupation, age and sex; the interest expressed in these talks by their listeners.

THE METHODS OF RESEARCH: IN BRIEF

Tests of basic comprehensibility were made on twenty-six talks in the "Topic for Tonight" series. Some 35-50 people were tested on each of these talks, the total being 1,072. The method of testing comprehensibility was to play a recording of a talk to a group of listeners, and then to test their understanding of it by means of their written replies to a series of questions about the major and minor points of the talk. After this, various personal details were collected from group members so that these could later be related to scores for understanding. An entirely separate group took part in the testing procedure for each separate talk. The twenty-six groups were matched for intelligence, age, sex. Later on, each of the twenty-six talks were analysed in order to relate their various characteristics to their tested comprehensibility.

THE METHODS OF RESEARCH: IN DETAIL
Which Talks Were Tested?

The twenty-six talks selected for testing were meant to constitute a fairly wide and not unrepresentative range of the talks in the 'Topic for Tonight' series as presented over a three month period in 1951. Thus, they were selected at intervals over that period, with routine variation as to day of presentation. Their subject matter ranged from 'jet aircraft' to 'gambling', and from the 'Festival of Britain' to 'bush fires in Australia'. Moreover, there was direct evidence that the level of their difficulty was considerably varied too.

Sampling Requirements

The following requirements of sampling had to be met. (1) For the total sample, people in each educational and occupational subgroup of the population had to be represented in sufficient numbers to allow the calculation of separate comprehension scores for each of those subgroups. This applied also for intelligence, age and sex. (2) These population subgroups had also to be such that they would allow the calculation of comprehensibility scores for each of the target audience, the actual audience and the general population. (3) The total sample was to be made up of twenty-six sub samples, one for each of the twenty-six talks, and these sub samples were to be made equivalent to each other in terms of age, sex, occupational level and possibly other variables, as a necessary basis for comparing them in terms of tested comprehensibility.

Accordingly, the recruitment of subjects was not designed to yield a representative sample of listeners, but to provide adequate numbers in terms of each age, sex and social class subgroup, it being recognised that the different analyses to be made would call for different weightings of the various (relevant) subgroups of the total sample taking part.

Methods of Recruiting Subjects

About half of those taking part in the comprehensibility testing had been interviewed by the BBC during the previous two to three weeks in the course of its Daily Survey of Listening. All had included "Topic for Tonight" amongst the programs they claimed to have heard. They now came to Broadcasting House by written invitation, bringing with them a 'friend' who tended to be the invitee's husband or wife or some adult member of the invitee's household. The system of invitation has been described already in general terms in Chapter 3, the important point about this system being that it could be used to control approximately the composition of the sample of people coming to Broadcasting House[b]. Obviously further adjustments would be needed (and were in fact made) once the testing procedure had established the precise background of those who actually came (including the 'friend').

Approximately 32% of those invited came, though this higher-than-average figure is due partly to the fact, as planned, that more than a due proportion of the better-off section of the population was invited. The composition of the subjects for the whole enquiry, prior to any re-weighting to match the different samples involved in it, is given in Table 1.

---

[b] The Survey of Listening had provided the name, age, sex and social class of "Topic for Tonight" listeners in Greater London (where the study was to be carried out). The percentage of people who usually come in response to written invitation had already been established in terms of age, sex and social class. Since the Survey of Listening provided these details about each of its respondents, it was possible (when inviting them to come) to exercise an appreciable control over the composition of the accepting sample with respect to these three variables. This meant that the special sampling requirements of the enquiry could be met initially in an approximate way, though obviously further adjustment would be needed once testing procedure had established the precise background of those who came.

TABLE 1.

Sample composition

Occupational Level	%	Age	%	Sex	%
Professional and		15 – 24 years	17	Male	46
semi-professional	9	25 – 34 years	27	Female	54
Highly skilled	25	35 – 44 years	24		
Skilled	28	45 – 54 years	17		
Moderately skilled	21	55 – 64 years	10		
Semi- and unskilled	17	65 +	5		

Test-Room Procedure

On arrival at the test room at about 7.15 p.m., those who had heard "Topic for Tonight" the previous evening were taken out of the group to another test room and so excluded from those who were now to hear last night's program for the first time and to be tested for comprehension of it. The latter were almost all people who had heard "Topic for Tonight" at some time in the past[c]. On average, about 40 of these people were tested on any one evening, all on the one talk, but usually in two separate test rooms so that the average size of a group was about 20 people. None of them was given any indication at all beforehand that tests of any kind would occur, though all knew that the evening would "include general discussion of programs."

After preparatory work aimed at the development of co-operative attitudes, group members were introduced to the standard rules of test room procedure: no discussion, real effort, frankness[d]. After this, they went through various procedures which included the following, using paper and pencil to register their replies. (1) They indicated whether or not they had ever listened to "Topic for Tonight" and how often. (2) They listened to the talk and were immediately tested for their comprehension of it (see later for further details). (3) They indicated their interest in the talk on a verbal rating scale. (4) They provided information about their educational background, completed a timed intelligence test and gave various personal details about themselves.

Group members had been instructed, with respect to procedure (2), that once a question had been dealt with there was no going back to it. They wrote in small booklets with a single page for a single question and the 'no going back' rule appeared to be fully observed.

---

[c] This was indicated by the Survey of Listening records on the basis of which they were selected for invitation, the only exceptions being a small number of the 'friends'.

[d] See Chapter 3 for details.

Assessing the comprehensibility of these talks.

Group members were asked to listen to a sound recording of a single talk, knowing that they would then be tested to find out how well they had taken in what the talk was about. Thus there was a deliberate attempt to give the talk the benefit of careful attention, this being vital to the concept of the 'basic comprehensibility' of programs. See Chapter 13 for a development of this point.

After this came the tests. These consisted of a series of about ten questions, each dealing with some particular point in the talk, and between them covering all its main points and various of its minor points[e], [f]. These points had been selected as major and minor by a panel of three judges. The questions themselves were prepared by the same three judges working together and every attempt was made to word them in simple language so that the question itself would not prevent the respondent from giving evidence of what he had in fact understood from the talk. Most questions required only a short reply.

Assessing subjects' interest in the talk

Interest in the talks was rated just after hearing it and before any testing for comprehension of it. This rating took about a minute and was done on a verbal rating scale running from "extremely interesting" to "extremely boring".

Assessing occupational level

The information requested included respondent's present job (housewives gave job before marriage and retired people gave last job), what they did in that job, training and qualification required for it, number of people working under their authority. This led to their being classified on a 7-point occupational scale, which itself was based upon skill and training required for the job. The occupational scale, which is given in the appendix to this report, had been developed on largely empirical lines and it drew also upon reports by Foulkes and Raven [122], Lingwood [128], Spielman and Burt [140], Vernon [152].

Assessing educational level

Respondents gave information about age of leaving school, any further education since then, examinations passed, type of school or educational institution attended, subjects taken, scholarships won. On the basis of this information they were classified in terms of educational level.

[e] This method of testing comprehension through a series of specific questions (the Specific Question method) was selected after preliminary work in which the Specific Question method had been compared with another possible measuring technique. For details of this experimental work, see Chapter 13.

[f] Since the recording of a "Topic for Tonight" talk could not be available till the morning after its broadcast, and since comprehension testing had to be done that evening, there was usually about six hours for the preparation of the questions.

Assessing respondents' intelligence

Respondents completed a 15 minute intelligence test[g]. It was described to them as a test to see how quickly they could think. Apart from intelligence it depended upon only a minimum knowledge of primary numbers and of letters. Respondents appeared to work keenly at this test and gave no evidence of objecting to the use of a stop watch.

Marking the Replies to Questions

The number of marks allotted to any one question tended to be proportionate to: the relative importance of the point to the meaning and the purpose of the talks; the pervasiveness or extensiveness of reference to the point. In effect, this meant that most major points were allotted a maximum score of 2 marks (and occasionally 3 or 4 marks) and that minor points in the talk tended to be allotted a score of 1 (with some points getting $1^1/_2$). Results were to be presented separately for major and minor points. A partially right answer got part of the full score for its question.

Marking was lenient. The emphasis in all marking was on the sense or the ideas of the speaker's message. Poor expression in writing an answer was not knowingly penalized. A reasonable grasp of a point would most certainly get full marks.

Content Analysis

After the completion of comprehension testing, the contents of all 26 talks were analysed by another three judges. For each talk, a count or an assessment was made of the following things: (1) the number of major and minor points presented in it; (2) the average level of difficulty of its hardest 30 words, difficulty level being judged by Vernon's Vocabulary Scale [153]; (3) the average number of words per sentence; (4) the simplicity of its average sentence as assessed by judges studying the script; (5) the straightforwardness or otherwise of its logical structure; (6) dependence upon the listener having certain background knowledge of a specialized kind; (7) the number of *figures* in the talk (a 'figure' being a number, a fraction, a date, a percentage, a cardinal number); (8) the Flesch Readability index[h]; (9) frequency of occurrence of various parts of speech per 100 words (i.e. active verbs, adverbs, abstract nouns, adjectives, personal pronouns, prepositions); (10) speed of presentation of the talk (i.e. number of words spoken per minute); (11) assessment of the ease or difficulty of a talk by a set of judges reading them. It was planned to correlate each of these with the comprehensibility scores of the talks, in the hope of identifying those elements in a talk which are most associated with communication success or failure.

[g] The Vernon Abstraction test (40 items).

[h] This index is calculated through the formulae $Xs + .06Xm - .07Xh - 0.75$ when s = average sentence length, m = average number of affixes per 100 words, h = average number of personal references per 100 words (115).

THE FINDINGS
The Size and the Nature of the 'Topic for Tonight' Audience and Reactions to the Series

The separate survey, based upon 1,849 adult respondents in Great Britain, provided the following estimates of the coverage achieved by the 'Topic for Tonight' series. On the average night 11% of the adult population in Great Britain hear it, and this compares with the 24% listening to the 10 o'clock news just before it. A total of 31% hear it in the course of each week and a further 11% hear it at least occasionally. As can be seen through Table 2, the 31% hearing 'Topic for Tonight' in the course of a week are similiar to the general population in terms of proportion of men and women; they have among them somewhat less than a due proportion of working-class people, of the under 24 year olds, and of the over 65s. Since the DE class group constitutes 70% of the population, it follows that a large proportion of the 'Topic for Tonight' audience comes from this group or class.

TABLE 2.

The composition of the "Topic for Tonight" audience*

	All	Sex		Age					Class		
		M.	F.	16 24	25 34	35 44	45 64	65 +	AB	C	DE+
		%	%	%	%	%	%	%	%	%	%
Once or more per week	31	30	32	24	29	32	36	28	38	35	28
Occasionally listens	11	11	10	9	15	11	10	7	11	11	11
Very rarely listens	8	9	8	9	6	11	8	5	8	10	8
No longer listens	18	19	17	19	22	18	17	12	16	19	18
Have never listened	32	31	33	39	28	28	29	48	27	25	35

* Survey based on 1849 adults in Great Britain, interviewed during January 1952.
+ AB = top 10% of population of Great Britain in terms of social class; C = =Next 20%; DE = next 70%.

Interest ratings of the talks

Those hearing the talks in the test-room rated them for interestingness on a scale ranging from 'extremely interesting' to 'extremely boring'. The distribution of the 1072 ratings, spread over the whole series of 26 talks, is given in Table 3, p. 138.

This result testifies strongly to the success of speakers in presenting in an interesting way topics which often looked complex and remote. Nor did these test room ratings differ appreciably from the ratings the talks were

T A B L E 3.

Distribution of 1072 interest ratings of "Topic for Tonight"
(unweighted sample)

	extremely interesting										extremely boring
Interest rating	1	2	3	4	5	6	7	8	9	10	11
Distribution ratings	25%	35%	15%	7%	6%	4%	4%	2%	1%	1%	0%

given after being heard under normal conditions at home. It is true that their subject matter had the advantage of being topical, but it is doubtful that this alone is always enough to catch a listener's interest. On this point the comments of listeners are illuminating. Perhaps because "Topic for Tonight" talks were not usually preceded by a title, and generally opened with an attention-catching lead-in, listeners often said they were 'in the midst of a talk' and their interest held by it before they fully realised what the talk was about. Moreover, many said that the talks seemed to be over before their interest had a chance to flag or to disappear.

What this means is that "Topic for Tonight" was reaching a very large and varied part of the population, a large proportion of these people being of working class background, and that its talks were overhelmingly regarded as interesting. This augured well for the talks, provided they were basically comprehensible.

The Basic Comprehensibility of Talks in the "Topic for Tonight" Series

The people who normally listened to "Topic for Tonight" talks had among them slightly more of high intelligence (and middle class background) and slightly fewer of low intelligence than would be found in the general adult population. The theoretical *target* audience contrasted with actual audience in that it left out the top 15% and the bottom 30%, intellectually, of the general population. Where possible, results will be given in terms of these three different populations.

Variability in the Level of Comprehension Scores for all Persons Tested

Those tested varied widely in their ability to understand "Topic for Tonight" talks when they listened to them attentively and without distraction. This while some of the duller listeners had comprehensibility scores of nothing at all, a few of the brighter ones scored between 80% and 90%.

In the same way, there was much variation in the comprehensibility scores for the 26 different talks, for these ranged from a figure of 11% for a talk on the European Army to 44% for one on Australian bushfires.

T A B L E   4.

Distribution of comprehension scores of 1072 individuals
(unweighted)

Comprehension Score in percentage	Distribution of Test Room Respondents	Comprehension score in percentage	Distribution of Test Room Respondents
0	5.0%	46– 55	8.9%
1– 5	12.3%	56– 65	6.7%
6–15	19.0%	66– 75	2.5%
16–25	19.5%	76– 85	1.1%
26–35	16.2%	86– 95	0.2%
36–45	8.6%	96–100	0.0%
			100.0%

T A B L E   5.

Comprehensibility of 26 different talks*

Talk	Comprehension Score %	Talk	Comprehension Score %
European Army	10.8	Telephones	28.3
Raw Materials	15.9	Argentina	28.6
Education for Management	17.8	Controlled Rents	31.4
Jets	18.3	Prime Minister's visit to	
Meat Supply	19.4	Paris	31.5
Atomic Energy	20.6	Korean Armistice	33.4
Prisons	20.9	Cuts in Expenditure in	
Australian Referendum	23.5	Education	33.5
N.A.T.O.	23.6	Submarines	37.6
Divorce	23.8	Festival	39.2
Heating Systems	23.9	Railway accidents	40.0
United Nations	24.3	Election Notes	40.7
Gambling	26.8	Banditry in Malaya	41.9
Sudan	27.4	Australian Bushfires	44.3

* The samples tested in each of the 26 talks were matched in terms of intelligence distribution.

Tables 4 and 5 present important findings in that they indicate that some people are missing out to a major degree, and that some talks are much less successful than others.

Average Scores for all 26 Talks

For people who ordinarily listened to "Topic for Tonight" talks, the overall average comprehensibility score was approximately 28%, much the same as the estimated average score for the general adult population (27%). For the target audience, the average was approximately 28%. The fact that the figure for the target audience came out at much the same level as the average for the *total* population in spite of the former being truncated at each end, is due to a fortuitous balancing out of the contributions of the excluded groups.

An average of 28% means that only about a quarter of the ideas and information in the talks were capable of being taken in under optimum conditions. This can hardly be regarded as a successful basis for the educational and informative purposes of the series.

The overall average of 28% might be thought to hide rather different results for *major* as distinct from *minor* points in the talk. In fact, *major points* were 'taken in' somewhat less than *minor points*, though the difference is relatively small. Table 6 compares scores for points ranked 'first in importance' in the talk (a 'top' major point), second in importance, third, fourth and so on. The figures given are averages for 12 of the 26 talks. For these 12 talks (which were meant to be representative of the 26) the point of first importance got a comprehensibility score of 29%, that of second importance got a score of 21%, that of third importance a score of 31%, that seventh in importance a score of 31% and so on. In other words, points which the speaker had in mind as central or of major importance did not get across any better then his minor points.

TABLE 6

Comprehension scores according to whether the point is a major or a minor one

	Major point						Minor point		
Order of Importance	1st	2nd	3rd	4th	5th	6th	7th	8th	9th
Comprehension Score*	29%	21%	31%	24%	34%	29%	31%	33%	34%

* These figures have not been weighted to the requirements of representative sampling, though there is no reason for supposing that this disturbs their relationship to each other.

Comprehensibility Related to the Background and the Abilities of Listeners

There were differences in comprehension scores according to the listeners' intelligence, occupational level, educational background, age and sex. Some of the differences were quite marked.

Men versus women

Men scored appreciably more than did women and the men's advantage held for 24 of the 26 talks tested. On average, men scored 1.34 times as much as did women. This appears to be due to the fact that men frequently have a better background knowledge of current affairs than do women—good understanding of a talk being dependent very much upon good background knowledge of the subject it dealt with.

Educational level

Not surprisingly, comprehensibility scores varied with the listener's educational background: the higher the listener's educational level the more he was likely to understand. What *was* surprising, however, was that even university graduates, when listening under optimum conditions, scored only about 50% on the average talk. The majority of the population left school at 15 years or less: their average comprehension score under the same favourable conditions was only about 25%.

TABLE 7.

Comprehension scores by educational level

Educational Level	Average Comprehension Score
University degree	48.4%
Higher School Certificate or General Certificate of Education (advanced level) or equivalent.	45.1%
General School Certificate or General Certificate of Education (ordinary level) or equivalent.	42.2%
At Grammar School or Technical School until 16/17 years but without G.S.C. or G.C.E.; equivalent education.	32.4%
At Central or Technical School or Grammar School to 14/15 years; equivalent education.	32.7%
At Elementary school to 14/15 years or Secondary Modern to 15/16 years. Pre-1944 Elementary school or equivalent to 11–13 years, or no schooling.	21.4%

Occupational level

Comprehension scores for different occupational groups were more evenly graded than were those for the different *educational* groups. Nonetheless, because of the appreciable correlation between educational and occupational levels, the indications are much the same: the higher the occupational level, the higher the comprehension score. But even for the professional, semi-professional and executive groups, the score for the average talk was only about 45%.

TABLE 8.

Comprehension scores by occupational background

	Comprehension Score*
Professional, semi-professional and executive	45.1%
Highly skilled	40.8%
Skilled	30.0%
Moderately skilled	21.5%
Semi-skilled and unskilled	16.9%

* These figures have been weighted to render them representative of the different occupational groupings in terms of age and sex.

One of the special merits of an occupational classification (see the Appendix for the one used in this enquiry) is that when its categories are filled in with actual jobs, it can give the broadcaster a fairly graphic description of the audience in terms of ability to understand his output. In the present case it will tell him that he achieved only 17% basic comprehensibility for people like: bus-conductors, truck drivers, semi-automatic machine operators, waiters, hospital orderlies, milk roundsmen, porters, laundry hands, stokers, labourers. Nor did he do much better (22%) with: brick-layers, sheet metal workers, plumbers, dispatch clerks, railway guards, barbers, filing clerks, tailors, machinists, telephone operators. Moreover, the level was only 30% for people like: fitters and turners, pattern makers, cabinet makers, cashiers, wages clerks, senior storemen, typists, qualified children's nurses.

Intelligence level and age

Comprehensibility is related more closely to the respondent's intelligence level (i.e. +0.62) than it is to education (+0.55), occupation (+0.53) or any other of the personal characteristics figuring in the analysis of results. Age, on the other hand was but little related to comprehensibility score, except for the drop in going from the under 64 years group to the 65 and over group.

TABLE 9.

Comprehension score by intelligence and by age

Intelligence Level		Comprehension Score	Age	Comprehension Score
Top	10%	45.2%	15 – 24 years	29.5%
Next	20%	38.2%	25 – 34 years	30.6%
Next	20%	28.0%	35 – 44 years	26.8%
Next	20%	21.6%	45 – 54 years	27.3%
Next	20%	14.9%	55 – 64 years	26.2%
Bottom	10%	14.8%	65+	16.6%

Summing up upon individual differences

The indication of this evidence is that for all major sections of the population, whether classified in terms of educational level, occupational background, intelligence, age or sex, the average "Topic for Tonight" talk was subject to an appreciable amount of communication failure. For the dull, the least educated, the unskilled and the old, the failure was of a major kind. Interestingly, the decision to exclude the lower 30% (intellectually) from the definition of the target audience as being least able to cope with these talks seems to have been justified. But the elimination of the top 15% on the grounds, say, that these people were 'beyond' the "Topic for Tonight" talks, would seem not to have been justified at all.

Characteristics of a Talk
Associated with the Amount of it Comprehended

Most of the foregoing results relate to the 'average talk'. There were, however, differences in score for the 26 different talks, ranging from 11 % for the talk on the European Army to 44 % for that on Australian bush fires. It was to increase insight into such differences that each talk was analysed in terms a number of characteristics. Some of these proved to be quite closely associated with the comprehensibility of talks and some did not. Table 10 gives results.

TABLE 10.

Comprehensibility related to the characteristics of the talk

'Variables' studied	Correlation with comprehension score
The degree to which the talk is dependent upon the listener having somewhat specialised knowledge about the background to the topic	− 0.66
Goodness of logical structure and emphasis on main points	+ 0.65
Frequency of difficult or unfamiliar words	− 0.56
Estimated ease of the talk (three outside judges; *not* respondents)	+ 0.52
Frequency of numerical references	+ 0.47
Flesch Readability Index	+ 0.27
Estimate of simplicity of sentences (three outside judges; not respondents)	+ 0.24
Sentence length	− 0.12
Speed of reading	+ 0.05
Frequency of use of various parts of speech (per 100 words):	
adverbs	+ 0.23
number of active verbs	+ 0.21
personal pronouns	+ 0.24
prepositions	+ 0.02
abstract nouns	− 0,27
adjectives	− 0.34

The three factors most closely related to how well a talk could be understood were (i) the degree to which a talk's meaning depended upon the respondent possessing a somewhat specialised knowledge of the background of the topic; (ii) the degree to which the talk was systematically presented, with its main points emphasised; (iii) the frequency with which difficult or unfamiliar words were used.

The use of difficult words

Any speaker with a message to impart has to make certain assumptions about his audience's knowledge of the words which he is going to use. If he assumes too much, the listener's understanding of what he says is likely to be impaired.

It appears, on the evidence of Table 10, that this is one of the things which reduced the comprehensibility of talks in the "Topic for Tonight" series. In fact, every eight seconds in the average "Topic for Tonight" talk, there came a word which was unfamiliar to about 50% of the population[i]. For the less comprehensible talks, the rate of occurrence of such words was higher.

Dependence upon special knowledge

Talks differed widely in the degree to which a set of judges rated them dependent (for meaning) upon listeners having certain rare or specialised background knowledge of the subject matter. Subsequently it turned out that the higher a talk's rating for such dependence, the lower was its comprehensibility score. This finding does not clinch the case for concluding that speakers were assuming too great a background knowledge in their listeners, for we are dealing here with the estimates of judges and not with empirical evidence of what the public does or does not know. Nonetheless, the evidence is highly suggestive.

Logical structure and emphasis on main points

Talks which were presented in a well organised, economic way and which emphasised the main points, tended to be the better understood talks. These are to be contrasted with those in which the argument was not systematically developed, where summaries and other ways of emphasising points were neglected and where the task of organising the material was left to the listener. Such talks tended to be poorly understood and the overall correlation of structure and comprehensibility was +0.65. Though talks differed quite a lot in terms of structure, structural weaknesses of at least some degree tended to feature the series as a whole and it is perhaps not surprising that the average listener appeared to have gathered to himself random pieces of information, with major points doing no better than relatively unimportant snippets of information. Had the listener had time to ponder over the talk, perhaps *reading* it twice, he might have been better able to grasp the main message. But in radio, one must move at the speed of the broadcaster and there is no going back.

Other characteristics

Perhaps surprisingly, neither sentence length nor speed of reading was associated in any appreciable way with the comprehensibility scores for these particular talks. However, we should note that variability in terms of speed of presentation, and also in terms of sentence length was relatively small — a situation that usually works strongly against the emergence of high correlations.

[i] Going by Vernon's Vocabulary scale [153]

In the twenty-six talks analysed, greater frequency of numerical references went along with greater comprehensibility. To some extent this contrary-seeming result is an outcome of the fact that various of the talks with little dependence on background knowledge carried a lot of numerals and vice versa, so that when all the talks are equated for dependence on background knowledge, the 0.47 correlation for numerical references reduces to 0.22. It does, however, remain a somewhat surprising finding, though it seems possible that a limited use of numerical references may go along with compactness and system in presentation.

Frequent use of adverbs, active verbs and personal pronouns were each associated, to some small degree, with greater comprehensibility. On the other hand, frequent use of abstract nouns and of adjectives had a small tendency to go with a lower level of comprehensibility.

Two indices of the difficulty of talks

The Flesch Index of Readability [121] based upon counts of sentence length, number of affixes per 100 words and number of personal references per 100 words was predictive of comprehensibility to only a small degree (0.27). Table 10 makes it clear enough why this is so: two of its three constituent counts are themselves of only low predictive power and there seems to be no reason for expecting the third (affixes) to be appreciably better. By contrast, direct rating of comprehensibility by a number of judges provided a much better predictor of comprehensibility (0.52). These judges had, it is true, the advantage of rating the talk in terms of all the variables in Table 10 before getting to the ease/difficulty rating of the talk as a whole.

SUMMARY OF FINDINGS AND SOME SUGGESTIONS

"Topic for Tonight" reaches a very large audience. A typical single programme is heard by about a tenth of the adult population and in the course of a week about a third of the population hears one or more of the five broadcasts of that period. This third is predominantly working class[j] though it includes a little more than a due proportion of the middle class. On present evidence, the overwhelming reaction to the talks was that they were interesting and this applied whether the talks were heard at home or in the test room. The nature of the audience and its reactions to the talks augured well for the effectiveness of "Topic for Tonight" provided the talks were basically comprehensible.

The talks were, however, written at a level which is above the head of the average listener: even when people listened carefully, they took in (on average) less than a third of the ideas and information presented; even those with University degrees took in only half of the average talk. Moreover, for these talks, even major or central points were no better understood than were minor points and small details.

[j] 28% of the 70% of the population making up the DE group, versus 35% of the 20% Cs and 38% of the 10% ABs.

The main reasons for the comparative failure of these talks to communicate their messages to listeners appears to have been (i) that broadcasters wrongly assumed that the listener had the background knowledge necessary for grasping what was being said; (ii) that the talks were deficient in logical structure and that main points were not highlighted or emphasised; (iii) that broadcasters frequently used language which was not familiar to listeners.

What seemed necessary was the use of simpler language, the development of a greater awareness of the paucity of specialized knowledge in the general public, the repetition of important points and the greater use of summaries.

APPENDIX

THE CLASSIFICATION OF OCCUPATIONS ACCORDING TO SKILL AND TRAINING REQUIRED FOR THEM

The following classification of occupations was used in the treatment of "Topic For Tonight" results. It was based upon estimated ability and training required for an occupation.

GROUP 1. HIGHER PROFESSIONAL AND ADMINISTRATIVE WORK

This group includes occupations which require university training to *at least* a three-year standard, and senior administrator occupations in commerce and industry.

Examples are: medical practitioners, professional engineers, dentists, graduate architects, research scientists, university lecturers, graduate teachers; higher management with Board status; men holding directive responsibility for an organisation; employers in more than a small way.

Other Examples

Research Manager, Barrister at Law, Company Secretary (if Solicitor), Chief Assistant in Chemistry Laboratory, Minister of religion (if university qualified).

GROUP 2. LOWER PROFESSIONAL, TECHNICAL AND EXECUTIVE WORK

This group includes: jobs which require several years of specialised training (and in most cases a background of advanced education); a variety of executive jobs of a more responsible kind needing acumen. With few exceptions they are of a 'white collar' kind.

Examples are: school teacher, pharmacist, surveyor, architectural draftsman, scientific technician; manager of medium sized factory or business house or of major branches of big organisations, buyers, managers, departmental managers.

Other Examples

Transport Manager (50+ employees), Hospital Matron (qualified), Articled Solicitor, Company Secretary of Accountant standing, Engineering Draftsman and Designer, Advertising Executive, Chief Accountant, Probation Officer, Journalist.

GROUP 3. HIGHLY SKILLED WORKERS

This group includes: highly skilled craftsmen with special training and a fair amount of responsibility; some of the more responsible and exacting commercial jobs.

Examples are: tool-maker, electrical fitter, machine shop foreman, clerk of works; senior accounts clerk, legal clerk, teller, private secretary, commercial traveller, senior retail salesman in large establishment, shorthand typist with qualifications, senior monitor.

Other Examples

Bank Clerk, Clerk with responsibility (4+ persons under him), Accountant's Clerk, Stockbroker's Cashier, Manager of small store (Outfitters), Masseuse (female) with qualifications, Certificated Nurse, Carpet Planner (measuring, making up and laying carpets), Assistant Accountant, Solicitor's Clerk.

GROUP 4. SKILLED WORKERS

This group includes trained, skilled workers (technical, clerical, etc.)

Examples are: fitter, turner, machinist, lithographer, pattern maker, boiler maker, carpenter, cabinet maker, wood machinist, upholsterer, tailor; cashier, superior shop-assistant, station master, routine typist with qualifications, general clerk, policeman, monitor.

Other Examples

Senior Storeman, Coach Builder, Insurance Salesman, Accounts Clerk, Ladies' Hairdresser, Dressmaker with training, 'Middle range' Clerk, Wages Clerk, Children's Nurse (qualified), Airlines Booking Clerk, Ledger Clerk.

GROUP 5. MODERATELY SKILLED WORKERS

This group includes: certain of the less technical tradesmen such as bricklayer, plasterer, house painter, sheet-metal worker, welder, plumber; a wide range of the more skilled factory operatives in the metal, textile, etc. industries; a wide range of store and transport workers such as despatch clerk, railway signalman, railway guard, bus driver; a wide range of workers in certain of the personal services, such as senior waiter, junior or ordinary shop-assistant, barber.

Other Examples
Panel Beater, Telephone Operator/Telephonist, Filing Clerk, Storeman, Low grade Clerk, Tailor's Machinist, Dressmaker's Cutter, Proprietor of small boarding house, Dressmaker (inexperienced or poor grade), Child Nurse (unqualified), Butcher (hand), Typist (unqualified).

GROUP 6. SEMI-SKILLED WORKERS

This group includes: many factory operatives engaged on semi-automatic machines, assembly, etc.; domestic transport and personal service workers of the sort waiter or waitress, postman, porter, conductor, truck driver, deliveryman, better grade domestic servant.

Other Examples
Cook, Routine Machinist (single items only), Lady's Maid, Cinema Usherette, Mother's help, Park-keeper, Hospital Orderly, Ticket Collector, Caretaker, Milkman.

GROUP 7. UNSKILLED WORKERS

This group includes persons engaged in unskilled labour or coarse manual work and includes: automatic machine operator, labourer, chimney sweep, labeller, packer, lower grades of domestic servants.

Other Examples
Laundry Hand (folder, junior), Stoker, Presser (automatic), Kitchen Maid, Dockworker, Bus Cleaner, Daily Help, Chambermaid, Parlourmaid.

[15]

The comprehensibility of "Facts and figures"[a]

A television series of short programs presenting the facts of current economic and related trends.

BACKGROUND AND AIMS

This report describes the second of two studies of "Facts and Figures". This was a monthly ten-minute television broadcast which gave, in diagrammatic form and with a spoken commentary, information about economic and related trends. The earlier study (22) was concerned with the familiarity of the program's target audience with various technical terms and concepts which it was thought might be used in the commentary. That report was submitted to production staff as a guide for the formulation of future programs in the series.

The success of "Facts and Figures" was ultimately to be judged by the extent to which it communicated its contents to members of its target audience viewing it in the ordinary way at home. While this depended to an important degree upon the interestingness of the programs, little communication could occur unless the material being presented was basically comprehensible. The aim of this enquiry was to assess the basic comprehensibility of two of the "Facts and Figures" programs, that is, to find out how far these two *could* be understood by their target audience provided the latter gave their full attention to them.

The program's target audience had been defined as the 'top' 70%–80% of viewers in terms of occupational background. However, since this large group could be expected to include a wide range of people in terms of capacity to understand "Facts and Figures", provision was made for describing performances at each of four distinct occupational levels. These were: (i) the professional, semi-professional, executive and administrative;

[a] This report is based upon work conducted in 1955 in the Audience Research Department by the writer and Dr. J. D. Hundleby, and reported in the BBC document, VR/55/411 [108].

(ii) the highly skilled; (iii) the skilled; (iv) the moderately skilled. Details of these occupational sectors are given in Chapter 10 and in the Appendix to Chapter 14.

THE METHOD OF RESEARCH

The sample

In all, 550 viewers took part. They came by invitation, in groups of about 40 at a time, to a small theatre in central London. The invitation system, which is described in detail in Chapter 3, was such that the 550 who took part were drawn equally from each of the four occupational sectors described above. Test room members of each of these four groups[b] were also approximately representative in terms of age and sex.

The programs studied

The study dealt with two "Facts and Figures" programs, each on film. Each was made up of a series of seven to eight independent units, averaging a little over a minute in length. The content of these units varied. Thus in one of the programs the first unit was about changes in retail prices, the second was about wages rates, the third about Britain's foreign trade, then came Britain's gold and dollar reserves, the number of men compared with the number of women, the proportion of women who marry, birth rates. The transition from one to the other unit was usually brief and to the point.

In each unit, presentation was through animated drawings which were themselves extremely simple and which were geared very closely to the verbal exposition. The drawings varied from unit to unit, but in the course of a ten minute program there were line charts, histograms, moving arrows, and cartoon-like drawings of people and things. When sections of a drawing moved, the words of the expositor were geared to the change produced. Visual and verbal elements in a unit were focused on only one point at a time and meaning was rarely dependent solely upon the words. There was a major effort to communicate.

The research design

Tests were to be made of the comprehensibility of eight individual (and independent) units of these programs. Since the testing of as many as eight units seemed more than any one respondent could go through without fatigue interfering with his results, the total sample was broken into two matched[c] subsamples, and each was tested on four units.

The test-room procedure

On arrival at the theatre, viewers were given light refreshment and heard a brief description of the work done by the Audience Research Department.

[b] Generalizations about the target audience as a whole were arrived at after re-weighting the scores of these four groups.

[c] Matching was in terms of age, sex, occupational and educational background.

They were then told the purpose of the meeting and the administrator laid stress on the importance of their giving the filmed presentation their careful attention. After this, group members went through the following main steps in the experiment. (i) A practice unit was projected, questions being read out immediately the lights came up; viewers used small booklets to write down their answers to the administrator's questions about the film. (ii) The administrator then went through his questions again and gave illustrations of adequate answers. (iii) Viewers were then rested for several minutes before being shown and then tested on the second practice unit. This too was followed by illustrations of correct answers. (iv) Then came the four test units, *one at a time*, with questions following each unit immediately it had been shown; adequate rest periods came between the end of a set of questions and the showing of the next unit. (v) During the evening, viewers completed a personal detail form, stating age and sex and giving information about occupational and educational background. (vi) The evening finished with general discussion of programs. Before the tests began, viewers had been asked not to talk during either the showing of the films or the questioning, to work entirely alone and to make every attempt to answer each question. As a matter of course, reminders of these points were given at intervals during the evening. Observation of the groups gave every indication that they were attending to the film and that there was very little collusion.

The coverage of the questions

The questions for testing comprehension were developed according to the principles set out in Chapter 13. Though a good many minor points were in fact tested, the chief concern of producers was to find out if the major points in the programs could be understood. Decisions as to *what* were the major points were reached in collaboration with the producer. Thus in a unit dealing with wheat production, there were two major points, namely (i) 'The world price of wheat has been falling during the last two years', and (ii) 'The reason for this fall is that wheat stocks have increased enormously during the last two years'. In a unit on beer consumption in five different countries, the major point was simply that, 'The Briton is not the biggest beer drinker'.

THE FINDINGS

The results as set out in Table 1 indicate that this program's target audience was capable, to a marked degree, of grasping the major points presented in the units tested. For the target audience as a whole, 70% showed a 'sufficient grasp of the average major point' being presented, while nearly 80% had a 'sufficient grasp of at least a useful part of the average major point'[d]. At the same time we must notice that for the

[d] The meaning given to these terms (i.e. a 'really good grasp of the average major point', 'a sufficient grasp of the average major point' and 'a sufficient

average major point, only 31% qualified at the admittedly very high standard of "a really good grasp".

TABLE 1.

Showing differences in grasp of major points and of detail by viewers, according to occupational background

Percentage showing:	Occupational Background*				Weighted average for total target audience
	I %	II	III %	IV %	
A sufficient grasp of a useful part of the (average) *major point*	88	84	81	71	79
A sufficient grasp of the (average) full *major point*	82	75	71	62	70
A really good grasp of the (average) full *major point*	40	35	33	24	31
A sufficient grasp of the average point of detail	78	76	75	68	73

* I = professional, semi-professional, executive and administrative workers, constituting 7% of the viewing population; II = highly skilled workers (13%); III = skilled workers (30%); IV = moderately skilled workers (27%).

grasp of the least a useful part of the average major point' may be illustrated as follows.

(1) In a unit dealing with Britain's share of the world export trade in cars, *one* of the major points presented concentrated on the fall-off in Britain's share of the trade since 1950, and the reason for this fall-off. A viewer was said to have '*at least a sufficient* grasp of the point' if he knew (a) that there had been a fall-off since 1950 *and* (b) that this had been due in part to increased competition. He was said to have '*a really good grasp of it*' if he also knew the approximate extent of the fall-off *and* that the competition was from Germany. Any who grasped only that there had been a fall-off since 1950 were said to have a '*sufficient* grasp of a *useful part*' of the major point'.

(2) In a unit dealing with the relative number of men and women in the United Kingdom population, a viewer was regarded as having '*at least a sufficient* grasp of the major point' if he knew that the population of men was increasing *and* that there would be more men than women in 1961. A viewer would be rated as having '*a really good* grasp of the full major point' (a) if he had understood also that the males had been in a minority for the last 33 years (the number of years was given in the question) but had been gradually catching up *and* (b) if he was aware that the number of males in 1961 would be only slightly greater than the number of women. Where, however, a viewer knew of the increase in the number of men (during the last 33 years) but had *not* grasped that the number of men would be greater in 1961, he was regarded as having 'a *sufficient* knowledge of a *useful part*' of the point being presented'.

In going from one to another of the four occupational groups, the difference (in grasp of major points) was comparatively small, with even the moderately skilled doing quite well. Thus 62% of the moderately skilled showed a sufficient grasp of the average major point and 71% a sufficient grasp of at least a part of it. In other words, the programs tested appear to have transcended those intellectual and educational differences between social class which ordinarily make for big differences in their intake of information. This bridging of a traditional gap may well have sprung from the deliberately unsophisticated treatment of program contents and from the special features of the visual aids used. Whatever the cause, the important thing is that apparently it can be done. On the other hand, the occupational differences are larger when it comes to getting "a really good grasp" (of a major point).

Table 1 also shows that the grasp of points of *detail* in the programme was also quite high and that here too there was little fall-off in going from one occupational grade to another.

The effects, upon comprehensibility of a particular unit, of the preceding and the following units

In interpreting these findings, it must be remembered that the units being tested were presented in comparative isolation from other units: respondents were given rest pauses between items. While it is important to know whether or not the content of a unit is pitched above the heads of the target audience, it is also important to know if its placement in a series of other units affects its comprehensibility in any way. Is it likely, for instance, that a sequence of, say, six units, each about a different subject and each one following rapidly upon the other, tends to weary and confuse the viewer so that his perception of the contents of units progressively decreases? Existing psychological evidence provides a good case for thinking that this might happen with some kinds of material [158]. Accordingly, an experiment was conducted to detect any changes in a unit's comprehensibility score as the number of units preceding it was increased.

A fresh sample of 250 viewers took part in this supplementary enquiry. The research design was such that different units were tested with systematic variation in the number of other units preceding them, the number of these preceding units varying from 0 to 6. The results of this work, which dealt with the comprehension both of major and of minor points, are presented diagrammatically in Figure 1.

There was no tendency for the comprehension of a unit's major points to decrease as the number of units preceding it grew from none to six. In fact there seemed to be a slight tendency for the understanding of a major point to increase through the presence of preceding units. The evidence of increase is not fully conclusive, but if in fact there is an increase, one possible explanation might be that exposure to the preceding units progressively increased the viewer's familiarity with the diagrammatic form of presentation being employed.

Comprehension scores as the number of preceding units is increased.

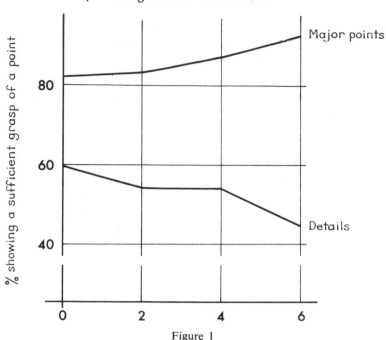

Figure 1

However, the results for details were different. Viewers' grasp of detail decreased as the number of the preceding units increased. This result might possibly be explained in terms of increasing confusion as a welter of detail built up — something less likely to occur with a more limited number of *major* points differing in kind. However, this is only speculation. What is clear, and what matters, is that grasp of detail seems to be impaired when the unit concerned is preceded by other units in the program.

SUMMARY OF THE ENQUIRY

This enquiry was conducted to measure the basic comprehensibility of two programs in the "Facts and Figures" series. These ten minute programs each consisted of a series of relatively independent short units, each one dealing with a different subject (e.g. birth rates, car exports, the gold and dollar reserves). The results suggested that the great proportion of the target audience for the series was capable of getting a "sufficient grasp" of major points in the programs tested. This applied also to minor points. Moreover these two programs appeared to have bridged some of the intellectual and educational differences within the target audience, in that the proportion achieving a sufficient grasp of points was, on average, not markedly different in going from the moderately skilled to the highly skilled. However, in terms of a really good grasp of major points, the target audience's performance was poorer and there *were* appreciable occupational differences in comprehension score. When a specific unit of the program was preceded by other units, there was a reduction in the grasp of its minor points, but not in the grasp of its major points.

MEASURING THE EFFECTS OF PARTICULAR PROGRAMS

An introductory note

This Section in concerned solely with the measurement of the effects of television programs. These measurements may relate to a single program or to five or six programs in a series, but they are not concerned with the broad social or psychological effects of television as a whole. Studies of such effects are introduced in Section IV.

If, in developing a program, a broadcaster has called for and made good use of a planning study, the chances of that program failing to do what was intended of it will be considerably reduced. The fact that a planning study has been made is not, of course, a *guarantee* against that sort of failure. The planning study provides guide lines, but the rest is up to production staff and to individual performers. Obviously the operation can still go wrong, and because of this there may well be a case for conducting an enquiry to find out precisely what the effects of the program actually were. If the issue being dealt with in the program or series is important, and if there has been no planning study beforehand, the case for measuring effects is quite a strong one. The extent of failure evidenced by past research of this kind adds to that case.

A program which is basically comprehensible (as indicated by its pre-broadcast test) is of course more likely to achieve what is intended of it. This applies particularly to its being understood when actually broadcast. But here too, this does not *guarantee* that the program will inform, make aware, stimulate thoughtfulness, make attitudes more kindly or tolerant, or whatever else the program was intended to do. A study of effects may still be warranted.

Chapter 16 sets out the case for conducting studies of the effects of television programs, Chapter 17 describes two techniques for carrying out such work, while Chapters 18 and 19 are reports of two enquiries of this kind. Each is given in sufficient methodological detail to illustrate the application of one of the methods, and the results are also given in detail.

References in this Section to articles and books will be found in alphabetical order, on pages 377–380.

[16]

The place and the function of studies of the effects of particular programs

Why is it desirable to conduct studies of the effects of programs?
The main case for conducting studies of the effects of programs is that, for better or for worse, particular programs may not do what was intended of them. With an operation as expensive and as time-consuming as broadcasting, neither the industry nor the public can afford to remain in ignorance over what the effects of programs really are.

The case for suspecting that a program may do less than or other than intended lies partly in the results of studies of program effects. But there are other grounds for concern, some of which have been referred to in earlier chapters. Thus much has already been said about the difficulties which arise when a broadcaster uses language which is not the common working property of his audience. To do this is to invite failure in the transmission of facts and ideas. Then again it is common experience that, try as they may to keep concentrating, many people have periodic lapses of attention [158] sufficient to cripple their understanding of any tightly argued thesis or case. The least that these involuntary lapses will do is to reduce understanding of intake of different small sections of the program. They may well do much more than this.

Perhaps as damaging as involuntary lapses of attention are the inevitable distractions of the home and, of course, lack of interest in the program or the speaker. Inattention for such reasons is likely to be considerable at times. The advertiser in particular is likely to lose through it. Some people attend carefully to advertisements, but others don't. Thus many people talk during the advertisement break; some glance at a newspaper; others turn down the volume or temporarily change stations; some say they just 'switch off mentally'. Over and above this, there appears to be a not inconsiderable amount of leaving the room when the advertisements come on and there seem to be all sorts of cases for doing this: to make coffee (it helps if it is *instant* coffee); to fetch cigarettes; to go to the toilet; to see that the children are all tucked up in bed; to fill the hot water bottles. Naturally enough, advertisers use various counter-measures to try to attract and to hold the viewer's attention and interest. One is to lift the advertisement's volume level above that of the ordinary program, though some viewers react to this by going in annoyance to the volume control and turning the sound *right down*. Another method of the advertiser is to introduce into the advertisement something of an arresting, startling, or possibly beautiful kind. This may well work, but certainly there are cases where the viewer does not get past the attention-getter, being satisfied with it in its own right or failing to transfer his attention to the product itself.

This sort of reaction to an advertisement brings me to another source of trouble in broadcasting, applying to general programming as much as to advertising and already touched on in Chapters 2 and 12. This is a process whereby people *select* from what is put before them, or distort it one way or another or interpret it differently. These processes are quite frequently reported in the literature of psychology[a] and they appear to be related to the personal values, needs, attitudes and pre-occupations of the person concerned. Selective and distorting processes have also shown up in broadcasting research. Thus in one program, an attempt to enlighten viewers by presenting all sides of a controversial issue led to the strengthening of existing biasses on the part of the viewer. What appears to have happened in this case was that viewers took the ideas of those with whom they agreed and rejected the views of the opposition. This rejection was made relatively easy because their own champions showed them how to reject ideas which previously they had tolerated for lack of an argument against them. Here is another case. A broadcaster attempted to portray the improved welfare services of our modern times by showing old and destitute people lining up for soup at a welfare centre:many viewers found it hard to interpret this as 'improved welfare', feeling that much more than this could be done for such people. In another program, the presentation of an American talking proudly about certain technical developments in his country was regarded by some members of an English audience as another case of American 'big talk'. A policeman shown being tough with a young criminal was regarded by some viewers as brutish. A woman, seeing some hot and enticing soup in a television advertisement by Bloggs, failed to think of it as Bloggs' soup but thought instead of the other brand she happened to have in the cupboard.

Obviously many things presented in the programs are perceived and interpreted without distortion or omissions, particularly where the viewer is not emotionally involved or ideationally committed. But this is by no means the case all the time and the writer's experience is that most programs are subject to at least some of this distorting or this selecting process.

So far, in talking about things that can go wrong with respect to the impact of a program, the reference has been mainly to informational pro-

[a] See references: [6, 31, 38, 47, 68, 98].

grams and to those meant to persuade. It is quite conceivable, however, that major changes will be produced by programs meant simply to entertain. For instance, many people suspect that there may be some unfortunate side effects to programs featuring crime and violence and they ask questions of the following kind. Do people, particularly children, learn to be more callous or agressive as a result of exposure to programs featuring killing and violence? Is some element of gentleness thereby taken out of them? Does human life become just that much cheaper through exposure to such programs? And do children and young people, seeing crime in action — and some portrayals can be rather informative — learn certain of the techniques of crime? Are young people with limited moral training thereby encouraged to try out these methods? Do some of them get the idea that crime could be made to pay? Are they led into taking the side of the crooks against the police? It can of course be argued that programs about crime teach young people that crime does *not* pay, for after all the crooks are usually caught. It is also argued in support of such programs that the forces of law and justice are usually characterized by various virtues and that because of this, they can be morally constructive. However, in the present state of knowledge, arguments about good and bad effects[b], however strongly stated, remain opinions. Hard facts, derived through research, are needed.

Still other views are frequently expressed about adverse effects of television: that many programs are sexy and so may encourage sexual promiscuity or latitude; that infidelity and broken marriages are too frequently featured and may serve to cheapen the concept of marriage; that alcoholic drinking to excess is presented as permissible; that top people in society are shown smoking on television and that this will encourage

[b] Adults in discussion groups make many comments about television and young people, and some of their ideas have included the following. "Programs with crime and violence in them can prey on a child's mind and it encourages teenagers to do the same." /"I think with younger children too much shooting and hanging and knifing is not a good thing, but I expect that children were doing the same before TV". "With some children it goes further but with others it is a game." /"As far as my own children are concerned, crime and violence have no effect at all. The violence is really so far fetched that they are very sceptical about it and say that it is obviously fiction. Although they sit goggle eyed throughout the program, it passes out of their minds completely by the next day." /"I don't think it affects normal children. I think perhaps that highly strung nervous children might take some of the violence to heart but I don't think it makes much impression." /"The main effect of crime and violence is on the teenagers. They see people get away with these terrible things and they think they can do the same." /"I think children get these things firmly in their minds and parents trying to bring them up the good way are usually wasting their time and children will take no notice of them." /"The ones that affect a child unfavourably I think are the ones where violence seems to triumph and be an easy way of life". /"I don't think it hurts them. It's really an outlet for some of their high spirits."

young people to take up smoking. As an integral part of such objections, it is claimed that many programs of the kind referred to are readily available to children either because they are shown at times when children could be expected to be up and around, or that children are frequently up and around much later than programmers allow for. Not all people who express concern about the effects of such program material limit themselves to the question of the impact on children and young people: some ask if this sort of material may not be affecting *adults* in an adverse way as well. Some of the ideas of viewers about such programs make interesting reading. However, suspicion is one thing: the fact may be something quite different. Only empirical studies of effects can provide us with the facts.

It may be felt that when a planning study has been conducted for the preparation of a particular program, an assessment of the effects of that program will not be necessary. In all probability an 'effects' study is less necessary where such empirical preparation has been made. This is because a planning study should have reduced considerably the likelihood of mishap. Nonetheless things can still go wrong, for the producer has yet to translate the recommendations of the planning report into concrete terms: the science of communication and persuasion is as yet too little established at this level of detail for such translation to be a safe and sure procedure.

Using the results of effects studies

What has been said so far is that effects studies are necessary in that they tell us what the programs have and have not achieved. They are, in a sense, the watchdogs of efficiency and of certain aspects of social welfare. In the writer's opinion this is enough in its own right to justify such studies, for they cannot help but make the producer 'effects conscious', so that his talents and his broadcasting techniques take on a more purposive character.

However, effects studies can be made to provide more positive and specific help than this, for it is ordinarily possible to make them yield quite a lot of information, or at least hypotheses, about the possible causes of success and failure in programs. Thus in an advertisement, a hair preparation was felt by some to be greasy partly because the advertisement showed, in close-up, a girl running her fingers through a young man's hair which was all glossy with the hair preparation. This was enough, it seemed, to produce a reaction of the kind: "Ugh! She'll get her fingers greasy". In a program on mental health, the forms of treatment which were demonstrated concretely were better understood and better accepted than those that got only verbal exposition. In another program meant to interest people in going to another country, too much realism appears to have put people off the idea of going (the program was trying to be realistically helpful). In another, the very favourable presentation of an unmarried mother (she appeared in pleasant surroundings, was well spoken and clearly she loved and wanted to keep her child) appears to have had a lot to do with the fact that the program made viewers more tolerant towards sexual relations outside marriage. Some viewers rejected an advertiser's message about a beverage because the use of classical ballet as a vehicle for transmitting a sales message was seen by them as 'sacrilege'.

Though such insights or understandings are in a sense 'wisdom after the event', they are useful and usable for they can promote and guide the elimination of certain failure elements from other programs in the same series or from similar programs. Such elements might include an over-technical commentary, an over-concentration on verbal expositions, an attempt to persuade people towards some point of view or some sort of behaviour on the basis of the less acceptable of the arguments available. On the other hand, evidence about how a program or parts of it succeeded can lead to the more deliberate use of the treatments or tactics found to be successful.

The long-term and general use of the results of effects studies is at least as important as their application for the betterment of other programs in the same series. Provided that some attempt is made in each study of effects to find out what lies behind successes and failures, there can develop a store of information which may then be used for the general guidance of programming. Information so derived could be built into a body of principles of communication and persuasion, each richly illustrated by examples of success and failure. The dissemination of any such information within a station or service ought, I think, to be partly the responsibility of those training new producers and certainly it should be made part of any formal training course provided within the broadcasting service. A major advantage of the formalization of this aspect of training is that this could help to maximise the use made of the available information about communication processes, including that available in psychological and other technical sources.

The formalization of such training could well hasten another necessary development from effects studies, namely the carrying out of basic research in order to test or to follow up certain of the hypotheses or leads derived from the 'effects studies'. The fact that the leads pursued in such basic research had come out of what was happening under real life conditions would increase very much the likelihood that the basic research would be of direct relevance and use to broadcasting.

When should such studies be carried out?

In principle, effects studies should be carried out as often as possible because only in this way will the broadcaster be kept up to date with the impact of his programming, and because frequent studies of effects will add more rapidly to the necessary store of knowledge about the principles of efficient broadcasting. However, studies of the effects of programs are at present time-consuming and rather expensive. This means that there must be some selectivity in the application of such studies. The most obvious application is to program material intended to inform or to educate or to persuade. This means programs such as talks, documentaries, educational programs and services, advertisements, political broadcasts, religious programs, those of a cultural kind. However, the choice of material for effects studies ought also to include certain programs broadcast for general entertainment, including some portraying crime and violence. For any long-term purpose, some variety in the selection of the programs to be studied is most important.

Within this setting, various things will determine what is studied at any particular time. The case for an effects study, or a short series of them, is particularly strong when a new venture in public service is being launched, as for instance a new service in adult education or a television service to schools. Obviously we need to know as early as possible if programs in the service are in fact doing what they were intended to do.

It is also sensible to measure effects: when a program or a series of programs is particularly expensive (as in advertising); where the aims of a series are of major social importance (as in mental health campaigning); where the broadcaster is sufficiently unsure about one of his decisions to want to have it checked; where there is a body of public opinion expressing concern at what certain kinds of programs might be doing to people.

Some special uses of effects studies

There is one rather important use to be made of effects studies. This one concerns long-term campaigning on television. It is perhaps best illustrated in terms of television advertising, but it applies equally to public service campaigning, political campaigning and to general propaganda work. The advertiser who aims to impart certain information about his product and to create an effective kind of interest in it may decide to conduct effects studies at various points in his campaign in order to find out at what point the return for extra money spent tails off or becomes negligible. At this point he may decide, on the basis of some of the explanatory data derived also from his effects studies, to reduce his expenditure on television for the time being, or to change the character of the television campaign, or something else. On the other hand, the enquiry may quite well indicate that a current campaign should be continued rather than stopped, or perhaps that it should be stepped up. With effects studies built into the campaign in this way, the progress of the campaign can be watched and the best steps taken at appropriate times.

Properly handled, this observation system can be made to tell the advertiser things like: what he gets for that extra money spent; the relative benefits of spreading his money 'thick' or 'thin'; the case for changing the character of his advertising or even his choice of mass media as he moves on to sections of his target market which are as yet unclaimed.

I see no technical reason why we should not consider using the same technique or strategy in studying and controlling the progress of other types of campaigning, whether these be related to road safety, to good manners in motorists, to adult education (through television), to cultural enlightenment or to political campaigning. If the money is available, this sort of work can be done. If the campaign is important, then it *should* be done. Obviously the technique can become expensive: but campaigning is expensive too — and so is failure.

[17]

The techniques for measuring the effects of programs

Measurements of the effects of programs are realistic only to the extent that such programs have been seen or heard under normal conditions of exposure. This situation is to be contrasted with that where people are deliberately exposed to programs under test-room conditions. Test-room exposure is appropriate for tests of program *comprehensibility*, where optimum exposure is a basic requirement of what is being measured. But it is unlikely to be appropriate if we are interested in measuring *the extent of the changes actually produced by a program in viewers at large.* We are also likely to get misleading results if people are *asked* to view the program at home before coming to some centre for a test, of if they *know beforehand* that some kind of test will follow home viewing. Just as soon as artificiality of any kind enters into the viewing or the listening process, there is a very real likelihood that what is assessed will be something other than the actual effects of the program. On this important matter, more will be said later on.

At the same time, the requirement that exposure be quite normal puts some serious difficulties in the way of measuring program effects. This chapter is intended to bring out the nature of these difficulties and to describe various of the research techniques which are meant to overcome them.

DIFFICULTIES PECULIAR TO EFFECTS STUDIES

The nature of the difficulties surrounding measurement of the effects of programs is best illustrated by referring to a very simple — but inadequate — approach to the task. Suppose a program about America was intended to change certain of the viewers' attitudes towards America and to provide them with facts about America. A naive researcher might make various measurements of attitudes and of knowledge on a sample of viewers *before* the program was broadcast, repeat the measurements on the same people *after* the broadcast, and then conclude that any differences in the two sets of scores were the result of exposure to the program.

There are several reasons why any such conclusion would be dangerous. To test people before the broadcast of the program would in all probability affect seriously the way they reacted to the program if and when they subsequently saw it at home or elsewhere. Thus we could expect these people to attend to it more carefully, to notice particularly the points about which they had been questioned earlier and to remember its content better than they might ordinarily have done. If these same people were tested again *after* the broadcast, their performance in the second test would be liable to be affected by the special nature of their exposure to the program. But over and above this, the fact that they were tested on the very same points earlier on must be regarded as likely to affect their performances in the second test. Here, to start with, is an experimental bias arising out of the two-test situation. The second source of danger is that factors *other than*, but additional to, exposure to the program are quite likely to enter into the situation. For example, it is certainly possible that between two tests of knowledge about the content of a program dealing with, say, Russian or African affairs, a newsworthy situation of one kind or another will develop and get publicity. Unless special precautions are taken, this cannot but distort an assessment of the effects of that program. This sort of difficulty applies particularly to current affairs programs, but the danger is present with any kind of program material. When the second test comes very soon after the broadcast (for example, next day), the degree of post-broadcast confusion of this sort is minimised. However, this is rarely possible. In any case it may be necessary to study the *long-term* effects of a program or series: in that case there is abundant room for the intrusion of extraneous influences, many of them unidentifiable.

Stated in more general terms, these two dangers are as follows. (a) Influences other than exposure to the program itself can enter into the experimental situation in such a way that the effects of these influences become confused with the effects of the program. (b) Misleading results are likely to emerge whenever the same people are tested both before and after the program. This is particularly likely when the tests are concerned with learning or awareness of facts or situations presented in the program.

These dangers are particularly relevant to any use of the over-simple 'before and after' design in the context of which they were just now introduced, and they apply especially to studies of the affects of informational programs. However, their relevance is more extensive than this, and in the assessment of the effects of programs they have to be recognised as rather pervasive factors against which certain precautions have to be taken no matter what research design is used.

Because of difficulties of the kind outlined, any realistic attempt to measure the effects of exposure to a program must be an exercise in tactics. The aim of any such attempt must be to reduce as much as possible the likelihood that results regarded as effects of a program are *in fact* the effects of something else. In the present situation this is the essence of scientific method. It calls for the use of checks and controls for detecting and for excluding sources of ambiguity. At the same time, the level of success to be expected in excluding ambiguity is a matter of degree. With more care and greater financial outlay we can go on reducing ambiguity, though, as is the way with practically all social research, it is doubtful that we will ever achieve anything like certainty. Just how far we go in this direction must depend upon our aims, upon the margin of uncertainty which can be tolerated in any given case and upon the funds available for research.

Apart from the over-simple before and after design, various research strategies have been used or proposed for use in effects research. Some of these are outlined below, along with comments on their weaknesses.

Strategy I: A 'Before and After' Design with the Use of Control Material

The simplest research design that might be considered reasonably safe to use is a development of the 'before and after' system just described. In it, two separate samples are used, each drawn randomly so that, barring sampling error, one might be considered equivalent to the other. Either one of them is regarded as the 'before' sample and the other as the 'after' sample. The 'before' sample is tested just before the broadcast and the 'after' sample just after the broadcast. The two lots of tests are of course identical. Tests relate to whatever the program is expected or intended to modify or change: knowledge, attitude, certain kinds of behaviour.

This two-sample technique is meant to eliminate the effect of double-testing (that is, test-retest influences). However, there still remains the possibility that events which are other than the program itself (e.g., a newspaper item, another program) but which nonetheless affect test score, could occur between the administration of the two sets of tests. This is the situation referred to under (a) above. If this happened, the difference between the two sets of scores could not be interpreted simply as an effect of the program. Accordingly, some further caution or system of control should be linked to this design in order to eliminate or at least to identify the influence of non-program events upon the difference between the test scores of the before and the after samples.

One such control involves extending the tests to include knowledge of a range of facts relating to the topic of the program but *not* given in the program itself (that is, non-program facts). The idea is that differences in score for the non-program facts could point to the operation (and influence) of factors other than the program itself. Along with this attempt at control, a careful watch should be kept for any events (e.g. news items, other programs on the same subject) which might possibly influence the second set of scores for either program or non-program content.

However, one cannot really assume that all relevant extraneous events will have been noted by the observer. Nor can one assume that non-program items are completely free from influence through exposure to the program. Also, and the most important, we cannot assume that a difference between the before and the after scores for non-program material will properly reflect what the factors responsible for this difference will have done to the test scores for the *program* material. At best, differences between the before and after scores for non-program material can simply alert the investigator to the operation of extraneous factors which may be important. He has still to try to determine how *much* influence these factors have had upon the test scores for *program* material. This in turn means that he cannot say *how much* of the difference between the scores (program material) of the samples is an effect of exposure to the program.

The ambiguity surrounding a difference in the test scores, on programme material, of the before and the after samples might be reduced to some extent by the application of further control materials. One such is information which was not included in the program *and* which was different in subject matter from the program. This system can be taken further in advertisement testing. The control complex could consist of: (i) differences (before and after) for *all* competing brands classified according to the amount and nature of the advertising given to them in the period between the before and after tests; (ii) differences (before and after) for similar products (classified by amount of advertising); (iii) information about the weather, selling activities, and other factors known to influence sales within the complex of products concerned. A web of evidence of this sort can reduce ambiguity, though it still does not tell the investigator *how much* of the difference between the before and after 'scores' is due to the campaign or, for that matter, how much bigger the effect may be than the raw difference indicates.

With programs presented as a short series and with most advertising campaigns, it may well be possible to conduct a *series* of tests (on a series of equivalent samples) at chosen points in time: just before the campaign starts; several times during it; after it. If at each of these test points control material of the kind indicated above is gathered, then ambiguity as to whether or not the program or the campaign is producing changes should be reduced to a considerable degree.

There is one other feature of this research strategy which is noteworthy. It detects changes for the sample as a whole and not simply for those sections of it which underwent exposure to the advertising or to the program material. The advertiser or program planner may be content with information about the sample as a whole but he will be in a much stronger position to plan and to act if he knows the impact of his material upon those who actually saw or heard it. Strategies 2 and 3 (below) can provide this kind of information as well as a greater safeguard against the misinterpretation of research findings.

Strategy 2: The Modified 'Before and After' Design,
Using Control Groups

To reduce the ambiguity inherent in the more usual version of Strategy 1, it is highly desirable to introduce control *groups* into the research strategy (that is, over and above such control *material* as is available). A control group will consist of people who did not undergo exposure to the program being investigated. The idea behind using a control group is that it can be employed to detect and to measure the influence, upon test scores, of factors other than the program itself, so that some form of subtraction will leave the researcher with a *quantitative assessment of the impact of the program.*

There are several different kinds of control groups. Thus a control group may be drawn from an area other than that in which the program (under study) is broadcast. On the other hand, it may consist of people who for one reason or another did not happen to see the program when it was broadcast. Then again, its members may be people who are somehow prevented (by the investigator) from seeing it. Each kind of control group has its own weaknesses and strengths.

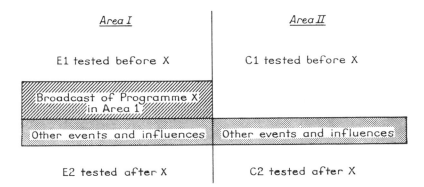

Figure 1

(a) Control groups drawn from another area (See Figure 1)

In the first of these control systems, two control groups may be drawn from an area (let it be called Area II) in which the program under study (let it be called Program X) is *not* broadcast. The total design of which this control system is a part is as follows.

In Area I where the test program (call it X) is to be broadcast, two equivalent samples of the population are drawn on random principles. Either one of them is regarded as the 'before' sample (El) and the other is regarded as the 'after' sample (E2).

In the *control area*, II, two equivalent samples are selected in the same way, each representative of the population in Area II. Either one of them is regarded as a 'before' control (C1) and the other as an 'after' control (C2).

All four groups are given exactly the same tests under equivalent conditions. E1 and C1 are tested at the same time shortly before the broadcast of program X. E2 and C2 are tested at the same time *after* the broadcast.

The rationale of this design is that the difference in the test scores of C1 and C2 is a measure of the effects, upon the exposees, of events other than exposure to the program itself. In other words, the effect of exposure to the program is assumed to be given by the formulae:

$$\text{Effect of program } X = (\text{E2 test score} - \text{E1 test score})$$
$$- (\text{C2 test score} - \text{C1 test score})$$

However, in considering this design, it is essential to be aware of the weakness of its control system: we cannot assume that the effect of non-program events upon people in Area II is the same as the effect of non-program events upon people in Area I. In the first place, the non-program events (that is, events other than the broadcast of X) in the two areas may be different in terms of such things as local happenings, press publicity, weather, local television programs. A prime case of this sort would be the broadcast in Area II, but not in Area I, of a program similar in character to program X. This could wreck the purpose of the control system, as indeed could a program, broadcast in Area II alone, which produced effects contrary in direction to program X.

However, quite apart from differences in the extraneous events of the two areas, it is quite possible that there will be differences between the people in them and since different people can react differently to even the same event, we have another reason for being wary about the interpretation of the difference C2 − C1. For instance, suppose that there was a national news story about police being physically violent with people in their custody and suppose that attitude towards the police was one of the things being studied as possibly affected by program X. If in Area II the populace already regarded violence by the police as a usual state of affairs, whereas people in Area I did not, we could well expect that particular news story to have different effects in the two areas.

To sum up, there are two kinds of reasons why the control groups in Area II would not necessarily reflect the extent of purely extraneous factors (that is, other than program X) upon test scores in Area I: (a) the extraneous events in Area II will not necessarily be the same as the extraneous events in Area I; (b) the effect of an event in Area I will not necessarily be equal to the effect of that same event in Area II. It may be that in a given study these difficulties will not happen to be of practical importance. Nonetheless they cannot be ignored and the practice of drawing control groups from another area must be regarded as a potentially dangerous one.

(b) *Control groups drawn from those who did
not happen to see the program*

It follows from the foregoing argument that if control groups are to be used to detect and to measure the effects of influences other than exposure to the program under study, such control groups should if possible be drawn from the areas in which the program is received.

In what is perhaps the best known of research designs for measuring the effects of a particular program (call it program X) the controls are people *who live in the region receiving the broadcast* but who, either by chance or by choice, did not see it. The total design within which the controls are used is as follows:

(i) Just as with strategies 1 and 2(a), this design begins with the setting up of two randomly developed samples of people in the program area. They are intended to be equivalent and either one is designated as a 'before' group and the other as an 'after' group.

(ii) Shortly before the broadcast of program X, all members of the 'before' group are put through tests directly concerned with whatever it was thought program X might do. Thus for a programme aimed at increasing people's interest in going to France, the test used would be one designed to measure 'interest in going to France'. If there are aims additional to this, further tests are used. After the completion of these pre-broadcast tests, there is no further contact with or testing of these people except to find out if, in due course, they happened to watch program X when it was broadcast. On the basis of this information they are then categorized as "Exposee, pre-broadcast" (E. 1 in Figure 2) or as "Control, pre-broadcast" (C. 1 in Figure 2). In other words, they provide pre-broadcast test scores for those who eventually see the program (E1) and for those who eventually don't see the program (C1).

(iii) *After* the broadcast of program X, members of the second sample are contacted and tested for the first time. Exactly the same tests are used on these people as were used on those who were tested before the broadcast of the program. At the end of this testing session, additional information is gathered to allow the classification of members of the post-broadcast sample as "Exposee, post broadcast" (E2 in Figure 2) or as "Control, post-broadcast" (C2 in Figure 2).

Score E2—Score E1 is regarded as measuring the combined effects of the program *and* of all other possible influences operating upon the exposees in the period between the two tests. Score C2—Score C1, on the other hand, is felt by those who advocate the method to provide a separate assessment of the effect, upon the program's exposees, of influences other than the program itself. Accordingly the effect of the program is regarded as being given by the formulae:

$$\text{Effect of Program X} = (E2 - E1) - (C2 - C1)$$

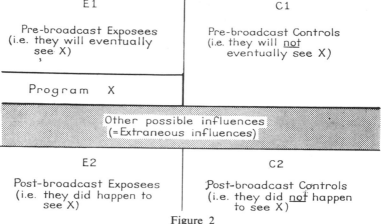

Figure 2

The argument can be put another way. The people exposed to the program or to the campaign are also exposed to extraneous events. The controls are exposed to *only* the extraneous events. Hence the effect of the program or the campaign can be assessed (it is argued) by subtracting the change (in score) for the controls from the change (in score) for the exposees.

This strategy is an advance upon the previous ones because it goes further than they do in reducing the ambiguity of findings. If control *material* is included in the strategy, ambiguity can be reduced even further. Moreover the method offers a measurement of the effect of the program upon the people who actually saw it.

On the other hand, this method is expensive and it has technical weaknesses. Let me deal first with its expensiveness. Suppose that the program to be studied was expected to have an audience of 20% and that each of the four groups in the design was to have a minimum of 300 people in it. For a 20% program to yield 300 exposees, the total 'before' sample would have to number 1500 and the same would apply to the total 'after' sample. Prior to the broadcast, all 1500 of the 'before' sample would have to be tested because there could be no telling at that stage which of them would eventually see the program. Very strictly speaking, all 1500 of the 'after' sample would have to be tested as well because the questions necessary to establish viewership should come only after all testing is completed (just as with the 'before' sample). Even if this admittedly stringent requirement is waived, so that only 300 of the non-exposees (and the 300 exposees) go through the testing procedure, there is no escaping a heavy testing operation. In fact, the minimum requirement for the project would be tests for 2100 people (to yield the required 1200 test results). For a 10% programme and a minimum of 400 in each of the four groups in the design, the minimum number for testing would rise to 4800. It is always possible to try to reduce the large numbers of people to be tested before the broadcast by developing predictive devices which will indicate beforehand which survey contacts will and which will not probably view the program. This, however, is usually a complicated and risky process and is not one which should lightly be recommended.

Let us turn to the technical weaknesses of this design. Just as with design 2(a), the impact upon the *control group* of what have here been called extraneous events is not necessarily equal to their impact upon the *exposees*. As in 2(a) this is because exposees and non-exposees (controls) are not necessarily the same kinds of people and so are not necessarily affected in the same way by the same things. Suppose the program under study dealt with the relations of management and labour and that its exposee group included more union members than did its control group. Then the occurrence of a strike in the area (or of industrial unrest) would in all likelihood affect the exposee group and the control group differently with respect to whatever the program was supposed to do. *Because exposee samples are self-selected in relation to the program under study, we must always be prepared for difficulty of this kind.* Certainly further examples are not hard to think of. The trouble is that the present strategy rests upon the assumption that the exposees and the controls are comparable. Yet when self-selection comes in, this may not be so.

One means of increasing the efficiency of the control groups is to equate them to E2, through matching[a], in terms of variables associated with test score — provided of course that such variables are not themselves open to influence by the program. These matching variables must always be established empirically.

Another difficulty is that there is no certainty that E1 will in fact be equivalent to E2 in terms of characteristics related to test scores (in spite of their similar random origin). Accordingly, it is sound policy to match E1 to E2 as well. In other words, E1, C1 and C2 are all matched to E2 (in terms of correlates of test score). Details of suitable matching techniques are given in the context of Strategy 3.

[a] The techniques for selecting matching variables empirically and for employing these to match one group to another are extremely important and are given in detail under Strategy 3. In the meantime, however, the following points should be noted. (i) In the first place, the selection of matching variables is a rigorously empirical process. Its purpose is to determine that combination of matching variables which jointly maximises correlation with test score and discrimination between the groups to be matched. (ii) A large number of variables, heterogeneous in character, should be introduced into the testing procedure as a pool from which to derive matching variables. (iii) The derivation of matching variables must be from analyses of the combined control and exposee groups.

Strategy 3. The Stable Correlate Technique

In spite of the seeming firmness of Strategy 2(b), it has a serious tactical weakness. It requires that the investigator should know, at least a week before the broadcast of the program, what its form and its detail will be. Only if this is so will he be able to formulate the necessary tests and use them prior to that broadcast. After all, it may take all that time to get through the necessary pre-broadcast test sessions. Without this foreknowledge of program content, the 'before and after' design cannot be used. In the writer's experience, such foreknowledge is frequently not available sufficiently far ahead, and 'live' broadcasts are automatically ruled out in practically all cases. In such circumstances, a special form of 'after only' design has to be used.

This is the method which in its original form the writer called the Stable Correlate method. He has since modified it in various ways, and it is the modified form of the method which is described here. Carefully handled, it can provide relatively unambiguous results. It is much less expensive than the modified 'before and after' technique.

The strategy of the stable correlate technique

Suppose that a program X was intended or expected to produce changes in its viewers with respect to a particular attitude, A. Suppose also that after the broadcast of program X, tests to measure attitude A were made on a sample of people who *had* seen program X and on a sample of those who had *not* seen program X. Any difference between the test scores of the two samples would have to be interpreted as a mixture of the effects of exposure to program X *and* the effects of any *original differences* between the two samples[b]. Thus if the two samples were different *to start with* in terms of characteristics related to test score, then these original differences could be expected to have contributed to the post-broadcast difference in test score. This situation is illustrated in Figure 3.

If an assessment of the effects of program X is to be gained from such a comparison, a means must be found for sieving out of the comparison the effects (on test score) of any original differences between the two samples. The Stable Correlate method is a means for attempting to do this.

The Stable Correlate method is a matching technique of an empirical kind. Its purpose is to render the non-exposee sample equivalent to the exposee sample in terms of all characteristics which are correlated with test score. If this can be done fully and provided these characteristics are not themselves open to influence by program X, then according to the Stable Correlate method any remaining difference in test score ought to represent an effect of exposure to program X.

[b] This includes differences in the impact of extraneous events arising out of differences in characteristics of the two samples. Note also that if exposure to the program X means that a person is unexposed to certain extraneous events, this is a genuine effect of exposure to X.

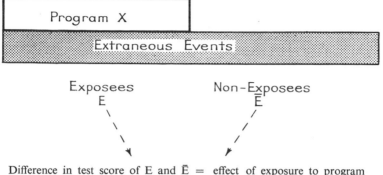

Difference in test score of E and Ē = effect of exposure to program
X + effects of original differences between exposees and non-exposees

Figure 3

Some requirements of matching variables

There are, however, some basic requirements for matching variables which must be made quite clear.

(1) *The matching variables must be associated with both test score and sample differences.* If a characteristic is in no way related to the test score in whatever is being studied, then differences between the exposee and the non-exposee samples in terms of this characteristic cannot produce differences between them in test score. They are irrelevant to the study and there is no point in trying to get rid of any differences of this kind that exist between the two samples. On the other hand, if a variable is highly associated with test score, then a difference between the two samples in terms of it would automatically produce a difference in their test scores (quite independently of any program effects). It would be essential to equate the two samples in terms of such a variable. When a variable is highly associated with test score but is not a source of difference between the exposee and non-exposee samples, there is no point in matching for this because they are matched for it already. Accordingly, the matching variables which are wanted are those which are associated with test score but which are also sources of difference between the two samples. Matching variables are thus selected for their *joint* associations — association with test score plus association with whether or not people saw the program. In other words, the matching technique turns upon the identification of characteristics which are predictive of test score and in terms of which the two samples are different[c]. There are special methods for achieving this selection and to these we shall be returning.

[c] The technician may care to think of this requirement as the identification of the correlates of both dependent and independent variables.

(2) *The matching variables must be stable.* Another requirement of the matching variables is that they should be *stable* in relation to the program under study (X in this case). To match the two samples in terms of variables which are themselves open to change by the program would be to whittle away the evidence of the effect of the program itself. This means that the matching variables cannot, with safety, be attitudes of any kind, but must be either (i) fairly enduring characteristics of sample members such as age, intelligence, or (ii) past behaviour sufficiently open to accurate recall for it to be firmly classed as occurring *before* the broadcast of program X. Thus for assessing the effects of program X (about Americans, say) upon attitudes towards Americans, the past behaviour variables tried out as possible matching variables might include such things as: personal acquaintance with any American prior to the broadcast; personal acquaintance with other non-English people prior to the broadcast; travel abroad prior to the broadcast; newspapers taken prior to the broadcast; programs similar to X which were seen prior to the broadcast of X.

(3) *Matching variables are selected as a small composite of variables all of which must be relatively independent of each other.* The point of this requirement is that no single variable, however well it qualifies under condition (i) above, will be sufficient to remove all relevant differences between the exposee and the non-exposee samples. Further or supporting matching variables are needed and these will be effective only if they do not duplicate the functions of the first selected matching variable. And they themselves must not duplicate each other.

To meet this and other requirements, the matching variables must be drawn from a large pool of *proposed* matching variables. There should be as many as 50 of these. Their derivation should be controlled by the requirements (i) and (ii) above and in addition they should be as varied as possible in their points of reference. The composite of matching variables to be drawn from this pool is intended to have in it as much matching power as the whole pool (see page 178), and accordingly the original heterogeneity of that pool is of great importance.

The Nature of the pool of proposed matching variables

Most of the variables in the pool are brought into it on the basis of (i) their known or suspected association with whatever variable is under study as possibly affected by program X and or (ii) whether or not a person will have watched program X. The 'best bets' are of course those variables which are thought to be associated with both. Suppose that program X dealt with mental illness and was intended to produce certain changes in attitudes towards the mentally ill. In this case, items proposed as possible matching variables might deal with such things as: respondent's personal (past) experiences with the mentally ill; whether or not he has ever visited a mental hospital; religion; whether married or single; number and age of children if married; whether a reader of 'quality' or 'popular' papers; whether or not he has ever seen certain films such as "Snake Pit"; occupation and educational background; age; sex; urban or rural residence. These *and possibly many others* could be brought into the pool on the basis of their likely or their suspected[d] association with (i) attitudes towards the mentally ill and or (ii) membership of exposee or non-exposee sample.

Whatever the source of proposed matching variables, it is essential that the total pool of them should be both numerous and heterogeneous. The requirement of heterogeneity is meant to ensure that the different variables will be as independent as it is possible to make them or, putting it another way, that they should between them rule out the possibility that some variable which is independent of them all has been left out. Indeed it is necessary that some variables be included without their seeming to be associated with the two criteria, simply because they are different from the other variables already included. What must be remembered is that an *expectation* of a relationship between variables is no more than expectation, and that a risk of missing a relevant source of difference between two samples is not worth taking.

With as many as 50 heterogeneous variables chosen in this way, it is most unlikely that any major and relevant source of difference between samples will be missed[e]. After all, it is the very common and disappointing experience of researchers that once three or four variables have been selected empirically as the best multiple predictors of some criterion, it is extremely difficult to find a further variable that will add anything appreciable to their joint predictive power. In other words, there is a lot of overlap between many variables. When an investigator is setting up a pool of *possible* matching variables, this situation works strongly in his favour.

Wherever possible, proposed matching variables should allow the respondent to answer with a "yes" or a "no". There are several advantages if this is done. First, it allows the investigator to include a lot of variables in his pool of proposed matching variables and this is much more important to the search for independent matching variables than is the obtaining of fine detail on a relatively small number of variables. Secondly, a

[d] On the basis: of past analyses; of (preliminary) intensive interviews with viewers; of the indications of related theory; of the hunches of the research team.

[e] This is not to say that a larger pool should not be used if it is feasible to do so, for that would provide greater safety against the danger of omitting some important factor from the total pool. The continuing reduction of ambiguity is, after all, a 'must' if there is any scope at all for doing this. In the present situation, the fact that all test room work must be completed within two hours puts a limit upon the number of pool items about which the necessary questions can be asked. In studies of the long term impact of TV, it is usually possible to ask many more such questions (see Chapter 21) though part of the reason for this is that more matching composites are usually needed.

'yes/no' type of response fits well into the procedure for selecting matching variables (see below for details).

The selection of matching variables

The first step in the selection of matching variables is to calculate the numerical association (that is, the correlation) of each of the proposed matching variables with test score on the matter being studied. There is a shortened technique for doing this, described fully in a footnote[f]. Next, the 10–15 variables with the highest numerical associations with test score are selected for further processing. Thus for each of them, two items of information are combined in a particular way[g]. These two items of information are: the measure of association just calculated[f] and the percent-

[f] *Calculating the extent of association between variables and test score.* Members of the combined exposee and non-exposee samples are classified as higher and lower in terms of their test scores, 'higher' being those in the top 50% for test score and 'lower' being the others. Each of the 'higher' and the 'lower' subgroups is then sub-divided in terms of the variable whose association with test score is to be measured. As shown in the following table, this leads to the derivation of four subgroups.

Test Score	Trial Variable P		Totals
	'Yes' in P	*Not 'Yes' in P*	
Higher 50% in test score	250	250	500
Lower 50% in test score	150	350	500
Totals	400	600	1000

The number of people in each of these four subgroups is then noted and this may for convenience be called the *actual* distribution of the sample. An entirely separate record is then made of the number of people who would be found in each of these cells if the variable being tested had *no* association with test score.

200	300
200	300

The difference is then calculated, cell by cell, between the 'association' distribution of figures and the 'actual' figure. The sum of these differences, ignoring the signs, is a realistic and easily calculated index of the numerical association of the proposed matching variable with test score. The bigger this figure, the higher the association. In the example given, the four differences are each 50, giving a total index of 200.

[g] *Combining indices to arrive at a joint association figure.* Suppose that a choice is being made betwen variables A and B. Let variable A have a numerical association index of 62 (calculated by the method described in footnote (f) and let it be the source of 15% difference between exposee and non-exposee samples. Then its joint index of power as a matching variable is 62×15 (= 930). Let variable B have equivalent figures of 75 and 10% giving it a joint index of 750. Then variable A would be selected ahead of variable B in spite of the latter having a higher numerical association with test score.

age difference between the two samples with respect to the variable concerned (that is, the one being tried out as a possible matching variable). The combining of these two items of information[g] provides the necessary index of that variable's *joint* association with test score and subsample membership. The variable with the highest *joint* association figure is selected as the first matching variable[g]. Let us imagine that this variable is number 24 among the 50 in the pool. The total sample (exposee plus non-exposee) is then split two ways[h] in terms of this variable. If responses on variable 24 were 'yes' and 'not yes', the split would be as follows.

All Cases

yes on 24   *no* on 24

Within the 'yes on 24' subgroup a further matching variable is chosen in the same way as was variable 24. Let this one be variable number 37. Next, the best matching variable within the 'not yes on 24' subgroup is chosen, quite separately, but in the same way. Let this variable be number 8. The sample is now sub-divided further as in Row II Figure 4. The important point to notice about the selection of the second order of matching variables is that different matching variables may emerge within the two subgroups (namely the 'yes on 24' and the 'not yes on 24' subgroups). This could be because the correlates of test score in one subgroup (e.g. young people) are not necessarily the same as those in a different subgroup (e.g. old people). It might also arise through exposees and non-exposees being similar (in terms of a particular correlate) in one subgroup but different in the other.

The selection of third, fourth, etc. levels of matching variables is continued to the limit of statistical meaningfulness and in the example in Figure 4

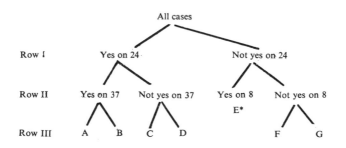

* In this subgroup there were insufficient cases (say 84) to warrant the further splitting of it.

Figure 4

[h] If variable 24 offered more than two response categories, its several categories would be sorted into two groups: those categories which were associated with the higher test score would go together in one group and those associated with lower test score would go together in the second group.

the process yields seven subgroups defined in terms of the chosen matching variables. These are best called matching subgroups and together they constitute a matching composite.

Using the matching variables to achieve matching

To achieve matching, the exposee and non-exposee samples are now each sub-divided into the 'matching subgroups' (seven in this example). Let these be as follows.

	A	B	C	D	E	F	G	Total
Exposees	65	68	73	44	50	39	61	400
Non-Exposees	56	94	112	83	34	121	100	600

Matching is usually achieved by taking the necessary steps to render the non-exposee sample the same as the exposee sample in terms of the proportion of them falling into the seven matching subgroups. For the above example, the following steps would be necessary.

1. The numbers in each of the seven cells in the exposee sample distribution would be multiplied by some common integer to make all of them larger than the corresponding subgroup in the non-exposee sample. In the above example, the common multiplier would be 4 (that is, all cells in the exposee distribution would be multiplied by 4).
2. The record cards of non-exposees would now be replicated systematically (that is, subgroup by subgroup) so that they were numerically equal to the record cards of exposees, cell by cell. This would lead to the following distributions and to matching without any casting out of record cards.

	A	B	C	D	E	F	G	Total
Exposee	260	272	292	176	200	156	244	1600
Non-Exposee	260	272	292	176	200	156	244	1600

Assessing the effects of the program

With the exposee and non-exposee samples matched in this way, average test scores are computed and the difference between the exposee and the non-exposee averages is interpreted as an approximation to the effects of exposure to the program.

If several different effects of the program were being investigated, this whole procedure, from the selection of a composite of matching variables to the equation of non-exposees to exposees, would have to be carried out anew. This is because it cannot be assumed that the matching variables appropriate for the study of one kind of effect are appropriate for the study of some other effect.

Challenging the findings

Since we cannot be certain that the matching variables used have in fact eliminated all relevant original differences between non-exposees and exposees, it is good policy to build certain checks into the analytical procedure. (i) One of these involves control *materials*. For instance if a program is intended to impart certain facts, then it should be possible to identify some further facts on the same general subject which were not given in the program and which could not be inferred or worked out from what *was* presented in the program. When the two samples are matched in the manner suggested, test scores for *these* 'control' facts should be the same. 'Control' attitudes would be a different matter, however, because one could not be sufficiently sure that a 'related' attitude would in fact remain unchanged. (ii) Another device is to split the non-exposee sample so that its two halves are as much different with respect to test scores as were the exposee sample and the non-exposee sample. The use of the matching variables for the mathing of these two sections of the non-exposee sample should eliminate all score differences between them, that is, if the matching variables for the matching of these two sections of the non-exposee type of check might be applied to the exposee group. No doubt further checks will be developed for this method in the course of time. Certainly checks of the kind indicated should be applied whenever they are appropriate and possible.

The origin of the samples to be used in the Stable Correlate technique

The people taking part in an 'effects' study based on the Stable Correlate technique may be contacted initially through a sample survey conducted on the day after the broadcast. Survey contacts are questioned to find out which programs they watched 'yesterday', and on the basis of their replies it is possible for office staff to classify them as exposees or as non-exposees to the program which is to be studied. The invitation system described in Chapter 3 may be applied.

The questions asked in the survey must relate to all programs viewed yesterday and must not be focussed upon the program in which the researcher is really interested. In fact the recruiting survey is carried out as if it were no more than a check to establish viewing figures for yesterday and the interviewers themselves see it as such.

Though a random sample survey may be used for the identification of exposees and non-exposees, it is much cheaper and much quicker to conduct this preparatory survey through a quota sample controlled in terms of age, sex and social class. When the questioning procedure is reduced to a minimum length, a single interviewer working on a quota basis can conduct a large number of these identification interviews in the one day. A team of about 40 interviewers can conduct enough identifying interviews in a single day for a full 'effects' study.

This *preparatory* survey must not be confused with the testing procedure to which many of these people will soon be subjected (see later for details). The latter is a very demanding and time-consuming procedure, whereas the preparatory survey is nothing more than a means of locating appropriate people for the tests.

The size and some other features of the control group

The people who eventually make up the non-exposee sample (the test-room 'controls') must number more than those who make up the exposee sample. This stipulation is made in order to reduce the possibility that one of the subgroups amongst the non-exposees will be too small to allow its magnification to the number of cases in the corresponding exposee subgroup. This requirement is not hard to meet because the number of people *not* seeing a program usually greatly exceeds the number who see it (as for instance with programs with audiences of 30% or less). Indeed the investigator is much more likely to be concerned with preventing the number of non-exposees tested from becoming *too* large.

*The conditions under which the testing of
exposees and non-exposees is to be carried out*

It is conceivable that in the course of time all the necessary testing of exposees, and of a sufficient proportion of the non-exposees, could be carried out in respondents' homes. However, since testing usually takes about two hours, and as it would be extremely difficult or impossible to get adequate testing conditions in some homes, there is usually little alternative to conducting the tests at some centre. Here, the necessary conditions for testing can be set up and maintained and, most important, it is possible to give the respondent a high degree of anonymity. Another advantage of testing at a centre is that about forty people can be tested at a time by just one skilled administrator.

The bringing of people to a test centre automatically raises problems of unrepresentativeness amongst the people who actually come: the proportion who come is usually about 25%−30% of those invited[i]. However, as explained in Chapter 3, it is possible to do a great deal about 'unrepresentativeness through volunteering', because ordinarily most of the unrepresentativeness is related to occupational level and to social class. If this information is gathered at the time of the preliminary survey (as advocated here), the total sample coming to the test centre can be held fairly representative of the program's audience in terms of these three variables and the necessary further trimming or adjustment of the sample can be achieved afterwards. Since the sole purpose of the non-exposee group is to fulfil the purpose of a control group, its composition is controlled (through the invitation system) to resemble the program's actual audience in terms of age, sex and occupational level. It is against this background that subsequent matching of the non-exposees and the controls, in terms of the empirically derived matching variables, takes place.

Of the Several Research Strategies Described in this Chapter

If the necessary money and time are available, and if the program to be tested has been filmed prior to the broadcast, then Strategy 2(b) is

[i] Each usually brings a friend rather like himself or herself in terms of social class and age; in most instances the friend is the invitee's husband or wife.

the obvious choice of method for measuring program effects. Unfortunately these conditions are only infrequently fulfilled: money for research is often scarce, there is usually little time available and often enough the content of a program will not really be known till the broadcast is actually made. The same applies to an important degree to Strategies 1 and 2(a). This means that very often Strategy 3, the Stable Correlate method, is the only one that can be used.

Having said this, I want to make it quite clear that Strategy 3 will not stand up against corner cutting, limited thinking, or general lack of care. Its successful application demands hard work, attention to detail, and the inclusion of large numbers of items for trial as matching variables, including some that may be unusual or untraditional. If these requirements are met, the Stable Correlate Method can provide a very useful service at comparatively low cost. In many cases, particularly for live broadcasts, there is no real alternative to it as a method.

[18]

A study of learning and attitude changes resulting from viewing programs in the television series "Bon voyage"[a]

BACKGROUND AND AIMS

"*Bon Voyage*" was a series of four television broadcasts included in successive editions of "Leisure and Pleasure" (a Tuesday afternoon program for women) from August 11th to September 1st, 1953. It was broadcast because the large annual flow of English visitors to France suggested that viewers contemplating a first visit to France might welcome a program which, in an entertaining way, taught them useful words and phrases and gave them information such as where to get a passport, the value of French money, how to use the Paris Underground Railway. It was hoped that the program would also serve to allay apprehensions about making a first visit to France, particularly those apprehensions which might spring from an inadequate knowledge of the French language.

The program was built around conversations between two people, one of them asking questions and the other answering with facts. There were frequent visual illustrations, sometimes in the form of film, sometimes through the showing of objects (e.g., items of French money), and on one occasion through a dramatised sketch. The first program dealt mainly with what was involved in actually getting to France, the second with the buying of food and drink, the next with sightseeing and the last with buying useful items and returning to England.

Many of the French words and phrases which were to be taught were presented in caption form. Where possible, they were illustrated pictorially and in all cases they were presented in the type of situation in which the visitor would be likely to need them. There was quite a lot of planned

---

[a] The chapter is based closely upon a paper by the writer in the *British Journal of Educational Psychology*, Vol. 26, Part I, 1956, p. 31. [165] Though the sample used was relatively small, the enquiry is reported here as one of the first of its kind.

repetition of the French words and of their English meanings, and in the last of the programs there was a re-presentation of the words taught during the series.

The purpose of this study was to find out to what extent the aims of the program were achieved. Accordingly the inquiry was addressed to three questions, namely, to what extent did viewers (a) learn the French words and phrases presented, (b) learn the general information presented, (c) sustain a reduction in their apprehensions about language and other difficulties involved in making a trip to France.

THE METHODS OF RESEARCH

Research design[b]

A research design sometimes advocated for studying the effects of exposing people to certain conditions involves the making of measurements before and after that exposure, a control group being used to assess (and thereafter to eliminate) the effects of purely extraneous events or influences. For two reasons, however, it is often not generally possible to use this approach in studies of the effects of broadcasts. In the first place, it is essential that the listening or viewing upon which the results are to be based should be entirely normal (i.e. not influenced either by pre-broadcast testing or by any knowledge that tests are to occur). Secondly, it is often impossible with television broadcasts, to say in advance of the program precisely what its content will be − as would be necessary in a comparison of 'before' and 'after' knowledge of specific words or facts. For these and other reasons it was necessary that in the present study a research design be used which allowed *all* the necessary testing to be done *after* the broadcast.

Accordingly, immediately after the last broadcast in the *"Bon Voyage"* series (of four programs) relevant *knowledge* and *attitude* tests were made on each of two large groups of people. One group was made up of viewers who had seen one or more of the four *"Bon Voyage"* programs, while the other group consisted of people who did not have television sets *and* who had not seen any of the *"Bon Voyage"* programs. Each group was tested for its knowledge of the French words and phrases and of the facts presented and after this came an assessment of those attitudes which it was thought the series might affect.

Differences between the two groups in terms of these tests results would be attributable to a combination of (a) the effect of the program and (b) pre-broadcast differences between the two groups (e.g., members of the viewing group might, prior to the broadcast of the series, have known

[b] This study was an early application of the Stable Correlate method. At that time, (i) traditional correlational methods were still being used and (ii) the double criterion method described in Chapter 18 had not yet been developed. See further details of the methods employed in this enquiry in "A Technique for Studying the Effects of a Television Broadcast" [164]

more or less of the words and phrases eventually presented than did the non-viewing group). To eliminate that portion of the difference between the two groups which arose out of such pre-broadcast differences, a refinement of normal matching technique was used.

The general principle of this refinement can be stated quite briefly.[c] What *usually* happens in matching procedure is that some members of either group are rejected until the two groups are the same in terms of one or more characteristics which the research worker *thinks* are the important ones (e.g., age, educational level, intelligence). The technique used in this enquiry differed from the traditional method in two ways. First, the various characteristics in terms of which matching was to be done were selected *empirically* as the best of those immediately available (that is, using correlational methods — see Table 1). Second, there was no discarding of subjects: instead, the score of the non-viewer group was adjusted through a regression equation to provide an estimate of what it *would* have been had the non-viewer group *not* differed from the viewer group in terms of the matching characteristics.[c] A comparison of this adjusted score with the score of the viewer group then provided a direct estimate of the program's real effect.

Since in this study the non-viewing group was being used to provide estimates of the pre-broadcast scores of the viewing group, the convention was adopted here of referring to these adjusted scores as the pre-broadcast scores of the viewing group.[c]

To put this method into effect however, it was necessary to include in the testing procedure questions in terms of those characteristics which seemed likely to be relevant as matching variables. At the end of testing it was then possible (through correlation methods) to determine which combination of these characteristics gave the highest multiple correlation with the variables being studied[d] — that is, which of them were the best available for matching purposes. Since in this project three separate things were being studied,[e] separate matching variables had to be set up for each. Some details of these matching variables are given in this section (i.e. Methods), and there is a brief account, under Findings, of the selection procedure and its outcome.

Subjects

Viewers who had seen one or more of the "*Bon Voyage*" programs were available from either of two sources. In the first place, the B.B.C.'s

[c] This study was based upon an early application of the Stable Correlate method. At this time, (i) traditional correlational methods were still being used and (ii) the double criterion described Chapter 18 had not yet been developed.

[d] Using the Wherry-Doolittle formulae and traditional correlational methods [185].

[e] Knowledge of French words, knowledge of certain facts, attitudes related to going to France.

Audience Research Department conducts daily surveys of listening and viewing which provide information about *which* programs people happened to hear or view on the previous day. In the course of this survey a record is made, for each person interviewed, of name, address, social group, occupation, age, sex, and various other details. The names and addresses of persons who happened to hear one or more of the first three *"Bon Voyage"* programs were, therefore, available before the last broadcast. In the second place, members of the B.B.C.'s viewing panel normally complete reports on programs which they happen to view in the ordinary course of events. Here, too, it was possible to note the names of those people who had been exposed to at least one of the *"Bon Voyage"* programs. Letters of invitation were sent to people selected from each of these two sources, provided they lived within travelling distance of Broadcasting House (where the tests were to be made). In all, 42 per cent of those viewers who were invited attended the session. Non-viewers were recruited mainly from the records available from the Survey of Listening and Viewing and some 35 per cent of those invited attended. Group members did not know, prior to coming, that the evening's procedures would include work on *"Bon Voyage"*.

In the selection of each group (i.e., those exposed to *"Bon Voyage"* and those not exposed) a standard technique was used to reduce volunteer bias. The normal audience of "Leisure and Pleasure" (the program within which *"Bon Voyage"* appeared) was classified in terms of age, sex and social class. Previous work had established the attendance rate to be expected, using standard letters of invitation, within each 'age/social class' sub-group, and these rates were taken into consideration in issuing invitations, the aim being to ensure that the exposees and non-exposees who actually came were closely similar to the "Leisure and Pleasure" audience in terms of age, sex and social class. This resulted in an *initial* rough matching of exposees and non-exposees, though it could never be assumed that matching only in terms of age, sex and social class would be *sufficient* for the purpose in hand.

In all, approximately 100 viewers (exposees) and 120 non-viewers (non-exposees) came as invited to Broadcasting House, meeting in the evening in groups of 15 to 25. Viewers and non-viewers met separately. The first of the viewer meetings occurred two days after the last of the *"Bon Voyage"* broadcasts and the other meetings followed on consecutive evenings, viewer and non-viewer meetings being held the same night or alternately.

Test procedure

While a certain amount of each evening was devoted to orienting the groups to the tests ahead, the essential steps were as follows. Members of groups: (a) were 'reminded' in some detail of the four *"Bon Voyage"* programs and were asked of each one of them to write down whether or not they had viewed it; (b) were given a list of twenty-six of the French words and phrases presented in "Bon Voyage" and were asked to write down each one's English meaning opposite it; (c) were later given the same list of twenty-six words and phrases and asked to choose the correct meaning from six proffered words (multiple choice)[f]; (d) were asked to write down answers to a number of questions about facts actually presented in the program; (e) were given an attitude test dealing with issues concerned directly or indirectly with making a trip to France.

The list of French words and phrases contained such terms as '*parlez-vous Anglais*', '*où est*', '*l'addition*', '*timbre*', '*douane*', '*pourboire*', '*la gare routière*', '*toujours tout droit*'. The twenty-six words and phrases were, it should be pointed out, all presented in the program with a serious teaching intention, practically all of them being shown in caption form, and the appearance of no one of them in the program being merely incidental.

In the test of factual knowledge there were questions about twenty-nine of the facts presented in the program and some examples follow: (i) About how many French francs are there to the English pound? (ii) If you were tipping a porter in France, how much would you be expected to give him for each piece of luggage he handled for you (answer in English or in French money)? (iii) If you were getting a passport, where would you expect to get it? Here, too, of course, each of the facts selected for testing had been presented in the program with a serious teaching intention. In marking answers, a fair margin of error was allowed (e.g., that there was anything from 800 to 1,200 francs to the English pound).[g]

The attitude test consisted of a set of twenty-eight statements each dealing with one of the various issues which it was intended to treat in the program and they took the following forms: (i) You don't need to know much French to 'get-by' on a short visit to France; (ii) It would probably be quite a lot of trouble making arrangements about passport, money, transport, customs, and so on; (iii) I know so little about French money that I would probably be swindled. The twenty-eight statements were listed and the respondent had to indicate, with respect to each of them, whether he 'agreed strongly', 'agreed', 'disagreed', 'disagreed strongly', or simply had 'no opinion' on the matter. The response chosen was underlined[g].

To provide proposed matching variables the following information was also required: (a) age and sex; (b) educational level achieved; (c) job at present or before marriage; (d) whether or not the subject had ever (i) visited France, (ii) studied the French language; (e) score on a short test

---

[f] The reason for testing by *both* creative response and multiple choice methods was to provide an estimate of learning at each of two different levels of intensity, thereby broadening the picture of learning achieved. The written replies to the creative response test were collected before the delivery of the multiple choice test.

[g] The classification of occupations is given in the Appendix to Chapter 14.

of French terms *not* presented in "Bon Voyage"[h]. The latter test included only five words and these are referred to hereafter as 'control words.' For the purposes of testing, they were scattered among the other twenty-six French words. The answers to (d) (i) and (ii) required only a 'yes' or a 'no'. The information about education and occupation was collected on a standard form developed by the writer for general research purposes and on the basis of this information occupational and educational classifications were made[g].

The tests were all of a paper and pencil kind. All subjects were assured of their *anonymity* and there was a lot of emphasis on the need for constant effort and for frankness. In all tests, abundant time was given and no respondent was knowingly penalised for poor expression.

THE FINDINGS

Details Related to the Derivation of the Matching Variables

The first phase of the analysis was designed to identify, for *each* of the three separate matters under study, that combination of the proposed matching variables which had the highest multiple correlation with test score. Table 1 gives the results of this part of the analysis.

TABLE 1

The proposed matching criteria

Variable under study	Stable correlates selected (in order of priority)		Multiple Correlation* Achieved
	Variable	*Correlation**	
Knowledge of	Control words	+0.78	+0.82 (first two)
French words	Educational level	+0.59	+0.85 (all three)
and phrases	Occupational level	+0.47	
presented in			
"Bon Voyage".			
Knowledge of facts	Control words	+0.54	+0.63 (first two)
presented in	Visit to France**	+0.46	+0.65 (first three)
"Bon Voyage".	Educational level	+0.51	+0.65 (all four)
	Occupational level	+0.48	
Attitude on issues	Control words	+0.48	+0.54 (first two)
related to visiting	Visit to France	+0.34	+0.55 (all three)**
France.	Occupational level	+0.39	

* The use of standard correlations and of standard multiple correlations was abandoned in later applications of the Stable Correlate method. In those later applications, modified (and more appropriate) measures of associations were used.

** Those who had made a visit in the past were more favourably and confidently disposed to making a further visit.

[h] In this early use of the Stable Correlate method, the number of variables tried out for matching purposes was relatively small. Larger numbers of trial variables would have made for safer and more powerful matching.

For the study of change in *knowledge of French words*, the variables which emerged as maximising the matching power of the whole pool of proposed (matching) variables were: control words; educational level; occupational level. Taken together, these provided a correlation with test score of +0.85. The Wherry-Doolittle technique [185] had been used to identify them. According to this technique, the addition of a fourth matching variable would have added nothing to the multiple correlation. In fact, the third variable, occupational level, added too little to the multiple correlation to warrant the additional processing of data which its inclusion would have involved and for this reason the matching variables actually used in the study of word knowledge were control words and educational level. For the same sort of reasons the matching variables selected for use in the study of *factual knowledge* were limited to control words and whether or not the respondent had ever visited France. Their multiple correlation with test score was +0.63. The same two variables emerged as the appropriate ones to use in the study of *attitudes* (multiple correlation of +0.54).

These, then, were the matching variables used for the adjustment of the test scores of the people who had not seen any programs in the "Bon Voyage" series (i.e., the non-viewers or the non-exposees). The adjustment was carried out through regression equations, there being a quite separate adjustment for each of the three scores. The results are set out in Table 2.

The Effects of the Program

The degree of exposure to the program

The number of *"Bon Voyage"* programs seen by persons coming to Broadcasting House as members of the viewer group (post-broadcast) was, expressed as an average, 1.6 out of 4. Some 59 per cent saw only one of them, 28 per cent saw two, and the remaining 13 per cent saw either three or four. Even when *two* of the four programs were viewed, these two tended not to be consecutive programs. This suggests that exposure to the program was not more than partial and that there was relatively little continuity of viewing.

The changes produced

Table 2 sets out the main findings and shows also the influence of the correction procedures used.

Changes in knowledge

There was a very small (but statistically significant) increase in viewers' ability to give or to recognise the English meanings of French words amongst the 26 the broadcasters set out to teach. Knowledge of the *facts* presented increased from an average of 9.1 of the 29 tested to 10.1. This statistically significant difference is also very small.

Several circumstances appear to have contributed to the relative smallness of these gains — circumstances which, it is important to note, are likely

TABLE 2.

Changes produced (post-broadcast groups)

Variable under study	Non-viewers' Scores		Viewers' Scores	Significance of Difference
	↓ *Unadjusted Averages*	↓ *Adjusted Averages*	↓ *Averages*	∅
Knowledge of words presented in *"Bon Voyage"*				
Creative Response*.	4.89	5.31	6.21	P = .02
Multiple Choice	9.47	9.97	11.68	P = .01
Knowledge of facts presented in *"Bon Voyage"***	8.54	9.08	10.10	P = .02
Attitude on issues related to visiting France.†	+ 15.38	+ 17.65	+ 11.80	P = .01

* Score out of 26, ** Score out of 29.
† 17.65 represents a relatively favourable and confident attitude.
∅ The closely matched character of the two groups was taken into account in calculating the P values.

to dominate or to condition those teaching programs which are meant to reach a wide or general viewing public. In the first place, *"Bon Voyage"* was presented within the context of a larger, regular, Tuesday program for housewives. While this gave it a wide audience, it seems rather unlikely that the persons exposed to it tuned in specially for the teaching aspect of this somewhat atypical section of the full program. They appear, rather, to have been fairly ordinary housewives, undistinguished by any particular determination to improve their French—as distinct from, say, an adult education class in French. In the second place, to hold this wide audience the program had to be a piece of genuine entertainment and this put an obvious limit upon the rigorousness of the teaching methods which could be used. Thirdly, while there was no progressive fall in the size of the audience seeing successive programs in the series, there was relatively little *continuity* of viewing, viewers having seen on the average only 1.6 of the four *"Bon Voyage"* programs. The absence of continuity also meant that the summary and the repetition (of words and facts) in the last of the four programs did not, in fact, operate as such to any marked degree. Of course the tests were carried out several days after the broadcast of the *last* program, so that quite a lot of time had passed since the first broadcast. This must mean that an appreciable amount of forgetting of French words and phrases and of facts had occurred between their presentation and the delivery of tests, so that what remained at the time of the tests was of a more durable nature. From a practical point of view this is as it should be, for the study was concerned with practical effects — that is, with more or less useful learning rather than lightly held impressions which fall away fairly readily. At the same time, this means that the assessment actually applied constituted no easy or generous test of the program's effectiveness.

Despite these important qualifications, the gains considered in any absolute sense are small and the educationist will want to evaluate them against gains in other situations — perhaps against the results of formal instruction. In doing this, however, one thing which it is important to keep in mind is that for most of the housewives receiving instruction through this program, the only real alternative was no instruction at all.

Changes in attitude

Turning to changes in *attitude* produced by the program, it may be taken that the pre-broadcast score of +17.65 represents a relatively confident and favourable attitude towards making a visit to France, and that a drop in score to +11.80 is a fairly substantial drop — though that final score still represents a somewhat favourable attitude.

Looked at in greater detail, the evidence indicates that, prior to seeing *"Bon Voyage"*, some 78 per cent agreed that "you don't need to know much French to 'get by' on a short visit to France", whereas only 55 per cent were in agreement with this after seeing the program. In the same way the program increased the number of viewers who felt that they knew "so little about French money" that they "would probably be swindled". After seeing the program, there was appreciably less belief that "the arrangements for going to France are quite straightforward", slightly *more* apprehension about "what to order in a French café", and more uncertainty about the "interestingness" of French food. Apprehensions concerning what to do about tipping were substantially increased. Confidence in ability to cope with the French transport system and with French money was somewhat reduced and there was a reduction in the proportion who had a "strong desire to spend a holiday in France".

On the other hand, the program appears to have increased the number who held that "France is a country of great variety and charm" and that "the French put more emphasis on politeness than we do".

While the direction of most of the changes may at first occasion some surprise (that is, an *increase* rather than a decrease in apprehensions), it is easy enough to understand how they occurred and there is profit of a general kind in trying to do so.

The main effort in this program went into the provision of useful pieces of information aimed at helping the traveller to solve her difficulties and at making her visit a smooth and enjoyable one. This was done vividly and in an interesting way, but nonetheless the giving of advice generally involves highlighting some difficulty: unless the viewer is *already* aware of this difficulty, the outcome is likely to be the *creation* of apprehensions and worries rather than an allaying of them. In fact, discussions with viewers suggest that far from being conscious of difficulties, the bulk of this audience had not, prior to the broadcast, given any informed thought to what actually would be involved in such a visit. Thus, prior to the broadcast, the great majority of them knew little French, had not been to France, and yet were reasonably confident that the visitor could 'get by' without knowing much French! In fact, what the program seems to have done is have to introduced the viewer, vividly and realistically, to the new and bewildering situations in which she would, as a foreigner in France, find herself. Language difficulties assumed their real importance as did cultural and other differences and, perhaps for the first time, she saw something other than a travel agent's version of France. The nature of the program's effect is not really surprising. What the result does suggest, however, is that there are some real hazards inherent in any attempt to provide a mass audience with an informational service of this particular kind.

Summary

(1) "*Bon Voyage*" was a television series designed to teach the viewer, in an interesting way, some French words and phrases and some general facts of the kind likely to be of use to the English visitor to France. It was hoped that the program would also serve to reduce such apprehensions as the intending traveller might have about an inadequate knowledge of the language. This study was designed to find out to what extent the aims of the program were achieved. Paper and pencil tests were used.

(2) For various reasons, it was inadvisable to try to deliver the necessary tests both *before and after* exposure to the program. The method used was to compare, after the broadcast, two groups of people, one of them being viewers who had seen all or part of the "*Bon Voyage*" series and the other being made up of people who had not seen any part of it. Special adjustments were then made to the scores of the non-viewers to eliminate that portion of the difference in test scores between the two groups which arose out of conditions other than the exposure of the viewers to the program (i.e., pre-broadcast differences). The exposure of the viewers to the program had been quite normal, had taken place at home and had occurred without any knowledge on the part of the viewer that she would be tested subsequently.

(3) The results indicated that the program had produced a slight increase in viewers' knowledge of the words and phrases, and of the facts presented, but that this was accompanied by an *increase* in viewers' apprehensions about language difficulties, and in general about visiting France. It is suggested that such an increase in apprehensions is one of the hazards inherent in an educational broadcast of this kind.

[19]

A study of some of the effects of viewing programs in the television series "The hurt mind"[a]

BACKGROUND AND AIMS

"The Hurt Mind" was a series of half-hour television programs produced by the British Broadcasting Corporation and broadcast on successive Tuesday evenings early in 1957. The series dealt with the problems and the treatment of mental illness, the first four programs being concerned, respectively, with 'conditions in mental hospitals', 'the causes of mental illness', 'psychological methods for treating mental illness', 'physical methods for treating mental illness'. In the last of the series, a panel of medical men talked about aspects of treatment raised in viewers' letters, and the Chairman of the series went on to talk about the importance of some of the social consequences of mental illness and to rate mental illness as a major social problem.

Each of the broadcasts in the series was seen by approximately 15% of the adult population in the United Kingdom, equivalent to about $5\frac{1}{2}$ million people. The reaction indices [b] for the five broadcasts were 80, 62, 70, 78 and 77 in order of transmission, the mean (73) being well above that for all talks and discussions televised in the preceding quarter of the year (64). On this evidence, it is reasonable to conclude that the series provided very acceptable viewing to a large audience.

The primary aim of the series, however, was to inform viewers about the nature and treatment of mental illness, and it was hoped that one result of this would be a change in people's views and attitudes on that subject. Accordingly, research was carried out to answer the following questions.

---

[a] A report of a study conducted by the author as a member of the Audience Research Department of the B.B.C. [172].

[b] The B.B.C.'s viewing panel rates reaction on a five point scale running from markedly favourable reaction to a markedly unfavourable reaction. The average rating is expressed as a percentage of the maximum score feasible. This percentage figure is the index of reaction referred to above.

(1) To what extent did the series affect viewers' knowledge of and ideas about mental illness?

(2) In what way did the series affect viewers' confidence in the ability of medical men to cure mental illness?

(3) In what way did the series affect viewers' willingness to accept back into society (as a normal person) the ex-patient of the mental hospital?

(4) In what way did the series affect viewers' attitudes towards the mentally ill?

(5) To what extent did the broadcast increase awareness of mental illness as a social problem?

THE METHODS OF RESEARCH

In any realistic measurement of the effects[c] upon its audience of a television broadcast, it is essential that the results be based upon completely normal viewing—i.e. that the people who will eventually act as the sample should not have had any idea at the time they saw the broadcast that they would subsequently be asked questions about it by the B.B.C.

The following special procedure had therefore to be used to recruit the sample. On the day following a given broadcast in the series, a special survey was conducted in which people were asked which programs they had viewed 'last night'. A check list of all the previous evening's programs was used. The name and address of each person interviewed was recorded together with age, sex and occupational level. This was done after each of the second, third, fourth and fifth broadcasts, and a "pool' was thus built up of people who *had*, and of people who had *not* seen the series (or some part of it) in the normal course of events. Subsequently groups of those who *had* seen the selected broadcast and similar groups who had *not* seen it, received invitations to attend a meeting of listeners/viewers in Broadcasting House. There was no reference in the invitation to the series or topic under study, and those coming had no way of knowing beforehand that the "Hurt Mind" program was to be dealt with in any way.[d] Special methods were used to ensure that those attending were approximately representative, in terms of age, sex and social class, of the people who saw the series (or some part of it).[e]

The meetings were held 1–14 days after the last broadcast in the series, and those attending it went through a set of prepared tests. The test scores of people who had, and of people who had not, seen the program,

[c] See Chapter 18 for a detaied description of the methods used for isolating program effects.

[d] Those who came knew beforehand that the evening would include general discussion of programs. At the test session itself all were asked if they wished to proceed after being told about the special enquiry which was to be included in the evening's procedure. Nobody opted out. There was every evidence, at the end of the session and during it, that group members enjoyed the session and found it very interesting.

[e] For details of the controlled invitation system, see Chapter 3.

were assessed and recorded. Standard techniques[c] were then used to eliminate that portion of the difference between the scores of these two samples which was *not* an effect of the broadcast, but was a result of the two samples being different to start with. The remaining difference was regarded as approximating to an effect of the broadcast on a sample of its viewers.[f]

In all, approximately 800 people were tested, and checks administered in the test-room indicated that the methods used in recruiting them had yielded a sample approximately representative of the series' actual audience in terms of age, sex and social class. The subjects, who were highly cooperative, remained strictly anonymous. All tests were conducted under classroom conditions and all answers to questions were written or marked on paper. In the analysis of results there was, naturally, no penalty for poor English. Most of the groups numbered between 40 and 60. Because quite a lot of points were to be covered in the tests, no single group was asked the full battery of questions, a system of rotation being used. Taken altogether, however, the questions required that subjects should write down what they felt on specified issues, should try to answer various questions about facts, and should select one or another of a range of statements as giving the nearest to their own opinion on some specified point. The purpose of the tests was partly revealed early in the session and fully disclosed at the end of it. Subjects also indicated which of the five broadcasts in the series they had seen.

A large quantity of information came out of the enquiry. It concerns not only the effect of the series, but the ideas and beliefs (about mental illness) of the viewers who elected to watch the series.[g]

THE FINDINGS
Knowledge and Ideas About Mental Illness

Subjects were asked, in stages, to name the various kind of mental illness, to write down as many as they could of the different causes, and to list the kinds of treatment which are used in mental illness. Later on in the session, they were asked to write down what was meant by specified kinds of treatment, where treatment could be obtained for mental illness (apart from mental hospitals), what proportion of patients entered mental hospitals of their own free will, and so on. All questions were geared to information actually given in the series. Responses were, in all cases, written in small books under conditions of silence and strict confidence. The time

---

[f] Theoretically, it is possible to regard the adjusted score of the group which did *not* see the broadcast, as approximating to the pre-broadcast score of the group which *did* see it. For convenience, the two groups are therefore referred to in the rest of this report as 'before' and 'after' viewing groups.

[g] The content of this chapter is limited to a description of the effects of the program. Other of the results, and a detailed description of the methods used, are available elsewhere [172].

allowed for answering to those who *had* seen the series, was precisely the
same as that allowed to those who had *not*.

Types of mental illness

Members of test-room had been asked to name (in writing) as many as
they could of the different kinds of mental illness. The evidence indicated
that viewing led to a slight increase in the number referring to 'depression'
and in the number referring in general terms to something meaning neuro-
sis. Each of these illnesses had in fact been featured in the program.
There was little or no change in the frequency with which the other types
of mental illness were mentioned. Table 1 gives details.

TABLE 1

The different kinds of mental illness

Proportion Referring to it		Type of Mental Illness Referred to
'*Before*'* %	*After* %	*(The terms used were nearly always less specific than the main titles given below)*
61	65	Neuroses, referred to in general terms (such as: 'neurotic anxiety', 'mental strain', 'repression').
14	13	Neuroses referred to more specifically (such as: 'neurasthenia', 'imagines he is ill', 'hysterical').
20	20	Paranoia (with references to: 'imagines others talking about him', 'delusions of greatness', 'complaining of neighbours').
22	21	Obsessions, fixations, phobias (with references to: unfounded fears, compulsive acts, kleptomania, 'sex mania', 'drug taking').
24	30	Depression (with references to: 'melancholia', 'suicidal').
30	33	Schizophrenia (with references to: 'split personality', 'lack of interest in anything', 'retiring from company of others').
7	8	Psychopathic personality (with references to: 'alcoholism', 'chronic liar', 'cries easily', 'no conscience').
13	14	Others (including mental deficiency, epilepsy, 'inferiority complex', amnesia, brain injury, 'demented', 'sleeping sickness', 'without Christian beliefs').

* The estimated 'before' scores (in fact the adjusted scores, the adjustment
being as referred to under 'Methods' and as described as detail in Chapter 18).

Causes of mental illness

Subjects were asked to write down all the causes of mental illness that
they could think of. The effect of the series on people's ability to enumer-
ate these is shown in Table 2.

From this it will be seen that there was a small reduction in the very
large proportion (90%) who named 'strain, worry, shock' and a small
reduction also in the proportion naming 'heredity' (34%−27%). There

was a small increase in the number referring to 'disturbances in the mother just after child-birth' or 'menopause' and a large increase in the proportion who blamed it on 'surroundings as a child' (22% 'before' the series, 33% after).

TABLE 2

Causes of mental illness

Proportion Referring to it		'Causes' (of Mental Illness) Referred to
'Before' %	After %	*(The terms used were sometimes less specific than those given below)*
90	83	'Strain, worry, shock' (with references to: anxiety, 'money worries', 'air-raids', 'grief', 'overwork', 'present-day living', 'noise', 'guilt', etc.).
44	48	Circumstances in which we are at present placed (with references to: 'frustration', 'housing conditions', 'family trouble', 'malnutrition', 'loneliness', 'conflict').
22	33	Surroundings in the past (with references to: ill-treatment as a child, divorced parents, 'shock', 'child feels he is not wanted', etc.).
34	27	Heredity
43	45	Injury or illness or disease (with references to: 'injury to the head', 'physical ill treatment', 'ill health').
11	11	Bad way of life (with references to: 'too much drink', 'drugs' etc.).
6	13	Menopause (and disturbances in the mother after child-birth).

TABLE 3

Treatment of mental illness

Proportion Referring to it		Type of Treatment Named or Referred to
'Before' %	After %	*(The terms used were usually less specific than those in this table)*
81	*74*	*Psychological Type Treatment*
25	23	occupational therapy
36	25	'rest'
13	12	'kindness'
31	20	analytical methods
31	27	humane treatment (e.g. 'special care', 'outings', 'visits from friends', and so on).
7	6	others
68	*80*	*Physical Type Treatment*
14	20	surgery
47	67	shock treatment
29	43	'drugs and injections'
21	25	general or non-specific references

Treatment of mental illness

Statements about methods of treating mental illnesses were elicited in the same way. 'Before' the broadcast, people thought more in terms of psychological-type treatment (81%) than in terms of physical treatment (68%). The series appears to have produced a more equal balance, increasing the reference to physical treatment and reducing reference to psychological treatment.

More specifically, there seems to have been a reduction in the number naming 'rest' as a method of treating mental illness (36% 'before' and 25% after), and a reduction also in the reference to psycho-analysis (31% 'before' and 20% after). But there was an *increase* in the number naming electric shock treatment (47% : 67%) and also in the numbers referring to surgery (14% : 20%) and 'drugs and injections' (29% : 43%). In other words, the series seems to have turned the ideas of viewers somewhat in the direction of physical-type treatment. The series did in fact stress this form of treatment.

Knowledge about other aspects of mental illness

The series appears to have produced a large increase in the proportion who realized that treatment for mental illness could be received in Outpatient Departments. This information was given in the series (33% 'before' and 49% after). A small increase (14% to 20%) occurred also in the number who believed that the majority of patients enter a mental hospital of their own free will. There was an increase from 27% to 36% in the number who believed that less than a third of those entering stayed there for more than a year. On the other hand, the program led to a large reduction in the number who thought that the *inheritance* of a mental illness affected the chances of curing it (53% before and 39% after). And it seems also to have led viewers to underestimate less than formerly the proportion of the population likely to have been mental patients at some period in their lives.

There were also questions about what was involved in different kinds of treatment, namely: occupational therapy, psychotherapy, leucotomy. There was a moderate increase (25% to 35%) in the number who thought of occupational therapy as a means of keeping people busy and of preventing them from engaging in morbid thoughts; there was a small increase also in the proportion who thought it gave patients self-confidence — that is, as an aid to re-entering society (6% 'before' the series and 14% after). There were no appreciable changes in the various other views of what occupational therapy was and of what it is supposed to do for the patients. When it came to *psychotherapy*, the series did not increase the proportion giving answers which were correct to some degree (about 50% both 'before' and after) but it *did* appear to increase the number who *wrongly* thought of psychotherapy as some form of physical treatment (11% to 22%). Presumably this was related to the program's emphasis on physical treatment.

Leucotomy was dealt with at some length in the fourth broadcast in the series, and in it an attempt was made to differentiate between the old and the modern method of performing a leucotomy. 'Before' seeing the series, practically no one could differentiate between the two methods. After the series, however, about 20% could do so on at least one point. The series also produced an increase in the proportion who had at least some idea of the type of patient on whom a leucotomy might be performed (23% before and 39% after). On this point one big increase was in terms of those suffering from 'severe depression' — an increase which might have been expected, for the point was both stressed and illustrated in the broadcast. However, viewers were not convinced by the program that leucotomy would leave the patient's personality unaltered, about 46% believing, both 'before' and after, that personality *could* change and about 40% remaining uncertain.

There emerged several points not already mentioned, but seemingly of importance. Thus both 'before' and after the series, about 90% of the viewers felt that there was a difference between mental illness and insanity, saying that mental illness tended to be curable and insanity incurable and that whereas with insanity the brain was 'far gone', the cause of the trouble in mental illness was only temporary. Again, when asked 'to whom mental illness might happen', about 60% selected the response 'anyone', about 30% the response 'the more intelligent', but only 2% 'the *less* intelligent'. A third point worth noting is that both 'before' and after the broadcast, viewers markedly underestimated the proportion of hospital beds given over to the mentally ill. Thus 'before' the series was transmitted, nearly 7 in 10 of those venturing an opinion believed the proportion to be 5% or less and only one viewer in 20 believed the proportion was between 30% and 50%. The series did not alter this balance in any discernible way.

Confidence in the Ability of Medical Men to Cure Mental Illness

Subjects were asked to indicate, on a prepared form, what they thought were the chances of curing mental illness 'these days'. They were also asked about their confidence in, and approval of, a number of different methods used in the medical treatment of mental illness. Finally, there were checks on their confidence in the ability of medical men and in the 'authorities' concerned with the mentally ill.

Take first changes of a fairly generalized or unspecific nature. The series seems to have increased the number who could agree that 'there's been great progress' over the last 20 years (45% 'before' and 58% after), cutting down the small proportion who held that there has been 'little or no progress' or who simply had no opinion (16% 'before' and 8% after).

As might be expected from this, there was also an increase in the proportion who felt that the majority of the mentally ill can be cured (73% 'before' and 85% after), and a small increase in the number who felt that the cure could be 'really complete' (37% 'before' and 43% after). 'Before'

TABLE 4

Views about progress over the last 20 years

Proportion		Statement Selected
'Before' %	*After* %	
1	1	None at all
3	2	Not much
39	34	Quite a lot
45	58	There's been great progress
12	5	I've no idea/no reply

the series was broadcast, over 70% were already fairly confident that psychiatrists and other medical men treating mental illness 'know what they are doing', but the broadcasts seem to have increased slightly the number with a really high degree of confidence (22% 'before' and 29% after). There was no increase of this kind, however, in respect of 'the authorities' concerned with this public service: about 53% believed, 'before' seeing the series, that they 'care very much' and about 50% believed this after seeing it.

Turning to matters of a fairly specific kind, the evidence indicates several large changes. The most striking of these was a substantial increase in viewers' confidence in the value of electric-shock treatment ('before' the series, 45% were confident that it could be a 'good thing', and 65% after); there was a corresponding increase in approval of it as a method of treatment (60% 'before' and 77% after). There was also an increase both in confidence and in approval concerning leucotomy (described to viewers as a method of treatment which means making a cut in the brain). The increase in approval of leucotomy as a method of treatment (29% to 48%) could be accounted for to a large degree by its reduction in the percentage who simply did not know what it was, but at least some of those concerned in the change were people who formerly disapproved of it.

'Group therapy' also gained in terms of public approval (50% 'before' and 64% after), as did 'talking it out under the influence of ether' (38% to 50%) and 'giving them drugs and injections' (47% to 55%). The gains for group therapy and for ab-reaction seem each to be dependent largely upon the series telling people what the treatment was, whereas such gain as occurred in respect of 'drugs and injections' was largely the result of a conversion from disapproval to approval. There was no meaningful increase however in approval of certain of the psychological-type treatments, namely: occupational therapy (80% 'before' and 82% after); psycho-analysis (69% : 70%); 'talking about it to a psychologist' (86% : 85%).

As a further probe into changes in viewers' confidence that mental illness can be cured, subjects were asked to say how they felt about statements of the following kind.

There's been progress all right. But there's no complete cure for mental illness. They may *seem* to be cured, but it's always there just under the surface.

Some of the things that medical people do in treating mental illness are just plain guesswork and may do more harm than good.

If someone dear to me needed treatment, I'd be very worried about him going along to the hospital for treatment, and I think it would be better for him to be looked after at home.

For each of these and other statements, respondent had to select his response from one of the following:

There's a lot in this/there's something in this/it's quite wrong

The ten statements differed quite widely in their references, but with one exception, the series produced changes in the direction of greater confidence. For instance, the series reduced the number who took the view that "Many of the mental hospitals in this country are just dumping grounds" (20% 'before' and 14% after).

From this set of results, the picture which emerges is one of a moderate but widely based increase in viewers' conficence that modern medical methods can cure mental illness· — an increase which occurs against a background of already considerable confidence.

Acceptance by Society of the Ex-Patient of the Mental Hospital or the 'Mental Out-Patient'

Questions were asked concerning informants' feeling towards people who are receiving treatment for mental illness or who have done so in the past. The questions also dealt with willingness to associate with such a person in various ways. In brief, the series produced only a small change which, nonetheless, was in the direction of increased acceptance. Details follow.

The first set of questions was about reaction to the people who, whilst still mixing freely with society, are in fact getting treatment for mental illness at an Out-Patients' Department of a General Hospital. Respondents were invited to agree or disagree with seventeen statements representing ways in which they might feel about this. (The patient referred to in these statements was supposed to have much the same education as the respondent, to 'seem all right' and to 'seem as pleasant as anyone else'). The seventeen statements and the reactions of respondents to them are given in Table 5 below.

From this it will be seen that as far as mental out-patients were concerned, the series appears to have increased only very slightly the number who said they wanted to help or who expressed interest in their well-being. At the same time, this feeling was already so general that there was really little that the series *could* have done.

TABLE 5

Feelings of acceptance or of rejection concerning the 'mental out-patient'

| Proportion Agreeing | | Statements Offered |
'Before' %	After %	
86	85	I'd feel sympathy for this person
89	90	I'd be glad he or she was getting treatment or help
87	90	I'd hope he'd get well quickly
76	80	I'd feel I wanted to help somehow
12	11	I'd feel a certain amount of fear
31	23	I'd be a bit uneasy
4	6	I'd feel a bit repelled by this person
30	34	I'd wonder what was going on under the surface
6	8	I'd never feel quite the same towards this person
21	19	I'd feel a bit strange and embarrassed in his presence
4	2	I'd feel I wanted to avoid this person
10	8	I would not like to be left alone with this person for long
21	19	I'd feel I couldn't rely on him or trust him as much as before
2	3	Somehow, I'd have less respect for him as a person
14	15	I'd feel it was unfair to the people who did not know about him
21	19	I'd feel that people ought to be warned in some way
15	14	I'd feel that he really ought to be kept in a mental hospital while ill and not left to mix freely with ordinary people

It reduced somewhat the number who said they'd feel 'a bit uneasy' but did only very little to reduce the proportion who felt that 'they could not rely on him as much as before' (1 in 5), or the number who felt that 'people ought to be warned about him' (1 in 5).

TABLE 6

Acceptance of the 'mental out-patient'

| Proportion saying 'YES' | | Questions Asked |
'Before' %	After %	
82	89	Would you feel quite willing to mix with such a person IN THE STREET OR IN THE SHOPS?
79	85	Would you feel quite willing TO LIVE NEXT DOOR to such a person?
76	81	Would you feel quite willing to WORK WITH such a person?
72	80	Would you feel quite willing to allow such a person to DROP IN ON YOU just as others do?
49	52	Would you feel quite willing to EMPLOY such a person?
7	7	Would you feel quite willing to allow this person to LOOK AFTER CHILDREN?

The results concerning association with this person in various ways were as in Table 6. (In the various questions asked, the person referred to could have been male or female.)

There was a small but well-spread increase in acceptance of this kind. Within this table the figure which is, perhaps, the most worth noting concerns willingness *to employ* 'this person' (about 50%), and it is specially worth noting that, despite the large margin for change, the program had very little effect. That only 7% would be willing to have 'this person' look after children may be understandable enough, and presumably the series did not set out to change this.

The same kind of question was put in relation to the *ex*-patient of the mental hospital — one who is now considered cured. Here too, he or she was supposed to have much the same education as the respondent, to 'seem all right' and to 'seem as pleasant as anyone else'.

T A B L E   7

Mixing with the ex-patient of the mental hospital

	Yes %	Not Sure %	No %	Statement Presented
	Percent Replying			
'Before'	93	5	2	Would you be quite willing to MIX WITH
After	96	4	0	this person IN THE STREET or IN SHOPS
'Before'	89	8	3	Would you be quite willing to WORK NEXT
After	92	6	2	TO such a person?
'Before'	87	9	4	Would you be quite willing to have this person
After	89	9	2	AS A NEXT-DOOR NEIGHBOUR?
'Before'	82	10	8	Would you be quite willing to have such a
After	87	10	3	person DROP IN ON YOU JUST AS OTHERS DO?
'Before'	74	16	10	Would you be quite willing to INTRODUCE
After	77	18	5	such a person TO YOUR CLOSE FRIENDS?
'Before'	64	23	13	Would you be quite willing to EMPLOY
After	67	22	11	such a person?
'Before'	50	32	18	Would you be quite willing to WORK FOR
After	59	28	13	such a person?
'Before'	45	21	34	Would you be quite willing to BECOME
After	46	28	26	FRIENDLY ENOUGH TO DISCUSS YOUR PERSONAL AFFAIRS WITH such a person?
'Before'	25	37	38	Would you be quite willing to HAVE such a
After	27	42	31	person IN AN IMPORTANT POSITION?
'Before'	19	40	41	Would you be quite willing to HAVE this
After	21	44	35	person MARRY SOMEONE CLOSELY RELATED TO YOU?
'Before'	15	38	47	Would you be quite willing to ALLOW such
After	20	36	44	a person TO LOOK AFTER CHILDREN (i.e., AS A BABY-SITTER, AS A NURSE-MAID, AS A TEACHER, and so on)?

For the report of results, the items in the 'degree of mixing' question-naire were put in order according to the number of people endorsing them and so they now form a scale of 'willingness to mix'. Thus at one end of the list, almost everyone would be willing to 'mix with this person in the street and 'shops', and at the other, only 1 in 5 would be willing to 'have him/her look after children'. Presumably many people do not really consider him/her fully cured. Perhaps as could be expected, people seem to be less unwilling to mix with the ex-patient of the mental hospital than they are with the person who, whilst in their midst (and whilst seeming to be all right) is receiving treatment (compare Tables 6 and 7).

Here, too, the apparent effect of the program was small, even where there was a large margin for change. All the same, the change which occurred was spread over just about the whole scale and was always in the direction of increased acceptance.

Attitude Towards Treatment for Mental Illness

Early in the session, subjects were asked what they, personally, would do if someone in their own family or someone known to them very well seemed to be developing a mental illness of some kind. The question is of course hypothetical and the distribution of answers cannot be regarded as giving a prediction of future action. The answers probably mirror the position at a level which is more intellectual than emotional — more a matter of knowing than of feeling or intending.

TABLE 8

What to do in cases of mental illness

Proportion Suggesting this 'Before' %	After %	Action Suggested by Subjects
37	34	*Non-Medical Action*
6	7	Seek advice of a lay kind (e.g. go to vicar, ask family) or personally advise
29	28	Look after them myself/at home
90	90	*Medical Type Treatment*
18	23	Advise them to seek medical treatment
51	49	Seek medical advice on their behalf
20	19	'Take early action' (with medical treatment in mind)
6	10	Support or urge treatment
17	20	Try for hospital or institutional treatment

Table 8 reveals little or no change in this respect produced by the program. Thus both 'before' and after the series, about 90% thought in terms of seeking medical help, though in this case there was very little room for change in the desired direction.

Later on there were questions about subjects' own feelings over the prospects of: entering a mental hospital; receiving outpatient treatment; having a brain operation. These questions too were distinctly hypothetical in nature, and their purpose was simply to gauge the 'climate of acceptance' as far as various kinds of treatment were concerned. This 'climate of acceptance' is, of course, different from 'approval' of a method or process or 'confidence that a particular treatment can do a patient good'. The question as put concerned the subject's feeling about the method being applied to *himself.* There was a small but well-spread increase in acceptance of this kind.

There was also a small increase in the proportion who said they 'wouldn't mind who knew' if they themselves were to undergo treatment for mental illness (22% ,before' and 30% after). When, however, it came to members of one's own family there was little or no change of this kind. See Table 9.

TABLE 9

Attitude towards others knowing of self or member of own family treated for mental illness

Statement Chosen	Self Treated		Someone in Family Treated	
	'Before'	After	'Before'	After
	%	%	%	%
I'd keep very quiet about it	25	23	32	31
I might tell a few people	53	49	46	45
I wouldn't care who knew about it	22	30	22	24

Summing up on 'attitude towards having treatment', it appears that whereas the series produced no change in the already very large proportion who, at a rational level, accept the idea of medical treatment for mental illness, there was a small increase in personal acceptance of it in relation to oneself, and a small increase in the number who would not care *who* knew if they themselves had such treatment.

Awareness of Mental Illness as a Social Problem

In the last broadcast in the series, mental illness was presented as one of our main social problems, and much was said to urge people to see it this way. An attempt was therefore made to find out the extent to which this effect had been produced. The attempt took this form: at the beginning of the test session, and before there was any indication at all that it was to be concerned with 'mental illness', subjects were asked to write down any of the things which in their opinion were the 'main social problems of today'. They were informed that as soon as they had finished doing this, they would be told why the question was being asked. The aim, of course, was to see if mental illness figured in their thinking as a social problem. On the results, it appears that the series increased the percentage thinking of mental illness in this way from 5% ('before') to 10% (after).

Attitudes Towards the Mentally Ill

In a sense, the whole of this report bears on attitude towards the mentally ill. In addition, however, a *direct* check was made with reference to some rather specific attitudes towards mental illness and the mentally ill. Here, subjects were free to agree or disagree with statements presented to them, or to indicate 'no opinion'. The statements, based on opinions set down by viewers who took part in an earlier study, [8] were of the following kind:

When a man's mind is ill, it's just like losing him altogether.
I feel I can't really be bothered with them.
I pity them.
Mental illness is just another illness and can be cured like any other illness.
Whenever I think of the mentally ill, I think how easily it might have been me.

There were 24 of these statements in all. The series appears to have produced changes in respect of many, but not all of them. Thus it appears to have reduced the proportion who feel disposed to reject the mentally ill as being 'unfit to mix with ordinary people' and who feel 'mental illness is best not talked about': it also reduced slightly the proportion (40%) who expressed feelings of wariness and suspicion about them (you 'never know what they're planning and it may be harmful'). Consistently, it built up somewhat the proportion who expressed feelings of pity or sympathy for the mentally ill (80% expressed feelings of sympathy 'before' and 89% after; 60% expressed *pity* 'before' and 68% after). It increased sharply the number who saw mental illness as 'no different from any other illness' (64% 'before' 76% after). There was also a slight increase in the proportion who felt·that 'they can't help themselves' (26% 'before' and 34% after). Interestingly, these changes went along with a slight increase in the number who saw the mentally ill as 'somewhat humorous'.

Since most of these changes are fairly small, too much weight must not be put upon them individually. Nonetheless, taken together they suggest a pattern of change of a fairly plausible kind. It is a pattern in which a reduction of the feeling that the mentally ill are 'different', goes along with a softening of feeling towards them and an increased insight into their condition. That there should have been a slight increase in the large proportion (40%) who thought of them as somewhat funny is not necessarily inconsistent with this: it could well be related to a reduction in their 'menacingness' and to an increase in 'familiarity' with them.

SOME COMMENTS ON THE FINDINGS

There is little in the way of comparative information to help us to evaluate the size of the changes apparently resulting from seeing programs in this series: so far, only three other programs have been studied in the same way. In comparison with these three, however, "The Hurt Mind" series comes out well: the apparent changes were practically all in the intended direction and quite a lot of them were moderate to large in extent.

Several general observations about these results should be made. One of them is that where the presentation of a point was made either in concrete terms or by confronting viewers with the patients themselves, the desired changes in attitude or knowledge tended to occur. In this category came the presentations of: leucotomy, electric shock treatment, ab-reaction; the effect of childhood surroundings'; 'depression as one of the mental illnesses'; 'occupational therapy as a means of diverting morbidity and developing self-confidence'; 'the availability of treatment at outpatient departments in general hospitals'. On the other hand, where the exposition was in verbal or in abstract form only, change in the desired direction tended *not* to occur. In this category were: the presentation of information about the causal significance of early habits of an inadequate kind, of anxiety, worry and guilt, of chemical deficiencies or imbalance, of heredity; purely verbal references to the different kinds of mental illness; information about the nature and the function of psycho-analysis and of some forms of psychotherapy. This does not prove that there is a causal relationship between the concrete form of presentation and a positive change, but the evidence is highly suggestive, and it may well lie behind the tendency (indicated by the results of this enquiry) for the public's awareness of ways of treating mental illness to swing somewhat away from psychological methods towards the more physical methods.

A second point of importance is that while there was but small margin for change on some issues, the margin was large and remained large on many other issues. Some of the more striking of these concern: the distinction which is made by the great majority between mental illness and insanity; the unwillingness of many to accept the 'ex-patient' in certain occupational and other roles; the generality of feeling that mental illness is something to keep fairly quiet about. Many more instances of this kind are to be found in the tables in this report. This is not to suggest that this series should or should not have produced a change with respect to any one of these aspects of mental illness. However, such information may prove useful for planning purposes in further broadcasts on one or another aspect of mental illness.

SUMMARY OF THE ENQUIRY

This enquiry into the effects of the television series "The Hurt Mind" was based upon the test room performances of 800 people whose decision to view or not to view had been made without foreknowledge of this inquiry. Special steps were taken to ensure a high degree of representativeness in the subjects and in their test results. The findings indicate that the series achieved a number of its objectives.

(1) It increased somewhat viewers' knowledge about mental illness, especially with respect to methods of treatment.

(2) There was a moderate but broadly based increase in viewers' confidence in the ability of medical men to cure mental illness; in this, there were appreciable increases in viewers' confidence in the usefulness of certain kinds of treatment, namely electric shock treatment, leucotomy, abreaction, group therapy.

(3) There was a small but well-spread increase in viewers' willingness to associate with the ex-patient or with the person who is at present receiving treatment for a mental illness, though the series did little to reduce the proportion who would be unwilling 'to employ' the ex-patient.

(4) There was a small increase in the large number who readily think in terms of 'medical treatment for mental illness', and a slight reduction in the large majority holding that treatment for mental illness is something to keep fairly quiet about.

(5) The series increased somewhat the public's feeling of sympathy and pity for the mentally ill, and produced also some increase in the public's insight into the condition of the mentally ill.

(6) The series increased from 5% (before) to 10% (after) the proportion actively aware of mental illness as a major social problem.

THE SOCIAL IMPACT OF TELEVISION

An introductory note

Section IV is concerned with the broad or global influence of television: its effects on such things as sporting attendances, sociable behaviour, family life, the use of leisure time, and so on. Its concern is thus different from that of Section III, which dealt with the effects of particular programs or series of programs.

Chapter 20 describes the growth of television in Britain and abroad and it presents the case for trying to learn the nature of television's impact on society. This is followed in Chapter 21 by a description of techniques which have been used for conducting research into the impact of TV. Chapters 22, 23 and 24 are reports of enquiries of this kind.

References in this Section to articles and books will be found in alphabetical order on pages 380-387.

[20]

Television's growth and the case for studying its social impact and other of its general effects.

THE PLAN OF THE CHAPTER

First in the United States and then in Britain, television ownership rapidly became widespread. In addition, the amount of time which families spent viewing was considerable. In these circumstances, it is not surprising that there should have been speculation about the impact on society of this new medium.

In this chapter are set out some basic facts about the spectacular spread of television in Britain and abroad, along with some of the published conjecture about its effects. From this, the chapter goes on to present the case for conducting research to determine what its effects actually were. The chapter ends with a descriptive enumeration of the ideas of viewers about television's effects upon themselves and others. This enumeration was developed from exploratory work as an aid for formulating realistic questions *for research* and it was used as such in two of the major enquiries reported in this section.

Against this general setting, but in the next chapter, there is a critical appraisal of the methods which have been used in this very difficult branch of research, along with suggestions for modified procedures.

THE GROWTH OF TELEVISION

In Britain

British television broadcasting began in 1936 from the B.B.C.'s transmitter at Alexandra Palace in London. It was the world's first television broadcasting service. At that time, programs were broadcast for about 13 hours each week and there were approximately 10,000 television receivers. Early growth was slow so that by 1939 the number of receivers had risen to only about 20,000[a] in spite of a substantial increase in the amount and the variety of the programs offered. Then, with the outbreak of war in that year, the service was closed down for nearly 7 years.

[a] Not all were necessarily licensed.

When transmission was resumed in June of 1946, growth in the number of television receivers was again very slow and by the end of 1949 only about 2% of the adult population of the United Kingdom had sets. Thereafter came a sharp increase in the rate of growth: 9% by 1951, 22% by 1953, 49% by 1956 and approximately 91% by the end of 1964. Table 1 gives the rate of growth year by year in terms of the percentage of adults who were viewers and in terms of the number of licensed television sets in the country.

TABLE 1.

Growth in TV reception in the United Kingdom

Year	% with a TV Set in the Home* at end of the year.		Number of TV Licences at *31st March* and total population	
(End of)	*All with Sets* **	*Receive I.T.A. as well as B.B.C.*	*All Licenses* (,000)	*Estimated Size of Population (incl. children)* (,000)†
				June each year
1936				
1947	0.2		15	49,571
1948	0.7		46	
1949	1.8		127	
1950	4.3		344	
1951	8.7		764	50,290
1952	14.0		1,449	50,431
1953	21.8		2,142	50,592
1954	30.6		3,249	50,765
1955	39.8	4.5	4,504	50,947
1956	49.4	19.7	4,740	51,184
1957	58.4	32.5	6,966	51,430
1958	65.0	45.0	8,090	51,652
1959	74.4	60.7	9,255	51,956
1960	81.8	71.9	10,470	52,352
1961	84.2	78.9	11,268	52,816
1962	87.4	83.7	11,834	53,341
1963	88.8	86.5	12,443	53,678
1964	90.8	88.0‡	12,885	54,066

* Figures provided by the Audience Research Department of the B.B.C.
** Prior to 1960, percentage figures are for adults (= 16 years and over). From 1960 onwards, they refer to all aged 5 years and over.
† Mid-year estimates, Monthly Digest of Statistics, May 1965, No. 233, HMSO, London. Figures for 1936 to 1950 not available on the same estimating bases as for 1951 to 1964. The figure for 1947 was taken from a 1951 estimate (Monthly Digest of Statistics).
‡ Figure estimated by writer from percentages 1955–63.

Until 1955, the B.B.C. had been the sole broadcaster of television programs in the United Kingdom. In September of that year, however, the Independent Television Authority began commercial broadcasting. At the

end of its first year about 5 % of the adult population were able to receive
I.T.A. broadcasts. By the end of 1960 the figure was approximately 72 %
and by the end of 1964 they could be received by approximately 88 %.

Transmitters and Coverage. Behind this great growth in television's reception was not only a growth in public demand for television but an
increase in the number of transmitting stations. Unlike radio, the range for
television transmitters was relatively limited, so that national coverage,
combined with the requirements of regional broadcasting, necessitated
the establishment of transmitters throughout the country.

The original transmitter at Alexandra Palace made programs available in an area in which about 24 % of the United Kingdom population
was living. In other words, if they had sets, these 24 % would have been
able to receive television programs. In 1949, a second transmitter was
opened at Sutton Coldfield in the Midlands, lifting the coverage figure
from 24 % to 42 %. In 1955, when the I.T.A. opened its first transmitter,

TABLE 2.

*Showing growth of transmitters and of coverage in the
United Kingdom*

Year	Number of main transmitting stations			% of population* living in areas in which television programs are available	
(end of)	*BBC*	*ITA*	*ALL*	*BBC*	*ITA*
1936	1		1	24	
1945	1		1	–	
1946	1		1	24	
1947	1		1	24	
1948	1		1	24	
1949	2		2	42	
1950	2		2	42	
1951	3		3	65	
1952	5		5	81	
1953	9		9	86	
1954	12		12	91	
1955	14	1	15	93	24
1956	15	4	19	97	59
1957	18	5	23	98	66
1958	21	7	28	99	76
1959	22	10	32	99	86
1960	22	11	33	99	88
1961	22	17	39	99	94
1962	22	18	40	99	97
1963	22	22	44	99	97
1964	22	22	44	99	97

* All population, all ages.
† In addition, the B.B.C. had (at the end of 1964), 26 relay stations.
– No transmissions during this period.

the B.B.C. had 14 main transmitting stations around the country and claimed a total coverage of 93%. By the end of 1964, the B.B.C.'s coverage was 99% and the number of its main transmitting stations was 22. At that time the I.T.A. had 22 stations and a coverage of 97% Table 2 gives details of this growth, year by year.

The growth of television in the different regions of the United Kingdom
As new transmitters brought to additional regions the possibility of receiving television programs, a fairly rapid growth in set ownership followed. Moreover, this rate of growth was remarkably similar from region to region. This may be seen from Table 3, which also indicates that by the end of 1963 many of the earlier regional differences in set ownership had either disappeared or been reduced very much indeed. Certainly these figures don't suggest that any one area is going to be specially resistant to television becoming near-universal in its homes.

TABLE 3.

Television's spread in the regions

Region	Percent with a TV set in the home, given by regions												
	1952	*53*	*54*	*55*	*56**	*57*	*58*	*59*	*1960*	*61*	*62*	*63*	*64*
South East (including London)	20	25	35	41	51	60	67	74	81	84	86	87	90
Midland	23	27	41	45	54	61	68	76	82	86	88	90	92
Northern	13	18	30	37	50	58	68	77	85	88	89	91	92
Western	6	9	19	28	43	53	63	73	80	84	86	88	89
Wales	7	12	30	36	46	54	63	76	83	87	89	90	92
Scotland	4	6	20	25	36	47	56	69	80	84	87	89	91
Northern Ireland	—	—	8	12	22	33	42	53	69	73	78	81	83

* 1956–64 figures are averages for the fourth quarter each year. Figures provided by the Audience Research Department of the BBC.

Television's growth in America
In the U.S.A., television got under way before the re-opening of the British television service and by the end of 1949 about 9% of homes had television sets in them. Ten years later the percentage had risen to 87% and by the end of 1963 to approximately 93%. At that time nearly 52 million of the country's 56 million homes had TV sets in them and there were 657 TV stations on the air. Over and above this, about 8 million homes had in them more than one TV set. The growth figures, year by year, are given in Table 4.

The very large number of transmitters in the United States of America is of course a function of the size of the country coupled with the limited reception area of a single TV station. The rate of the spread in ownership is the more remarkable for this.

The Social Impact of Television
TABLE 4

Showing growth in number of receivers and transmitters in the U.S.A.
(end of year)

Year	TV Set Ownership*			Year	TV Stations on the Air†		
	Homes with TV (,000)	*Secondary sets in Homes (,000)*	*% Homes with sets*		*Commercial*	*Educational Non-Commercial*	*All*
31st Dec.				31st Dec.			
1941	–	–	–	1941	3		3
2	–	–	–	2	4		4
3	–	–	–	3	4		4
4	–	–	–	4	6		6
5	8	–	.02	5	6		6
6	14	–	.04	6	7		7
7	172	1	.4	7	17		17
8	940	10	2.3	8	50		50
9	3,875	50	9.0	9	97		97
1950	10,320	165	23.5	1950	107		107
1	15,300	315	34.2	1	108		108
2	20,400	505	44.7	2	125	2	125
3	26,000	800	55.7	3	349	10	331
4	30,700	1,000	64.5	4	411	10	421
5	34,900	1,620	71.8	5	442	16	458
6	38,900	2,500	78.5	6	471	22	493
7	41,924‡	3,668	83.2	7	492	27	519
8	43,950	4.550	85.9	8	509	35	544
9	45,750	5,950	87.1	9	517	45	562
1960	47,200	6,700	88.8	1960	530	52	582
1	48,855‡	7,520‡	90.0	1	543	62	605
2	50,300	8,650	91.3	2	564	76	640
3	51,600	10,075	92.3	3	563	82	645
4**˙	53,100	11,400	93,5	4	572	99	671

* Set figures based on data provided by National Broadcasting Company, U.S.A.
† Figures drawn from F.C.C. sources. These include a number of satellite and booster stations (41 at the end of 1963).
– Figures not available.
‡ Advertising Research Foundation – Census.
** Preliminary figures.

Television's growth in other countries
In Table 5 are listed those countries with a population of five million or more, where regular TV broadcasting had begun by 1963. It gives the number of television sets per thousand members of the population (all ages) for each of four well-spaced years (in order to bring out growth patterns). 'Sets per 1,000 members of the population' is, it should be noted, very different from 'sets per 1,000 *families*': in fact, the American figure of

TABLE 5

*Number of receivers per 1000 population in countries with
5 million population or more and where there was regular TV
broadcasting by 1963*

Name of Country	Date when Regular TV Broadcasting Began (1)	No. of Receivers per 1000 People				Estimated Population in 1963 (in millions) (6)
		1953 (2)	1958 (3)	1960 (4)	1963 (5)	
Algeria	1956	—	2	5	6	10.00
Argentina	1951	2*	11	21	42	20.80
Australia	1956	—	46	108	146	10.55
Austria	1957	0.01*	7	27	56	7.07
Belgium	1953	2	25	68	109	9.25
Brazil	1952	2	13	18	20	70.00
Bulgaria	1958	0.03†	0.06	0.6	3	8.00
Cambodia	1962	—	—	0.06	0.06	5.00
Canada	1952	40	194	218	245	18.50
Chile	1959	—	—	0.06	0.5	8.00
Columbia	1954	1*	10	11	14	15.00
Cuba	1950	14	49	74		6.91
Czechoslovakia	1954	0.3*	24	58	100	13.80
Egypt. U.A.R.	1960	—	—	2	7	26.00
France	1949	1	22	41	75	45.73
Federal Republic of *Germany*	1952	0.2	39	83	139	56.75
Eastern Germany	1952	0.1*	18	60	90	17.08
Great Britain	1936	58	171	211	238	53.68
Hungary	1958	0.02*	2	10	27	10.00
Iran	1958	—	0.1	2	3	20.89
Iraq	1956	—	1	5	7	7.00
Italy	1954	2*	22	43	70	51.00
Japan	1953	0.1	17	64	140	94.93
Kenya	1962	—	—	—	1	7.29
Korea Republic	1956	—	0.1	0.3	1	24.99
Mexico	1951	2	6	19	28	36.90
Morocco	1962	—	—	—	0.4	10.00
Netherlands	1953	1	35	69	114	11.73
Nigeria	1959	—	—	0.03	0.1	45.00
China, P.R.	1958	—	—	0.03	0.03	650.00
Peru	1958	—	0.4	3	7	11.00
Philippines	1953	0.2*	0.7	1.4	6	27.45
Poland	1954	0.01†	3	14	33	30.23
Portugal	1957	—	2	5	12	9.00
Rumania	1957	0.01†	0.9	3	6	18.30
Spain	1956	—	1.7‡	8	26	30.00
Sweden	1956	0.1	33	137	220	7.54

Table 5 (Continued)

Name of Country	Date when Regular TV Broadcasting Began (1)	No. of Receivers per 1000 People				Estimated Population in 1963 (in millions) (6)
		1953 (2)	1958 (3)	1960 (4)	1963 (5)	
Switzerland	1958	0.2	10	24	46	5.43
Taiwan (For- mosa)	1962	–	–	0.01	0.4	11.21
Thailand	1955	–	1	3	6	24.60
Uganda	1963	–	–	–	0.04	6.52
U.S.A.	1941	169	284	310	332	186.00
U.S.S.R.	1947	1	12	19	32	216.00
Venezuela	1952	6‡	31	37	60	7.52
Yugoslavia	1958	–	0.4	1	6	18.54

Notes

Column (1) from "Statistics on Radio and Television 1950–1960",
    U.N.S.E.C.O., Table 7, pages 74–76, 1963. In several cases, information was
    provided by embassies in London.
Columns (2), (3) and (4) from "Statistics on Radio and Television 1950–1960",
    U.N.E.S.C.O., Table 8, pages 77–79, 1963.
Columns (5) and (6) from "World Communications", U.N.E.S.C.O., 1964.
* † ‡ = indicate 1954, 1955 and 1957 figures respectively.
–   = indicates no receivers.
Blank = no information available.

332 for 1963 is equivalent to 93 % of all families having a TV set; the figure of 238 for the United Kingdom is equivalent to a family penetration
figure of over 95 %
    There are, of course, many countries where regular television broadcast-
ing had not started by 1963 or where the viewer population is as yet relatively small[b]. Nonetheless, the figures in Table 5 give some indication of
the worldwide penetration of television and of its almost universally high
rate of growth wherever it has started.

THE COMPOSITION OF THE TV-OWNING POPULATION

In the United Kingdom
The earliest buyers of television sets in the United Kingdom were by no
means a cross-section of the whole population. They were, of course,
drawn from the London region alone, but one of the other differences between viewers and non-viewers was in terms of family composition. Thus

[b] It was reported in "World Radio and TV Handbook" for 1964 that 150 million
    of the world's 3,000 million people were viewers. This indicates both tremend-
    ous growth and considerable scope for *further* growth.

in 1950, viewing families were somewhat larger than non-viewing families and had in them more children aged 5–15 years and fewer adults aged 55 or more. The difference with respect to children under five was quite large amongst the middle classes though it did not appear to occur amongst working class families. In both classes, the tendency for viewing families to have fewer older people in them was appreciable, though it was quite marked in the working class.

TABLE 6

Early buyers in terms of family size and composition†

Age Group	Composition of Average Family		Average for Middle Class		Average for Working Class	
	Viewers	Controls*	Viewers	Controls	Viewers	Controls
0– 4⎱	.35⎱	.34⎱	.88	.67	.73	.76
5–15⎰	.50⎰ .85	.39⎰ .73				
16–24	.31 .31	.32 .32	.27	.23	.37	.39
25–34⎫	.49⎫	.47⎫				
35–44⎬	.71⎬1.74	.53⎬1.47	1.75	1.59	1.72	1.39
45–54⎭	.54⎭	.47⎭				
55–64⎱	.30⎱	.39⎱				
65+ ⎰	.23⎰ .53	.35⎰.74	.49	.59	.59	.85
Total Family	3.43	3.26	3.39	3.08	3.41	3.39

† Table drawn from the B.B.C.'s "Television Enquiry (1950)", Part II.
* The controls were (for certain technical resons) all next-door neighbours of the viewer sample. Hence the differences between viewers and non-viewers are possibly greater than those indicated here.

TABLE 7

Showing the distribution of viewers in terms of income level†

Year Ending	% With Sets	Income level* of the Owner of the Set			
		Top 12%	Next 20%	Lower 68%	All
1947	0.2	48	27	25	100
1948	0.7	41	32	27	100
1949	1.8	34	32	34	100
1950	4.3	28	32	40	100
1951	8.7	24	33	43	100
1952	14.0	22	33	45	100
1953	21.8	19	29	52	100
1954	30.6	16	25	59	100
1955	39.8	14	24	62	100

† Parts of the data in this table were calculated from one presented by Emmett on p. 294 in his "The Television Audience in the United Kingdom" [273].
* Top 12% were those who, in 1954 terms, earned over £15 per week; the next 20% were earning between £10 and £15 a week; the lower 68% were earning less than £10 per week.

However, the really large difference between the early viewers and the non-viewers was in terms of income level, as illustrated in Table 7. Thus in 1949 some 34% of viewers were drawn from the top 12% of the population in terms of income level and this equalled the number coming from the lower 68%. In other words, viewers were over-represented by people in the upper income levels and they were markedly under-represented by those in the lower income levels.

However in the course of the next few years, this situation rapidly changed. By 1954, when about a third of the adults in the country were viewers, only 16% of viewers came from that upper 12%. Some of the other facts about the situation in 1954 are given in Table 8.

TABLE 8

Showing differences between viewers and non-viewers at the beginning of 1954*

Occupational Level	View-ers %	Sound Only %	All %	Age of Ceasing Full-Time Education	View-ers %	Sound Only %	All %
Professional, administrative,				18 or over	5	4	4
				16 − 18	20	18	19
executive	8	5	6	Less than 16	74	78	77
Highly skilled	12	9	10	Unknown	1	0	0
Skilled	29	23	24				
Moderately skilled	20	21	21	*Further Education*			
Semi-skilled	17	20	19	*or Training*			
Unskilled	10	16	15	Yes	30	35	34
Unclassified	4	6	5	No	70	65	66
				Mean number of persons per household			
Weekly Income				0− 4 years	0.20	0.22	.22
Over £25	5	1	2	5 − 15 years	0.70	0.50	.55
£15 − £25	13	7	9	16 − 25 years	0.33	0.33	.33
£10 − £15	26	17	19	26 − 45 years	1.18	0.88	.96
£5 − £10	42	47	46	46 − 65 years	0.78	0.91	.93
£5	9	20	17	66+ years	0.23	0.33	.31
Not known	5	8	7	All	3.42	3.17	3.30

* Tables based upon figures in Emmett's "The Television Audience in the United Kingdom". [273]

Though it is clear from Table 8 that in 1954 there were still differences between viewers, non-viewers and the general population, notably in terms of family composition, the overwhelming indication of Table 8 is that by 1954 television had spread on a large scale into many different sections of society. It was this situation or the tendency towards it, which gave such momentum to the speculation of the times about what television was doing to the people of Britain.

In America

In America, the study of differences between viewers and the rest of the population presented a picture very similar to that found in the United Kingdom. Thus the 6% found by the Market Research Corporation to have TV sets in September 1949 had the following characteristics: they were under-represented by the least well-off quarter of the population and by those with only Grade School education; they were under-represented by families of only 1 or 2 persons and by those with no children; they were sharply under-represented by housewives aged 45 and over. In addition, those with sets were drawn almost completely from towns of 500,000 or

TABLE 9

Showing changes year by year, in the degree of representativeness of viewers*

	Sept. 1949 (6%)	July 1951 (27%)	July 1953 (49%)	July 1955 (68%)	July 1956 (76%)
Income					
Upper fourth	7	33	58	81	87
Next fourth	7	32	55	76	85
Next fourth	6	28	50	69	76
Lowest fourth	3	18	32	48	58
Education					
Grade School	4	23	43	62	70
High School	7	34	57	75	83
College	6	24	48	73	79
Family Size					
1 & 2 members	4	19	38	59	69
3 members	6	30	52	73	81
4 & 5 members	7	35	58	78	85
6 & more members	6	27	53	66	74
Age of Housewife					
Under 35 years	8	36	58	75	82
35 – 44 years	8	37	60	74	82
45 years & over	3	19	40	61	70
Presence of Children					
5 years & under	7	36	54	75	81
6 – 12 years	7	35	56	76	83
13 – 20 years	6	28	49	71	78
No children	4	21	37	61	70
City Size					
Farm	–	7	23	43	54
Under 2,500	–	9	26	56	67
2,500 – 50,000	–	16	31	53	65
50,000 – 500,000	–	28	51	75	82
500,000 & over	14	53	77	87	89

* Part of a table presented by Bogart in "The Age of Television" page 15 [241] and based on data from the Market Research Corporation in America.

more people. Table 9 presents details for 1949 and for some subsequent years[d].

With the spread of television facilities during the next seven years, the viewer figures for smaller towns and for farming communities came to resemble much more those for the larger towns, though even in 1956 the farming communities were appreciably under-represented amongst the nation's viewers. The extent of some of the other early differences had also been reduced over time, though in mid-1956, when over 70% had sets in the home, there were still differences between viewers and the population as a whole.

Table 10, which refers to American housewives in 1954[e], confirms the nature of the differences presented in Table 9 and presents several more. Thus at that time rather more viewers than non-viewers owned their homes, owned an automobile, were in employment outside of the home, and were white.

TABLE 10

Some other differences between viewers and non-viewers: 1954*

	TV Homes %	Non-TV Homes %
Children under 18 years	60	48
Under $3,000 income	20	53
Professional, semi-professional, managerial occupation (head of house)	23	14
Grade school education or less (housewife)	24	39
Own automobile	77	63
Own home	58	51
Live in single-family dwelling	63	72
Metropolitan area	77	37
55 years and older (housewife)	18	28
Married (housewife)	80	71
Employed outside the house (housewife)	35	28
White	93	84

* Figures from Bogart, "The Age of Television" [241], drawn originally from a study by W. R. Simmons and Associates for the National Broadcasting Company, 1954.

A New Haven study in 1952 by Parker, Barry and Smythe indicated that when differences in social class were held constant, Catholics and Jews had a higher rate of TV set ownership than had Protestants. The difference was particularly noticeable at the upper and upper middle social levels.

[d] As reported by Bogart in "The Age of Television", pp. 14–15 (241)
[e] As presented by Bogart in "The Age of Television", p. 18 [241].

With passing time and with the eventual rise of the television penetration figure to 93% by the end of 1963, many of the above differences
between viewers and the total population inevitably became less and
tended to disappear. In the present context, however, the point that matters most is that only a few years after the start of television in America,
and certainly by the time that 20% had sets, TV ownership was a feature
of just about all sectors of the American society. In this respect, the situation was very much like that in the United Kingdom.

THE AMOUNT OF VIEWING BEING DONE

Speculation about the effects of television did of course spring in large
part, too, from the fact that people in all walks of life were giving the
screen so much of their time.

The total amount of this allocation of time is indicated in Table 11.
It refers to the viewing population in the United Kingdom and it gives
the estimated number of hours per week which owner-viewers spent
watching TV.

TABLE 11

Estimates of actual and potential exposure*
to TV programmes per week

Year† (ending 31st Dec.)	Average Hours Viewed Per Week.			Average Hours Transmitted Per Week‡	
	Morning till 7 p.m.	*Evening from 7 p.m.*	*All Day*	*B.B.C.*	*I.T.V.*
	(Hrs.)	(Hrs.)	(Hrs.)		
1953	2.3	11.1	13.4	39	—
1954	2.5	11.6	14.1	43	—
1955	2.1	12.7	14.8	47	50
1956	2.3	13.2	15.5	52	50
1957	3.2	12.5	15.7	58	62
1958	4.1	12.9	17.0	64	71
1959	4.2	14.1	18.3	64	74

† From 1953–9, figures limited to U.K. adults (= 16 yrs. and over).
‡ Average number of hours when TV programs are available, based on sample
of weeks throughout year.
* Estimates based on BBC figures for all programs broadcast in a sample of
weeks throughout each year.

The data in Table 11 make it clear that viewing by those with sets was
very heavy even in 1953: an average of 13.4 hours per week by adults.
It also shows that there has been a distinct tendency for the amount of
it to increase over the years, up to 1959. The available evidence relating
to the period since then suggests that the 1959 level has been at least

maintained.[f]. The increase shown in Table 11 no doubt has been assisted by the increase in the hours of TV broadcasting, but whatever the reasons, the fact of the matter is that viewing was very heavy from the early years of television's growth and has remained so.

Reporting on a B.B.C. enquiry conducted in 1954, Emmett [273] presented further evidence of the degree to which television was being used. He reported among other things that the average evening rate of television consumption per viewer was two programs out of every five and that it was normal for between 60% and 80% of owner-viewers to see at least something in the course of the evening.

In the same report Emmett gave details for 1953, 1954 and 1955 of variations in set usage in the four quarters of the year. This information, presented in Table 12, shows a fall during the summer months in the percentage viewing the average evening program, but the table's general indication is that heavy viewing goes on throughout the year.

TABLE 12

*Showing quarterly averages amongst the adult television public**

		Average Daytime TV Audience	Average Evening TV Audience
January–March	1953	10.2	41.6
April–June	1953	9.8	35.9
July–September	1953	9.6	36.9
October–December	1953	9.9	41.7
January–March	1954	9.9	45.0
April–June	1954	10.2	38.7
July–September	1954	8.7	36.9
October–December	1954	9.7	41.6
January–March	1955	10.0	43.8
April–June	1955	7.6	36.1
July–September	1955	6.4	30.0
October–December	1955	8.4	36.6

* Table as presented on page 300 in "The Television Audience in the United Kingdom", B. P. Emmett, 1956 [273].

[f] The following yearly averages were calculated by the writer from data provided by the Audience Research Department of the BBC. They represent average time devoted to viewing each week out of a standard 47 hours made up as follows: 2 to 5 p.m. on Saturday; 3 to 5 p.m. on Sunday; 5 to 11 p.m. on all seven days of the week. They relate to the U.K. viewer population aged 5 and over.

> 1961 . . . . 14.5 hours (out of 47)
> 1963 . . . . 14.5 hours (out of 47)
> 1964 . . . . 14.4 hours (out of 47).

If we base these averages on the whole 60+ hours available (since 1960) to any one viewer, they would convert in all cases to over 18 hours.

In America, the position as presented by Bogart through the following Nielsen figures (Table 13) was also one of massive viewing. (It must be noted that the figures given are the averages for TV homes rather than for individual viewers and so are not directly comparable with the figures in Table 11. Also, of course, they are for an average day, whilst those in Table 11 are for a whole week.) The Nielsen data suggest a slight increase, in the long-term, in the amount of viewing done. Another set of American findings dealing with a single town (New Brunswick) and reported by Cunningham and Walsh, gave levels of evening viewing for individuals and these are similar to those for the United Kingdom.

TABLE 13

Average hours of daily TV viewing per TV home

	Hours*		Hours*
1950	4.5	1954	4.8
1951	4.7	1955	4.9
1952	4.8	1956	5.0
1953	4.7	1957	5.1

* Source: A.C. Nielsen, Co., through Bogart [241].

PUBLISHED CONJECTURE ABOUT WHAT TV WAS DOING TO PEOPLE

To sum up on the foregoing: such was the growth of television and the amount of time given to it in all sectors of society that conjecture about its effects was inevitable.

One major source of complaint and of warning was the British sports promoter. Warnings referred particularly to boxing, football, dog racing, motor racing, and they appear to have arisen from poor attendances at local sporting functions, backed by the experiences or impressions of American promoters in the period of television's growth in America. Some sports promoters in Britain tended for a time to restrict or to rule out altogether the televising of sporting events under their control. One of them is reported to have commented publicly to the effect: "Television is the number one menace. I have decided never to allow the televising of my big fights."

Cinema attendances fell drastically in the period of television's growth and television alone was named the cause by many in the cinema industry. With a fall-off in the public's use of transport in the evenings, a Chairman of the London Transport Executive was reported in the press as saying: "We can't persuade people to come into town as they used to. Television is the major criminal...."

It was widely claimed and publicly stated that television was interfering with homework. An alleged 22% fall-off in attendances at adult educational classes in London was also credited to television and there was a published claim that it was responsible for the closing of village halls and of literary societies. It was also suggested through the mass media that television was drawing people away from election meetings, cutting down on the total amount of gambling and, it seemed, "boosting the biscuit trade". At its door too was laid reduced attendance at branch meetings of trade unions.

During the television growth of 1953, seaside resorts had a rather hard time and a Brighton official was reported as stating that thousands of people were spending their money on television sets. He was reported as going on to say: "Every town is the same. The buying of television sets has been the terror of us all".

Publicans were reported as saying that television was a threat to their trade and that viewers were, instead, buying bottled beer to drink at home. One reported that even putting a set in the bar didn't help because customers watched the set instead of drinking up. There was a press statement as well to the effect that miners in Nottinghamshire had forsaken an age old custom of having a pint of bitter and a chat with friends when the underground shifts were over.

Wherever there was change, television seemed to many of those who made public statements to be the obvious and logical cause. There was a fairly marked tendency, too, to name it as the *only* cause. But was it the only cause? Were there cases where it was not a cause at all? And how much strategy and policy and fear were mixed up in the various published claims? At that time, however, there was little to guide opinion beyond the seemingly obvious, and the temptation to blame television, that growing and absorbing new medium, must have been very difficult to withstand.

Many of the public statements about television referred to its power for good or for evil. Some of these presented it as offering culture and learning to vast audiences, and a popular broadcaster talked of the "whole vast untapped future of a wonderful invention". Other optimistic speakers saw it as re-establishing the family and making of the home a more pleasant and enticing place. In the same vein, a Deputy Postmaster General was reported as expressing his confidence that British character was quite strong enough to be able to drag itself away from a television set and not to be mastered by it.

Not all were as optimistic, however, and a church leader warned: "It would be foolish to deny that television could be used for evil as well as good, and like any other new invention, it has brought with it possible dangers..." Another churchman went much further, saying: "Television is potentially one of the world's greatest dangers". There was a statement too about bringing "the demoralizing influences of the music hall right into the home".

In this same foreboding mood, fears were expressed publicly that television would kill people's interests, dull their initiative and make them generally lazy and inert. There were serious warnings that television would impair imaginative and creative activities, and dull the corporate character of family life. A prominent surgeon said that universal television would mean subjecting all to "the lowest common level of intelligence — that of the average cackling studio audience".

THE CASE FOR CONDUCTING RESEARCH INTO TELEVISION'S EFFECTS

Conjecture of this kind invited research. The immensity of the phenomenon out of which the conjecture sprang established a very real case for that research. Certainly mere conjecture and speculation about such important matters was not enough. If television was affecting society, particularly in any negative ways, it was essential that the facts of the matter be established as quickly as possible. And mere conjecture, however sensible its originator may seem, is no substitute for empirically established fact. This, of course, applies today in just the same way as it did then: if television is changing its viewers, it is highly desirable that the public and those who control television should be aware of the nature and the extent of these changes and of precisely how they come about. Such information seems to the writer to be essential in any attempt to control the television medium in the interests of society.

This is the simple and obvious case for conducting studies of the general effects of television — social, psychological, economic or physical. It is a case which has already motivated a great deal of research in America and elsewhere. It is a case which exists still.

THE SELECTION OF APPROPRIATE ISSUES FOR RESEARCH

Publicised conjecture as a guide for selecting research topics

Research into television's effects may indeed be focused upon publicised conjectures of the kind set out in this chapter. Thus the research may perhaps be made to deal with: television's effects upon attendance at sporting events, literary societies, union meetings, the cinema; television's effects on beer drinking and on gambling; its effects on the general level of morality, or of imaginative activity; its effects upon adult education. Publicised conjecture may in fact be a source of important questions for research into television's effects. At the same time, publicised conjecture has some dangerous limitations in this respect. The most general of these is that in all probability such conjecture will not provide as realistic and as complete a guide for question formulation as is available and necessary. In the first place the conjectures that get publicity may well have been selected and processed by the newsman, and inevitably the more striking, and the more controversial will have tended to get a degree of precedence over others. Apart from this, there is a real danger that some of the public utterances concerned are at least tinged with emotion or with a desire to find a scapegoat or with vested interest of some kind. A more serious limitation to publicised conjecture (as a source of questions for research) is that many of the people who pronounced public judgement on television were not themselves owners of TV sets and it is hard to see how such people could really know what they were talking about. As is often the case, many who were called experts were in this position. Indeed, the writer has for a long time found it particularly interesting to note the differences between the conjectures of the so-called experts and the conjectures of the viewers themselves.

However, the point that needs particularly to be made here is that the formulation of questions for research ought not to be based upon publicised conjecture alone. In all probability the latter is neither wide enough nor wise enough to be used as a sole source.

The ideas of viewers themselves as guides to what should be studied

A major and fruitful source of ideas which may be used *along with other sources* in formulating questions for research, consists of the ideas of the viewers themselves. Such ideas have the advantage of being grounded in real experience. Properly elicited, they tend to be realistically wide and ranging in the total spread of their points of reference. Let us be quite clear however that they cannot be regarded as providing *facts* about television's effects: they are simply *ideas* and as such they are part of the necessary raw material for the formulation of questions to be investigated through rigorous research procedures.

The collection and grouping of such ideas has in fact been carried out by the writer as part of the preparation for research described in this book. Details of the methods used and of the results derived are given in the Appendix to this chapter.

A Combination of Sources

At the same time, it would be wrong to base the formulation of research topics *solely* upon viewer ideas about what television was doing to them, for certainly it is conceivable that viewers could be undergoing changes of which they were themselves quite unaware. Sound practice requires that the selection of topics for research be based jointly upon at least the three sources set out below.

(1) The leads and suggestions available from past research (much of this being American.)
(2) Conjecture presented through the mass media or in general circulation (some of which has been presented in this chapter.)
(3) The ideas of a large number of viewers and, for contrast, of some non-viewers.

All three of these sources were used in the formulation of research topics for the two major enquiries reported in Chapters 23 and 24 in this Section.

COLLECTING AND CLASSIFYING THE IDEAS OF VIEWERS (AND OF SOME NON-VIEWERS) ABOUT THE EFFECTS OF TELEVISION

METHODS USED FOR COLLECTING IDEAS

Ideas were collected in a number of different ways.

(a) Large groups of viewers, 25 in each group, met on BBC premises on different evenings. They were drawn from the general population and the invitation system used to recruit them had led to their being broadly similar to the general population in terms of occupational level, age and sex. They met in Broadcasting House and they knew in advance that they would be required to give their opinions as to what the effects of television were. They spent the first 10 minutes (before the start of discussion) writing down their ideas in order to facilitate their later offering of ideas for discussion and as a precaution against one or another important idea not coming up for discussion. Then came the discussion itself. Into this the Chairman did not intrude as a discussant or to offer an opinion of any kind. He limited himself: to seeing that one point was discussed at a time; to asking for 'anything else' before requesting a 'next point'; to seeing that all members of the group took part. Discussion lasted for over an hour; it was vigorous and highly productive of ideas. It was recorded verbatim. On analysis of the results from the fourth and fifth sessions, it was fairly clear that these had added relatively little to what had come out of the first three sessions and so this procedure was then discontinued. The number of people offering ideas through the five sessions was about 100.

(b) In addition, discussions were held with 16 different family groups, in their homes, after an earlier indication to them of what the discussion would be about, namely television's effect on *their own family members*.

(c) Thirdly, letters were sent to 300 viewers, all of them reserve members of the BBC viewing panel, asking them to set down what they thought television was doing *to them*. In addition, 100 non-viewers on the BBC listening panel were asked for their opinions about what television was doing to viewers. 82% of the 400 replied, giving their ideas.

The many ideas of viewers, gathered in the way described in *(a)*, *(b)* and *(c)* above, were content analysed and found to yield over 40 fairly distinct ideas about what television was doing. These are set out below, under five broad headings:

I.   Relationships with others, with special reference to family life, to visiting, and to general sociability.
II. Interests and state of mind.
III. Education and schooling.
IV. Morals and manners.
V.   Physical well-being.

These ideas, along with others from the literature of research and from press and other public statements, were highly influential in the formulation of the major studies reported in this section, namely: 'The Effects of Television Upon the Interests and the Initiative of Adult Viewers' and 'The Effects of Television Upon Family Life and Upon Sociable Behaviour'.

Group I

IDEAS ABOUT TELEVISION'S EFFECTS UPON RELATIONSHIPS WITH OTHERS, WITH SPECIAL REFERENCE TO FAMILY LIFE, VISITING AND GENERAL SOCIABILITY

Television Promotes Family Life

It brings the family together in the home
This idea was offered by many viewers, with some arguing as follows: 'father comes straight home now without lingering at the pub, and he doesn't go out again after dinner'; parents now stay together at home, whereas before TV, they sometimes went out separately; "the young people are drawn off the streets and away from cinema"; "we do less visiting now"; TV makes it unnecessary to go out for entertainment; "home is now a good place to be in" because it has some real entertainment in it.

It makes the family more united
Arguments for and against this idea were raised. Suggestions that there was *increased* unity involved the following kinds of argument: it brings the family together in the home and "they are having enjoyment together"; children are not out at night so much now, so that parents worry less about juvenile deliquency; the husband and the children often have to pitch in with the household chores in order to get them done in time to watch television programs; since the program is seen by all, "the whole family has a common topic of conversation afterwards"; it may make their interests more similar; it reduces irritability and relaxes members of the family;

parents have a better hold over their children (i.e., because of the bargaining power given them by their possession of the set); "mother is now a better cook" (due to programs about cooking).

Others, however, held that television produces friction and discord in the family: the husband and other members of the family may leave the housewife to finish the chores while they sit down to view; the children are annoyed with parents when they (the children) are not allowed to stay up to view; parents sometimes differ over what the child can and can't be allowed to view; the housewife or the husband may neglect household jobs (or the children) to view; sometimes, when the home is small or when only one room is heated, there may be disagreement about whether the set should or should not be on; where there is interference with someone's hobby or studies, there could be friction; persons disturbing viewers are told to "Shush"; the 'shush habit' can restrict conversation within the family for a large part of the evening, and "there is not much time for talk after the service closes down"; the new centre of the family is the TV set and members of the family become impersonal to each other, "like people in a cinema"; "viewing goes on in the half-darkness"; TV cuts out self entertainment in the family; TV breaks up routine in the home, viewers often rushing to get things done or leaving them undone.

TV produces co-operation between members of the family in getting household jobs done

Arguments to this effect were: "We all pitch in with the odd jobs so that we can all go in together and enjoy the programs without someone being left out"; "my two children work together to get their jobs done in time"; "I'm dashing about doing the washing up and ironing so that the wife can sit down with me to see it". Some, however, claimed there was all too little co-operation and that this, in itself, became a source of friction.

The interests of members of the family become more alike as time passes

This suggestion is based on claims to the effect: that television interferes with the interests and activities of anyone standing out from the viewing group, tending strongly to draw him to the set; that the topics featured in television programs lead to the growth of interest in these, at the expense of areas of interests *not* so featured.

It helps to unify the standards of family members

This suggestion rests on the claim that television offers, through its programs, the one set of morals, values, and ideas to the whole family.

TV makes for common experiences and common thinking in the family

There were claims to the effect that television provides a common experience for the whole family and that this leads to a similarity in thought and in action. It also appears from comments that it may sometimes be difficult, particularly in small homes, for anyone to stay outside of this common experience ("We keep the light on so that those who don't like the program can do other things").

TV makes members of the family less interested in each other

With television accepted as the new centre of attraction, members of the family are said by some to find less of interest in other members of the family, especially as (it was felt) television reduced the individuality of the things that family members used to do.

The house is now a quieter place with adults and children silenced by television

Other ideas

Television interferes with household activities. Family members have a warmer feeling for each other. Married couples spend more time together. The breadwinner gets home earlier. Routine in the home is broken. A good television program can form the basis of—or lead to—a discussion of a knowledgeable kind.

Television Affects Sociability

Television has altered the amount of visiting done

There were numerous claims to the effect that non-viewers call on viewers to see programs, though some held that this was temporary and would stop when more people got sets. On the other hand viewers claimed that they went visiting less, preferring to stay at home and watch television.

Television has reduced the amount of entertainment provided by viewers (as Hosts)

Claims implying this idea varied. Some said that viewers insist that guests simply sit and view and that conversation is discouraged. Others said, of entertaining their guests, that they now "let the telly do it for them". Some viewers admitted that they resented the arrival of visitors when viewing, and several said they refused to answer the door or the telephone when a good program was on.

Television makes people less sociable in their day-to-day activities

Some opposed this view on the grounds that "television provides topics for conversation at work next day" or that "when neighbours call to see a program you have at last broken the ice with them". Those claiming a reduction in sociability argued: that there was less attendance at social functions, at pubs and at clubs; that there was less going out; that people mixed less in crowds; that when they have television, people don't need social outlets so much.

Television helps in the growth of nationalism

It is held by some that "the nation is being drawn together" by participation (through television) in national events such as the Coronation, Wimbledon lawn tennis, Test cricket.

Group II

IDEAS ABOUT TELEVISION'S EFFECTS UPON INTERESTS AND STATES OF MIND
Television Reduces Interests

Viewers' claims were frequently to the effect that television had caused them to lose interest in the things to which they had formerly been drawn and about which their behaviour had been oriented. Their references were made with respect to a wide variety of interests: cinema going, attendance at sporting events, reading books or newspapers, hobbies, woodwork, pub and club attendances, playing of sports, going out, sewing, library membership, odd jobs about the home, theatre going. Moreover, their admissions tended not to be accompanied by evidence of regret. Some held that the interests were not lost — "it's just that television is a greater attraction". Nonetheless comments suggested that the diversion was of an enduring kind, and two television repairmen agreed that viewers were "simply lost" when their sets were out of order.

On the other hand, viewers not infrequently claimed that television had introduced them to new and interesting things with which they would not otherwise have had experience.

Some interests got special mention as being affected in one way or another and details follow.

Television reduces cinema-going

This was the most frequently mentioned single interest. Some said that they don't go at all now, and others that television had made them more selective. A few held that in their cases there was a return to the cinema after the first six months and some others that paying for the television set keeps people too poor to be able to afford cinema-going as much as before. Other explanations of reduced cinema attendance were of the following kinds: "television is *real* entertainment"; "we have to dress up to go to the cinema"; "we have to go out in bad weather for the cinema"; "often enough the picture turns out to be very poor"; "getting to and from the cinema can be a problem"; "we have to get a baby sitter"; "going to the cinema is expensive". A few implied that television sets up standards against which the cinema cannot compete.

The TV program "Current Release" came up for discussion as affecting cinema attendances. It was thought by some to have re-stimulated cinema-going, but not to have produced a return to anything like normal. On the other hand, some blamed it for a large part of the fall-off, saying that it produced *selective* attendance: "people have learned to want to know about a show before going to see it, and unless it gets a good preview they won't go — in the old days they used to go to anything".

Television reduces reading

While some viewers say that television has made them seek out a particular book, viewers claim, almost without disagreement, that television

has reduced the total amount of their reading. Their claims include statements to the effect that: they don't use the library as much now; books
taken out are either not read or only partly read; it takes longer to read
books now; even though they still take the same newspapers, they don't
read them as much now; "sometimes the newspapers don't even get opened". However, several viewers held that television was, because of its
drain on time, making people more selective in their reading.

Television affects attendance of football matches

About TV's effects upon attendance at football matches, there was a lot
of disagreement, some saying that television kept people away and others
that it did not. Some of the arguments put for its keeping people away
were: "it is easier to sit at home than to stand in the snow waiting to get
in"; "I don't like crowds"; "I'd watch at home if the weather was bad";
"You can see it better on TV". Those claiming it made no difference tended to say that: it won't affect the enthusiast; the atmosphere of the crowd
is important; the TV cameras can't follow the game as well as the person
who is actually there.

With sporting events generally, the position was much the same: a difference of opinion.

Television makes events and people become realities for viewers

A limited number of viewers volunteered ideas of the following kind:
"TV lets you see things you only *heard* about before"; "it turns names into
real people"; "it makes people you've only heard about seem like ordinary
people".

Television makes people physically and mentally
lazy and reduces initiative

There was repeated comment to the effect that television makes people
lazy, namely: household jobs are left for it; viewers don't make the effort
to go anywhere or to follow their old interests; "it stops you doing things
for yourself"; "you sit and watch television when you ought to be doing
something else"; "it seems to sap your interests"; some people just sit on
and on and then they say they are too tired to do anything else; "it makes
you put off the jobs you want to do".

Television reduces imagination in the viewer

A number of viewers made claims to the effect that television is such a
complete form of presentation that it leaves nothing to the imagination of
the viewer, and this was contrasted with the position of radio. It was also
held by some that television was so convincing and compelling that it
stopped the viewer from having his own thoughts about the matters por-
trayed.

Television reduces boredom

This was stated directly by some and implied by others. Thus some said: "it's real entertainment"; "it gives you something pleasant to do in the evening"; "it is something the majority has been waiting for and it fills a great gap"; "it's a boon for cripples and invalids who can't get out"; "it's entertainment for people who can't leave the house because of the children"; "I'm away a lot and it's a comfort to the wife".

Television makes people relax and reduces irritability

Television was said by some to be compelling in a way that radio never was and that it forces people to relax: it makes housewives "put their feet up"; "my husband works long hours and used to be irritable, but now that we have television he relaxes"; "I find it a great relaxation"; "it certainly makes you rest".

Viewers learn habits of concentration

It was frequently claimed that during the viewing of a program there is silence in the family circle; a few went further and claimed that this teaches viewers habits of silence and of concentration which are carried over to other activities.

Viewers learn improved methods of thinking

Several viewers implied that television incidentally taught people to think in a tidier way, because it gripped them as the program went ahead in a logical sequence.

There is an increase in spectatorism and in passivity

There were direct statements to this effect: "I find it's easier to look at television than to read a book"; "I will sit down and watch TV when I ought to be doing something"; "I'd rather stay indoors to watch than go out in the weather to see something".

Television leads to a feeling of futility or failure

Just a few made claims to this effect, on the grounds that it prevented people from doing the things they wanted to do. Many did, of course, admit to neglected duties of one form or another, but only rarely did they seem worried or frustrated about this.

Group III

IDEAS ABOUT TELEVISION'S EFFECTS UPON EDUCATION AND LEARNING

It interferes with homework and study

Statements presenting this idea were to the following effect: children hurry through their homework to watch television; "what with looking in here and there, it's 9.30 before he gets finished"; it draws young people away from evening study courses; "children will always find some excuse for dodging homework and television is *it*"; "I find it a great battle to decide whether I'll study or watch television"; some children have to try to do their homework in the room where the TV set is; "it may be a deterrent to study by teenagers"; "I was training to be a nurse and I know it would have kept me away from study if I hadn't pulled myself together".

This sort of suggestion was opposed by some who claimed that they kept control over the children and television, and that "it is up to the parents to see that homework is done".

Television is educational (*in the broader sense*) ·

Many acclaimed television as an educator, both in the sense of providing specific items of information and as broadening the outlook of viewers: "It shows you different things which you didn't know before and I think it's a great thing for improving one's knowledge of the world"; "Since George Cansdale has been on television, I know so much more about animals than I ever did before"; "Now we know a great deal more about the Philharmonic Orchestra"; "It's educational for my children and educational for me too because I have to look up the darned thing to answer them"; "My boy learns a lot just through incidentally picking it up from the programs he watches"; "Lots of things come up that people would never come by otherwise, and often when they see it, they're dumbfounded because they didn't think those things really happened"; "It's very instructive"; "You get the information so much more easily through television"; "It gives you educational subjects and it makes you want to read and learn more about them".

Some viewers disagreed, saying that instructional programs were frequently too difficult, and 'put them off' that sort of program. However, this type of objection came up with reference to programs focused on formal instruction rather than those which were meant mainly as entertainment but wich incidentally offered information.

Others, concerning education

It broadens the outlook.
It introduces people to new ideas and to new concepts.
It keeps people up with current affairs.
It develops critical ability.
Television means that the children are 'too tired' for school next day.

Group IV

IDEAS ABOUT TELEVISION'S EFFECTS UPON MORALS AND MANNERS

Television is cutting down on juvenile delinquency

This claim is really based on the argument that television is keeping the children and young people off the streets by giving them something interesting to do at home. Against this argument must be set the view, frequently offered, that it teaches them crime and helps them to accept violence.

Television is Spoiling our Manners

Viewers frequently referred to 'bad manners' as an effect of television: "you develop the Shussh habit"; "It is not entertaining visitors to make them sit and view"; "You don't attend properly to what the guests are saying"; "It makes people unsociable"; "It makes people insincere because all they visit you for is television, and you know it".

Television is lowering our moral standards

Where this claim was made, the reference was often to the pattern of morality in plays, namely to: "a lot of drinking"; "loose standards in marriage"; "lots of divorce". Light entertainment was blamed for "jokes in poor taste"; "dirty jokes"; "too much showing" (e.g., "plunging necklines", 'legs', "men in tights"); "bad language".

Group V

IDEAS ABOUT TELEVISION'S EFFECTS UPON PHYSICAL WELL-BEING

Television makes viewers go to bed later

With some, television was said to be like a magnet, keeping people up till the programs were over. Others, saying they were selective, held that waiting for particular programs kept them up. Quite often there appear to be unfinished or unstarted jobs to be attended to after viewing ends. Children were said to be affected. However, some viewers claimed that since they didn't go out so much in the evening now, they saved the time they used to spend in travelling home, and so got to bed *earlier*.

Television is Bad for the Eyes

Many claimed that television hurt their eyes: "I do find that if I view for too long, it makes my eyes run"; "My son has had to have glasses and the optician definitely put it down to television viewing"; "I have found out from the school clinic that there are many thousands of children that now have what is known as 'television eyes' "; "My eyes started playing up on me". There were suggestions from some viewers, however, that television was being made a scapegoat to at least some extent. Others again claimed that the trouble was due partly to poor lighting: "Well, I have had eyestrain, but I don't think that's the fault of the television entirely — I think it's our lighting"; "Yes, we had it, but we find it's much better with the lights on".

Television causes a loss of health

There were claims to the effect that the constant sitting of the viewer and a reduction in outdoor activity led to a loss of health and to an increase in physical weight.

[21]

The techniques for measuring television's social impact

Chapter 17 dealt with techniques for measuring the effects of exposure to particular programs. The present chapter is concerned with techniques for assessing the long term as well as the short term effects of being a viewer. In some ways, the methods appropriate for these two kinds of measurement are similar. This is because the difficulties to be overcome are also similar. The basic difficulty here too is that experimental controls cannot be applied to studies of TV's effects without interfering with the normality of the viewing process: yet in the absence of such controls it is extremely difficult to distinguish between those changes (in viewers) which are the results of exposure to television and those which are due to something quite different. This difficulty is probably more acute in the second kind of assessment — that is, the assessment of the general effects of television — because there can be no question at all of using controls over *which* members of the community do, and which don't, buy sets. Nor can there be any long-term control over who views what. To a large extent, the researcher must take the situation as he finds it and sort it out. Even where the researcher is fortunate enough to be able to conduct tests just before television comes to an area and again afterwards, he is by no means out of trouble because he cannot control *who* buys the sets, nor what is viewed, nor the many events which can effect people without these being in any way related to television. To this situation I shall be returning with comment later on, but in the meantime, the hard fact remains that there is much sorting out to be done.

In my opinion, this is not a problem which can be solved by laboratory experiments in which real life conditions are copied or simulated in some way. Such studies can, if well done, help us to discern some of the principles whereby certain things happen in society, and in this respect they can be of great value. On the other hand they cannot tell us the extent of television's long-term impact under normal conditions of viewing.

Social scientists trying to determine the causes of juvenile delinquency have of course been faced by the same problems, for in testing an hypothesis that some specified condition helps to produce deliquency they must find some means of sorting out how much of it is due to something else

239

altogether. They must take the situation as they find it and then must try to sort it all out afterwards, bringing to bear on the problem the tactics and the methods of social science. It can be done to a considerable degree, but the operation is technically demanding in the extreme. It is not only television research and crime research which are beset by this problem however: it affects that great range of social phenomena which, in human society, cannot be interfered with (that is, for the purposes of experimental control), without a breach of the law or of the moral code or without loss of the normality of the reaction process. Whenever we face the task of finding out what did what in society, the problem is basically the same: there is a lot of sorting out to be done.

THE DIFFERENT METHODS USED IN TELEVISION RESEARCH

In television research, many different methods have been used to try to assess the general effects of being a viewer. I shall present and comment on a number of these in order to bring out some of the requirements of an adequate sorting-out procedure.

Getting viewers to report on what they think television has done to them

A number of the earlier investigators concerned with television's effects tried to get viewers to tell them, directly, what television had done to them or to their families. This is usually called the 'Retrospection' method because the viewer has to look back over time — to see things in retrospect, as it were. In one study of this kind [222], viewers were asked to give estimates of how often they did certain things prior to getting a television set, and how often they did them at the time of the survey. The difference was attributed to television's influence. In other studies using basically the same method [279, 356] viewers were asked if they did certain things more or less frequently now, than they did before they got TV sets. In yet another version of this method, viewers were asked directly if television had affected their behaviour in certain ways [278, 356] and, in some cases, to what extent.

The weakness of the Retrospection technique as a method for assessing effects, particularly when applied to quantitative estimates of impact, lies in the fallibility of human judgements in such matters. In the first place, estimates of frequency, particularly with respect to irregular behaviour, are known to be subject to a lot of error and the extent of this can vary with the recency of the events being recalled [237]. Secondly, it is difficult to see how a viewer can really *know* that what he thinks is a real change in his behaviour is due, wholly or partly, to television. Consider the possibilities: the change may be due only *partly* to television; the behaviour concerned may be of an occasional or of an irregular kind; the *total* change may be in a direction opposite to that produced by television (as when TV changes behaviour in one direction and some other factor changes it to a greater extent in the other direction). It is not being suggested that viewers will always be unaware that television has done something to their behaviour: with big changes in formerly regular behaviour (e.g. weekly cinema going), there may well be a general awareness of TV as a cause. But even in such cases, it is too much to expect a correct attribution of a specific part of a change to television. The viewer will be in even greater difficulty with behaviour of an irregular kind (like occasional attendance at sports events) or with behaviour subject to fads or fashion or bursts of interest. It seems quite possible too, that he may be unaware of changes of the more subtle and personal kind. For instance, what about changes in his sociability, his initiative, his considerativeness for other members of his family? An understanding awareness of our own subtle processes, particularly at a quantitative level, is neither universal nor readily available to the researcher.

Because of its many uncertainties, the Retrospection method must be ruled out as a tool for reliably detecting or measuring TV-produced change. On the other hand, it can be of considerable value for the development of *hypotheses* about the kinds of things that television *may* be doing to people. Some of those using the method have regarded it in this way. It was, in fact, the technique used for developing the hypotheses set out in the appendix to the previous chapter.

There is one development of the Retrospection method which probably reduces somewhat the uncertainties of ordinary retrospection. This development consists of getting retrospective accounts of behaviour changes from *both* viewers and non viewers [351], and regarding the difference between the two sets of estimated change as a measure of the effects of being a viewer. This development appears to be designed to take account of the possibility that *part* of the perceived change is due to factors other than TV, the assumption being that this part will be indicated by the *non-viewer's* perception of change. In all likelihood, this assumption would be justified to some degree. Nonetheless, it must be remembered that to the extent that viewers and non-viewers are different in their characteristics or in their background, there is a likelihood that they will react differently to non-television events. To this important point I shall be returning in the context of discussing other research techniques later in this chapter. In the meantime, the least that can be said of the assumption is that it is by no means beyond challenge. Quite apart from this, the modification does nothing to resolve the difficulties already described in relation to the perception of changes and to the accurate perception of the extent of these. Thus though the modification is certainly an improvement from the point of view of scientific method, it does not take us far enough for it to be regarded as anything like a safe technique[a].

[a] On the other hand, it does offer us an improved technique for developing *hypotheses* about *possible* effects of TV. The improvement lies in the fact that the use of non-viewer estimates of change provides a form of challenge to the estimates of the viewers.

Comparing viewers and non-viewers

In a number of the early studies of television, straightforward comparisons were made of the behaviour of people with TV sets and of people without them [227, 367]. Generally speaking, many such studies do not appear to have been meant to provide assessments of the effects of television, but rather to provide comparative information about the new and growing television population. This, however, did not prevent the behavioural differences they revealed between viewers and non-viewers from being interpreted by some as effects of television. This tended to be on the grounds that the main difference between the viewers and the non-viewers was that the former had been exposed to television and that the latter had not. Whilst the serious researcher of to-day would be unlikely to draw such a conclusion, it is well that I say here why it cannot safely be drawn. The reason is important because it affects the whole strategy of 'effects research'.

So long as we have any reason for considering that viewers and non-viewers may be somewhat different kinds of people, present differences in their behaviour must be attributed, at least in principle, to a combination of TV's influence *and* of *original* differences between the viewers and the non-viewers. In other words, the behaviour of the two samples may have been appreciably different *before* the start of television.

There is, in fact, a very good case for considering that there *were* certain basic differences between viewers and non-viewers at any given time. The evidence presented in the previous chapter makes it clear that in Britain and in America the early buyers of sets were sharply different from other people in some respects at least (e.g. income). Some of those early differences were, it is true, much reduced after several years. But did they disappear entirely?

We know, of course, that after a few years TV ownership became common in all sectors of the population. Moreover we can expect that in due course viewers and the total population will be very similar indeed — in that just about everyone will become a viewer. However, for research into the effects of television, the two populations that matter are *not* viewers on the one hand and the whole population on the other; they are viewers and the *remaining non-viewers*. As television spreads upwards from the 50% level, the differences between these people in terms of their basic characteristics are likely to become greater rather than less. Thus when the non-viewers are some residual 5% of the population, we can expect them to be a fairly atypical set of people — just as were the viewers when *they* were only 5% of the population. However, important differences between viewers and non-viewers are likely to develop well before the 95% level of penetration is reached. This is illustrated in Table 1 which relates to mid-1959 when about 70% of Londoners had TV sets. Whereas most of the differences (between viewers and non-viewers) shown in it are small, several are quite large, particularly those in terms of age and family composition.

TABLE 1

Comparing some characteristics of viewer and non-viewer samples in London*, 1959

	Viewers %	Non-Viewers %		Viewers %	Non-Viewers %
Age			*Occupational Level*		
21 – 39	42	42	Professional and		
40 – 59	45	36	highly skilled	24	30
60+	13	22	Skilled and moder-		
			ately skilled	38	29
Sex			Semi and unskilled	23	17
Male	49	46	Unclassifiable	15	24
Female	51	54			
			Number of Adults		
Marital State			*in Household*		
Married	79	66	1 – 2	60	71
Others	21	34	3 – 4	36	25
			5 or more	4	4
Age of Leaving					
School			*Number in House-*		
13 or less	5	5	*hold Aged 20 or*		
14	53	38	*less*		
15	15	17	0	47	64
16 – 20	24	34	1 – 2	45	30
21 or more	3	6	3 or more	8	6
Further Educa-			*Number in House-*		
tion			*hold Aged 7 or*		
Yes	27	40	*less*		
No	73	60	0	60	66
			1 or more	40	34
Occupational					
State†			*Number in House-*		
Full employ-			*hold Going to*		
ment	61	57	*Work*		
Part-time	13	11	0 – 1	39	42
Self-employed	5	5	2	35	30
Retired	5	11	3 or more	26	28
Housewife	38	34			
Others	4	8	*Ownership of*		
			a car	34	25
			a refrigerator	33	26

* Sample sizes: 746 viewers and 269 non-viewers, each excluding the same small sectors of the population.

† These will not total 100% because some respondents appear in more than one category.

What about differences in the years leading up to 1959. The available evidence makes it quite clear that differences of one kind or another separated viewers and non-viewers throughout this period. One such source of difference was family composition, as illustrated in Table 2.

In 1950 the average viewer family was only a trifle larger than the average family in the total population, while non-viewer families (accounting then for 96% of the population) had an average size just about the same as that for the whole population of families. Over the years through to 1959, the *viewer* average has remained much the same, whereas the non-viewer average has fallen, slowly at first and rather rapidly since 1956. By 1959, major differences had developed between viewers and non-viewers. Table 2 gives some details of this process of change as well as details of change in terms of the proportion of family members aged 5 to 15 years. In this respect, viewers were well above average in 1950 though in time this numerical advantage appears to have been somewhat reduced. On the other hand, the figure for non-viewers, starting in 1950 at the average for the general population, fell steadily and appreciably, till in 1959 it was only about half the average for the families in the viewer population.

TABLE 2

Indicating variations in the family composition of the
non-viewers (1950–1959)

Date and area of survey	Viewer and non-viewer families compared with *all* families			
	In terms of family size		In terms of number of childred aged 5–15	
	Viewers	Non-Viewers	Viewers	Non-Viewers
1950 London & Midlands (i)	1.02	1.00	1.27	0.99
1954 United Kingdom (ii)	1.02	0.97	1.27	0.91
1954 – 5 London (iii)	1.04	0.95	1.20	0.89
1955 – 6 London (iv)	1.03	0.96	1.22	0.83
1958 United Kingdom (v)	1.03	0.88	1.20	0.63
1959 London (vi)	1.03	0.82	1.18	0.58

Data (i)–(vi) are calculated indices based upon figures provided in the following documents: (i) "TV Enquiry (1950)", BBC [245]; (ii) "Viewers, Viewing and Leisure", BBC [246]; (iii) "The Effects of Television Upon the Interests and the Initiative of Adults in London", W. A. Belson, [232]; (iv) "Television and the Family", W. A. Belson for the BBC [231]; (v) "The public and the Programmes", BBC [247]; (vi) "The Effects of Television Upon the Reading and the Buying of Newspapers and Magazines", W. A. Belson [234]. The use of an index (e.g. viewers as a per cent of total population) was necessary for rendering comparable the diverse data of (i) to (vi).

Although in the early days of television the number of children aged less than five was much the same in viewer and non-viewer families, differences did in time develop, viewing families coming to be constituted somewhat more of those with children under five. Another source of difference has been the ages of *adult* viewers: over the years, viewers have been quite markedly under-represented by those aged over 65.

Early differences in income level had been reduced very much by 1954, though there were still quite marked differences between the proportion of viewers and of non-viewers in the *really low* income levels — differences which were still present in 1959. Moreover in 1954 the age of leaving school of those in the upper income groups was slightly lower for viewers than it was for non-viewers, though this did not apply for people in the lower income groups. In line with this, there is evidence of a tendency for more non-viewers than viewers to have had some form of further education or training after leaving school, particularly of the non-vocational kind. This sort of difference was certainly present as late as 1959.

If we go beyond the more traditional variables, other differences appear. Thus in a 1954 study by the writer dealing (in its methodological aspects) with the pre-television background of viewers and non-viewers, differences of the following kind were found. Viewers tended MORE than non-viewers: to have bought a home, to have made some furniture, to have owned laboursaving gadgets, to have owned a refrigerator; to have attended a Daily Mail Ideal Homes Exhibition; to have had an outside garden, to have owned a pet; to have run a car; to have owned a gramophone or a camera; to have employed others; to have been a cinema-goer. On the other hand, in the pre-television period the average viewer had done the following things LESS than the average non-viewer: had been a member of a debating society; had defied authority, had gone against the advice of others in choosing a career; had helped pay for his or her own education; had been a member of a lending library; had played a musical instrument, had attended a ballet performance, had gone somewhere to hear music played; had taken holidays in the country, had done some bird watching; had owned sporting gear, had played sport regularly. No pre-television differences were found with respect to political activity, club membership, going to see a music hall performance.

Amongst these many differences there seems to the writer to be a vague pattern. In particular, the viewers of this period seem to have been drawn somewhat more than non-viewers from those with a materialist outlook. By this is meant that they tended somewhat to be people who associated themselves with or expressed themselves in terms of material pleasures, material welfare and the possessions of things. By contrast, the non-viewers seem to have tended more than the viewers to be people who could 'live within themselves' as it were. This line of thought must not be taken too far because the differences found are matters of *degree only*, and because similarities tended to be much greater than differences. Nonetheless the differences found give us clear warning of the existence of original differences of the less traditional kind between viewers and non-viewers.

While neither these, nor the differences of the more traditional kind, indicated in other parts of this chapter, present any final block to 'effects' research, they do serve to make it clear that it is unwise to interpret behavioural and attitudinal differences between viewers and non-viewers simply as effects of television: they may well have sprung in part at least from *original* differences between those who had, and those who had not, become viewers at the time of the enquiry concerned.

Comparing viewers and non-viewers who have
been matched on an intuitive basis

It was an awareness of this kind of difficulty which led various re-searchers in the early 1950's to base their studies of TV's effects upon *matched* populations of viewers and non-viewers [275, 303, 324]. The tendency in these studies was to equate (i.e. to match) non-viewers to viewers in terms of characteristics which the research worker judged to be important or relevant. Usually the characteristics chosen for 'matching' included age, sex and social class. Occasionally additional or alternative matching variables were used, such as: residential nearness, education, intelligence, income, family size.

The thinking behind this sort of method is straightforward and appealing. Through matching, the non-viewer sample was to be reconstructed so that it closely resembled the viewer sample in terms of the latter's basic characteristics. This, it was expected, would much reduce or would eliminate altogether the influence of original differences upon the comparison of viewer and non-viewer test scores. This in turn would make it possible, so it was thought, to interpret the differences in test-scores between the viewers and the matched non-viewers as *effects of television.*

The *weakness* of the method is that the relevance and the completeness of the matching done is dependent very largely upon the hunch or the intuition of the researcher. *For matching to be effective, it must eliminate all those basic differences between viewers and non-viewers which influence the behaviour being studied (i.e. for change by television)*[b]. Yet how can this possibly be done by hunch or by guesswork? Tracking down all the differences between viewers and non-viewers existing at any one period in time can be a major process of detection. Moreover, knowledge as to which of these differences is associated with the behaviour under study can only be derived empirically.

Matching by hunch was, I have said, a basic feature of various early studies of television's effects. However, it was used in a much later and major enquiry in Britain [284]. In the latter study, which dealt with children in two age groups, the chosen matching variables were age, sex, intelligence and social background. In one of the towns in which the research team worked it was possible to examine pre-television differences in behaviour between viewers and non-viewers matched to each other in

[b] Suppose for instance that the differences between viewers and non-viewers included differences in family composition, as indeed they did in London in 1959. Family composition happens also to be correlated with newspaper readership. If in a study of television's effects upon newspaper reading, differences in family composition were not eliminated, their continuing presence would affect the estimated difference between viewer and non-viewer newspaper-reading scores.

terms of the chosen matching variables. The report presents very little of this vital information (about residual differences) in quantitative form, but the one exception to this indicated major disparity in terms of comic reading. In other words, in this case at least, matching by hunch did not eliminate a major pre-television difference (in behaviour) between the viewer and the non-viewer samples. The report also indicates, though not quantitatively, that there were further pre-television differences which were not eliminated by matching.

I am not suggesting that studies of effects which are based upon matching by hunch *cannot* yield meaningful estimates of television's effects. If the chosen matching variables happened by good fortune or by good judgement to eliminate all or most of that part of the pre-television difference which is associated with the behaviour under study, then sound results will have emerged from the enquiry. Moreover I think that the know-how of the experienced researcher can be of great help. In the last analysis, however, the fact remains that matching by intuition or by know-how is too much a 'hit or miss' process to be considered a reliable tool of the scientific method. If matching is to be used in a study, the researcher must *know* what the current differences in viewer and non-viewer characteristics are and he must *know* which of them are important for his particular enquiry. Their importance will depend jointly upon the size of the difference, and upon the size of the correlation of the variables concerned with whatever is being studied. This demanding task can only be tackled on a strictly empirical basis. To this important point I shall be returning later in this chapter.

Comparing people in television and non-television towns

Several studies have been based upon a somewhat different research technique, namely a comparison of two towns which are deemed similar in their basic character but which differ in that one receives television broadcasts while the other does not. The thinking behind this technique is very similar to that of the method which employs intuitively matched samples of viewers and non-viewers: the people in the non-television town are assumed to be matched to those in the television town and to be, as it were, what the people of the viewer town would be like if television had not come to them. This design tends to be used when the matching of viewers and non-viewers in the one area is deemed impractical or impossible. This judgement may spring out of a scepticism about the whole principle of matching non-viewers to self selected viewers or it may arise out of the fact that television is practically universal in those areas where it can be received.

Whatever the reasons, however, the 'similar towns' technique has its weaknesses and dangers. One of the dangers is that the researcher may be quite wrong in his assumption that the two towns were the same prior to the coming of television. How can he be reasonably sure that they were the same? The challenging fact of the situation is that for some reason or other a particular town does not yet have television: *Why?* If it is because the town is isolated, does this not imply possible (pre-TV) differences between the activities of its people and those of less isolated towns? Or, could it sometimes be that the non-TV town is insufficiently prosperous to be of much interest to the television proprietor? Quite apart from the selection problem, there is the possibility that people in different towns may be of different racial or religious backgrounds. The two-town system does not escape from the problems of matching. It simply introduces them in a form with which it is extremely difficult to deal.

This is not the only trouble however. Two towns, separated from each other by perhaps considerable distances, are quite likely to be subject to rather *different* sets of local events — events which are quite distinct in character and origin from television. It is also quite feasible that the effects of these local differences will in due course build up to a considerable degree.

One recent use of this sort of two-town design was made in a study conducted in Canada [331], the two towns being situated in the same province and each having a population of approximately 5,000. While the report indicates that there were many similarities between the two towns, it indicates too that the one without television was the more isolated of the two with respect to larger communities and that it got big-city newspapers later than the other town. Moreover it appears that the television town was fairly close to the American border. The claim that they both had weekly newspapers cannot be taken to guarantee a closely similar presentation and treatment of news. Nor should we assume that their having a similar school system guaranteed a closely similar educational input.

This is not to say that the 'two town' system of research is necessarily misleading. Nonetheless its obvious weaknesses must leave us in doubt about the interpretation of findings derived from it and I think that we would be well advised to use such a design only with the utmost caution and care.

Just as the technique of 'matched comparisons' gains from having check comparisons built into it, so does the 'two town' technique. An example of this was a study of television's impact on cinema going [223]. The areas involved in this study included one in which television programs could be received and one in which they could not. The ultimate comparison of cinema going rates was between viewers in the TV area, non-viewers in the TV area, *and* non-viewers in the non-TV area. This extra element in the comparison did not necessarily clinch the matter, but it did provide an extra safeguard against the researcher being misled by original differences between the areas concerned in the comparison. After all, the extra check was nothing more than a small application of the scientific method, namely the method of building into an otherwise ambiguous situation every possible check and challenge as a guard against arbitrary or intuitive interpretation of research findings.

BEFORE AND AFTER STUDIES

One of the more satisfactory but demanding methods for measuring the effects of television is what is frequently called the "before and after" method. This method was described in Chapter 18 in the context of measuring the impact of particular programs. However, its use and its weaknesses as a means of assessing the long term social impact of television call for special comment and this in turn requires a brief repetition, here, of the basic form of the technique itself.

In its simplest form, the method is as follows. Just before the expected opening of a TV service in an area, interviews are conducted with a sample of the area's population. Some time after the service has been set up — possibly a year later — those members of the sample who have since secured sets are re-interviewed and asked precisely the same questions as before. A sample of those who did *not* secure sets is also re-interviewed with the same questionnaire. The pre- and post-television responses of the set buyers are compared and differences between them are worked out to provide a measure of TV's effects *plus* the effects of any non-TV influences which may have operated on the viewers between the two interviews. The differences between the pre- and post-TV scores of the *non-viewers* are taken to represent the effects of the influences other than television. These differences are then subtracted from the differences for the viewers and the result is regarded as an estimate of the effects of television. Figure 1 indicates the main features of this research strategy.

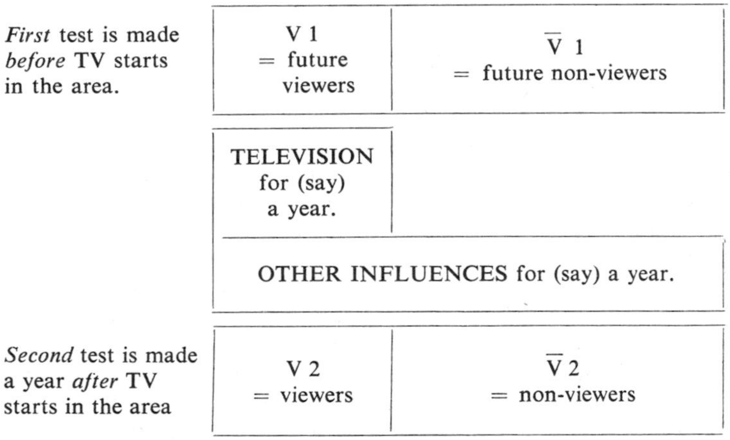

First test is made *before* TV starts in the area.	V 1 = future viewers	$\overline{V}$ 1 = future non-viewers
	TELEVISION for (say) a year.	
	OTHER INFLUENCES for (say) a year.	
Second test is made a year *after* TV starts in the area	V 2 = viewers	$\overline{V}$ 2 = non-viewers

ESTIMATED EFFECT OF TELEVISION =

(Scores for V2 − scores for V1) − (Scores for $\overline{V}$2 − Scores for $\overline{V}$1)

Figure 1.

Illustrating the 'Before and After' method

This particular version of the design has certain weaknesses. The first of these is that we cannot be sure that the comparison of the two lots of non-viewer scores will in fact yield an accurate estimate of the effects of events other than television upon the *viewers*. Thus if the non-viewers are different from the viewers in some way, it is possible that *their* reactions to these extraneous events will not be the same as the reactions of the *viewers* to them. Thus if the non-viewers are *older* than the viewers, then presumably they will react differently from the viewers to at least some kinds of events (e.g. sporting events, political events). If they have fewer material possessions than viewers, they may well be affected differently by economic changes; if they have fewer children, the ideas and the fashions of the young will, in all probability, affect them somewhat differently. In the circumstances, it is desirable that the non-viewers included in this particular design be matched to the viewers in terms of the more powerful correlates of whatever it is that is being studied (as possibly affected by television). It may be that in the study of some issues, matching will make but little difference to the outcome. On the other hand, it may well matter. In any case it is a step towards greater precision to use this device and accordingly it is a step which should be taken if the circumstances allow it.

Another difficulty about this 'before and after' technique is that the double testing of individuals could possibly have an effect (in its own right) upon the second set of test results. After all, the respondent is required to answer the very same questions as he did a year ago. Where the tests are concerned with *behaviour* of some kind, this danger does not seem to be very great. But with tests of knowledge, performance on the second test might well be affected by the experience of going through the first test. Whilst we might hope that the test-retest effect on viewers would be balanced out by a similar test-retest effect in the control group (i.e. the non-viewers), it is by no means certain that this would happen if the controls were not well matched to the viewers.

One of the more serious limitations of this technique is a practical rather than a technical one. After about a year of television, it may well be that only 5% to 10% of the sample tested before television started will have become viewers. If the study is restricted to this one year period, the wastage of cases will probably be very high and the number of people in each of the four cells of the design may possibly be too small for statistical adequacy. An enquiry conducted in Norwich [284] ran into difficulties of this very kind. The first test was made with 2,200 children. After a year only 185 of these qualified and were tested as viewers. To these were matched 185 non-viewers to be used as controls. Hence over 1,800 of the original (i.e. pre-television) tests were wasted. Moreover to have secured a sufficiently large number of viewers, the original number of individuals tested would have had to be much larger and the eventual wastage much greater.

With the 'before and after' design, it is usually sound economy to continue the enquiry for several years, because by then the total number of viewers available from the pre-TV sample will have increased substantially, especially if the rate of TV growth accelerated in its usual way. There is, however, another very sound reason for continuing this sort of enquiry beyond the one year. A one-year study can tell us nothing more than the nature of the early effects of television upon the first small section of the population to buy sets. This is useful, but we need to know much more. On the other hand, a long-term enquiry is administratively most demanding and the writer knows of at least one major long-term enquiry of this kind which faded out in the waiting period.

There is yet another difficulty about the long term enquiry based upon the 'before and after' design. If it is desired to measure effects from time to time in the course of the test period, then we become involved in test-retest problems with a vengeance, for now we may well have two, three or four tests to make on the one person. This is not necessarily disastrous, but it needs watching, and it might be deemed necessary to make a major alteration in the research design so that each year of the enquiry a fresh but equivalent sample of the population is brought in for testing. This very costly procedure was, it will be remembered, one of the designs discussed in the context of assessing the effects of specific programs (Chapter 17).

All things considered, it is probably not surprising that 'before and after' designs did not come into major use in television research. Several enquiries of this kind have of course been attempted [264, 284, 298]. However, the greater scientific adequacy of the technique must be set against its expensiveness, its demandingness in terms of administration and maintenance, and also against the ever present risk that the eventual yield of viewers will be too small in statistical terms.

THE STABLE CORRELATE METHOD AS A MEANS OF MEASURING LONG TERM EFFECTS OF TELEVISION

The Stable Correlate method offers a way round some of these difficulties: it is relatively inexpensive to use, it does not require that tests be made in an area *before* the advent there of television, and there is little or no likelihood that the eventual yield of viewers will be too small for meaningful analysis.

The nature of the Stable Correlate method: basic strategy and application
The Stable Correlate method has already been described (Chapter 17) as a means of measuring the effects of specific programs or series of programs. Its application in the present context is rather similar, though there are sufficient differences to warrant re-description of some aspects of the method and its application.

For the purposes of this description, let us assume that our aim is to assess the effects of television upon activity X and that activity X can be expressed through some form of score. The method starts with the assessment of score X for each of 2 samples: those who have got television in their homes (i.e. viewers) and those who have not (i.e. non-viewers). *The non-*

viewers are then equated to the viewers in terms of those correlates[c] *of score* *X which are also sources of difference between the two samples.* Amongst other things[d], this strictly empirical matching or equating process is intended to remove that part of the difference between the X-scores of the two samples which has nothing to do with the effect of television but which arose out of *pre-television* differences between them. If the extent of the matching is complete, and provided the matching variables are not themselves open to influence through television, then the difference in X-scores between the viewers on the one hand, and the reconstituted sample of non-viewers[e] on the other, should approximate to the effects of television on activity X.

The empirical choice of the matching variables is made from a large pool of proposed matching variables (e.g. age, family composition, area of residence and many others). These pool variables are based upon a large number of questions, heterogeneous in character, which are asked of the respondent in the course of the survey which was used to establish the X-scores. The selection of matching variables is made through a preliminary correlational analysis, this being followed by the equating of the viewers and the non-viewers in terms of the selected matching variables.

Some requirements of efficient matching

The form and the principle of the Stable Correlate method appropriate for studies of the general and long-term effects of television are, then, very similar to what is appropriate for assessing the effects of specific programs. The requirements for adequate matching are also very similar. They have been described at length in Chapter 17 and so are only summarised here.

(1) The selected matching variables must be associated with both X-score and with whether or not the respondent is a viewer. Differences between the viewer and the non-viewer samples in terms of characteristics which are not related to the X-score may be ignored because these differences cannot influence the size of the X-score difference between the viewer and the non-viewer samples. Where differences in their characteristics *are* related to the X-score, they certainly *can* affect the X-score difference between the two samples. This intrusive and misleading influence would be removed by equating the non-viewer sample to the viewer sample in terms of all such variables. There is a special way of identifying these particular characteristics or variables, and this method is described in working detail in Chapter 17. The method entails the calculation of an index of the association of a proposed matching

---

[c] In other words, variables which are numerically accounted with test score.
[d] See later section called: "A Complication Related to the Effects of Extraneous Events".
[e] By this time, the different (relevant) sections of the non-viewer sample will have been differentially weighted, so that the non-viewer sample would, in fact, have been 'reconstituted'.

variable *jointly* with the X-score on the one hand and with membership of the viewer (or non-viewer) sample on the other. The proposed matching variable with the highest index of joint association is chosen as the first-order matching variable. Second-, third- and fourth-order matching variables are then chosen on the same principle to provide an empirically derived *composite* of matching variables. The building of this composite is stopped when the addition of further variables would add nothing to its total power as a means of eliminating relevant differences between the viewer and the non-viewer samples. Here again, working details are given in Chapter 17.

(2) A separate composite of matching variables must be derived for each separate activity under study as possibly affected by television. Thus the composite appropriate for the study of activity X would not necessarily be suitable for the study of activity Y. The reason for this is that the correlates of X-scores may not be the same as the correlates of Y-scores.

(3) The matching variables chosen must be stable in the sense that they are not themselves open to the influence of television. Thus 'age' in years is stable whereas 'interest in sport' may *not* be stable. If the chosen matching variables are not stable in this sense, then the very process of matching will whittle away the evidence of TV's influence on activity X. In the present state of knowledge, there are likely to be many cases where we cannot be certain about the stability or otherwise of a proposed matching variable, but if there is any doubt at all about a variable's stability, that variable should not be considered as a matching variable.

(4) Though the selection of any one composite of matching variables is a relatively straightforward procedure, its efficiency does depend upon there being a carefully developed pool of variables from which to select them. The necessary information for building up this pool will have been gathered through questions asked of respondents at the same time as the survey procedure which was being used to establish the X-scores. This pool of variables must have certain features. (a) The variables brought into it must be known to be or expected to be sources of difference between viewers and non-viewers; they should be known to be or expected to be numerically associated with the behaviour under study as possibly affected by television. Possible sources of these variables are past research, sociological or psychological theory, intensive interviews with viewers, the suggestions of other research workers. (b) The pool of variables should be large and highly varied. For the study of the long-term effects of television, as many as 200 variables may be included in the pool. On the other hand there should not be less than 50 of them. The requirement that the pool be large and varied is made because this is the soundest available form of insurance against missing some factor which is both a source of difference between the two samples and a correlate of activity X. This particular point is developed in

Chapters 13 and 17. Indeed, variability in the pool is so important that it is good procedure to introduce into the pool 10–20 items simply for the sake of variability. They should be different from the items already in the pool and it will not matter if some or all of them might be considered completely unlikely as sources of either difference or of correlation. A few of these additions may even be regarded as a bit odd. Nonetheless, these should be included because heterogeneity in the total pool is of the utmost importance[t]. (c) It is an advantage if the questions used to develop pool items are answerable by a simple 'yes' or 'no', for this allows a lot of questions to be asked in a short space of time and it facilitates the efficient selection of a composite of matching variables.

Using the matching composite once it has been developed

The methods of *applying* the composite of matching variables have already been described in detail in Chapter 17 and accordingly only brief reference to these methods will be made here.

One of these methods is that of re-weighting. Both viewer and non-viewer samples are subdivided in terms of the matching composite and this may yield as many as 30 subgroups in each sample. The composition of the non-viewer sample is then made equal to the composition of the viewer sample in terms of these sub-groups. The method of equating them is to replicate cards in the sub-groups of the non-viewer pack. The replication is done on a random system. There is no throwing out of non-viewer cards and this is achieved by multiplying the whole of the viewer sample by some integer sufficient to raise the number of cards in all viewer sub-groups above the numerical level of all corresponding sub-groups in the non-viewer sample. Different sub-groups in the non-viewer pack are then separately weighted up to the levels of equivalent sub-groups in the viewer sample. This whole process leads to a considerable reconstitution of the composition of the non-viewers — who in this new form are the controls.

The other method of applying the matching variables to the matching process is the Multiplication method. It begins also with the splitting of each sample into the sub-groups defined by the matching composite. The average score for the activity or attitude under study is then calculated for each of the non-viewer sub-groups. Next, each of these is multiplied by the number of cases in the equivalent sub-group in the viewer sample. These various products are then added and a sample average is calculated. This is the score for the controls.

[t] At the same time, it should be noted that the multiple correlation derived from a total pool, large and varied in character, is usually accounted for almost completely by as few as four to six relatively independent elements in that pool and that the extension of the pool from 100 to 200 items usually only leads to the discovery of a slightly more powerful version of a predictive element already present in the pool of 100. In fact there seems to the writer to be a strong case for thinking that the number of independent predictors, of any general value, for a single criterion, is strictly limited, and that with care of the kind indicated above, all of them will be found.

For each method of matching, the difference between the activity score (X) for the viewers on the one hand and for the controls on the other may be regarded as an estimate of the effects of TV upon activity X. One disadvantage of the Multiplication method is that it makes it difficult to apply to the resulting estimate of effects any standard form of statistical evaluation.

A complication related to the effects of extraneous events

The application of the Stable Correlate method to the assessment of the long term effects of television involves a complication not met with in any marked form in studies of the effects of seeing specific programs. This complication concerns the differential effects, on non-viewers as distinct from viewers, of events other than exposure to the TV set.

Since in a study of the long term effects of TV, extraneous events will have been operating upon viewers and upon non-viewers for a lengthy period, there is a real possibility that the two samples will *not* have been equally affected by these events. If this were the case, then the difference, in terms of score for activity X, between viewers and non-viewers would have to be interpreted as a mixture of at least three things: the effects of TV; the differential influence of pre-television difference between the viewers; *the differential influence of extraneous events between viewers and non-viewers.*

However, and fortunately, the empirical matching system which was used to reduce or to eliminate the unwanted influences of pre-television differences, serves also to reduce distorting differences between viewers and non-viewers with respect to purely extraneous events. This assertion requires explanation on several different grounds.

1. One of the reasons for extraneous events affecting viewers and non-viewers differently is that viewers and non-viewers are not necessarily the same in terms of various characteristics. Thus a family with several children in the 5–15 age range may be effected rather differently by school holidays than is the family in which the children are all under 5 years. In other words, different kinds of people may well react to the *same* event in different ways simply because they are different kinds of people. However, the elimination, through matching, of such differences in kind should automatically eliminate this source of bias.
2. It may be that differences in people's area of residence will lead to their being exposed to *different* extraneous events and, presumably, to the occurrence in them of different sorts of reactions and changes. This is an undesirable situation to have intruding into an effects study and it calls for the matching of viewers and non-viewers in terms of residential area. Where viewers and their 'controls' come from a single random survey conducted within one area, differences between viewers and non-viewers with respect to the kinds of events that happen around them should be much less marked than when they are drawn from separate

communities. Indeed, with tight empirical matching, such differences should be quite small. Even in this circumstance, however, it is desirable, where it is possible, that the matching variables used to reconstitute the non-viewers into a control system should include 'local area of residence'.

3. There is one difference in the degree of viewer and control exposure to extraneous events which it is necessary to *avoid* eliminating. If viewers are less/more exposed (than controls) to certain non-TV events *just because they are viewers*, this is an effect of television and it would be misleading were we to reduce or eliminate it through the research design we use. In fact the matching system used in the Stable Correlate method does not reduce or eliminate it, for the method operates solely through the elimination of relevant original differences between viewers and their controls.

Summing up, the Stable Correlate system of matching can be expected to reduce or eliminate any existing differences in the influence of extraneous events where the difference in exposure to or in reaction to these is a result of viewers and non-viewers being different to start with (including being somewhat different in the distribution of their homes within the survey area). It can be expected to leave alone those differences in exposure to non-TV events (and reaction to them) that are a result solely of becoming a viewer.

Measuring TV's effects according to length of set ownership
If we can get from viewers accurate information about the length of time they have had sets, then it is possible to derive estimates of television's effects year by year. This does not involve long term follow-up studies: it can be achieved through special analyses of the data collected through one large scale enquiry. An enquiry carried out six years after the start of television can be made to yield trends for television's effects over the first six years. For this kind of result, it is necessary to match the non-viewers first to those who have had a set for up to a year, then (separately) to those who have had it for one to two years, then (separately) to those who have had television for two to three years, and so on. Each of these matching processes yields a separate control average and a separate estimate of television's effect. This method was used in the two major enquiries reported in Chapters 22 and 23.

When should the Stable Correlate method be used?
One final point about the Stable Correlate method. The writer would not use it if he had the funds, the time and the opportunity to use a thorough-going 'before and after' design. Conducted on the lines advised here, the 'before and after' method is the safest method to use. Most times, however, the researcher is not in a position to use it, particularly with respect to the assessment of long term effects, and for this more usual situation

the Stable Correlate method is a valuable alternative. It is administratively simple to use, and is relatively inexpensive. At the same time, its operation requires of the researcher a lot of hard work, much care over detail, no corner cutting and a certain amount of creativeness in the derivation of items for the pool of proposed matching variables. If these elements and qualities cannot be brought to the use of the method, it is better that it be not used at all.

SEVERAL CONCLUDING COMMENTS

One of my purposes in presenting this methodological chapter has been to introduce the three 'effects' studies reported in this section: each of them was based upon one or another form of the Stable Correlate technique[g]. In addition, however, I have sought through this presentation to put the reader in a better position to evaluate the many different findings reported in the literature about television's social impact. Rigorous appraisal of the methodology of reported research is necessary in any field of enquiry, but it is particularly important in this one. In television research, findings are too often accepted simply on the basis of the amount of publicity given to them.

It may be disappointing to some readers to realize, from what is written here, that it is now virtually impossible to conduct studies of television's general social impact (though not of the impact of particular programs) in either the U.S.A. or the U.K. — for the simple reason that television is now so widespread in these countries that there are left no suitable samples for use as controls.

However, there is still ample opportunity for such work to be done in the many countries where television is not yet received by the large majority. In these countries, the measurement of television's social impact is certainly possible still, both in major population centres and in scattered rural areas.

[g] This is not to say that these particular applications of the Stable Correlate method are without methodological inadequacies of one kind or another. Each has its own weaknesses and each falls below the standard of matching recommended in this chapter. This is largely because the rigorous matching techniques recommended here were slowly developed through enquiries such as these. While the matching inadequacies concerned were not in my view, of a serious kind, they do exist and the reader will do well to note this in studying the chapters and the reports concerned.

[22]

The effects of television upon the interests and initiative of viewers[a]

BACKGROUND AND AIMS

In Chapter 20 there was a description of the rapid growth in television ownership in Britain and reference to the considerable use which owners made of their sets. Chapter 20 also presented something of the resulting conjecture about television's effects upon society — conjecture which was sometimes given considerable publicity but which in Britain remained almost untested. It was this situation which triggered off the enquiry reported in this chapter. It was aimed at providing firm evidence in place of some of the conjecture.

In deciding upon the precise issues for investigation, preliminary study was made of the available reports of research (most of it American) and of the publicised conjecture about television's probable effects. However it was regarded as imperative that a major consideration in formulating issues for study should be the impressions of the people actually exposed to television's influence, namely the viewers themselves. The methods used for studying viewer impressions have already been described in Chapter 20[c]. Chapter 20 also gives details of the subsequent analysis of the impressions which were brought together through these methods. They fell into five broad groups, in one or another of which television's effects

---

[a] This chapter is based upon a report of an enquiry carried out by the author in the period 1954–5[b] at a time when approximately 35% of Londoners had television sets in their homes.

[b] The enquiry had financial assistance from the British Broadcasting Corporation and from the Central Research Fund of the University of London.

[c] Very briefly, these methods were as follows. Discussions were held with 16 viewer families (in their homes) and with 100 adult viewers in a series of group meetings. Discussions were strictly non-directive in character. In addition, written requests for their impressions were made to 300 members of the BBC's viewing panel and to 100 non-viewers on another BBC panel. Approximately 85% replied. The non-viewer opinions were sought in order to bring into the pool of ideas some of the impressions of the ordinary outsider.

upon the following were included: upon family life; upon sociability; upon interests and associated behaviour; upon various mental states and processes including boredom, irritability, imagination, passivity; upon initiative; upon education and learning; upon morals and manners; upon physical well-being. The publicised kinds of conjecture and the possible indications of the American research were also classifiable within this system.

Of the eight issues listed above, two were chosen for study. These were (i) television's effect upon interests and associated behaviour; (ii) television's effect upon initiative. Each of these, but particularly the first, had come in for repeated mention by viewers. Each seemed socially important in its own right. With respect to neither of them had the question of television's effects been anything like fully resolved by research.

The meanings given to the terms 'Interests' and 'Initiative'

The viewers who put forward the idea that television was affecting *initiative* had in mind the process of doing something without being told to do it or how to do it. Some used the expression "doing things off your own bat". The concept of 'initiative' as held by viewers, had to it overtones of *real effort generated by oneself*, of *originality* or ingenuity and possibly too of some degree of *departure from normal or accepted procedures*. More will be said about how viewers understood this concept in describing the methods used for measuring initiative, but the point which is vital in the present context is that it was the *viewers'* concept of initiative which was to be studied. The suggestion that television had affected initiative had, after all, come primarily from viewers; accordingly, *their* meaning for the term was the one to use.[d]

By 'interests', viewers tended to mean things that they liked to do or to see or to read or to think about. These 'things' included hobbies and spare time activities but they included also events in the world around them, various forms of art, ideas, concepts — indeed, anything at all on which their attention tended to be focussed in some voluntary, continuing and pleasant way. It is this interpretation of the term 'interests' which was used throughout the enquiry. Here, too, the reason for adopting this definition is simply that the suggestion that television affects 'interests' came primarily from viewers, and so it was *their* concept of 'interest' that was studied.

Specific questions for investigation

Several different aspects of interests were to be considered. One was the *behavioural* aspect of viewers' interests (that is, *doing* something about

[d] In Warren's *Dictionary of Psychology*, 'initiative' is defined as "the capacity of certain individuals to produce compositions (works of art, mechanical devices, etc.) which are essentially novel or which were previously unknown to the producer". H. C. Warren, "Dictionary of Psychology", Houghton Mifflin Co., New York, 1934 [363]

one's interests), while the other was the aspect which might best be described as the *strength of feeling* for or about one's interests. For instance, television may change not only the amount of a person's cinema going, but also his *desire* to go to the cinema. It may change not only the amount of reading he does on international affairs, but also his feeling of interest in international affairs. It may affect not only what a woman does about home decoration but also her feeling of interest in such activity as well. This distinction has practical importance. Suppose a viewer ceased to attend club meetings. If in addition he lost *all interest* in attending — all desire to go — that would seem to indicate a more thorough-going loss of the interest than would be the case if the *desire* to go had remained. Where a positive feeling for the interest remains, it is always possible that a regeneration of the original behaviour may occur or a substitute for it be found. Where even the *feeling* of interest has gone, regeneration of previously associated behaviour seems much less likely.

One further distinction was made with respect to viewers' interests. Since television programs constantly present material intended to foster or to develop new areas of interest or to feed existing interests, it seemed possible that such interests might be affected differently from those which tended *not* to be featured in programs. Accordingly, the enquiry was designed to provide, additionally, an assessment of television's effect upon those interests which happened to be more frequently featured in television programs.

These various considerations led to the formulation of the following three questions about interests.

To what extent, if at all, does television affect the behavioural aspects of viewers' interests? If there is an effect, how long does it last? ...   .   Project I

To what extent, if at all, does television affect the strength of viewers' feelings for or about their different interests? If there is an effect, how long does it last?   ...   .   Project II

What are television's effects, if any, upon those of the viewers' interests which tend to be featured in television programs? What is the duration of any such effects?   ...   .   Project III

The question for investigation concerning initiative required no such diversification. It was as follows.

To what extent, if at all, does television affect viewers' initiative? What is the duration of any such effect?   ...   Project IV

The methods of research: a summary

The enquiry began with the construction of the necessary measuring devices. These included: a representative sample of the fields of interest of Londoners; scales for assessing the intensity of an interest; a representative sample of the acts of initiative ordinarily occurring in London; a very large pool of variables to be used for matching purposes. Their development was based on work with various samples of adults, totalling in all approximately 3,000. The measuring devices were built into a special kind of questionnaire which was then administered to samples of viewers (440) and of non-viewers (342) in Greater London. After this, the Stable Correlate technique was used for the empirical matching of the non-viewers to the sample of viewers and estimates of television's various effects were calculated. In addition, separate matching of the empirical kind was carried out for each interest about which an estimate of television's effect was required. The fieldwork for the enquiry was spread over a full year, starting in late 1954.

The methods of research: in detail
Making the Measuring Instruments

It was a feature of this project that more work went into the making of measuring devices than went into their *use* in the final survey. This lengthy preparation was necessitated partly by the type of research design which it was necessary to use (that is, the Stable Correlate method), and partly by the absence of existing measuring instruments of a suitable kind.

The measurement of interest
If we are to conduct research upon interests in general and to conclude about the effects of TV upon interests *in general*, it is essential that such work be based upon a *representative sample of the public's interests.* If all interests were affected by television in just the same way, then it would matter little *which* of them we studied. This, however, cannot possibly be assumed. (As it turned out it would have been a wrong assumption had it been made.)

Nor can it be assumed that some 'reasoned' selection of different fields of interest would constitute a safe basis for a generalization, for we could not assume that the person doing the selection was sufficiently in touch with the interests of the general population for him to be able to make such a selection simply by exercising his personal judgement.

Accordingly, the necessary steps were taken, using rigorous sampling techniques, for drawing a properly representative sample of the public's interests.

Developing a representative sample of the public's interests
This sample was developed in three stages. (1) In the first stage a compilation tending towards exhaustiveness and based upon approximately

LIST 1.

The general sample of the public's interests

Selected Items	Percentage of Londoners at least mildly interested
The English countryside	91
Making new friends	89
Interior decoration of the home	87
Festive occasions (e.g. birthdays, New Year, Christmas and so on)	84
Gardens (e.g. looking at the gardens of other people, going to see well known gardens, cultivating a garden, and so on)	82
Labour saving gadgets and ideas	80
*Reading books for relaxation or entertainment or general interest	79
*Going to the cinema	78
Different ways of preparing food	77
The Royal family	76
Variety and vaudeville shows	75
Visiting people	74
Listening to light music	73
Strolling in the park	72
The ideas and doings of well known people	69
Military bands	68
International and world affairs (e.g. international relations, foreign affairs, American–Russian relations, international economy and so on)	67
*Playing cards	66
The animals and the birds of the world	64
*Playing gramophone records	62
*Politics in Great Britain	62
*Going to see sporting events	58
Fashions to-day	56
Crossword puzzles	56
Motor cars (that is, their design or development or maintenance)	55
Talking about the past or thinking about it	54

Selected items	Percentage of Londoners at least mildly interested
*Places of historic importance (e.g. historic houses or buildings, fields of battle and so on	53
*Modern developments in science	51
Physical culture	50
*Looking at paintings	49
Listening to or attending lectures or talks	47
History (e.g. ancient, modern, 19th century English, American, and so on)	46
Photography	45
Welfare work	44
*Ballet	42
Wimbledon tennis	42
Ice or roller skating	41
*Membership of clubs or associations	38
Talking about dreams or interpreting them	36
Playing darts	35
Trade Unionism	32
Bird watching	31
Chinaware and pottery	31
Collecting things (e.g. reproductions of famous paintings, postcards, insects, stamps, pictures of well known people and so on)	26
Railways (e.g. reading about them, train spotting, engine design, studying routes and time-tables, and so on)	25
Rifle or revolver shooting	24
Folk lore	21
Sculpture	18
Hypnotism	15
Weaving	8

* Those marked with an asterisk were to be studied for change in their own right. See later for reference and explanation.

300 diary records, was made of the public's interests. In its final form it consisted of over 400 different items ranging from cinema going to fashions of the past, to indoor gardening, soccer and playing darts. (2) In the second stage, this list was made the basis of a sample survey in Greater London, conducted to determine the proportion of adults professing an interest in the different listed items. It was then possible for distribution figures to be set against each of the 450 areas of interest in the compilation. (3) From the 450, a sample of 50 was then selected on random principles but within a tight control system in terms of the proportion professing an interest in the different items in the list. This important control ensured that the sample had in it only a due proportion of interests with large or medium or small followings. This procedure represents a new development in research methodology and for this reason its three stages are given in greater detail, in the appendix to this chapter.

The sample of 50 items so selected is given in List 1.

It was intended that this sample of interests should serve two purposes. In the first place, it would be used as a basis for developing a single but properly weighted estimate, of a quantitative kind, of TV's effects on interests *in general*. In addition, however, it would allow the calculation of TV's effects upon *individual* fields of interest within the sample. It was considered an advantage that this system would allow the changes for specific fields of interest to be seen in the broader perspective of what television was doing to interests in general. Where it seemed important to assess TV's impact upon a specific field of interest which did not happen to be included in the sample, this field of interest was brought into the study but was not regarded as part of the sample to be used for the generalization.

The interests to be studied in their own right

Though it would have been possible to have made a separate study of each of the areas of interest in the general sample, considerations of social importance, topicality and methodological ease led to a limit being put upon the number of them to be so treated. These are marked with an asterisk in Table 1. In addition to these, six more areas of interest which did not happen to be included in the general sample[e] were added to the number for individual study. These were as follows:

> Going to the theatre
> Events in different parts of the world
> Gardening (indoor or outdoor)
> Information about people in other countries
> Major soccer matches
> Horse racing and show jumping

The total number of interests for individual study was thus eighteen.

[e] These were in fact selected from a completely different sample of interests, namely a sample of the interests featured in TV programs. This particular sample is given later in the chapter.

Measuring the extent of interest

All the above named areas of interest, whether in the general sample or not, were measured to determine the *extent* of respondents' interest in them. Two kinds of measures were used.

One of these two measures was the *amount of behaviour* of a specified kind (e.g. I went to the cinema) which occurred in some particular period of time. In this enquiry the period was the 'last two weeks'. For most of the interests, the information sought was *how many times* if at all the specific behaviour had occurred in that period. These were interests of the kind cinema going, playing cards, going to see soccer played. However for some interests, like gardening and book reading, the most meaningful way of recording behaviour seemed to be in terms of *time* devoted to the activity (in the last two weeks). With such interests the information sought was which of three listed periods came nearest to the respondent's own outlay of time on the activity indicated. For either form of information, the respondent had been warned (in the questionnaire) that he must expect to find few activities with respect to which he had done anything at all. He was asked a preliminary question (for each activity) about whether he had done anything at all in relation to it (NO/YES/NOT SURE); only after this was he asked for frequency or amount.

The second of the two measures was of the *intensity of the respondent's identification with*, or feeling for, the area of interest concerned. After preliminary survey work, a simple five-item verbal rating scale was chosen to make this measurement. It was:

> Not interested in it
> Mildly interested in it
> Moderately interested
> Quite interested in it
> Very interested in it

For each area of interest, the respondent was required to underline that one of the five terms which best indicated the extent of his or her interest[f].

For the development of a *generalization* under Project I (i.e. concerning changes in behaviour related to interests), each respondent's behaviour scores for all fifty interests in the sample were to be aggregated into a 'total behaviour' score. (The Stable Correlate Method was then to be applied to the comparison of total behaviour scores of viewers and of non-viewers for the calculation of television's effect upon behaviour level associated with interests). The study of effects (on behaviour) for any *specific* area of interest was to be based upon the behaviour score for the interest concerned. Precisely the same approach was to be used in studying television's general and specific effects in relation to *strength* of

---

[f] For details of presentation and of lead-up questioning, see the section on the questionnaire.

interest. In this case, the aggregate score to be used in the study of effects *in general* was to be based upon the sum of all fifty of a respondent's ratings for strength of interest.

The two *aggregate* scores just referred to were of course fundamental to Projects I and II and each was based upon the general sample of interests.

A sample of the 'areas of interest' featured in television programs

It was necessary to base Project III upon a separate sample of interests, namely a sample of those areas of interest upon which television programs of the past tended to have been focussed. To derive such a sample, an analysis was made of the content of TV programs broadcast in the period 1950–1954. On the basis of this analysis, areas of interest dealt with in programs were listed in order according to the amount of time given to them. From this list a sample of interests was then drawn using the same selection principles as were used for the selection of the general sample. In this case the controls exercised were 'type of interest' (as with the general sample) and 'amount of program time given to the interest'. The final list, which happens to have twelve items in common with the *general* sample, was as follows:

L I S T 2.

A sample of the areas of interest featured in television programs

The ideas and doings of well known people	*Going to the theatre to see plays Ice or roller skating
Wimbledon tennis	*Gardening (indoor or outdoor)
*Events in different parts of the world	Architecture of churches and cathe-
Modern developments in science	drals in Britain
The English countryside	English towns
The jobs of other people	Different ways of preparing food
*The people of other countries	Places of historic importance in
The royal family	Britain
The animals and birds of the world	Fashions to-day
*Horse racing or horse jumping	Variety and vaudeville shows
Test cricket	Ballet
*Major soccer matches	Looking at paintings.

* These were selected for individual study as well as being items in this sample.

The whole sample of 23 was to be used to arrive at a generalization about the effects of television on interests actually featured in TV programs. In addition, however, some of the individual areas of interest featured in television programs were to be studied in their own right (along with others in the general sample) and there are marked with an asterisk.

The measurement of initiative

The measure of initiative was based upon a representative sample of the acts of initiative which ordinarily occurred amongst adults in the survey area. For each act in this sample, the information required was whether or not the respondent had done it in the last two weeks.

The sample of *acts of initiative* was developed in very much the same way as was the sample of the *interests* of the population. The description of its development is dealt with only briefly here, but details are given in Appendix 2.

There were four stages to its development. (1) A compilation was made, using approximately 280 diary records of Londoners, of the different kinds of acts of initiative which ordinarily occurred in London. (2) The relative frequency of occurrence of each of these was established through survey methods. (3) Data from this survey also made it possible to calculate an index of the validity of each of the acts of initiative in the total list and this was used as one of two controls in the selection, from the total list, of a representative sample of 30 acts; the other control was 'frequency of occurrence of the acts'.

The full sample of 30 acts of initiative is given in Appendix 2. Several of its items follow as examples.

I changed my doctor or dentist or one of my tradesmen because I was not satisfied.

When a hitch occurred in something I was doing, I quickly got things going again.

Rather than buy an article shown in the shops, I worked out a way of making it myself (for example: a piece of furniture, a dress, a gadget, and so on).

I started up a conversation with someone I didn't know before.

For each item in this list, the information to be sought in the final survey was how often the respondent had done it in the 'last two weeks'. Just as with the interest measurements, respondents were given early and repeated warning that they might find they had done very few of the listed acts in the very short period concerned.

The Pool of Variables from which Stable Correlates Were to be Drawn

Because each project within this enquiry was to be based upon the Stable Correlate technique, it was necessary to develop a large pool of variables from which to draw the necessary composites of matching variables. The number of different matching composites needed was in fact quite large. Thus two separate composites of matching variables were required for the study of television's effects upon interests generally, one for the study of change in strength of interest and the other for the study of associated behaviour. Similarly, two each were needed for the study of: TV-featured interests; the many different interests which were to be studied in their own right. In addition a separate composite was required for studying TV's effects on initiative.

There were approximately 160 variables in the total pool of items from which these different composites were to be drawn. Items were brought into this pool when it seemed that they might possibly be both sources of difference between viewer and non-viewer samples *and* correlates of one or another of the variables under study — for these are the joint requirements of effective matching variables. Pool items were also made as varied as possible, for only in this way could the danger be faced that some relevant source of difference between viewers and non-viewers was being left out of the pool entirely.

The variables brought into the pool were, broadly speaking, of two kinds. Some were straightforward characteristics of the respondent and of the respondent's backgound. These included things like: age, sex, marital state, job level (reflecting income level and social class), responsibility level at work, intelligence, age of ceasing full-time schooling, further education or training, examinations passed or certificates gained, family composition (including the number of children and young people of different ages, the number of adults), number of rooms in the house, proximity of relatives, a physical mobility index, area of residence (and juror percentage index of this area).

The other kind of pool item consisted of certain of the respondent's own past acts, ownerships, experiences, and activities in the period 1946 (end of the war) to the beginning of 1950. Memory aids were used[g].

---

[g] There were two reasons for including in the pool, items of this kind. (i) The first was that the respondent's past acts, experiences, etc., appeared to offer a fairly fruitful source of correlates. Thus past membership of a library (also known to separate viewers and non-viewers) seemed a good prospect for one of the correlates of book reading; similarly past ownership of a garden or past attendance at a Chelsea Flower Show seemed likely correlates of a present interest in gardening. (ii) Since such proposed correlates had to be *stable* as far as television was concerned, it was essential to refer them to the pre-television period, which for most people was prior to 1950. It was for this reason that the small proportion who had sets before 1950 was excluded from the present study. To have gone any further back would have put greater strain on respondent memory.

Even though memory aids were used, it is clear that pool items of this kind were open to memory error, particularly as to whether or not they fell within the designated period[h]. However the question that mattered was whether viewers were going to be biassed in their memory errors more in one particular direction than were the non-viewers and there seemed no good reason for supposing that this would be so.

Some of the items of this kind were straight forward, like "I owned a tennis

The many items in the total pool were to be fed into the questionnaire carrying the various measuring instruments. Subsequently analyses were to be conducted to develop composites of variables associated with test scores, these composites to be used for matching purposes within the context of the Stable Correlate method.

The Questionnaire

With the development of the necessary measuring devices and the preparation of a large pool of potential matching items, the next and final step was their application, through survey methods, to the study of television's effects. They were built into a questionnaire of a special kind.

Inevitably it was a long one and many of its questions required careful thought by the respondent. Accordingly it was designed so that after the interviewer had started the respondent on the first parts of it, the rest could be completed by the respondent in the absence of the interviewer. This *self completion* questionnaire was then collected by the interviewer about a week later by appointment. The necessary rules went into the questionnaire itself and were repeated at appropriate intervals. The questionnaire had also to be distinctly interesting so that the respondent would finish it.

In fact, the questionnaire consisted of a small book in which were fixed three booklets dealing respectively with: ratings of strength of interest (in the 63 different areas of interest); behaviour in relation to interests; the pool of stable correlates. With these three booklets, the layout of questions was as follows:

---

racquet", "I took an active part in trade unionism", "I won a sporting trophy". Others, however, needed special preparation and some examples of these follow:

I went to see an FA Cup Final (Winners during this period were: Derby County; Charlton Athletic; Manchester United; Wolverhampton Wanderers).

Did you attend any of the following art exhibitions between 1946 and end of 1949?

The exhibition of the King's Pictures (held in Burlington House between October 1946 and March 1947).
The Van Gogh exhibition (held at the Tate Gallery between December 1947 and January 1948).
The Indian exhibition (held in Burlington House between November 1947 and February 1948).
The Courtauld exhibition (held at the Tate Gallery in 1948).
The Viennese Art Treasures exhibition (held at the Tate Gallery in 1949).

(h) More recent research [237] has indicated that for long term memory of events of the kind involved here, there is a tendency in respondents to bring events nearer in time. This would suggest that respondents may on average have used a date during 1949 as a terminal point rather than the start of 1950.

From booklet 1 (after initial instruction).

HOW INTERESTED are you in each of the folowing things? Choose your answer from the ones given and *put a line under the one you choose.*

GARDENING (that is, looking after a garden yourself)	GOING TO SEE SPORTING EVENTS	NEEDLEWORK
Not interested in it	Not interested in it	Not interested in it
Mildly interested in it	Mildly interested in it	Mildly interested in it
Moderately interested	Moderately interested	Moderately interested
Quite interested in it	Quite interested in it	Quite interested in it
Very interested in it	Very interested in it	Very interested in it

When you have done these, please turn to the next page.

From Booklet 2 (after initial instructions)

Have you done any of the following things during the last TWO WEEKS? Choose your answer and draw a line under it.

If yes, EXACTLY HOW MANY TIMES IN THE LAST TWO WEEKS?

I did a crossword puzzle (even if it was not finished).	no/yes/not sure	. . . .
I went to see a pottery or chinaware display	no/yes/not sure	. . . .
I went to see some place of historic importance (for example, historic houses or buildings, fields of battle, homes of great writers of the past, and so on).	no/yes/not sure	. . . .
I did some physical culture	no/yes/not sure	. . . .
I attended a lecture or talk	no/yes/not sure	. . . .

From Booklet 3 (after initial instructions)

Did you own or do any of the following things between the BEGINNING OF 1946 and the END OF 1949?

Look at each in turn and choose your answer from the ones on the right. Draw a line under the one you choose.

I OWNED A CAMERA	no/not quite certain/yes definitely
I HAD A DRIVER'S LICENCE	no/not quite certain/yes definitely
I TOOK COOKING LESSONS (for example, at a Womens' Institute, a technical college, and so on) OR ATTENDED A COOKING DEMONSTRATION.	no/not quite certain/yes definitely

Now please go ahead with the rest.

Much use was made of colour in these booklets, and instructions (and reminders of instructions) were printed at planned intervals throughout each booklet. The instructions and reminders were all on coloured pages and never more than one instruction appeared on a single page.

The Sample and the Rate of Interviewing Success

The survey area was Greater London. The population to be sampled was limited to those aged between 21 and 65 and the polling districts in London representing the lower 15% economically were also excluded. In each case this was because it was doubted on the evidence of pilot work on the questionnaire that people over 65 years and those in the lower 15% economically would be able to complete the questionnaire in a sufficiently thorough fashion.

A sample of names was drawn from the remaining polling districts, with controls over area and economic level. People who proved to be over 65 years and the small number who had a TV set before 1950 were to be by-passed when either fact became known. To achieve the right balance of viewers and non-viewers for the application of the Stable Correlate method, only every second non-viewer was interviewed.

Fieldwork was spread over a whole year so that the study would not be unduly influenced by special events. In other words, about a fiftieth of each of the viewer and the non-viewer sample was interviewed each week.

Some 5% of the initial sample was not contacted; 6% of those eligible for interview refused to accept the booklet questionnaire; of the booklets accepted and started by eligible persons, 8% were either not completed or not recovered. The final sample of completed booklet questionnaires came from 440 viewers and 342 non-viewers.

Selecting the Composites of Matching Variables

The methods used for selecting composites of matching variables are described below in the context of Project I, namely the project dealing with television's effects upon behaviour associated with interests *in general*. The 24 other composites of matching variables were developed on the same principles.

Let the total behaviour score for non-viewers be called X. Score X was used as the criterion against which the composite of matching variables was to be selected (as a composite it was required to provide the highest available joint correlation with X). The following steps were taken (i) All past acts, achievements and ownerships were separately correlated with X and those which had the higher correlation indices were aggregated to form a single 'item', which was called C2. (ii) Next, all the variables in the pool, including C2, were correlated with X and that one of them with the highest correlation index was chosen as the first-order matching variable. In fact this variable turned out to be C2, and its correlation with X was +0.66. (iii) The Wherry Doolittle method [185] for maximising correlations was then applied to identify second, third, fourth and possibly fifth matching variables. The principle of this method is that each new variable brought into the composite is that one in the whole pool which adds most to the multiple correlation already achieved by the variables so far selected. The selective and additive processes are stopped when the addition of a further variable is found to add nothing to the existing composite's multiple correlation with score X. The total selective process was based upon the non-viewer records, for it was the non-viewer sample which was to be adjusted (through the matching composites) to yield control scores.

In the case of X (for Project I), the selection was stopped after the third matching variable had been identified, the threesome being C2, respondent's examinations success, the level of responsibility reached by respondent in the last job he or she held. Details are given in Table 1. Also in

TABLE 1

Showing five of the main composites of matching variables

Variable Under Study	Stable Correlates Selected for matching, shown in order of priority		Multiple correlation achieved	
			First two Variables	*All three Variables*
	Variable	*Correlation*		
Interests in General				
Strength of Interest	Past Acts/ownerships (C1)*	+0.61	0.615	
	Age	+0.13		
Associated behaviour	Past Acts/ownerships (C2)	+0.66	0.685	0.688
	Examinations passed	+0.20		
	Authority in job	+0.12		
TV-Featured Interests				
Strength of interest	Past Acts (C1)	+0.55	0.564	0.576
	% Jurors in Polling District	+0.16		
	Age	+0.18		
Associated activity	Past Acts (C2)	+0.58	0.582	0.579
	Age	−0.16		
	Authority in Job	+0.19		
Initiative	Past Acts (C3)	+0.77	0.783	0.784
	Children under 16 years	−0.13		
	Age	−0.19		

* C1, C2 and C3 are separate composites of past ownerships/activities/achievements. Each includes about 30 items selected on the basis of their correlation with the issues under study (i.e.: C1 items for their correlation with the grossed scores for strength of interest on 50 areas of interest; C2 items for their correlation with the grossed behaviour scores for the same 50 interests; C3 items for their correlation with the initiative score).

Table 1. are the matching composites developed for Projects II, III and IV[i].

Applying the Matching Composites to Eliminate Pre-Television Differences

All matching in this enquiry was done through reweighting the scores of the non-viewers in the different subgroups defined by the matching criteria. This re-weighting was through the multiplication system described in Chapter 21 and illustrated in Chapter 23. For example, in the present enquiry, one matching composite defined 10 different subgroups. For each of these, the average score for the non-viewers was worked out. Each of these averages was then multiplied by the number of people in the equivalent viewer subgroup and a new overall average (all subgroups combined) was calculated for the non-viewers. The difference between this adjusted non-viewer score and the score of the viewers was taken as an estimate of television's effects. Obviously, a completely fresh adjustment of non-viewer scores (based on a separate matching composite) was necessary for each separate study within the total enquiry.

THE FINDINGS
Television's Effects on Interests, Considered Generally

For Project I, the effect of matching was to close the gap between viewers and non-viewers not only in terms of the matching variables but in terms also of those many past possessions, achievements and past activities which were correlated with the issue under study. The same applied with respect to matching for Project II. More to the point, matching led in each case to modification of the non-viewer score. Details of these modifications are given in Table 2 along with the resulting estimates of television's effects upon viewer interests.

TABLE 2

The modification of non-viewer scores through matching and the resulting estimates of television's effects

Variable under study	Non-viewer scores		Viewer scores	Loss or gain	Significance of difference
	Before matching to viewers	After matching to viewers		%	P
Strength of interest	89.08	88.14	84.19	−4.5	0.01
Level of associated behaviour	18.32	17.80	16.07	−9.7	0.01

[i] Inevitably, the selection process led to the rejection of a majority of the items in the pool. The seeming wastefulness of this procedure is, however, unavoidable: the very size of the pool is part of the necessary precaution against matching variables of importance being left out of the enquiry altogether.

From this table it will be seen that there was a statistically significant reduction in viewers' interests in terms both of strength of interest (a 5% loss) and in terms of associated behaviour (a 10% loss). In interpreting this finding we must remain aware that viewing as such was not included as one of the 'interests' studied as affected by television. This was because the present study was one of the effects of the 'viewing interest' upon other interests.

Effects year by year

The 5% and the 10% losses are a population average for the whole period from 1950 to 1955. However, it is important to know how permanent these changes are and at what time after set purchase they were at their maximum. Since length of set ownership was known, the effect of television after different periods of ownership was also derivable. This required that the matching procedure be applied separately for each of the 'set-age' groups. Thus non-viewers were first matched to the viewers who had owned sets for one year or less, and an estimate of television's effects after that length of ownership was derived. The non-viewers were then matched afresh to the viewers who had owned sets for one to two years, to derive an estimate of effect, after that length of ownership. Similarly, with the 2–4 year group, and for those with sets for 4–6 years. By linking these results, it is possible, granted a reasonable matching of the viewer groups, to derive trend curves of the kind shown in Fig. 1.

Figure 1

Television's effect on interests and associated activity according to length of set ownership

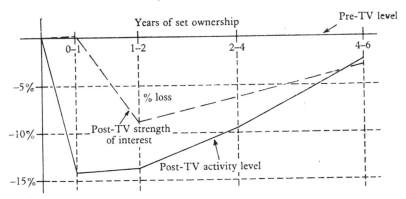

What Figure 1 suggests is that *activity* associated with viewers' interests undergoes a sharp reduction in the first year of set ownership (14.0%) and that this degree of loss is maintained during the second year (13.9%). It also indicates, however, that thereafter there is a steady tendency towards recovery (the loss is 9.7% after 2–4 years), and that after 4–6 years, activity associated with interests is almost back at its pre-television level. Moreover, the evidence leaves it quite possible that eventually there may be some overall *gain* in activity level.

With *strength of interest* — that is, a feeling of interest, irrespective of whether or not it is accompanied by activity — the position is somewhat different. In the first year there is no significant change; during the second, however, there is a fall by 8.6%. After that comes a tendency towards recovery: the loss is 5.9% after 2 to 4 years, and 3.3% after 4 to 6 years. The finding that there is no fall in strength of interest during the first year — despite a sharp reduction in associated activity — seems to have its explanation in the fact that television programs have, quite naturally, featured many of the interests in the sample (of interests) at some time or other in the past. Further reference will be made to this a little later on.

The extent and duration of change varies with the frequency with which interests are given active expression. Thus the number of interests which occasion activity fairly frequently is reduced by about 21% in the first year; this is followed by a partial recovery in the second year, but even at the end of about 5 years, the loss is still at the 10% level, and there is but little sign of it becoming less. On the other hand, the number of interests occasioning activity at a lower rate is reduced less sharply in the first year (7%), continues to decrease in the second year (12%), but thereafter undergoes a full recovery and possibly a long-term increase. The trends are given in Fig. 2.

Figure 2

Television's effects on number of interests pursued (a) very frequently, (b) less frequently.

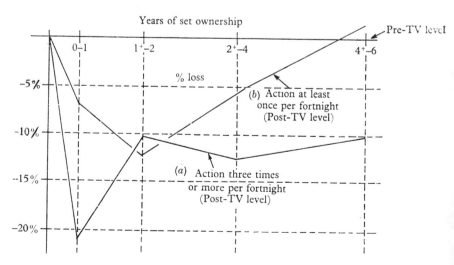

What all this means is that, from a long-term point of view, the main loss is in viewers' more intensely pursued interests, the recovery with those pursued less intensely being complete. Another way of putting this is to say that there is in the long-term a full recovery in the diversity or variety of behaviour associated with viewers' interests, but at a somewhat lower level of frequency. The position is much the same with the intensity of viewers' *feelings* of interest in various things.

Looked at from the long-term point of view, one might also say that television makes a difference at first but that, given time, people can 'take it in their stride' — as indeed, they appear to have done with many an earlier innovation. From the short-term point of view, however, the position is that there is an appreciable reduction in viewers' interests during the early years of set-ownership, and that though recovery tends thereafter to occur, the pre-television level is closely approached only after about 5 years. Moreover, if the buying of television sets continues at its present rate, it is likely that for society as a whole there will be an appreciable reduction in interests for some years to come.

Quite apart from the question of the size and the pattern of the loss, it is clear on the evidence that one of television's effects has been to render interests more passive, for the loss in behaviour is greater than that in 'strength of interest'. This passivity is specially marked in the first year, where the loss is only in terms of behaviour.

Television's Effects Upon TV-Featured Interests

It is an essential feature of the television scene that some interests are featured in programs, and that others (like visiting, being at home, playing darts, crossword puzzles, membership of clubs and associations) tend not to be. It is understandable that there should be some reduction with the latter group. But what happens with those that are directly featured? To what extent does this produce or enliven viewer interest in those things?

Project III was intended to answer this question. It dealt with 23 interests selected as a cross-section of those featured in television. The matching composites developed for the activity level and the strength of interest aspects of this enquiry were set out in Table 1. Their application led to the development of the following estimates of television's effects.

TABLE 3
Showing the extent of change in TV-featured interests

Variable under study	Non-viewer scores		Viewer scores	Loss or gain	Significance of difference
	Before matching to viewers	*After matching to viewers*		%	P
Strength of interest	44.74	44.80	44.63	−0.4	0.42
Level of associated behaviour	5.63	5.38	5.03	−6.5	0.01

This table indicates a non-significant loss with respect to strength of interest and a small but highly significant loss (6·5%) with respect to activity level.

Behind these averages were the year by year trends set out in Figure 3.

Figure 3

*Television's effect on interests when these are
featured in television programs*

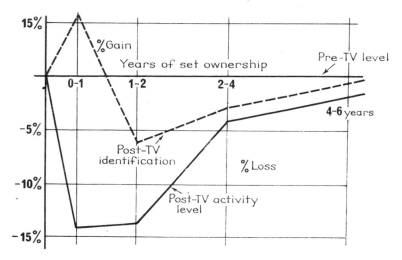

Very broadly speaking, these are quite similar to the trends for the overall sample of interests whether TV-featured or not: a loss, followed by recovery in the long term.

There are two things to be noted about these trends, however. One is that, despite a decrease later on, a strength of interest *increases* during the first year. Possibly this increase is associated with the novelty of first year TV ownership, though it is essentially a passive increase for it is accompanied by the usual sharp loss in associated activity. The second thing to notice is that the loss in activity tends to be slightly less than with the general sample (6·5%: 9·7%) and, by implication, less than the reduction for interests which are not so featured. The fact that the overall picture is one of reduction should not be interpreted to mean that merely to treat an interest in television programs is to reduce it. There is, in fact, evidence that with some interests this happens, but a more likely interpretation of the results is that treatment of interests in television programs makes up to only a small degree for the reducing effect which the process of continued viewing exerts on such interests in that longer period when they are not being so featured. It is as though the television medium carries a basic handicap, such that the person who wants to use it to develop interests of one kind or another has to start from 'well behind scratch'.

Television's Effects on a Number of
Specific Interests

Because this inquiry was based upon samples of the population's interests, it was possible to arrive at conclusions about television's effects on interests as a whole. These conclusions inevitably obscure much about the way in which the many specific interests making up the samples were affected.

Information about these could, however, be derived by applying the Stable Correlate method to each of them separately in order to establish television's effects. One of these interests was cinema-going and for this one, a detailed presentation of the problem and of the findings seems warranted.

Cinema going

One of the most common claims about the effects of television was that it was 'killing the cinema'. Here in Britain the main factual basis for the claim was that as the percentage of people with sets went up, cinema attendances went down and cinemas began closing. The year by year changes in set ownership and in cinema attendance are compared in Figure 4.

The same relationship had quickly emerged in American 'movie' statistics. Moreover, various comparisons in America of the movie going of viewers and non-viewers tied in with the indications of this relationship [227, 310]. So did the testimony of viewers themselves — namely that TV was reducing cinema going [222, 252, 351]. Indeed, the eivdence that television was a major factor in the decline of the cinema, was, in spite of its technical inadequacies (as evidence), too strong to be set aside. Nonetheless, both here and in America there were several discordant elements of information which suggested that the cause might not be television alone.

1. Lawton's 1950 study in Norman City and Oklahoma City [298] indicated that the decline in movie attendance amongst viewers was paralleled by an equal decline amongst non-viewers.

2. Bogart reported in *"The Age of Television"* [241] that at "the start of 1949, long before television became a force to be reckoned with, a *Wall Street Journal* survey of twenty cities found that attendance was down in all parts of the country. In November 1950, *Business Week* observed that the box office slump was as bad in Honolulu, which had no television, as in New York, which abounded in television homes."

3. In Britain there was an enormous wartime increase in cinema attendance, the level rising from 987,000,000 admissions in 1938 to 1,494,000000 in 1942 and reaching an all-time high of 1,635,000,000 in 1946. From that time, however, the decline set in and major losses had occurred *before* television restarted and long before television became anything of a force to be reckoned with. Indeed, the only reversal in that trend in the next ten or so years was in the first year of the resumed transmission from Alex-

andra Palace when cinema attendance temporarily went *up*. Indeed there is something about the steady downward trend that is suggestive simply of a return to the pre-war level of admissions.

Figure 4

Changes in cinema attendance and in percent with television sets.

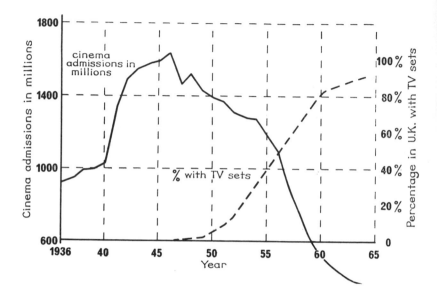

4. Finally, study (in 1953) of the opinions of cinema goers themselves had suggested that there was a considerable amount of dissatisfaction with the industry — a condition which might be expected to have contributed in at least some way to the decline in admissions.

None of these points is meant to argue away the possible influence of television on the cinema. All I am trying to do is to suggest that there could well be much more to the postwar decline in cinema admissions than a simple, direct influence of television, and that there was a strong case for research aimed at establishing precisely *what* the influence of television had been.

It was against this general background that cinema going was given special attention in that part of the present enquiry which dealt with television's effects in specific areas of interest. The special attention took the form of including in the pool of potential matching variables some thirteen different films which were box office successes in the period 1946–49 but which, on the available evidence, had not been shown in London since then. The questions asked were designed to find out for each of them if the respondent had seen it in that period. To help in the recall process, the names of leading members of the casts were given as well. Two of the thirteen follow as examples.

THE RED SHOES (with Moira Shearer, Anton Walbrook and Marius Goring).

PASSPORT TO PIMLICO (with Stanley Holloway, Margaret Rutherford and Hermione Baddeley).

Score out of 13 was then regarded as one of the 160 items from which the matching variables were to be selected. In fact this score emerged as a main matching variable both for the study of actual attendance at the cinema and for the study of desire to attend. It had a correlation of +0·61 with the actual attendance and 0·58 with 'desire to attend'. These figures rose respectively to 0·63 and to 0·59 when taken in combination with the best of the other matching variables derived. The two matching composites were then separately applied to produce the estimates of effects set out in Table 4.

It appears from this evidence that television has reduced cinema *attendance* of viewers by 33%, and the strength of *interest in* attending by 21%. Behind these totals lie differences in what happens year by year. Thus it appears that in the first year of set ownership there is an 11% decrease in attendance, that the loss increases to 42% in the second year, remains at about that level during the period between the second and fourth year, but that after this, a slight tendency towards recovery sets in, such that after about five years of set ownership, the loss stands at 31%. These

TABLE 4

Television's effects on cinema-going

Variable Studied	Set Age in Years	Viewers' Average	Non-viewer Averages (342 cases)		Loss or Gain	Significance of Difference
			Unadjusted Average	Adjusted Average		
					%	P
Attendance at	0 − 1	0.87	0.93	0.98	− 11	.01
the Cinema	1 − 2	0.67	0.93	1.16	− 42	.01
	2 − 4	0.54	0.93	0.95	− 43	.01
	4 − 6	0.66	0.93	0.95	− 31	.01
	0 − 6 (All)	0.67	0.93	1.00	− 33	.01
Strength of						
interest in	0 − 1	1.99	2.36	2.38	− 16	.01
cinema going	1 − 2	2.03	2.36	2.50	− 19	.01
	2 − 4	1.74	2.36	2.35	− 26	.01
	4 − 6	1.76	2.36	2.35	− 25	.01
	0 − 6 (All)	1.84	2.36	2.32	− 21	.01

trends have to do with actual attendance. But under the impact of television, even *interest* in attending decreases, the reduction reaching a maximum between the second and fourth years, and such recovery as occurs after that being of a very minor kind.

It is specially illuminating to compare these changes with those produced by television in interests generally — that is, as measured for the sample of 50 interests. This comparison is presented in Figure 5.

From this it appears that cinema going is affected to a far greater extent than are other interests and, perhaps more important, it appears to lack their resilience — their power to recover. Indeed, when the various interests in the sample were studied separately, there was no other interest amongst the 50 where the loss was as great or the lack of resilience as marked. Looking over the evidence, I think that there is a case for saying that here in Britain the cinema industry has yet to feel the full impact of television broadcasting[j]. This is partly because now, in 1956[j], there is yet no sign of a decrease in the rate at which people are becoming viewers; it is partly also because many viewers have yet to enter the period of really heavy loss[j]. In addition to this, however, the results given represent the effect of BBC television alone; with the rapid growth of Britain's commercial system, and the increased choice of programs which this provides, the power of television to draw people away from the cinema seems very likely to be increased.

Finally, there are several points which should, I think, be made. This evidence does not prove that television is the sole agent responsible for the decline in cinema attendance. It may well be that television's impact is facilitated by other things: perhaps by a return to some of the social conditions which influenced the prewar level of attendance; perhaps by something to do with the quality or the character of the films being shown now; perhaps by economic conditions. The evidence simply establishes television as a *contributor* to the decline.

Another point of relevance is that television's contribution to the decline ceases to increase after about three years, so that the question here in Britain is not one of whether or not television will 'kill the cinema'. Rather, it seems to be one of establishing the new level of operation to which the cinema industry is likely to gravitate in the absence of new developments or procedures.

Specific interests other than cinema going

Estimates of television's effects were also made for seventeen more specific areas of interest. Comments on some of these follow. The overall changes of all 17 are given in Table 5.

Gardening

When the changes for all viewers (irrespective of age of set) are combined, the overall change in the amount of gardening done is nil. This,

[j] As reported in 1956.

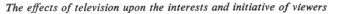

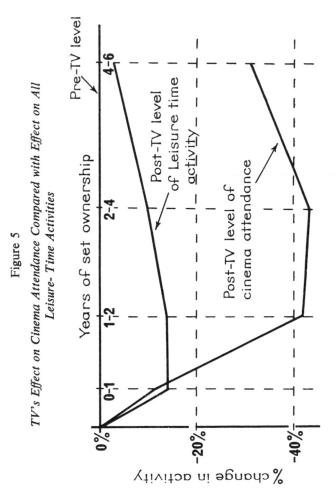

Figure 5

TV's Effect on Cinema Attendance Compared with Effect on All Leisure-Time Activities

however, masks what may be a telling trend. Thus a first-year reduction, by about 23%, is followed by a second-year gain of 13%. After that there is a tendency for gardening activity to return to its pre-television level.

Sport

Television led to a sharp increase both in attendance at and interest in major soccer matches by London viewers. The rises were 18% and 16% respectively. Though there was evidence of some fluctuations in this gain year by year, the tendency was for an appreciable increase to be maintained. In America in 1950, Jordan [289] reported that many more of his viewer informants were season ticket subscribers to football games than were the members of the total population (36% : 17%), but he interpreted this as evidence of pre-television differences between viewers and non-viewers. Sheatsley and Borsky, comparing a TV and a non-TV town for attendance at college football matches, reported a higher attendance in the latter and interpreted this as indicating a reducing effect of television in the TV town. In comparing this outcome with the present findings, it must be remembered that the latter dealt with *major* soccer matches whilst the American studies dealt with regular college football. Most important, the major soccer matches in Britain were *not* fully televised at the time, though frequently parts of them were shown later on.

There was a large increase in attendance at horse racing and show jumping and an appreciable rise in strength of interest in these sports. In this connection it may be highly relevant that show-jumping in particular had been featured frequently in television programs. There appear also to have been TV prompted increases in viewer interest in Wimbledon tennis and in skating: each had been featured in television programs particularly Wimbledon tennis.

Reading

The *number* of books read for pleasure or relaxation went down by 23% and even the strength of the viewer's interest in such book reading went down somewhat (9%). Moreover this effect appears to be of a continuing kind.

Along with this, there was a reduction in the *amount* of reading done in connection with such things as: events in different parts of the world (7%); modern developments in science (17%); international and world affairs (12%); politics in Great Britain (13%); people of other countries (26)%. If we are to attempt an evaluation of these changes, in social terms, it is well to note that most of the affected areas of interest had been the frequent subject of television broadcasts and that because of this, the above losses must be set against whatever intake there was of related program material by millions of people who would not in any case have read on those subjects at all. Various American studies also point to a drop in reading [252, 275, 303, 310, 351].

Attendance at clubs or association meetings

Contrary to expectation, television does not appear to have produced a permanent reduction in viewer's attendance at clubs or association meetings, though there are periods following the acquisition of a set when the losses are appreciable.

Going to see paintings

During the year of the study, television increased viewers' attendance at exhibitions of paintings. The increase was considerable, and it seems more than likely that it was associated with some of the televised presentations by Sir Gerald Kelly. Certainly the attendances at public galleries were greatly increased after certain of his broadcasts. The specially inter-

TABLE 5

*Television's effects in various fields of interest:
showing change in 'strength of interest' and in 'associated
activity'*

	Effect of TV	
	% Change	P
Cinema going		
Interest in going	– 20.6	0.01
Attendance	– 33.1	0.01
Theatre-going		
Interest in going	– 9.1	0.01
Attendance (at play)	– 43.7	0.01
Ballet		
Interest	– 11.2	0.04
Attendance	– 21.2	0.01
Looking at paintings		
Interest	– 7.0	0.09
Attendance at gallery	+ 52.1	0.01
Politics in Great Britain		
Interest	– 6.1	0.11
Reading about it	– 12.8	0.01
Membership of associations/clubs		
Interest	+ 0.8	NS*
Attendance	+ 1.7	NS
Book reading		
Interest	– 9.4	0.01
Books read	– 26.6	0.01
Gardening (indoors or outdoors)		
Interest	– 3.9	0.16
Amount done	0.0	NS
Card Playing		
Interest	– 1.3	NS
Time playing	– 10.3	0.14

* Where NS is shown, P = 0.17 or more

(Continued Table 5)

	Effect of TV	
	% Change	P
Playing gramophone records		
Interest	−17.5	0.01
Playing done	− 6.0	NS
Events in different parts of the world		
Interest	− 7.8	0.02
Reading about them	− 6.8	0.12
Modern developments in science		
Interest	+ 4.0	NS
Reading about them	−17.9	0.03
International and world affairs		
Interest	+ 1.5	NS
Reading about them	−11.9	0.01
Places of historic importance		
Interest	− 5.2	0.14
Made a visit	−29.1	0.01
Information about people in other countries		
Interest about them	− 5.2	0.09
Reading about them	−26.1	0.01
Going to see sporting events		
Interest in going	− 9.2	0.01
Attendance	+10.4	0.14
Major soccer matches		
Interest	+15.6	0.01
Attendance	+18.2	0.01
Horse racing or horse jumping		
Interest	+11.2	0.02
Attendance	+47.4	0.01

esting feature of this evidence, however, is that there was also an overall reduction in viewers' *feeling* of interest in looking at paintings. This paradox appears to have its explanation in the fact that the increase in attendance was largely on the part of the minority who had been before. *Their* feeling of interest in looking at paintings had *increased*. The reduction in interest involved the great majority who had not ever been to see paintings (at an art gallery).

The Lack of Generality in Television's Effects on Interests

One thing which these results make clear is that, despite the nature of television's effect on interests as a whole, there is considerable variation in what happens to specific interests. Some are reduced quite sharply, others remain little changed, while a few undergo increase. Moreover, a reduction in activity level does not necessarily go with a reduction in viewer's feelings of interest. Nor is the opposite the case. While it is only partly indicated here, television's effect on these interests, year by year, is also quite varied, there being a lot of deviation from the general pattern of early loss and later recovery. From both these lines of evidence, it follows that a knowledge merely of television's effects on interests as a whole does not allow us to say what happens in any specific field of interest. Nor does it help much to know whether or not the interest was television-featured, for in both the 'featured' and the 'not-featured' groups of interests, the variability in effect is very marked indeed.

It was only for the eighteen interests in Table 5 that the full matching procedure was carried out. For the remaining forty-two interests included in the various samples, only the unadjusted differences between viewers and non-viewers are presented. These are given in Appendix 3. While, taken along with other information, these differences provide grounds for speculation about the dynamics of television's effects, such speculation is not attempted in this report because the aim here is to stay as much as possible with a factual presentation. Nonetheless, the application of the Stable Correlate matching procedure to the remaining forty-two interests, and the development from these of a system of hypotheses, seems to be the logical follow-up to this inquiry. It should serve to show which kinds of interest are more affected and which are less affected by television, and it may serve to indicate why. In addition it may well indicate what can reasonably be expected when different kinds of interest are presented through this particular mass medium.

Television's Effects Upon Initiative

The matching criteria for the study of initiative were applied in just the same way as were those for the study of interests. The results are shown in Table 6.

Table 6

Television's effect upon initiative

Set age in Years	Non-Viewer Scores		Viewer Scores	Loss or Gain	Signif. of Difference
	Before Matching To Viewers	*After Matching To Viewers*		%	P
0−1	13.38	12.81	10.18	−20.5	0.01
1−2	13.38	13.37	11.34	−15.2	0.01
2−4	13.38	12.68	13.12	+ 3.5	0.21
4−6	13.38	13.21	13.82	+ 4.6	0.11
All	13.38	13.00	12.48	− 4.0	0.01

On the evidence of this table, the frequency of acts of initiative underwent a 21% loss in the first year of set ownership. Thereafter, however, recovery was fairly rapid and there appears to be even a slight gain by the third and fourth years, a gain which is maintained during the fifth and sixth years.

Effects in terms of *diversity* of initiative were also calculated. A diversity score is simply the total number of the thirty acts which were done at least once (in a two week period). As must be expected, effects in terms of this score are very similar to those already described, though they are not quite as extreme in the first year.

0—1 years	...	...	−15.8%
1—2 years	...	...	−15.7%
2—4 years	...	...	− 0.7%
4—6 years	...	...	− 0.5%
All	...	...	− 5.7%

SEEING THE RESULTS IN PROPER PERSPECTIVE

It is well to conclude by stressing some of the limitations of this inquiry. The first is that it is based upon the adult population of Greater London less the 'over 65 years' and less that 15% of the population living in the more economically depressed of the polling districts. As it happens, relatively few of the viewers were, at the time of this study, to be found in these excluded groups. But the main point is that the results for Greater London do not necessarily apply in other urban concentrations or in rural areas or small towns. The second defining point is that the study of interest was one of television's effects on interests other than the interest of viewing itself: thus there is a sense in which it has been a study of the effects of the viewing interest on other interests.

SUMMARY OF THE ENQUIRY

1. *Aims.* The aim of this study was to measure the effect of television upon the interests and the initiative of adult viewers in London and to relate the extent of the effect to length of set ownership.

2. *Methods.* The Stable Correlate method was used for the isolation of effects. There was extensive preliminary test construction, and the measurement of television's effects was made against a representative cross-section of the public's interest in the one case, and of their acts of initiative in the other. The final survey was based upon 782 cases and the construction of measuring devices upon about 3000.

3. *Results.* The effect of television has been to reduce both interests and initiative. The reduction of interests is not only in terms of activity level but in terms of viewers' *feeling* of interest as well. Even when interests are featured in television programs themselves, the loss to television is

made up to only a very small degree. Television's effects do, however, vary markedly from one group of interests to another. The loss in initiative and in interests extends over a period of five to six years. Generally speaking, the loss is greatest in the first few years, after which there is a gradual recovery.

APPENDIX I

DEVELOPING A REPRESENTATIVE SAMPLE OF THE INTERESTS OF ADULT LONDONERS

The sample was developed in three stages: (i) a compilation, tending toward exhaustiveness, was made of the interests of adults in Greater London; (ii) this list was made the basis of a survey to determine the relative size of the following for each interest (that is, the proportion endorsing each item in the list as something they were interested in; (iii) a sample of 50 of the 450 in the original list was then selected on random principles with a control over the size of the following of the listed items. Details follow.

Compiling a full list of interests
In the first of these three stages, 350 members of the London public who were waiting to join a BBC panel, were asked to write down as many as possible of their interests. They were asked to do this over a full week, adding more of their interests as they thought of them. The 85% of these who did so were fairly representatively varied in terms of occupational level, education and age; about half were women and half men.

From the returned forms, a compilation was made of the many listed interests. To a marked degree the forms of reference used by the contributors was preserved. A single mention of an interest was enough to get it into the compilation. A further source of items was then brought to the compilation, namely that part of the results of a national survey which dealt with the public's interests.

After a limited amount of generalization necessary to handle the enumerations at all, the final list consisted of approximately 450 'areas of interest'. Some of the features of the 'areas of interest' in this long list are worth special note.

(a) A lot of them were *fairly specific* (e.g., fashions of the past, going to watch soccer played, naval and military history, indoor gardening, playing darts).
(b) Some of the listed areas of interest were limited to one aspect of something which was already fairly specific (for example, '*playing cards myself*'), whilst with others this finer distinction was not made (for example, 'the royal family'). This was in line with the principle that 'areas of interest' should be reproduced in the form in which they tended to be given in the original enumeration by informants. Where the form alternated, each of the references was entered in the list (for example, 'local affairs' and 'taking part in local affairs').
(c) The list included many items of a kind tending not to occur in traditional classifications or lists of interests. Examples are: Old English hall-marks, mothercraft, bell ringing, wines, the British countryside, festive occasions, labour saving gadgets and ideas, my personal appearance, the United Nations Organisation.

Establishing the relative followings of all 'areas of interest' in the list
For convenience, the list was randomly broken into workably small sections, five in all, and a separate small-scale survey was conducted with respect to each of them. The five surveys were limited to Greater London, were random in character, and were conducted all at the same time. The effective sample size for each of the five surveys was approximately 225 adults (1125 in all). Respondents indicated, for each item on a list, whether or not it was one of their interests and, if so, the strength of their interest in it. The survey thus provided a general indication of the relative size of following for all 450 areas of interest.

Selecting a sample of 50 areas of interest
The aim in sampling was to draw from the 450 items a cross-section of the public's interest, properly weighted in terms of *kind* of interest and numerical size of following. The 450 areas of interest were set in order according to the size of following of each, running from small to large. Cumulative frequencies were set beside the listed items, working from the top to the bottom of the list of 450. The total was 17,690.

Since 50 items were to be selected, the list was divided into fifty sections, equal in terms of cumulative frequency. Thus the first cutting point, running down the list, was where the culmative frequency count reached 354 i.e., 17,690/50); the next was at 708, and so on up to 17,690. Within each of these fifty sections, one item was drawn on random principles (but under one further control as indicated below). Obviously the first of the 50 sub-sections included many items because in this section were the items with only small followings; on the other hand, the last of the sub-sections contained relatively few items. The fact that only one item came from each of the fifty sub-sections ensured that rate items occurred only in due proportion in the final sample (no matter how important they might seem to be). The first item selected came from the sub-section with the smallest number of items in it and the selection was random; the next selection was made from the section with the next largest number of items in it and so on, the last selection being made from the sub-group with the largest number of items in it. This order of selection made possible the imposition of a further control over the selection process. This was a control to ensure that the items selected were not unduly similar in kind. Thus if the second item, drawn randomly, had happened to be closely similar to the first one drawn, (e.g. 'meeting old friends' and 'mixing with people') another item in the second sub-section was drawn, namely the one next to it, working alternately downwards and upwards. The large number of items in the last sub-section was necessary in view of the amount of 'play' required at this stage.

The selected sample of fifty items is set out in List 1 in this chapter. This sample of *areas of interest* was to be used as a basis for generalizing about the effects of television on interests both in terms of activity level and in terms of intensity of the feeling of interest.

Appendix II

DEVELOPING THE SAMPLE OF ACTS OF INITIATIVE

There were three stages in the development of this sample: (i) the compilation of a list of the different acts of initiative ordinarily occurring in London; (ii) the establishment of the relative frequency of occurrence of each of the acts in this list and the calculation of its validity index; (iii) the drawing of the sample with frequency of occurrence and validity as controls.

Compiling the list
Approximately 300 adult Londoners of fairly representative background were asked to write down one or more examples of initiative drawn from their own everyday lives. The request put to these people had been as follows.

> "Please write down a description of one or more actions or incidents which in your opinion show *initiative. We would like you to draw your examples from your own everyday life*".

Approximately 800 acts were given. These were highly varied in detail, but on analysis they reduced to a relatively limited number of categories or kinds, namely 120 in all. This 120 was regarded as a universe from which a sample of 30 of the more valid items was to be selected with a control over frequency of occurrence.

Assessing frequency and validity

A small scale random survey (130 adults only) was conducted in London to establish approximately the relative frequency of occurrence of the 120 different kinds of acts in the total list. Data from this survey were also used to calculate the correlation between individual items and total score on the whole 120 items. This correlation index was regarded as a limited form of validity check and was used as one of several controls in the drawing of the 30 item sample of acts.

Selecting the sample

The 120 acts were set in order according to frequency of occurrence and cumulative totals were entered against them from top to bottom of the list. On the basis of these totals the lists were split into 30 sections in just the same way as was done with respect to the drawing of the general sample of *interests* (see Appendix 1). One item was drawn from each of these sections, namely the one with the highest validity index. Where this one happened to be very similar to an act already selected, the item with the next highest validity index in that subgroup was selected in its stead. The 30 items selected are set out in Table 7 below. For each of the 30, this table gives the percentage who claimed they did it in the last 4 weeks and its validity index. (The period '4 weeks' was used in the development of the sample, but in the final survey this qualifying period was reduced to 2 weeks).

TABLE 7.

List of the thirty acts of initiative included in the initiative sample

List of items Selected	Propor- tion so doing in last 4 weeks %	Validity index (+0.) (p.bis) r
I changed my doctor or dentist or one of my tradesman because I was not satisfied	6	.30
I took an active part in out-door sports of some kind (for example: football, tennis, cycling, athletics, shooting, hockey, bowls, fishing, and so on).	8	.22
When my transport was running late, I used another means of transport.	8	.26
I thought of something ahead of others (If possible, please give a few details of what it was).	9	.37
Rather than buy new materials for a job I had to do, I made do with odds and ends I had on hand (for example: in dress-making, in sewing, in carpentry, and so on).	9	26

List of items Selected	Proportion so doing in last 4 weeks %	Validity index (+0.) (p.bis) r
I made a firm decision to meet some particular person or went out of my way to get in touch with someone.	11	.38
I persuaded other people to do something (for example: something which I thought needed doing; something to benefit all concerned; something for my own benefit, and so on).	11	.46
I corrected some member of the public who was acting badly.	12	.33
I turned a mistake into a success or at least prevented an error from spoiling things (for example: in cooking, in carpentry or house-keeping, in dress-making, and so on).	12	47
I did some nature study of some kind (for example: bird-watching, botany, geology, biology, and so on).	15	.32
When a hitch occurred in something I was doing, I quickly got things going again.	16	.50
Rather than buy an article shown in the shops, I worked out a way of making it myself (for example: a piece of furniture, a dress, a gadget, and so on).	17	.33
I went to a lot of trouble to achieve something (Please say what it was and be sure that you have not counted it already).	17	.52
I introduced something different (into my work or into my home) or found a better way of doing one of my jobs (Please make sure that you have not counted it already).	18	.35
I went out of my way or made a special effort to get some information or news about something.	18	.61
I took part in a board game of some kind or in a parlour game (for example: darts, monopoly, chess, and so on).	21	.34
I decided on the spur of the moment to buy something.	23	.40
When I couldn't get what I wanted in one way or in one place, I tried another way or another place.	25	.40
I started up a conversation with someone I didn't know before.	27	.45
When the proper tool or instrument or material was not available, I made do with something else (for example: I made a rough and ready copy of the missing tool or instrument; I thought of a way to make another tool or instrument to do the same job; I thought of a way to use different kinds of material to do the same job; and so on).	28	.35
I travelled ten miles or more for the sake of an interest.	29	.30
I did someone else's job for him or her without being told to do so.	30	.41
I invited someone home to a meal or to stay for a period.	33	.25
When something broke or ceased to work, I mended it.	34	.34

List of items selected	Proportion so doing in last 4 weeks %	Validity index (+0.) (p.bis) r
I used a text-book or journal or newspaper to make a study of something (for example: a technical subject; history; current affairs; animals; home economy, and so on). *This does NOT mean ordinary newspaper reading.*	34	.35
I helped someone in difficulty of some kind or when help was needed (for example: a woman fell and I helped her with her parcels; I helped someone I didn't know to cross the street; I was able to help with advice or information; and so on).	37	.46
I used a dictionary.	39	.47
I did some work on a hobby or interest of some kind (for example: a handcraft; woodwork; pottery; embroidery; design; photography; gadgets; and so on).	43	.30
I wrote a letter to a friend or acquaintance or relation.	63	.27

APPENDIX III

DIFFERENCES BETWEEN THE INTERESTS OF VIEWERS AND OF NON-VIEWERS

Early in this list are those items for which the activity score of viewers was greater than that of non-viewers, and later on come those for which the non-viewer score was the greater. All fifty items making up the general sample of interests are included.

TABLE 8.

Area of Interest	Difference† between scores of viewers and non-viewers expressed as a percentage of non-viewer score	
	Activity level %	Strength of interest %
Visiting the Zoo	+183	—
Weaving	+ 78	+ 4
Ice or roller skating	+ 67	+26
Motor Cars	+ 66	+10
*Looking at paintings	+ 52	− 7
Trade Unionism	+ 51	− 9
*Horse racing or horse jumping	+ 47	+11
Interior decoration of the home	+ 37	+ 1
Variety and vaudeville shows	+ 26	+18
Tennis (Wimbledon)	+ 25	+13
The English countryside	+ 23	− 7
*Major soccer matches	+ 18	+16
Darts	+ 14	+10
Going to see sporting events	+ 10	− 9
The Royal Family	+ 8	+ 1
Rifle or revolver shooting	+ 8	−12
Fashions to-day	+ 4	− 5
Different ways of preparing food	+ 4	−11
*Membership of clubs or associations	+ 2	+ 1
*Welfare work	+ 1	− 6
*Gardening	0	− 4
Jobs of others	− 2	−11
Cricket	− 3	+ 2
*Playing gramophone records	− 6	−18
Talking about the past	− 7	− 8
*Events in different parts of the world	− 7	− 8
Labour-saving gadgets and ideas	− 8	+ 7
*Card playing	− 10	− 1
Physical culture	− 10	−14
Collecting things	− 10	−26
Festive occasions	− 11	− 3
*International affairs	− 12	+ 2
*Politics in Great Britain	− 13	− 6
Visiting People	− 14	−12
*Modern developments in science	− 18	+ 4
Reading about animals and birds of the world	− 21	—
Listening to or attending lectures or talks	− 21	−10
*Ballet	− 21	−11
Strolling in the park	− 22	− 7
English towns	− 24	− 8
Chinaware and pottery	− 24	−12

Area of Interest	Difference between Viewer and Non-Viewer scores as a percentage of non-Viewer Score	
	Activity Level %	*Strength of Interest* %
*People of other countries	− 26	− 5
Crossword puzzles	− 27	− 3
Photography	− 27	− 5
*Book reading	− 27	− 9
*Places of historic importance	− 29	− 5
History	− 32	− 14
Bird watching	− 32	− 17
*Cinema-going	− 33	− 21
Talking about dreams	− 42	− 17
*Going to the theatre to see a play	− 44	− 9
Listening to light music	− 49	− 6
Architecture of churches and cathedrals	− 50	− 8
Military bands	− 55	− 6
Hypnotism	−	+ 5
Needlework	−	− 1
Animals and birds of the world	−	− 1
Gardens	−	− 6
Ideas and doings of well-known people	−	− 9
Making new friends	−	− 11
Railways	−	− 24
Sculpture	−	− 39

− Not assessed.

* In these cases, differences in score have been corrected to eliminate 'original differences' between viewers and non-viewers, and hence the percentage shown approximates to an 'effect of television'.

† Where the percentage is positive, viewer score is greater than non-viewer score; where the percentage is negative, the opposite is the case.

[23]

The effects of television upon some aspects of family life and of sociability[a]

BACKGROUND AND AIMS

This enquiry, like the one on interests and initiative, had its origin both in the flood of speculation that accompanied television's rapid growth and in the desire to know what television was in fact doing to people.

Two broad issues were chosen for enquiry, namely television's effects on some aspects of (i) family life and (ii) sociability. This selection was based upon preliminary examination of the literature of research and upon the opinions of viewers themselves about television's effects. These opinions had been gathered in a preliminary study, the methods and results of which were set out in Chapter 20.

The 'family life' study was divided into five sub-projects, namely the effects of television upon:

(1) the degree to which members of the family stay at home together;
(2) the degree to which the married couple stays at home together;
(3) the degree to which the younger members of the family stay at home together;
(4) the total mount of activity of a home-centred kind which ordinarily occurs (at home);
(5) the degree to which the various members of the household do things together (e.g., do the washing up together, play gramophone records together).

The 'sociability' study also had several sub-divisions, one of which is reported here, namely the effects of television upon: the ordinary run of sociable acts as they occur in the day-by-day round of events (e.g., talking

[a] This enquiry was designed and directed by the writer and carried out during 1956 by the Audience Research Department of the BBC under a supervisory committee. Members of the supervisory committee were Professors A. R. Knight (Chairman), M. G. Kendall, P. E. Vernon and Barbara Wootton. The report was presented in 1959 under the title "Television and the Family", and it is on this report that the present statement is based.

to neighbours, taking a meal out with an acquaintace, lending a neighbour something, providing information to a stranger, going to a club.

Since it was by no means certain that television's effects would prove to be uniform everywhere and at all times, it was decided that separate surveys should be made in each of two large cities (London and Birmingham) and that there should be a third in a small town well away from these two cities (Wakefield was selected). Surveys were to be made in both winter and summer in London, the Birmingham survey was to be made in winter, and the Wakefield survey in summer.

THE METHODS OF RESEARCH

(Common to the Different Sub-Projects)

A considerable amount of methodological work was done in preparation for this enquiry, much of it for the development of the necessary measuring instruments. The latter were then built into a questionnaire and this was completed in the context of a research design based upon the Stable Correlate technique. The methods of this enquiry were closely modelled on those of the study reported in Chapter 22.

The research design

The Stable Correlate technique has been described in considerable detail in Chapter 21 and was referred to again in Chapter 22. Accordingly its description here is limited to its basic features and to those aspects of the technique which are specific to this enquiry.

The central feature of the Stable Correlate method *as used in this enquiry* is that non-viewers are matched to viewers in terms of variables derived in a strictly empirical way. This special form of matching is intended to remove as much as possible of the influence of original differences between viewers and non-viewers, so that the remaining difference between them may be regarded as approximating to an effect of television. The variables for use in matching are selected on the basis of the extent of their correlation with the behaviour being studied (that is, as possibly affected by television). The overall aim of the selection procedure is to derive a composite of variables which jointly have a high degree of matching power. For example, in the study of television's effects on sociability, this would mean a higher joint correlation with sociability. Matching variables must be 'stable' in the sense that they are not themselves open to change through television.

It follows from the above that the matching composite suitable for the study of television's effects in one field of behaviour (e.g. sociability) will not necessarily be suitable for studies in other fields of behaviour (e.g., the amount of activity of a home-centred kind). This makes the research process extremely burdensome, but this is unavoidable if the matching is to be satisfactory.

There were approximately 200 variables in the pool of items from which the different matching composites were to be selected. These items had been brought together on one or both of the following expectations: (i) they might possibly be correlated with one or another of the different fields of behaviour to be studied; (ii) they represented possible sources of difference between viewers and non-viewers. All these variables were introduced into the enquiry itself and from them fourteen separate matching composites were derived. These were applied separately for each different field of study and separate estimates of effects were developed. Within each field of study, non-viewers were separatel; matched to each of four groups of viewers classified according to age of set, and hence estimates were also developed of effects by 'age of set'.

The selection of each composite of variables was made in the same way. The one developed for the study of television's effects on joint activity in the home is presented as an example. In this case, the first matching variable to be selected was 'family type', this being a five-group classification of families running from the young married couple without children right through to the old couple whose children have all grown up and left home. This variable was selected because it had a higher numerical association with 'joint activity' than had any other of the 200 variables in the pool. For matching purposes, the sample was then split into two groups, namely 'younger families' on the one hand, consisting of young couples, young families and larger families, and on the other of 'older families' consisting of adult families and older couples. *Separately for each of these two groups*, a fresh search was made for the variable with the highest association with 'joint activity' score. In fact the variable which qualified in this way for the 'younger family' section of the sample was different from that which qualified in the 'older family' section of the sample. These two variables were respectively *sex* and *number of person in the respondent's household*. This selection of second order matching variables led to the splitting of the sample into four sections. The process was continued and eventually yielded 17 sub-groups as set out in Figure 1.

In using this matching composite (to achieve matching of non-viewers to viewers), each of the viewer and the non-viewer samples was separately split into the 17 subgroups. The average score for joint activity was calculated for each of the 17 subgroups in the non-viewer sample and each of these averages was then multiplied by the number of people in the equivalent subgroup of the viewer sample. These products were then added and a new average (for the whole non-viewer sample) was calculated. This process is called matching by multiplication and it is illustrated in Table 1. The new average for the non-viewers (i.e., their adjusted average) was then subtracted from the average for the viewers to yield an estimate of the effects of television upon 'joint activity' in the family.

In some of the other fields of study in this enquiry, the matching of non-viewers to viewers was through the *replication of non-viewer records* in such a way as to make the non-viewers equal to the viewers in terms

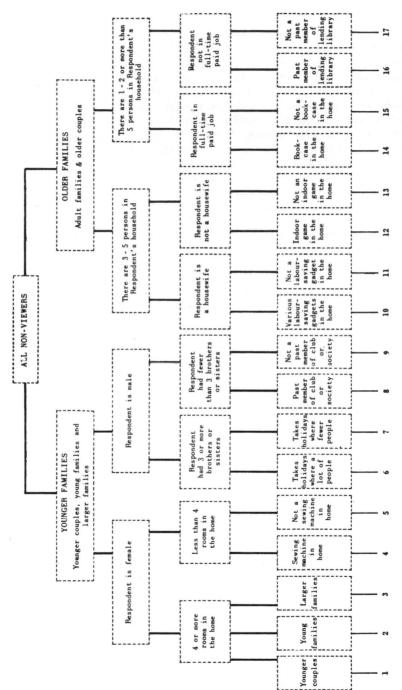

Figure 1

of the distribution of people across the various subgroups defined by the matching composite.

Making the measuring instruments

For some of the measuring devices to be used in the enquiry it was sufficient to pilot-test different ways of asking for information. For others, however, notably those to be used in the study of sociability, of home centred behaviour and of joint activity, a major program of test construction was called for. The reason for this was as follows. In each of these studies, the research aim was to find out whether or not television had changed viewers' behaviour. Had it for instance increased or decreased the amount of day-to-day sociable activity; had it affected the number of the viewer's home centred acts; had it changed the total amount of joint activity occurring in the home? The answer to these questions depended to a large degree upon which particular activities were studied, for it was unlikely that all activities within one or another of these groups would be affected by television in the same way. A balanced assessment of television's effects upon, for instance, society's sociable behaviour could be derived only if study were based upon *a truly representative sample* of the

TABLE 1.

Showing the multiplication method of applying the matching composites

Subgroup	Number in Non-viewer subgroup	Average score for those in non-viewer subgroup	Number in viewer subgroup	Product (2) × (3)
	(1)	(2)	(3)	
1	35	2.60	71	184.6
2	78	3.03	205	621.2
3	37	4.17	59	246.0
4	9	2.33	41	95.5
5	21	1.81	36	65.2
6	45	2.42	120	290.4
7	41	2.83	110	311.3
8	44	2.66	127	337.8
9	25	3.16	67	211.7
10	17	4.01	67	268.7
11	52	2.10	78	163.8
12	53	2.34	145	339.3
13	37	3.03	79	239.4
14	22	1.73	52	90.0
15	30	1.00	40	40.0
16	27	2.19	31	67.9
17	34	3.50	58	203.0
Totals	607		1386	3775.8

many different sociable activities which ordinarily occur within that society. The same applies to society's home centred activities and to the amount of joint activity going on within families.

Samples of *activities* had therefore to be developed. The method of their development was modelled upon that devised for the sampling of interests and of initiative (as described in Chapter 22) and it entailed two stages of research. In the first stage, survey methods were used to get records from a sample of 200 adults of (a) the different kinds of sociable acts which they had observed around them or had carried out themselves and (b) the different kinds of household activities occurring in the ordinary daily round of events in the home. These were then listed in separate sections of a questionnaire which was taken to a second survey sample of 500 adults, their task being to indicate how often, if at all, they had themselves done these various things during some specified period of time. This made it possible to set the frequency of occurrence against each item in the different lists, and from this information it was then possible to select weighted samples of (i) sociable acts and (ii) home centred acts.

A slightly different method was used in developing the cross-section of activities with respect to which there was joint activity in the family. In the second of the two surveys used in the construction process, information was gathered not only about the frequency of occurrence of a large number of specified home-centred acts, but also about *which* members of the family took part in these acts. This information provided a measure of the relative *amount* of joint activity ordinarily accruing to the different acts in the list and it made possible the drawing of a weighted cross-section of them — weighted, that is, in terms of relative *amount* of joint activity.

One other consideration entered into selection of the three samples. Once the first survey had yielded a list of acts regarded by their originators as representing either sociable or household behaviour, a panel of judges rated them for either sociability or for home-centredness. These ratings led to the throwing out of a limited number of items from each list. They were used also as a secondary control system in an otherwise random selection of the sample. In other words, the selection of home centred acts was random within the stricture of two controls: the frequency of occurrence of the acts concerned; the average ratings given them for home centredness by a panel of judges. The same system of selection applied to the sample of 'sociable' acts.

The three samples of acts are given in the context of the findings as are several fairly specific details about their development. For each of these samples, the basic information required for the study of effects was frequency of occurrence within some specified period. This information was collected through a sample survey using the form of questionnaire described below.

The questionnaire

The questionnaire consisted of a booklet with a number of different sections, each having to do with one or more of the nine studies in the project. One section provided for the making of a half-hourly record mainly of the times at which members of the family were at home. The next section was concerned with activities in the home, and it dealt with home-centred activities and joint activity in the family. There was also a section dealing with sociable activities.

Last of all came several pages asking questions about the respondent himself/herself. These questions had three purposes: (i) to establish whether or not the respondent had a television set and if so for how long; (ii) to get basic information about the respondent (e.g., age, sex, marital state, occupational level so that an assessment could be made of television's effects upon different sub-sections of society; (iii) to provide the necessary information for the selection of the various composites of matching variables. For this third purpose, a very wide range of questions was asked. There were questions about present or past job (e.g., whether in a part-time or full-time job, whether a housewife or not, whether retired, and so on); about sociable outlets at the respondent's place of work (if in employment); about educational background (e.g., age of ceasing full-time schooling, whether or not respondent had undertaken any further education or training since then); about family composition, the size of the home, whether the home was rented, whether there was a garden, how long the respondent had been in present home. There were also questions about the kinds of transport used, whether or not transport was used at a regular time; about the presence of any of a wide range of durable goods in the respondent's home and about a large number of past activities and achievements. There were in addition questions about the respondent's own childhood (e.g., number of brothers or sisters, whether respondent had a pet of any kind, played a musical instrument, took part in sports). The items under (ii) above were also to be included in this pool of potential matching variables. The full set of questions asked for this purpose, along with some asked earlier in the questionnaire, provided a basis for about 200 items in the pool of possible matching variables.

Clearly many of the items in this pool might be subject to memory errors. In this respect, it is most important to be aware that what matters about a matching criterion — whether it be an accurate measure of something or not — is its power to predict some specified test score. What we need to be wary about is the possibility that such errors as feature some statements by respondents are not influenced by television, for this would mean that the variable was not *stable* in relation to television.

The administration of the questionnaire

The interviewer was to introduce the booklet to the survey respondent, explain its purpose, and get the respondent to make a start on the completion of the early parts of it to show how it should be done. For several reasons, the greater part of the booklet questionnaire was to be completed in the interviewer's absence. Thus much of the questionnaire was in the form of a diary which had to be completed on a specified day. Further, some of the information required had to be checked with the whole family and it would have been too costly for the interviewer to have done this. Indeed, some of the questions could be much better answered if the respondent was free to get help (in remembering) from others in the family. The interviewer called back to collect the completed booklet at a prearranged time.

This self-completion technique, which had been highly successful in earlier surveys, and which had been piloted in the instrument-making phase of this enquiry, nonetheless imposed a number of conditions on the design of the booklet-questionnaire. The questionnaire had, above all things, to be simple and the instructions well placed and simply worded. It had to be interesting in itself and as attractive looking as possible. Hence the various sections of the booklet were in different colours, examples of what was required were frequently given, and slips reminding the respondent about certain of the more important rules were placed throughout the booklet.

Each booklet carried a statement drawing attention to the fact that part of it referred specially to a particular day, when a diary had to be completed. The day varied from booklet to booklet, the total sample of booklets for a given area being spread equally over a large number of consecutive days.

The surveys

The booklet questionnaire was used in four separate surveys, each based upon a representative sample of viewers and non-viewers. Two were conducted in Greater London, one in winter (approximately 2440 cases) and the other in summer (approximately 2320 cases). The third was in Birmingham in the winter (approximately 2340 cases) and the fourth in Wakefield in the summer (approximately 1130 cases). The two winter surveys (London and Birmingham) were made in October-November 1955, one of them starting a week after the other and each extending over 28 consecutive diary days (though of course a single respondent completed diary details for only one of these days. The two summer surveys (London and Wakefield) occurred in June – July 1956, the London survey running for four weeks and the Wakefield survey starting a week later and running for two weeks.

In each of these surveys a stratified sample was used, names being drawn on the random principle from the electoral registers. The stratification was in terms of geographical area and economic level. Just as in the study of interests and initiative and for the same reasons, these four samples were truncated in two ways: they excluded people living in the most economically depressed 15% of the polling districts in the total area; they excluded homes in which the survey contact proved to be over 65 years of age. In this enquiry, the non-viewer sample did not have to be as big as the viewer sample and so only each second non-viewer encountered amongst those listed for contact was interviewed. The selection of each 'second' non-viewer was closely controlled.

Interviewing success rates

For all four surveys taken together, about 5% of those listed for interview were not contacted after three calls and approximately 2% refused to co-operate. Of the 8,230 with whom booklets were left, 6% failed to complete at least one of the eight sections of the questionnaire.

THE DIFFERENT SUB-PROJECTS

SUB-PROJECT I: TELEVISION'S EFFECTS IN KEEPING FAMILY TOGETHER AT HOME

METHODS AND FINDINGS

Some Additional Aspects of Methods Used

A diary-type record had been used to establish the times at which each member of the respondent's household was at home during a specified day. The diary *day* varied from one household to another, each day of the week being represented by an equal number of diaries. The record kept was for each half-hour between 6·30 a.m. and 11.30 p.m.

The analysis of family togetherness was based upon the *primary family unit*. This was confined to the parent(s) and such dependent or unmarried offspring as lived with them. Persons living alone were not included in the analysis. The degree to which the family was at home together was measured in terms of the proportion of the family at home during a given half-hour. This measure was taken for each of the 34 half-hours in the period studied. This information, analysed within the stable correlate research design, led to estimates of television's effects for each of these 34 time periods.

The matching criteria selected were developed in the manner described in this chapter. They included, in order of matching power: the number of people in the primary family unit; the number of people in it who were in full-time employment; various characteristics of the family, including number of children under 5, number between 14 and 17; whether survey contact said he was, as a child, a member of a club of society of any kind; tendency of the respondent to leave parts of the questionnaire and diary incomplete. On the basis of these matching criteria, the viewer sample and the non-viewer sample were divided into those 38 sub-groups which were most relevant for matching purposes. The non-viewer sample was then weighted up so that its proportionate make-up across the 38 matching sub-groups was the same as the make-up for the viewer sample.

Findings

Let me first describe the pre-television pattern of 'family at-homeness', as indicated by the results for the 'control groups'[b]. In the control homes[b] studied, the average number of people in the primary family unit varied slightly from area to area: 3.17 in London in the winter and 3.10 in the summer; 3.14 in Birmingham in the winter, 3.05 in Wakefield in the summer. In the course of the day there are, of course, marked variations in the degree to which the family is at home together, but the pattern of these variations was strikingly similar for all four surveys. With minor exceptions, the pre-television pattern for London, in the winter, can be taken as typical and this is shown in Figure 2. One aim of this enquiry was to find out the degree to which television had altered this pattern.

Overall changes

Table 2 shows the estimated changes produced by television for the average half-hour of the whole period between 6.30 a.m. and 11.30 p.m. There are separate estimates for each of the four surveys.

TABLE 2

*Television's effect upon family at-homeness**

Survey	Average Size of Primary Family Unit	Average Number at Home During the Average Half Hour		
		Control Group	*Viewer Group*	*Diff-erence*	*Change*
	Persons	Persons	Persons		%
London (winter)	3.17	1.90	1.95	+ 0.05	+ 2.6
London (summer)	3.10	1.80	1.83	+ 0.03	+ 1.7
Birmingham (winter)	3.14	1.93	1.97	+ 0.04	+ 2.1
Wakefield (summer)	3.05	1.76	1.85	+ 0.09	+ 5.1

* Figures based on average for *all* half hour periods from 6.30 a.m. till 11.30 p.m.

Expressed as percentages of the average pre-television figure (as indicated by the scores for the control groups), there were increases of 3% in London in the winter, of 2% in London in the summer, of 2% in Birmingham and of 5% in Wakefield. These are but small overall changes. Though in fact these figures mask larger changes in certain parts of the day, they are themselves important is showing that whatever the impact of television upon the amount of time the family spends at home together,

[b] The controls are the non-viewers after they have been matched to the viewers.

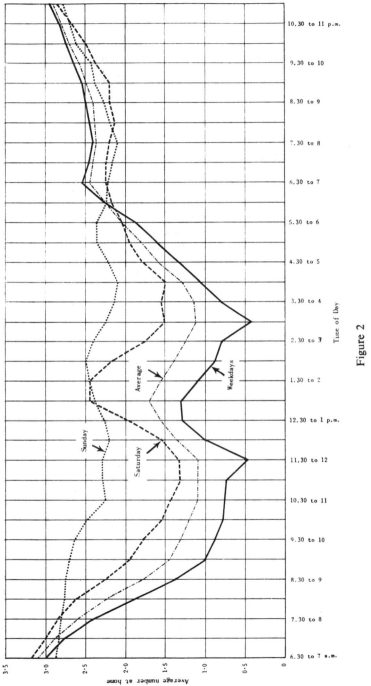

Figure 2

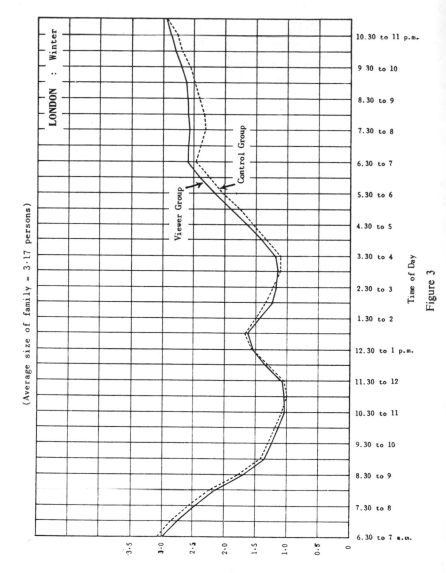

Figure 3

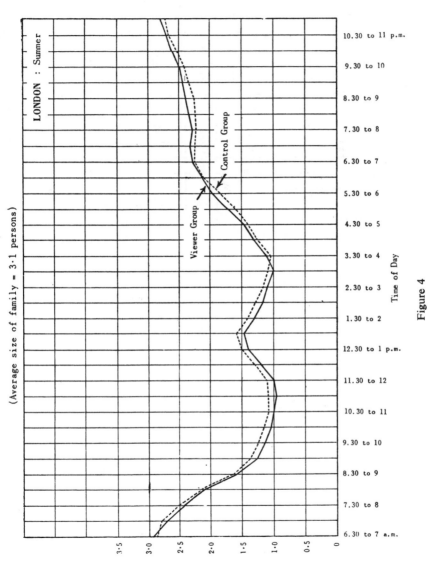

Figure 4

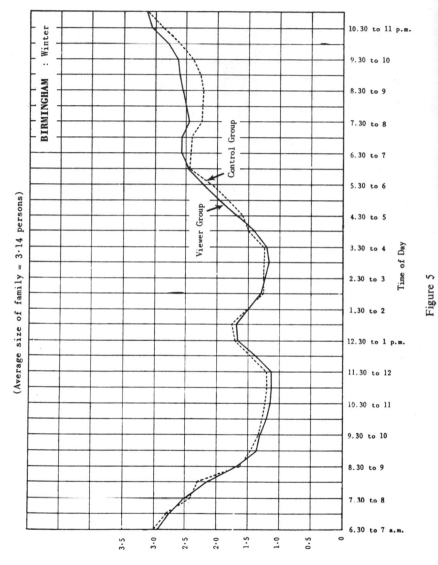

Figure 5

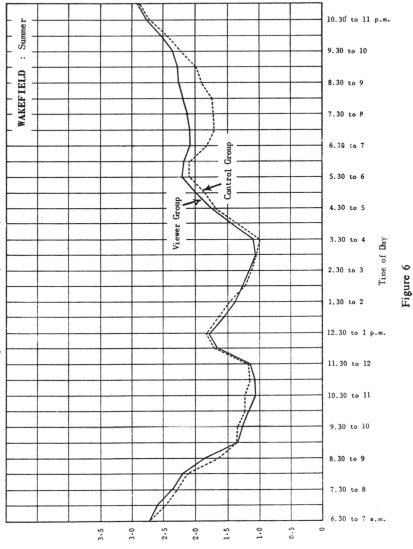

Figure 6

it does not take the form of any appreciable increase in the *total* amount of time so spent.

Figures 3–6 take us behind the broad averages of Table 2 by presenting changes for each half-hour of the day.

An outstanding feature of these figures is the greater at-homeness of the viewing families from 6 p.m. onwards, particularly from 7 p.m. when evening transmissions started. There was also a tendency towards increase, but with some exceptions, between 3 p.m. and 6 p.m., the period of afternoon transmission. However, the situation for the morning and early afternoon tended to be different: in all areas and surveys, there was a *reduction* in family at-homeness for a large part of this period.

Looking over the whole pattern for the day, it seems that television's effect was to increase family at-homeness during some periods (especially during evening transmission) but to reduce it at others (usually during the morning and the early afternoon). Considering this evidence along with that of Table 2, it appears that *television's influence on family at-homeness has been more to alter its distribution throughout the day than to change the total amount of it.*

Table 3 provides broad quantifications of these changes by time of day. The three periods referred to in it are 6.30 a.m. till 3 p.m. (morning and early afternoon), 3 p.m. till 6 p.m. (afternoon transmission period), 7 p.m. till 11 p.m. (evening transmission period).

Table 3 indicates: that *average* changes during the long morning and early afternoon period tended to be small decreases; that changes during the rest of the day were all increases; that the latter varied in size from about 2% in Birmingham's afternoon transmission period to about 14% in Wakefield's evening transmission period.

Changes by age of set

The non-viewers had been matched *afresh* to each of four groups of viewers defined in terms of the length of time they had owned TV sets: 0–1 years, 1–2 years, 2–4 years and 4–6 years. This led to the derivation of estimates of television's effects for each of these four groups. These estimates were expressed in terms of each half hour of the day and in terms of the averages for morning and early afternoon, for later afternoon, and for evening.

For any one of the surveys, there was some variation in effect year by year. However, this variations was by no means common to the four surveys. Indeed, the variability from year to year and from survey to survey is such that no general trends are discernible. All that can be said is that the evidence does not suggest any long-term return to the pre-television situation.

Changes by various characteristics
of respondent or his family

Analyses were made of television's effects in different sections of the population.

TABLE 3

Television's effects on family life at-homeness: percentage changes by time of day*

Average number of persons at home

Survey	Morning and early afternoon				Afternoon transmission period				Evening transmission period			
	Con-trols Pers.†	View-ers Pers.†	Diff-erence	% Change	Con-trols Pers.†	View-ers Pers.†	Diff-erence	% Change	Con-trols Pers.†	View-ers Pers.†	Diff-erence	% Change
London (winter)	1.65	1.62	−0.03	−1.8	1.48	1.58	+0.10	+6.8	2.50	2.65	+0.15	+6.0
London (summer)	1.57	1.53	−0.04	−2.6	1.38	1.45	+0.07	+5.1	2.37	2.51	+0.14	+5.9
Birmingham (winter)	1.69	1.66	−0.03	−1.8	1.57	1.60	+0.03	+1.9	2.41	2.64	+0.23	+9.5
Wakefield (summer)	1.62	1.62	0.00	0.0	1.52	1.60	+0.08	+5.3	2.05	2.34	+0.29	+14.1

* Excluding the periods 6.00 p.m. – 7.00 p.m. and 11.00 p.m. – 11.30 p.m.

† Pers. = Average of number of persons home each half hour of the period.

The different occupational sections

Occupational background was graded by the skill and training required for the respondent's job (or last job held). There were three such grades: (i) the professional, semi-professional and highly skilled; (ii) the skilled and moderately skilled; (iii) the semi-skilled and the unskilled.

Only in Wakefield in the summer was there any steady trend in terms of occupational level: there, television's effects on family 'at-homeness' varied from a small decrease for the professional and skilled group to an increase for the semi-skilled and unskilled. The other surveys brought out evidence of different amounts of changes in the different occupational sub-groups, but there was no obvious pattern to these changes. In any case such patterns as there might possibly be varied with area and season.

Type of family

The were five family types, namely: younger couples, small families, large families, adult families, older couples. Here too, television's effects varied with area and season. Thus: (i) in *London* in the winter there was a large increase (by about 11 %) in respect of 'small families', but no change for such families in Birmingham (in the winter). (ii) in Wakefield there was a large increase in the 'at-homeness' of younger couples (11 %) but very little increase in London; (iii) for older couples there was an increase in 'at-homeness' in summer-London but a decrease in winter-Birmingham. Within this context of variability, it does seem, however, that whereas television *tended* to keep younger couples at home together more, it did not do so with respect to 'large families'. Indeed, for the latter the tendency was for there to be a *reduction* in the degree to which they were at home together. Just why this should be so is by no means clear. However, discussions with members of large families suggest that a partial cause may perhaps be that in such families teenagers and others go out of the home for social activity, conversation, etc., because they find no scope for these in a living room that is fairly fully occupied by people who are viewing.

Presence of young children in the family

Amongst families that did *not* include a child of 5 years or less, television produced (in all four surveys) small increases in family 'at homeness'. Amongst families *with* one or more such infants, the increases were smaller or negligible. One highly speculative explanation of this small trend might be that in families *with* such children, the freedom of movement of the parents was automatically restricted whether there was a television set in the house or not, so that the scope for an increase in 'at-homeness' would seem to be smaller than for parents *without* such children.

Summing up about television's effect in
keeping the family together at home

Television led to some changes in the times at which family members were at home together. The main change was an increase during evening transmission, but there was a tendency also for viewers to make up for this to some degree by going out more when television was not on. There is evidence of variation in this pattern and in the total amount of the change according to area, season, and the various characteristics of the viewing family. There was nothing to suggest that the changes reported were only temporary.

Within the populations studied there were some groups where the total change was either nil or a decrease. One of these was the larger family: television tended to *reduce* the extent of its 'at-homeness together'. On the other hand it tended to increase slightly the 'at-homeness together' of families which did not include a small child.

SUB-PROJECTS II & III: TELEVISION'S EFFECTS IN KEEPING CERTAIN FAMILY
MEMBERS AT HOME TOGETHER:

(a) THE MARRIED COUPLE; (b) CHILDREN AND YOUNG PEOPLE

The enquiry also provided evidence about the effects of television in keeping the married couple at home together and about its effects in keeping children and young people at home. Separate matching composites were developed and used for each new issue studied in each of these two broad areas.

The At-Homeness of the Married Couple

All four surveys indicated that television had increased the degree to which the married couple stayed *at home together* in the evening period. The increase was greatest in Wakefield. During the rest of the day there were at least some periods when TV couples *reduced* the time they spent at home together, presumably in part compensation for increased 'at-homeness' in the evening. There was marked variation, by area and season, in television's effects on Saturdays, on Sundays, and on Monday-Friday.

Television's effect in keeping the couple at home together varied with the age of the set, but the particular pattern of change was not the same in each survey.

The effect also varied according to the type of family from which the couple was drawn, those from 'larger families' tending to spend *less* time them together at home was greater when both were employed than when only one was employed. Television's effect varied with the occupational only one was employed. Television's effect varied with the occupational background of the couple, but the nature and direction of the change depended to a marked degree upon the geographical area and the season.

The At-Homeness of Children and Young People

Five age groups were studied: the 3–6 years olds, the 7–10s, 11–13s, 14–17s and 18–22 year olds. Television had affected the extent to which each of these was at home, but the changes were more in terms of *redistribution* of the time spent at home than alterations in its total quantity. Quite frequently television led to reduced 'at-homeness' during the morning and early afternoon, and to an increase in the evening period.

There were however, few clear-cut differences between the five age groups, and even *within* age groups the nature of the change brought about by television was by no means constant, varying from one area to another and by season. The most that can be said is that *on balance* television tended to result in children and young people spending more time in the home — but not much more.

SUB-PROJECT IV: TELEVISION'S EFFECTS UPON THE AMOUNT OF THE VIEWER'S
HOME CENTRED ACTIVITY
Some Additional Aspects of the Methods Used

The object of this part of the enquiry was to discover whether, and to what extent, television had an effect upon what may be called 'home centred activity'. The best available definition of this concept is the representative sample of such acts which was developed specially for this enquiry and which is given in full in Table 4 below. Also in this table is the number of times each activity was performed on a typical day per 100 respondents in London. Details of how this sample was developed were given earlier in this chapter in the more general description of methods.

The list of acts was built into the questionnaire in the order shown. A respondent had to indicate, for each act, whether or not he or she had done it on the diary day and, if so, how many times. For each respondent, two scores were calculated: one of these was the number of acts out of the twenty which the respondent had done at least once. For the other score, each activity was credited with the number of times it was claimed as being done (up to a maximum of five) and these were added for all 20 items to give a total. These two scores were regarded as indices respectively of the diversity and of the total amount of home-centred activity.

The empirically developed composite of matching items for this project consisted of ten variables[c]. Their use in matching led to the splitting of both viewer and non-viewer samples into seventeen subgroups and the equating of the non-viewer sample to the viewer sample in terms of these subgroups.

Findings

Table 5 presents estimates of television's effects for each of the four surveys. For the *total amount* of home-centred activity, there was a tendency towards decrease. However, with the exception of Birmingham, these

[c] These ten variables included: whether or not the survey contact was a housewife; whether or not respondent's family included a child of up to five years of age; whether or not the time of catching transport varied from day to day; the numbers of the survey contact's brothers or sisters; whether or not the respondent owned or had use of various durable goods (e.g., bicycle, bookcase, piano, sewing machine).

T A B L E 4

The sample of home-centred acts

Items in the sample	Number of times each act was performed per 100 respondents, in London, on a single day
I fed pets or domestic animals (e.g. dog, fish, birds, and so on).	61
I did some gardening or tidied up the garden (not window boxes)	20
I chatted to a neighbour (e.g. over the fence, when she or he dropped in, and so on	38
I attended to plants or flowers *in* the house (including window boxes)	23
I bathed a child or put it to bed	27
I entertained a visitor	43
I cleaned some kitchen or bathroom equipment (e.g. fridge, bath, and so on)	45
I sorted out some papers (e.g. letters, bills, newspapers, patterns, and so on)	30
I entertained or played with a child in some way (e.g. romped, told a story, helped with stamp collection, and so on)	48
I prepared a shopping list	22
I washed the floor or did some polishing	33
I did some sewing (e.g. mending, embroidery)	28
I tidied up a child's toys	32
I cleaned out a cupboard or tidied a drawer	19
I did some baking or jam making	16
I moved some furniture around	18
I cleaned the windows	10
I gave a present to some member of the household	11
I did some household repairs (e.g. mended an iron, put washer on tap, cleaned out pipe)	9
I washed the paint	8

T A B L E 5

Television's effect upon home-centred activity

Survey	Score for Total Amount of Activity*				Score for Diversity of Activity†			
	Controls	Viewers	Diff.	% Change	Controls	Viewers	Diff.	% Change
London (winter)	5.76	5.63	−0.13	−2.3	4.44	4.46	+0.02	+0.4
London (summer)	5.84	5.82	−0.02	−0.3	4.50	4.58	+0.08	+1.8
Birmingham (winter)	6.63	5.89	−0.74	−11.2	4.90	4.63	−0.27	−5.5
Wakefield (summer)	5.91	5.69	−0.22	−3.7	4.39	4.41	+0.02	+0.5

* maximum score = 100 (= 20 × 5)
† maximum score = 20

decreases were quite small if not negligible. The *diversity* of home centred activity seems to have been affected hardly at all, again with the exception of Birmingham. In Birmingham, the reduction in *total amount* of home-centred activity was about 11 % and in *diversity* about 6 %.

Changes by age of set

Changes according to length of set ownership were calculated. In all areas, the total amount of home-centred activity fell in the first year of set ownership. However, what happened thereafter varied sharply from area to area. There was a suggestion in the findings of some tendency for the level of this activity to approach that of the pre-television state after about five years, but this possible tendency was not a clear or convincing one. Much the same applied for the year by year changes in *diversity* of home-centred activity except that changes were smaller and displayed a more distinct tendency to disappear after about five years.

Changes by respondent characteristics

Home-centred activity was compared for those who did and those who did not have children or young people (under 20) living with them. All four surveys showed television to have reduced this kind of activity amongst those with children. On the other hand, three out of the four showed it to *increase* this kind of activity amongst those *without* children. For the remaining survey, which was for Birmingham, the *trend* was the same, in that the reduction was less than that for people with children.

Any attempt to explain this pattern of findings can be only speculative. One possibility is that in families with children there is in the first place, a greater margin for loss in home-centred activity (their scores are higher to start with). Second, there is probably greater opportunity for one adult to escape to the TV set when there are other people around than when there is just the couple in the house. We know too that television leads the married couple without children to spend more time at home together, and presumably this ought to lead to more chores being done or perhaps having to be done.

Analyses of change were also made in terms of whether the respondent was a housewife, whether or not there were 'in-law' in the respondent's home, and the occupational level of the respondent. These analyses brought out evidence of reductions in different subgoups, the reductions sometimes being quite large. Yet no general trends emerged and what happened to any one of the subgroups seemed to depend upon the geographical area in which the respondent was living or the season or both.

SUB-PROJECT V: TELEVISION'S EFFECTS UPON THE AMOUNT OF JOINT ACTIVITY
IN THE HOME

Some Additional Aspects of Methods

The key concept in this sub-project was 'the joint activity of family members in or about the home' — that is, the extent to which they do things together in or about the home.

Just as in Project IV, the measure used was based upon a representative sample of activities. In this case they were the activities in respect of which family joint activity normally occurred. The method of deriving this sample has been described in an early section of this chapter. In its final form, it consisted of the following 20 acts, shown in the order of their presentation in the questionnaire.

TABLE 6

The sample of acts for which joint-activity occurs in the family

Items in the Sample	The number of times performed *jointly* per 100 respondents*
I washed up the dishes	35
I laid or cleared the table	22
I entertained a visitor	25
I prepared or served a meal	12
I made a cup of tea or some other hot drink	13
I had a serious discussion about something	15
I did some gardening or tidied up the garden (not window boxes)	6
I made the beds	8
I planned something (e.g., holiday, layout of garden, arrangement of furniture)	12
I looked for something which had been mislaid (e.g., keys, papers)	6
I fed pets or domestic animals	6
I tidied up a child's toys	7
I played some gramophone records	6
I gave a present to some member of the household	5
I entertained or played with a child or baby in some way (e.g. romped, told a story, helped with a stamp collection)	15
I tended plants or flowers in the home (including window boxes)	2
I did the washing (i.e. clothes)	1
I checked the shopping and put it away	3
I put things ready to give away or sell (e.g. oddments for a jumble sale, newspapers for the fishmonger)	1
I cleaned the windows	1

* If respondent did this when *alone*, it did not count in the derivation of the above figures. It was counted only if it was done *jointly* with at least one other family member.

The Social Impact of Television

In the questionnaire, these acts were presented along with the acts of the home-centred sample.[d]. Two items of information were sought for each of them: (i) whether or not the respondent was involved in the act on the diary day; (ii) if so, who, if anyone, helped or did it with the respondent.

An individual's score was the total number of instances of help or co-operation given to the respondent by members of his or her family. Thus two people helping the respondent with the garden counted as a score of 2 (though there was a ceiling of 5 on any single act.[e]

The matching variables which emerged as appropriate for this project were different from those used in the home-centred activity project (because the issue under study was different)[f]. Their use led to the equation of the non-viewers to the viewers in terms of 17 different sub-groups.

Since the criteria against which matching items were selected was based upon the *total score* for joint activity it is not legitimate to draw conclusions about any of the *individual* acts in the 20 item sample. This of course is also the position for the samples of home-centred acts and of sociable acts dealt with in Projects IV and VI respectively.

Findings

In three of the four surveys, there was evidence of a small reduction in the total amount of joint activity in viewer homes. In the fourth (Wakefield in the summer) there was evidence of an increase by about 8%. Details are given in Table 7.

Changes by age of set

For London (both winter and summer) and for Wakefield, there was a reversion towards the pre-television level (of joint activity) after about five

[d] Some of these acts were the same as those in the sample of home-centred acts, but there was little likelihood of *complete* overlap because the controls for selection were different, the vital one in the present case being the frequency with which the acts were done jointly.

[e] In the development of the sample of acts, the frequency of occurrence of joint activity was based on the number of times an act was done jointly with at least one other member of the household, so that if two people helped with the one act, it counted as *one* rather than two. On the other hand, the scoring of joint activity in the assessment of television's effects was based upon the total number of family members helping or co-operating.

[f] The present composite included the following: the type of the respondent's household; respondent's sex; the number of people in the respondent's household; the number of the respondent's brothers and sisters (when a child); whether respondent was a housewife or not; whether in a full-time job or not; presence in the home of certain durable goods or possessions; whether respondent takes a holiday at a crowded centre or elsewhere; library membership in the past. The full set is given in diagrammatic form as Figure 1, where it was used to illustrate the selection system.

TABLE 7

Television's effect on joint activity

| | Score for total amount of joint activity | | | |
	Control Group	Viewer Group	Difference	% Change
London (winter)	2.62	2.55	− 0.07	− 2.7
London (summer)	3.02	2.90	− 0.12	− 4.0
Birmingham (winter)	2.73	2.58	− 0.15	− 5.5
Wakefield (summer)	2.61	2.81	+ 0.20	+ 7.7

years. In Wakefield, the reversion followed appreciable increases in the early stages of set ownership, whereas in London it followed decreases. In Birmingham there was an early increase, and then a moderate reduction which tended to be sustained.

Changes by respondent characteristics

The nature and degree of television's impact with respect to each of the five types of family studied differed considerably from area to area. Indeed, the only consistent element in all four surveys related to larger families: in each area, their joint activity was reduced.

Analysis of effects was also made with respect to the following: whether or not there were any children in the home; whether or not there was a parent-in-law in the home; whether or not respondent was a housewife; the occupational level of the respondent. In some of the sub-groups defined by these divisions, TV's effects were quite marked, but there was little tendency for the extent and the direction of the changes in subgroups to be the same in the three areas surveyed, and they appeared also to vary with the season of the year.

Summing up on Project V

In London, both in summer and winter, and in Birmingham in winter, television led to a small reduction in the total amount of joint activity occurring in the home. In summer in Wakefield it increased it somewhat. In all four surveys, however, the total amount of change was small.

In the early stages of ownership, television led either to an increase or a decrease in the joint activity in the home, depending on the survey area or the season. But in three of the surveys there was evidence of a long-term tendency for the amount of joint activity to return towards the pre-television level. Television's effects on different subgroups of the population was quite marked, but there was very little tendency for the extent and the direction of these changes to be the same by area and season.

SUB-PROJECT VI: TELEVISION'S EFFECTS UPON SOCIABLE ACTIVITY

Some Additional Aspects of Methods

It had been felt that one possible result of the coming of television would be that viewers would spend more time at home and so less in those sociable situations which ordinarily occur outside the home. It seemed possible that such withdrawal might then lead to a more or less continuing loss in the ability and the will to mix with others. It might, on the other hand, be contended that an invitation to a neighbour to come and watch television might lead to a 'breaking of the ice' with people with whom there had previously been but passing contact. Another argument, in the same direction, was that the common experience of watching particular television programs would give people something more than the weather to talk about and that this would ease social contact.

As in the study of home centred activity, this part of the enquiry was based upon a sample of the sociable acts which actually occur in society. The methods used to select this sample have already been described in general terms in this chapter. The 20-item sample was as follows:

TABLE 8

The sample of sociable acts

Items in the Sample	Namber of times each act was performed per 100 respondents, in London, in the course of a week
I attended an exhibition, a display or a show (e.g. picture gallery, animal show, and so on)	9
I took part in an indoor game with persons *other than* members of my own family (e.g. table tennis, billiards, etc.)	22
I went out somewhere with one or more friends or acquaintances	112
I attended a conference or lecture or class	10
I invited friends or acquaintances to my home	68
One or more acquaintances *dropped in* and were entertained by me (e.g. a cup of tea, a chat, a meal, and so on)	75
I had a meal out with an acquaintance or business associate	49
I attended a party or a social gathering of some kind (e.g. whist drive, bridge evening, wedding, and so on)	14
I met some friends or acquaintances at a pub or hotel or went there with them for a drink	43
I performed a task or service for a neighbour or acquaintance (e.g. helped with shopping, baby sitting,changed library book, provided shillings for gas, prepared meal for member of neighbour's family, paid tradesman or fed pets while neighbour was away, and so on)	71
I lent something to a neighbour or acquaintance (e.g. sugar, paint brush, lawnmower, etc.) or offered him/her use of something (e.g. telephone)	55
I introduced myself to someone	26
I co-operated with a friend or acquaintance on something of common interest (e.g. a hobby, working on a motor, dealing with local authorities, and so on)	29

Items in the Sample	Number of times each act was performed per 100 respondents, in London, in the course of a week
I helped a stranger with information when this was needed (e.g. street directions, time of last bus, and so on)	72
I helped a child not known to me personally (e.g. helped child across road, comforted distressed child, and so on)	32
I said good morning to a stranger (e.g. while travelling, through my work, in a street, etc.)	63
I travelled to or from work with an acquaintance or friend	92
I asked about the family of an acquaintance	93
I talked for 20 minutes or more with a friend or acquaintance	115
I helped someone at work	114

The selected sample of acts was included in the questionnaire. Respondents were asked to say of each act whether or not they had done it in the last seven days and if so, how often. From this information two measures were derived. One was the total number of the 20 acts which the respondent had done at least once. This was called the diversity score on the assumption that it gave a measure of diversity or variety of the respondent's sociable activity. The second measure took into account the number of times each different act was said to have occurred, though as with other measures of this kind a ceiling of 5 times for a single item was set. This second measure was called the 'total amount of sociable activity'.

The criterion used for setting up matching variables was the 'total activity score'. Variables included in the final matching composite were: past membership of a club or society; time taken to get to work; whether or not respondent was in a full-time job; past membership of a lending library (pre-1950); the existence or not of a club at the respondent's place of work; ownership (ever) of a gramophone and of certain other durable goods.

Findings

Table 9 presents the findings expressed as averages.

For *diversity* of sociable activity, the effect of television was either negligible or a small reduction. For *total amount* of sociable activity, winter London showed a slight increase, summer London and Wakefield a slight decrease and Birmingham a decrease of about 8 %. Together, these changes are more suggestive of reduction than of increase. Taken together, they are not large changes however, and clearly they vary with area and season.

It does not follow from this that all the different kinds of behaviour which contribute to the *total score* in any one area are affected equally or in the same direction. However, short of developing a matching composite for each item in the sample it is not possible to say what is the pattern of change *within* the sample of sociable acts.

T A B L E   9

Television's effect on sociable activity

Survey	Score for Diversity of Activity*				Score for Total Amount of Activity†			
	Con-trols	View-ers	Diff.	% Change	Con-trols	View-ers	Diff.	% Change
London (winter)	7.16	7.21	+0.05	+0.7	15.52	15.96	+0.44	+2.8
London (summer)	7.42	7.15	−0.27	−3.5	16.00	15.56	−0.44	−2.8
Birmingham (winter)	7.65	7.26	−0.39	−5.1	17.22	15.85	−1.37	−8.0
Wakefield (summer)	7.19	7.17	−0.02	−0.3	16.53	15.98	−0.55	−3.3

* Maximum score = 20   †Maximum score = 100

Changes by age of set

The effects of TV during the early years of ownership were in some instances increases in sociable activity and in some instances reductions. However, there was a tendency, after changes during the first four years of TV ownership, for the viewer's sociability score to return towards the pre-television level.

Changes by characteristics of respondents

Changes were also studied in various sub-groups of the viewing population — in the different age groups, by sex, marital state, occupational background and type of family. There were differences in television's impact upon sociable activity for many of the different sub-groups. Thus in London in the winter, television's effect was to increase sociability amongst women (6%), amongst the married (6%), amongst the part-time employed (9%), amongst the semi-skilled and unskilled (12%) and amongst the younger couples (18%) and small families (10%). However, this pattern of results did not tend to be repeated in summer London and was appreciably different in Wakefield and Birmingham. It seems that for sociable activity too, area and season were important factors in determining *who* was affected and in what way.

Changes in diversity versus total amount of sociability

Whereas changes in diversity and total amount of behaviour have tended in other of these projects to run parallel with each other and to be broadly similar, this was not so in the case of sociability. It thus seems that in spite of the ceiling of five put upon the contribution to total score by any one act in the sample, one or several items in it contributed rather more change than did others.

SUMMARY OF THE ENQUIRY

Aims of the study

The study was designed to measure the effects of television upon some aspects of family life and of sociability.

Methods used

The enquiry was conducted in London, in Birmingham, and in Wakefield, through four separate surveys with a total of 8,230 respondents. The identification and measurement of effects was attempted through the Stable Correlate method in which non-viewers are matched to viewers using a large composite of empirically derived matching variables. In preparation for the study a number of special measuring devices had to be developed, this process taking as long as the final enquiry in which they were used.

Findings

The enquiry indicated the following.

(1) Television produced some changes in the time spent at home by the family. Though the total effect was a slight increase, the main character of the change was a redistribution of the family's at-homeness: there was an increase in the evenings but a partly compensating reduction in earlier parts of the day. For the larger family, in contrast with the majority of families, television's effect tended to be a *reduction* in the total amount of time spent at home. The evidence did not suggest that these changes were only temporary.

(2) The same pattern applied to the 'at-homeness together' of married couples and to the at-homeness of children and young people: the tendency was for there to be an increase in the evenings and a partly compensating reduction at some during the rest of the day.

(3) The enquiry dealt also with the home centred activities of viewers, for example, sewing, window cleaning, moving furniture round, household repairs, gardening, baking. With the exception of Birmingham, where there was a moderate reduction, television's effect on the total amount of home centred activity was either small or negligible. In all four surveys, the home centred activity of adults with children was reduced by television more than was that of adults without children.

(4) In London and in Birmingham there was a small reduction in the degree to which viewer families did things together or helped each other in the home. In Wakefield, television somewhat increased this 'joint activity'.

(5) The total amount of the viewers' sociable behaviour was also studied. Television's effect on this was to reduce it to a moderate degree in Birmingham but to change it by only a small amount in London and in Wakefield.

(6) In each survey area there were differences in television's effects in going from one to another sub-group of the population. However, the nature of these differences varied quite a lot and sometimes markedly by survey area and by season.

[24]

The effects of television upon the reading and the buying of newspapers and magazines[a]: A 1959 report

BACKGROUND AND AIMS

According to a 1958 report by the Central Office of Information (251), the British public buys more newspapers per person than does the public of any other country in the world. In that year the 16 million families in the United Kingdom bought over 16 million national morning newspapers, about $2\frac{1}{2}$ million London evening papers, about 27 million national Sunday papers, as well as huge quantities of weekly and monthly publications and over 9 million provincial morning and evening newspapers. This score does not include the many specialist publications or local weekly papers. There was then, and there is now, an enormous circulation of newspapers and magazines.

Even so, the circulation figures for the national publications have, for several years, been falling[c], and the general pattern of the decline is presented in Figure 1. This fall applies to (1) the combined circulation figures for the national morning newspapers — a fall of 4 per cent between 1957 and 1959, representing 680,000 copies; (2) the combined circulation for the national Sunday papers — a fall of 8 per cent since 1957 and of 12 per cent since their peak circulation year, 1951; (3) a wide range of weekly papers — a fall of about 10 per cent (since 1957) in the circulation of those for women and of over 30 per cent for those of a more general kind; (4) a fairly representative range of monthly papers — a fall since 1957 of about 15 per cent for women's publications and of about 6 per cent for the others.

[a] A report based upon the first and second of three studies by the writer, carried out to determine the causes of circulation decline in certain sections of the British press. [b] Reported in 1959.

[b] The series of three studies ("The British Press", Parts I, II and III) was financed by the London Press Exchange Limited. An article based on the first of them appeared in the Public Opinion Quarterly (Vol. 25, Fall, 1961) under the title of this chapter. The second study dealt with readers' reactions to their papers, and the third with factors related to Press economy.

[c] This statement was published in 1961.

Broadly speaking, then, the circulation figures of the national papers
have been going down, and by newspaper standards that decline is serious.
It is serious not only because it means a loss in revenue from sales and a
declining service to readers: it means also a loss in advertising revenue at
a time when production costs are extremely high. The decline is even more
serious in that it looks as if it may continue.

Figure 1.

Circulation trends and rise of television ownership in the UK

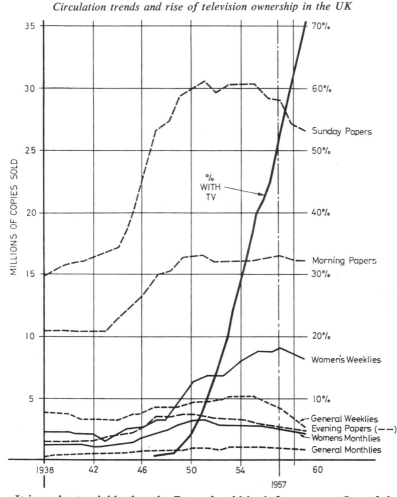

It is understandable that the Press should look for a cause. One of the
things that pressmen and others have seen is that this period of decline
coincided with a period in which the proportion of homes with television

sets in them was still rapidly growing, as shown in Figure 1. This comparison constitutes part of the case for a fairly widespread view that television is responsible for declining circulation figures. This case has the support of an appealing argument that if people are spending their time watching television they will have less time for reading papers and that if papers go unread for a long period they will cease to be bought. This is, in fact, a large part of the case for suggesting that television is responsible.

This suggestion may seem to make sense. But there is other evidence that makes the case against television much less 'cut and dried' than this particular argument may suggest.

1. The growth of television has been going on for quite a long time — much longer than the circulation decline of morning and Sunday papers (see Figure 1).

2. Whereas the aggregate figures for the national papers showed a decline, circulation figures of *some* of the papers were by no means declining. The predominantly middle class papers *(The Times, Daily Telegraph, Guardian, Sunday Times, The Observer)* do in fact have *rising* circulations. It is among the predominantly working class papers that decline tends to be taking place. This applies to morning papers, to Sunday papers, and also to magazines.

3. One other piece of evidence of a particularly suggestive kind can be found in the circulation trends for the period 1938 to 1951. These, given diagrammatically in Figure 1, are set out numerically in Appendix tables 4 and 5. The enormous circulation figures of the period 1950 to 1957 were reached during the second part of the war and in the period of austerity which followed it. The increases came about under a set of very special conditions which tend to exist no more: newsprint controls which kept papers small and which caused each new allocation of newsprint to be fed into increased circulation rather than into greater size; a wartime hunger for news; a general absence of competing entertainments during the war and in the five years after it. With the withering away of these conditions, it is conceivable that the recent decline is in fact the beginning of a return towards prewar levels of circulation.

The specific aims of the enquiry

Thus there is evidence both ways, and as it stands it leaves quite unresolved the question of television's impact on the British press. The enquiry I am reporting was an attempt to assess what that impact actually is — its nature and its extent. More precisely, the enquiry was addressed to three questions.

1. Does television affect the frequency with which the viewer reads or buys newspapers and magazines? If so, what is the extent of this effect, what is its duration, and in what sections of the population is it most pronounced? If there are changes, what are the reasons for them?

2. To what extent has television (as distinct from other factors) been responsible for changes, over recent years, in the *circulation* of British newspapers and magazines?

3. Does television affect the nature or the range of the items which the viewer reads about in his papers? If so, in what way?

PREVIOUS RESEARCH

Work done prior to this enquiry

At the time this enquiry was made, the available literature offered no ready and reliable answers to questions of this kind. Early U.S.A. research upon television and reading tended to take the form of comparisons of the reading behaviour of viewers and non-viewers[d]. Other enquiries were based upon retrospective accounts, by viewers, of what they thought television had done to their reading[e]. Straight forward comparisons of viewers and non-viewers cannot, of course, be regarded as studies of televisions effects, and those referred to were not necessarily presented as such. They can, however, be good material for hypothesis making as can the retrospection studies. Regarding them as material for hypotheses, one of the indications of these studies seems to be that television had reduced the use of *magazines*[f]. However, the indications with respect to newspaper reading were anything but constant. Thus several of the early studies might be taken as indicating that television had reduced the viewer's use of newspapers [e.g. 222, 351], several that television had *not* affected the viewer's use of newspapers [e.g. 227] and one that television had *increased* the viewer's use of them. [310]

In Britain, comparisons of viewers and non-viewers had been made with respect to newspaper and magazine reading. One of these, conducted by the BBC in 1954, had indicated: (i) that viewers tended slightly more than non-viewers to be readers of national newspapers (morning, evening and Sunday); (ii) that for 18 of the 21 individual papers with national circulation, the proportion of *viewers* who were readers was either slightly greater than or equal to the proportion of non-viewers who were readers; that the remaining three tended to be working class papers; that none of the differences (for the 21 papers) was large; (iii) that viewers tended slightly more than non-viewers to be regular readers of magazines or periodicals; (iv) that prestige, general interest and specialist magazines were (claimed to be) read regularly by a greater proportion of viewers than of non-viewers; that this balance was reversed for film, theatre and religious magazines; that women's publications were read by equal proportions of viewers and non-viewers. However, according to a later BBC

---

[d] For examples of studies based wholly or partly upon this method, see references [227, 310, 344, 263, 307].

[e] For examples of studies based wholly or partly on this material see references [222, 303, 351].

[f] See references [222, 227, 263, 310, 344, 351]

report [247] the position had changed somewhat by 1958. Whereas for most national newspapers the proportion of *viewers* who were readers was still higher than the proportion for non-viewers, the balance was reversed for four quality newspapers.

Valuable as were the results of these two enquiries, they do nonetheless rank as comparative data, as distinct from data about television's *effects*. On the other hand, two studies conducted by Coffin in America bore directly upon the question of television's effects upon newspaper and magazine reading. In the first of them, reported in 1951 [256], Coffin matched viewers and non-viewers in New York in terms of age, sex, family size, education, income, area of residence. He reported a small reduction in the number of viewers reading a newspaper on an average day (78 % for viewers compared with 83 % for their controls), though the fall was greater amongst viewers with low income or with only secondary school education. He also reported reductions for magazine reading. Thus for the average day, 23 % of his viewers, as against 27 % of his controls, spent at least some time in magazine reading. The average time so spent by viewers was reported as 11 minutes compared with 16 minutes for the controls. In 1953–4, Coffin got virtually the same results from a before and after study [257]: before television, the future viewers spent 17 minutes daily reading magazines compared with 16 minutes for controls; after television the figures were respectively 10 minutes and 17 minutes.

In the context of a wider enquiry ("Television and the Child"), Himmelweit, Oppenheim and Vince reported on the reading behaviour of children in Britain [284]. They compared viewer and non-viewer children *before* and then a year *after* the coming of television to Norwich. The results indicated that under television's influence, book reading by children 13–14 years of age had fallen appreciably, but for 10–11 year olds only slightly[g]. There was evidence also of a TV-produced reduction in comic reading for both age groups[h]. Unfortunately the final samples for the Norwich study were very small[i]. In addition, though very indirectly, the evidence of the enquiry seems to suggest that the number of 'children's newspaper or magazines' read each week by viewer children has not been reduced by television[j].

[g] See reference 284 page 327, Table 62.
[h] See reference 284 page 187, Appendix Table 52.
[i] In the book reading study there were 38 viewer and 45 control children respresenting the 13–14 year olds and 110 and 113 respectively in the 10–11 year old group. The numbers were much the same for the comic reading study (also part of the Norwich check).
[j] The enquiry does not offer direct numerical evidence about television's impact upon children's reading of newspapers or upon their reading of magazines, but merely upon the combined group "comics, children's newspapers or magazines". However, since matched groups of viewer and non-viewer children were much the same in terms of the number of publications (in this mixed category) which they read every week[k] and since the Norwich study

This then, was the situation at the time this study was planned. Coffin had conducted impressive studies of effects, in two towns, but these studies being in the American setting and featuring American papers, could not necessarily be projected to Britain. No comparable work on adults had been done in Britain. Moreover, Coffin's work had not been national in coverage and had not been designed to bring out differences between publication categories such as 'highbrow' or 'lowbrow' or, for that matter, 'quality' versus 'popular'. In the circumstances, it was clear that nothing like enough information was available for solving the problem of what lay behind the circulation trends for British publications or, to be more specific, for answering the three questions posed above.

Research reported since the present
study was undertaken

In "Television in the Lives of Our Children", Schramm, Lyle and Parker reported on child studies conducted in ten communities in the United States and Canada. In the context of this important contribution to the study of television and children, the authors compared children's reading in two Canadian towns. These two towns were referred to respectively as Teletown (because television programs could be received there) and Radiotown (because only radio programs could be received there). Each had about 5,000 people living in them and they were judged by the research team to be similar in many respects. It was reported that the number of comics read per month was much less in Teletown, but that the number of *books* read per month (by sixth and tenth grade children) was only slightly less there (3.18 : 3.41). There was practically no difference in terms of the number reading a *newspaper* more than once a week (74.4% in Teletown: 72.3% in Radiotown), though more children in Teletown than in Radiotown read a newspaper every day (45%: 34% for sixth grade children and 57% : 44% for tenth grade children). There was little overall difference in terms of the number of *magazines* read per month, though the Teletown average was a little lower (3.7 : 4.0). At the same time, this small difference appears to mask certain larger differences in the kinds of magazine material read. Thus: (i) 34% of the Radiotown children claimed that they often read confession, screen, detective or adventure pulp magazines, as compared with 20% in Teletown; (ii) for frequent reading of general magazines of the kind "Life" and "Saturday Evening Post", the order was reversed, with 52% for Radiotown and 65% for Teletown.

At the same time, we must take careful note of the fact that this was a 'two-town' enquiry, with the characteristic weaknesses of the 'two-town'

---

indicated that television reduced comic reading, it seems to follow that television did not reduce (or may have increased) the number of 'children's newspapers or magazines' read by viewer children each week. However, this tentative conclusion is weakened by the fact that the matching of the viewer and the non-viewer children appears to have been incomplete.

[k] See reference 284, page 487, Appendix Table 51.

The Social Impact of Television

design. In particular, it remains possible that the differences found between these two towns were present at least partly, even before television
came to Teletown. This is not to deny the usefulness of the findings, but
simply to underline them with the proper degree of reservation.

THE METHODS OF RESEARCH

The research design used was the Stable Correlate technique. Through it,
a representative sample of 288 non-viewers was matched empirically to a
representative sample of 869 non-viewers. The enquiry was conducted in
Greater London at a time when about 70% of the population had sets in
their homes but when the differences between viewers and non-viewers had
not yet become extreme.

Publications studied

The enquiry dealt with 53 different publications: nine national morning
papers; the ten national Sunday papers; the three London evening papers;
14 weekly magazines; 17 monthly magazines.

The matching variables

These were chosen empirically from a pool of 28 variables. The variables
in this pool represented (i) known or suspected differences between viewers
and non-viewers; (ii) known or suspected correlates of newspaper and
magazine reading. Correlation methods were then used to draw from this
pool a composite of variables which maximised the pool's power to
discriminate between viewers and non-viewers[1]

The final composite of matching variables consisted of five different
items, namely age of ceasing full-time school, the number of people in the
family aged 20 years or under, the number of adults in the household, presence of a refrigerator in the home, presence of a family car. The non-
viewers were then equated to the viewers in terms of these variables.
Automatically, this sort of matching achieved a fairly close equation of
the samples in terms of other variables in the pool as well[m]. Thus for
each of the following, the equation was in fact very close indeed: age, sex,
marital state; occupational state (i.e. full-time job, part-time job, housewife, retired, student, self-employed, unemployed), occupational level in

[1] Ordinarily, the primary criterion used for selecting matching variables is
test score for whatever is being studied as possibly affected by television
(reading behaviour in this case). In the present case, television ownership
(or not) was used as the primary criterion.

[m] The reasons for this are (i) that the maximising procedure used for selecting
the composite of matching variables ordinarily leads to the selection of the
major independent factors in the total pool and (ii) that the development of
this particular matching composite was stopped when the addition of further
items added little to the existing correlation between the composite and the
criterion (in this case, set ownership).

last job; number of children aged seven or less in the home; the number of adults going out to work; the size of the house, area of residence; possession/use of certain durable goods or services; respondent's estimate of own speed of reading; whether or not the respondent had any special responsibilities[n].

The questionnaire

The various questions to which answers were required were set out in a booklet which was taken to survey respondents, started with them and left for completion. Subsequently it was collected by appointment.

Most of the questions in this booklet were highly structured in character and had been developed out of preliminary discussions with groups of readers of newspapers and magazines.

The booklet questionnaire included sections dealing respectively with: the frequency of reading and of buying of each of the 53 publications: the amount of time spent reading about specified topics of the kind ordinarily presented in newspapers and magazines; the ideas and attitudes of respondents concerning particular publications and the British Press generally; various items of information about the respondent, these to be used in the selection of matching criteria. At the beginning of the booklet was a list of interests about which data was needed for a quite different purpose but which also served to develop co-operation in the respondent.

The sample and the interviewing success rate

The viewers and non-viewers successfully interviewed were made up of 71 % of a probability sample of London adults on whom interviewers were required to call[o]. Of the others, approximately 4 % had refused to take part and about 6 % had failed to complete booklets.

THE FINDINGS

Though the matching achieved is of a wide and multi-dimensional kind, it must still be remembered that the residual differences between the viewer and the control samples may yet be influenced to some degree by original differences between the two samples and by other extraneous factors. Accordingly the findings from this enquiry are best regarded as *approximating* to the effects of television. Internal checks strongly suggest, but cannot prove, that the approximation is close.

The Daily and the Sunday Papers

The national morning papers

Findings for the nine national morning newspapers are given in Table 1.

[n] See Parker [315] and Belson [236] for an exchange concerning the efficiency of the matching used in this enquiry.
[o] If those who had moved, or were ill or were away for a long period were excluded from the sample, the success rate would become approximately 80 %.

TABLE 1

*Television's effect on regularity of reading and on buying
for nine norning papers (in per cent)*

| Publication | Frequency of Reading | | | | Buying Trends* | |
	Regularly	Often	Now and Then	Not at All	Read and Buy	Read but Don't Buy
Daily Express:						
Viewers	23	5	17	55	25	20
Controls+	19	6	17	58	22	20
Daily Herald:						
Viewers	10	2	12	76	11	13
Controls	9	2	10	79	12	9
Daily Mail:						
Viewers	11	1	9	79	10	11
Controls	7	3	13	77	12	11
Daily Mirror:						
Viewers	43	5	16	36	40	24
Controls	25	7	24	44	29	27
Daily Sketch:						
Viewers	9	5	19	67	14	19
Controls	7	4	14	75	13	12
Daily Telegraph:						
Viewers	9	3	13	75	11	14
Controls	10	1	17	72	15	13
The Guardian:						
Viewers	3	2	5	90	5	5
Controls	5	1	5	89	6	5
News Chronicle:						
Viewers	8	3	11	78	10	12
Controls	13	3	10	74	14	12
The Times:						
Viewers	2	1	7	90	5	5
Controls	6	2	10	82	9	9

* Those who did not read at all bring these section totals to 100%.
+ Controls are non-viewers equated to viewers in terms of a large number of variables.

With respect to frequency of reading, one feature of the residual differences presented is their variability from paper to paper. Within this variability there is, however, a pattern: frequency of reading appeared to have been reduced for the predominantly middle class papers *(Daily Telegraph, News Chronicle, The Times)* but to have been increased for some of the predominantly working class papers (the *Daily Mirror* and the *Daily Sketch)*. It is noteworthy that whilst about half the papers in Table 1 were subject to only small or negligible change, two of them appear to have undergone quite large changes, namely the *Daily Mirror* and the *Daily Sketch*. Internal checks of a fairly rigorous kind indicate that this assemblage of results represents effects of television and is not simply an artifact of inadequate matching procedure[p].

Though the changes in the *buying* of these newspapers were relatively small (again with the exception of the *Daily Mirror*), they tended to parallel the changes in frequency of reading. In other words, whereas there appears to have been some tendency for television to reduce the buying of the predominantly middle class papers, this tendency is not apparent for the predominantly working class papers. For these there has been a tendency for television to increase buying.

One implication of this finding is most important. It is that television cannot be regarded as generally a cause of the circulation trends under study. This is illustrated by the following comparison of details from Table 1 and Table 4 (in the Appendix).

(i) The circulation figures for The Guardian, The Times, and The Daily Telegraph have been on the increase, yet television's effect on the

[p] In interpreting these results, we are bound to ask if any of them could have arisen out of inadequacies in matching. The results in Table 1 are sufficiently controversial for this question to warrant special attention. In an attempt to answer it, some fairly detailed analyses of the findings were made, with the following outcome: (i) The results for the individual papers, including the Daily Mirror, the Daily Sketch and the Daily Telegraph, did not arise out of the weighting up of some atypical sub-group of non-viewers; the differences being interpreted here as effects of television in no case arose out of single sub-groups and that for the Daily Mirror was present in all but one of the matching sub-groups. (ii) The matching of the samples in terms of the selected composite of matching variables was very close. This also applied to a large range of other variables which included occupational state and occupational level, speed of reading, the number going out to work, possession/use of various goods or facilities. This set of information is most important because clearly such variables could be related to the kind of paper a respondent reads and to the frequency of reading. (iii) For each of the variables for which matching was somewhat incomplete, correlations were worked out between that variable and each of the reading/buying indices involved in Table 1. In no case did these go beyond the 0.4 level. The smallness of this figure, taken in combination with the actual (small) size of any of the known differences between the matched samples rules out the possibility that these particular differences were responsible for any appreciable part of what is being interpreted here as effects of television. Certainly such differences would not appreciably reduce the larger of the 'effects' reported in Table 1 and they would not reverse the apparent direction of the smaller 'effects'.

It remains feasible of course that some matching variable of relevance has been omitted. For such an omission to make a difference to the results, the variable concerned (i) would have to be appreciably unassociated with each and every one of the variables in terms of which matching was achieved; (ii) would have to be a source of appreciable difference between viewers and non-viewers; (iii) would have to be appreciably associated with reading/buying behaviour of the kind under study. In all the circumstances, this is most unlikely, though it cannot be completely ruled out.

buying of these particular papers appears to have been a slightly reducing one. In other words, it appears that circulation figures for these papers would have been slightly *greater* had it not been for television.

(ii) For the *Daily Mirror*, the *Daily Mail*, and the *Daily Express*, circulation figures over recent years have fluctuated up and down a little without there being any distinct evidence of a general rising or falling tendency. The effect of television on these papers appears to have been to *help sustain* the circulation level. In other words, it appears that but for television the circulation levels of these papers would have fallen to at least some degree.

(iii) For the *Daily Herald*, the *Daily Sketch* and the *News Chronicle*[p], circulation figures had been falling for some years. Yet the evidence in Table 1 indicates that for the first and the second of them television could hardly have been a cause of the decline — indeed, its effect on the circulation of the *Daily Sketch* appears to have been to reduce somewhat the rate of its decline.

(iv) The one exception to this pattern of findings was the *News Chronicle*. With this one, television appears to have contributed, at least partly, to the decline in its circulation figures.

The conclusion to be drawn from this information is, then, that with the exception of the News Chronicle, television cannot be regarded as a cause of the changes (over the years leading up to 1959) in the circulation figures of the national daily papers. Television *does* appear to have influenced the final form of these trends, in that for some papers it has reduced the extent either of an increase or of a decline, and in that for others it has helped to stave off decline. But *an explanation of why some papers have rising circulations and why some are in decline must, with the exception of the News Chronicle, be sought in factors other than television.* Moreover, there is evidence (see page 338) that even for the *News Chronicle*, television was only one of the factors responsible for circulation decline.

The national Sunday papers

Table 2 sets out the results for the national Sunday papers. These results are very similar in character and in their implications to the results for the national morning papers.

Television appears to have reduced the frequency of reading of *The Observer*, of the *Sunday Times* and, to some small degree, of the *Sunday Express*. The first two of these are read predominantly by the middle class and the third tends also in this direction. *The People* and several others

[p] Its publication ceased in 1960. In a subsequent study of readers' satisfaction with their papers [233, Part 2], the *News Chronicle* had a relatively low rating in terms of reactions that make for retention of newspapers and a high rating in terms of reactions that make for rejection of newspapers.

TABLE 2

Television's effect on regularity of reading and on buying
for ten Sunday papers
(in per cent)

| | Frequency of Reading | | | | Buying Trends* | |
	Regul-arly	Often	Now and Then	Not at All	Read and Buy	Read but Don't Buy
Empire News:						
Viewers	4	1	4	91	6	3
Controls+	2	0	3	95	3	2
News of the World:						
Viewers	39	7	17	37	41	22
Controls	31	7	13	49	36	13
Observer:						
Viewers	6	2	5	87	8	5
Controls	12	1	8	79	14	7
The People:						
Viewers	32	4	12	52	34	14
Controls	31	4	12	53	32	15
Reynolds News:						
Viewers	2	1	3	94	3	3
Controls	1	1	2	96	3	1
Sunday Dispatch:						
Viewers	9	1	7	83	10	7
Controls	7	1	7	85	8	7
Sunday Express:						
Viewers	22	2	8	68	19	13
Controls	20	5	12	63	22	15
Sunday Graphic:						
Viewers	5	2	4	89	6	5
Controls	4	0	5	91	4	5
Sunday Pictorial:						
Viewers	39	7	11	43	39	18
Controls	32	4	9	55	31	14
Sunday Times:						
Viewers	6	2	4	88	7	5
Controls	9	2	9	80	12	8

* Those who did not read at all bring these section totals to 100%.
+ Controls are non-viewers equated to viewers in terms of a large number of variables.

appear to have been but little affected. Television increased the frequency of reading [r] for the *News of the World* and the *Sunday Pictorial,* both of them read predominantly by the working class. With respect to the *buying* of these Sunday papers, the effects of television were closely similar to those for frequency of reading.

[r] Though not enough to reverse its overall tendency towards decline.

Here too, there was nothing to suggest that television was the cause of rising or of falling circulation figures (as shown in Table 5). (i) For *The Observer* and the *Sunday Times,* circulation figures were rising whereas television's effect appears to have been a reducing one; for the *Sunday Express,* the same tendency was present. (ii) For the *News of the World, Empire News, Reynolds News,* and *Sunday Dispatch,* circulation levels had been falling whereas television's effect appears to have been to increase buying and thus to offset to some degree the extent of the decline in circulation. (iii) The circulation of the *Sunday Pictorial* had declined slightly over recent years in spite of television's apparent tendency to increase the public's buying of it and from this it would seem that the influence of other reducing factors had been offset to at least some degree by television. (iv) For *The People* and the *Sunday Graphic,* small increases in circulation over the last five years appear to have been assisted to at least some degree by television.

The evidence is thus against any general assumption that television was a major factor behind recent decreases in the circulation levels of certain Sunday newspapers. Television's effect seems rather to have been to reduce the extent of circulation decline for the predominantly working class papers, though on the other hand it appears to have damped down the circulation increases of predominantly middle class papers. At least partial exceptions to these trends were *The People* and the *Sunday Graphic.*

The London evening papers

The *Evening News* is more a working class paper than is the *Evening Standard,* while The Star was somewhere in between[s]. All three had falling circulation levels. Television's effect upon the frequency of reading and upon the buying of the *Evening Standard* appears to have been a reducing one. The opposite applies for the *Evening News.* For *The Star,* television's effect on reading and buying was negligible. See Table 3 and Table 4 (Appendix) for details.

Thus while it appears that for one of these London Evening papers television was contributing to circulation decline, it is clear that for the group as a whole we must look beyond television for any adequate or complete explanation of the circulation trends under investigation.

What then, are the causes of circulation change for daily and Sunday papers?

As soon as we are willing to consider that there might be factors other than television responsible for circulation declines, it is not very hard to speculate about what these might be: the content and the character of the newspaper itself; changes in the public's tastes; distribution tactics; changes in the content of competing publications. No doubt there are further

[s] It ceased publication in 1960.

TABLE 3

Television's effect on regularity of reading and on buying
for the three evening papers
(in per cent)

| Publication | Frequency of Reading | | | | Buying Trends* | |
	Regularly	Often	Now and then	Not at All	Read and Buy	Read but Don't Buy
Evening News:						
Viewers	32	9	24	35	41	24
Controls+	25	8	26	41	36	23
Evening Standard:						
Viewers	13	5	22	60	23	17
Controls	12	10	24	54	29	17
The Star:						
Viewers	21	6	24	49	31	20
Controls	19	5	25	51	33	16

* The percentage shown under 'not at all' brings these totals to 100%.
+ Controls are non-viewers equated to viewers in terms of a large number of variables.

possible causes. A follow-up to the present enquiry was in fact concerned with finding out what these other factors might be and in testing their validity as explanations. This was a major study in its own right [233, Part 2.] and its methods and findings can be presented here only in summary form.

This second enquiry rested on the same sample and on the same questionnaire (but a different part of it) as the study of television's effects. Preliminary discussions with groups of newspaper readers had led to the formulation of lists of readers' reactions to their *own* newspapers. Some of these could be regarded as referring to strengths of newspapers and some as referring to weaknesses. They were separately listed as such in the questionnaire and respondents were required to tick those that applied to specified newspapers which they themselves took or read. There was in fact a separate rating sheet for each such newspaper. The weaknesses and strengths so listed are set out below.

Possible strengths	*Possible weaknesses*
* Well written and presented	* Sensational
Good pictures	* Exaggerated
* Good coverage of news	* Not accurate enough
* Up to the minute news	* It makes too much of trivial things
* Gives the necessary details	* It's one sided
Gives me the things I'm interested in.	Too many advertisements
	* Not enough real news
* Good articles	* Dull
* Good sports coverage	The print is hard to read
Provides light reading and amusement.	* It repeats what I've heard already.
	* Too much scandal and gossip

Possible strengths	Possible weaknesses
Takes an interest in the man in the street	* Untruthful
	Not enough respect for people or things
* It's fair	
Outspoken	Takes too much on itself
Responsible and trustworthy	Irresponsible
Useful advertising	Too much crime and violence

* These are 'retention' factors (left hand column) and 'rejection' factors (right hand column). They were not marked with asterisks or in any other way in the questionnaire. See later for explanation.

The respondent had in addition to this to indicate: (i) which papers (if any) he had dropped over the past few years and *why;* (ii) if he had to drop one of his present papers, which it would be and *why* it would be this one; (iii) if he could retain just one of the papers he takes at present, which would it be and *why* that one. Reasons given under (i) and (ii) were used to identify or develop the more recurrent *rejection factors,* while the reasons given under (iii) were used to develop *retention factors.* The more frequently given retention and rejection factors so closely approximated to certain of the items in the above lists of strengths and weaknesses that certain of these may be regarded as retention or as rejection factors. These are marked in the above list with an asterisk (though this asterisk did not of course appear in the questionnaire itself.) Retention factors are included under 'Possible Strengths' and rejection factors under 'Possible weaknesses'.

For the morning and evening papers, circulation trends were fairly closely related to reader ratings in terms of grossed retention factors. In other words, if a paper had a comparatively high average for the retention factors, it tended to have a rising circulation; if it had a relatively low average, it tended to have a falling circulation. It is noteworthy, in this connection, that the *News Chronicle* and *The Star* were at the bottom of the list in terms of 'retention' factor scores.

The averaged endorsements of *rejection* factors tended to be relatively low, and interestingly these levels were not associated with circulation trends for the daily papers. From this, it seems that within reasonable limits it was the presence of retention factors rather than the absence of rejection factors which conditioned the public's buying of daily papers. For the Sunday papers, on the other hand, it was the average of the *rejection* factors which was closely related to circulation trends: papers with a low average for endorsement of rejection factors were the ones with the rising circulation figures, whilst those with high averages were the ones with falling circulations.

Though what is important for one paper may differ from what is important for another, it seems from the evidence available in Part 2 of *The British Press* that what was happening to the circulation of newspapers was a function of, amongst other things, two aspects of public demand.

In the case of daily papers, in appears to have been a demand for what is called 'real news' given in some detail, for fairness of presentation, and for variety of content, including sports coverage. In the case of Sunday papers, the demand was of a negative kind, whereby readers appeared to react against a paper in terms of it being: too much concerned with scandal and gossip and with crime and murder; too sexy; biased; sensation seeking; not serious enough. In understanding what I have said about Sunday papers, it is necessary to remember that what people might like and what they will be seen buying and reading could be rather different things. In other words, though it may perhaps be that many people like a bit of sexy reading, it does not follow at all that they will buy papers specializing in this sort of material or be seen to buy or read them.

Part 2 of *The British Press* also indicated that yet other factors or influences were operative as well: (i) papers with the higher delivery rate tended more than others to have stable or rising circulations; (ii) evening papers were rated as 'not important' much more frequently than were morning or Sunday papers and there was no difference in this respect between viewers and non-viewers.

These and other points are developed in the full report on the British Press, but enough has been said, I think, to indicate that there was much more behind circulation trends in the years leading up to 1959 than simply the effects of television.

Why does television have the kinds of effects described in this report?

Nonetheless we must ask why television's effects on reading and buying take the particular form described in this report. What we seek to understand is why it is that television appears to have damped down somewhat the reading and buying of predominantly middle class papers, and to have supported to some extent the reading and buying of predominantly working class papers.

There is no firm evidence on this matter and anything that is suggested here must rank as speculation. Nonetheless the close questioning of viewers suggests that one element of the answer may possibly be found in the special nature of behaviour in the viewing room. Not all the people going into the viewing room go there to view: the viewing room happens to be the family sitting room. But once there, with the set on, there is a strict limit to the number of things people can do. Talking is quite likely to be silenced by an irritated viewer. Letter writing and indeed anything that calls for continuity of thought is likely to be interrupted. Under these conditions, the reader of a rather demanding newspaper which requires continuity of thought would seem to be specially handicapped. On the other hand, the man whose paper has in it much that is short, easy and discontinuous is in a better position to complete with TV. Certainly it is the writer's experience that many working class viewers are quick to point out that they pick up their papers and read something between programs and during advertisement breaks. In this connection, it would be quite wrong to think that the morning papers are finished with by evening: 29% of the London sample said that they did their main reading of morning papers in the evening and this leaves plenty of room for television to differentially effect the reading of these papers. This is not to say that it *does* happen but that there is some scope for it.

Another possible element in the situation is that with some of the mass circulation papers a practice had been made of giving space to items which were featured in television programs the previous evening, the point being that what was on the 'telly' last night was known to be a good talking point amongst working class readers. It may well be, too, that the boldly printed schedule of TV programs which appears in certain of these papers was another factor which worked specially in their favour — they could be easily seen in the viewing room.

These speculations do of course seem to apply more to changes in reading than to changes in buying, but it is hard to see how the circumstances described would not in the end stimulate somewhat the buying of certain papers and work somewhat against the buying of others. For most papers, of course, the buying changes to be explained were not large.

The writer is well aware of an opinion put forward by some researchers that television tends to satisfy the viewer's desire for the light, the entertaining and the trivial; that this causes him to drop his lighter rather than his heavy reading material. This is a sort of displacement theory in the sense that light newspaper fare is held to be displaced by an *alternative* source of light and trivial things. This, however, is an unlikely explanation in the case of British newspapers, because the middle class reader tends not to take a working class paper and so tends not to be in a position to give up the latter rather than his middle class paper. In any case, if a displacement theory is to be invoked, it seems more likely that it would operate in rather a different way. Thus it seems possible that after a day in the office with his clerical or technical or business affairs, the reader of the middle class paper will feel inclined to relax with a TV program rather than give his attention once more to serious affairs in the form of somewhat heavy or serious journalism. For the working class reader of the working class paper, the contrast between the difficulty level of television material and that of the paper would seem to be very much less marked.

Too much must not be made of these several speculations, but they do seem to warrant at least some consideration.

Television's Effects on Weekly and Monthly Magazines

On the evidence of this enquiry, the effect of television on weekly and monthly magazines appears to have been broadly similar to its effects on newspapers. Thus (i) its effects appear to have varied from one magazine to another; (ii) the frequency of reading and the rate of buying of the predominantly middle class magazines appear to have been reduced by television, while reading and buying of various of the predominantly working class magazines appears to have been increased; (iii) there were several appreciable changes in buying and in frequency of reading, but many were small; (iv) TV-produced changes in the buying of magazines were approximately equal in size to TV-produced changes in the frequency of reading, *but in neither case were they consistent with circulation trends*. At the same time, there was a greater tendency for the changes in magazine reading to be decreases than was the case for the daily and the Sunday newspapers.

Television's effects on some of the magazines studied are specially worth noting. Those undergoing moderate change through television were: *Argosy, Housewife, The Lady, The Listener, New Statesman, Punch, Reader's Digest, Woman's Illustrated* (all decreases); *Weekend, Woman's Own* (both increases). In most cases, the reported change in reading arose out of both a change in the number buying the publication and a change in the number who read it without actually buying it. One of the exceptions to this was *Reader's Digest*, where the assessed reduction in reading appears to have been due wholly to reduced reading by those who did not actually buy it themselves but got it passed on to them.

Television's effect upon the total number
of newspapers and magazines read
An analysis was made of television's effects on the *total number* of papers which viewers read either regularly or often. On the evidence, television appears to have increased slightly the proportion of viewers who regularly or often read at least one morning newspaper. The same seems to be true with respect to the London evening and the national Sunday newspapers.

When the weekly magazines are considered, this slight tendency toward increase disappeared, and for the monthlies the effect of television was a slight *reduction* in the number read at least occasionally.

Changes Relating to Publications
Generally

Effects according to reader characteristics
Television's impact on the number of papers read was fairly evenly distributed throughout the sample. Nonetheless, there were some people for whom some aspects of reading appear to have been the more affected by television: (1) under the impact of television, older people increased slightly the number of newspapers read, at the expense of weekly magazines but not at the expense of monthlies; (2) the less skilled section of the sample appear to have increased the number of daily newspapers read (but not of Sunday papers), at the expense of both weekly and monthly magazines; (3) those in full-time jobs increased the number of Sunday papers read, apparently at the expense of weekly papers.

One possible explanation of these changes may lie in the differing functions or uses of magazines as distinct from newspapers. On the evidence of this enquiry, magazines were used much more as time fillers than were newspapers. But television is itself a great time filler. Hence, for people with time on their hands — the old, the unskilled, those not in a full-time job — magazine reading seems likely to have been displaced to at least some degree. The functions which different publications serve for specific sections of the community do in fact seem to be key elements in understanding how television is going to affect these people.

Effects by length of set ownership
A comparison was made of the impact of television upon the number of papers read by those who had been viewers for over four years and those who had secured sets within the previous four years. The comparison suggests that television's effect was to stimulate slightly, in the long term, the number of *newspapers* read and that it did the opposite for weekly and monthly magazines. Setting this out in greater detail, it appears that there was (1) an early increase for morning papers and a maintenance of this in the long term; (2) little or no change for evening and Sunday papers during the early period of ownership but increase later on; (3) an early small increase for weeklies, followed by a small decline; (4) a small reduction for monthlies, starting in the early phase of ownership and maintained in the long run. We must be careful to note, however, that the changes under (3) and (4) were far too small to explain the changes in magazine circulation figures, so that here too any adequate explanation of circulation declines must be looked for beyond television.

Television's effect on the kind and
range of things people read about
Another part of this enquiry was a study of television's effects on the sort of thing that people read about in their papers. Those taking part in the enquiry were presented with a list of 30 topics ordinarily presented in newspapers and magazines. For each topic or item they indicated whether or not they had spent at least *some* time on it in the last seven days. *This is not the same as asking about the total amount of time spent on them; in fact, we know from other work that television may reduce the total reading time* [232]. The list of thirty items included things like happenings in Britain, gossip columns, sporting events, front-page news, weather reports, letters from readers, fashion articles, world affairs, reviews of films and plays, the pictures in papers, comic strips and cartoons, gardening notes and hints. With one or two exceptions, most of the changes were relatively small. Indeed, there were only two large changes — reading about television programs, where, inevitably, television had brought an increase, and an increase in the reading of comic strips and cartoons.

Despite the smallness of the changes for most of the thirty items, it is still possible to detect something of a pattern within them.

1. The incidence of at least some reading about items calling for serious and lengthy attention seems to have been reduced by television, whereas topics calling for little concentration or allowing piecemeal attention tend to get slightly more readers (e.g. comic strips, cartoons, crossword-puzzles, gossip columns). This is very much in line with the description in this chapter of behaviour in the viewing room.

2. When the topics were of the kind dealt with in television programs themselves and offered either something of human interest or something of practical importance to the viewer, there was a tendency toward a greater incidence of (at least some) reading (e.g. television notes, sporting events, weather reports, advertisements, the views of ordinary people and of celebrities).

3. The incidence of at least some reading of articles concerning the "home" also appears to have been increased by television.

By counting the number of items out of thirty to which the respondent gave at least some attention, it was possible to assess changes in the range or breadth of reading. The viewer read or noted at least as many subjects as he did before television, and perhaps more. There was no major variation in television's impact on range of reading from one section of the population to another, but it appears that increases in range of items read were somewhat more frequent among older people, among those in full-time jobs, and among the unmarried. Effects concerning range of reading also varied with length of set ownership: change was negligible over the first five years or so, but appreciable increases occurred later on.

Television's effect on the noticing of press advertisements
The testimony of the survey respondents was brought to bear on an issue vital to the economics of the press industry, namely the degree to which readers notice press advertisements. On the evidence, television appears to have increased somewhat the number of people who spent time looking at press advertisements. Perhaps more important than this is the fact that a large proportion of viewers (33 per cent) claimed that seeing a television commercial caused them to notice press advertisements about the same product. Viewer testimony on this subject indicated that this bolstering effect was more likely to occur when the visual content of the two advertisements was similar or identical; where this occurred, there was some likelihood that the reader would come out with something like "Oh, that's the one we saw on television!"

Relating These Findings to Those From
Other Enquiries

In trying to relate these findings to those from other enquiries, one matter of discipline is rather important. I believe that the only studies which should be brought into such a comparison are those in which there has been a really serious attempt to eliminate from the results the influences of extraneous factors and of original differences between viewers and non-viewers. This reduces considerably the number of studies with which comparisons may meaningfully be made. If we impose also the requirement that the topics and the age range of respondents should be broadly similar, Coffin's two enquiries are virtually the only qualifiers. The present findings for monthly publications are much the same as those of Coffin. Hower, whereas Coffin reported a small reduction in the number reading a newspaper on the average day, the present study reports a slight increase in the proportion who read at least one morning newspaper regularly or often. Though these two sets of findings are expressed within different reference systems, they do seem to be contrary. This apparent difference in findings for newspapers may indicate that at least one of the two result is in error; on the other hand, it may reflect real differences in what TV has done in America and in England. Then again it may be that the two studies were concerned with different types of papers: certainly the present enquiry indicates that what happens with one paper may be rather different from what happens with another paper.

Having reduced in this way and to this extent the number of studies to be brought into a comparison of results, one published viewpoint is nonetheless worth noting. A number of writers have argued that the character of much television material is such that it facilitates escape from reality and tends to feed fantasy seeking. This, it is argued, lies behind its power to displace the sort of printed media which performs the same functions — material with a light, trivial and partly fictitious character (for example, comics). One writer extends this point of view to argue that we should therefore expect television to reduce the reading of the British popular press. Those familiar with these papers would probably be quick to point out however that the so called 'popular' papers are regarded by their readers as a quite proper and serious source of their news. These readers tend not to take a so called 'quality' paper as well (as a serious alternative) and they don't regard so called 'popular' papers as providing them with anything like fantasy — as would a comic. The main difference between the two types of papers is in fact in the selection of news and the way in which it is presented. The British 'popular' press emphasises the human interest side to news and presents this in an easier-to-understand form than do the 'quality' papers.

SUMMARY OF THE FINDINGS

This study indicates that, in the period under investigation, television's effect on the reading and the buying of publications tended to be small and to vary from one to another publication. There was, however, a pattern to the changes. (1) Where there were TV-produced increases, these tended to be among the predominantly working class papers with their simpler, shorter, material; on the other hand, the TV-produced *decreases* tended to be among the predominantly middle class papers. (2) Television appears to have increased somewhat the incidence of reading[t] of items actually dealt with in TV programs, and to have increased slightly the total range and variety of the press items read. (3) In the long term, television appears to have increased slightly the reading of daily and Sunday papers at the expense of weekly and monthly magazines.

The outstanding result of this enquiry is, however, that most of the changes produced by television were small and did not parallel the circulation changes. The direct implication of this is that we must go beyond television for any adequate explanation of the decline in press circulation figures. To assume that television has been the cause of the troubles of the press and to leave it at that, is to miss the possibility of dealing with the real causes.

---

[t] This does not mean that television increased the *total amount of time* spent reading— only the number of reading occasions. In fact, we know that television reduces the *total amount* of reading.

APPENDIX

TABLE 4

Circulation figures of nine national morning newspapers and three evening newspapers, 1938–1965 (figures to nearest thousand)

Year.	Daily Express*	Daily Herald*	Daily Mail*	Daily Mirror*	Daily Sketch*	Daily Telegraph+	The Guardian*	News Chronicle*	Times+	Evening News	Evening Standard	Star
1938	2,466	2,000	1,531	1,408	780	660	40	1,273	202	802	388	488
1939	2,546	1,850	1,533	1,571	750	737	40	1,299	204	838	382	488
1940	2,587	1,850	1,416	1,800	700	896	40	1,188	184	847	401	455
1941	2,633	1,850	1,420	1,775	725	762	40	1,152	165	817	461	425
1942	2,586	1,875	1,448	1,775	750	648	40	1,194	159	853	483	518
1943	2,604	1,875	1,413	1,800	781	650	40	1,180	158	850	521	529
1944	2,977	1,875	1,606	2,000	865	708	80	1,350	179	1,001	599	606
1945	3,239	2,000	1,752	2,000	883	822	80	1,454	195	1,072	656	651
1946	3,545	1,875	1,927	2,400	919	823	80	1,595	230	1,192	718	720
1947	3,805	2,096	2,016	3,490	762	902	80	1,579	271	1,641	763	1,074
1948	3,855	2,114	2,077	3,701	772	907	80	1,620	240	1,653	781	1,082
1949	4,044	2,072	2,201	4,390	769	970	137	1,603	262	1,742	839	1,214
1950	4,116	2,071	2,245	4,567	777	976	140	1,534	254	1,752	862	1,228
1951	4,169	2,003	2,267	4,514	794	998	139	1,507	232	1,678	839	1,230
1952	4,042	1,920	2,172	4,433	751	986	127	1,407	236	1,535	787	1,164

Year.	Daily Express*	Daily Herald*	Daily Mail*	Daily Mirror*	Daily Sketch*	Daily Telegraph†	The Guardian*	News Chronicle*	Times†	Evening News	Evening Standard	Star
1953	4,078	1,873	2,174	4,452	805	970	137	1,356	225	1,503	765	1,118
1954	4,069	1,811	2,127	4,665	826	1,041	146	1,316	221	1,431	761	1,103
1955	4,036	1,759	2,068	4,725	950	1,055	156	1,253	222	1,313	711	954
1956	4,042	1,654	2,072	4,650	1,123	1,062	164	1,441	221	1,221	663	927
1957	4,127	1,641	2,139	4,659	1,305	1,074	177	1,394	233	1,286	665	908
1958	4,041	1,523	2,106	4,526	1,224	1,134	179	1,267	248	1,225	590	789
1959	4,053	1,465	2,071	4,497	1,156	1,181	183	1,207	254	1,170	577	758
1960	4,143	1,407	2,066	4,565	1,117	1,177	199	1,162(a)	263	1,156	584	735(a)
1961	4,313	1,419	2,687	4,593	1,000	1,251	235		260	1,486	761	
1962	4,285	1,348	2,571	4,560	953	1,253	265		255	1,448	742	
1963	4,224	1,302	2,479	4,631	923	1,290	266		255	1,388	729	
1964	4,276	1,265	2,423	4,951	923	1,313	272		256	1,424	759	
1965	3,981	1,361‡	2,425	4,947	826	1,351	276		258	1,278	680	

* Audit Bureau circulation figures from 1948 on. Before that, as provided by London Press Exchange, by individual newspaper organisations, and by the Audit Bureau. All ABC figures from 1948 onward are for the January–June period.
† Figures provided by London Press Exchange, Ltd.
‡ Renamed "Sun".
(a) Ceased publication in October, 1960.

TABLE 5

Circulation figures of eleven national Sunday newspapers, 1938–1965 (figures to nearest thousand)

Year	Empire News*	News of the World†	Observer†	The People†	Reynolds News†	Sunday Chronicle*	Sunday Dispatch†	Sunday Express†	Sunday Graphic*	Sunday Pictorial†	Sunday Times*
1938	1,450	3,750	219	3,250	500	1,000	737	1,400	900	1,500	286
1939	1,456	4,000	225	3,250	500	1,000	824	1,498	900	1,500	324
1940	1,450	4,000	241	3,250	500	1,000	932	1,555	900	1,750	349
1941	1,450	4,000	244	3,250	500	976	992	1,676	850	1,750	370
1942	1,442	4,000	244	3,447	500	976	1,094	1,639	855	1,800	383
1943	1,625	4,000	254	3,250	500	1,093	1,116	1,687	956	2,000	415
1944	1,675	4,000	277	3,250	580	1,149	1,263	1,936	1,055	2,212	417
1945	1,812	5,000	299	3,447	580	1,150	1,372	2,114	1,026	2,500	460
1946	1,909	7,000	340	4,500	630	1,230	1,490	2,334	1,153	2,600	514
1947	2,033	7,725	370	4,626	720	1,164	2,060	2,437	1,154	3,755	557
1948	2,067	7,887	384	4,673	720	1,179	2,061	2,579	1,185	4,005	510
1949	2,241	8,382	388	4,958	732	1,199	2,187	2,735	1,234	4,735	533
1950	2,085	8,444	422	5,089	705	1,118	2,378	2,967	1,169	5,094	535
1951	2,029	8,407	450	5,163	712	1,051	2,631	3,306	1,139	5,170	535
1952	1,897	8,230	453	4,984	708	939	2,664	3,185	1,082	5,047	484
1953	1,940	8,169	476	5,129	689	918	2,744	3,247	1,114	5,263	507
1954	1,961	8,134	535	5,167	628	863	2,676	3,243	1,174	5,446	565
1955	2,049	7,971	564	5,075	579	830	2,549	3,235	1,220	5,539	606
1956	2,550	7,493	601	4,948	516		2,420	3,331	1,190	5,624	618
1957	2,473	7,241	641	4,954	452		2,334	3,412	1,152	5,676	740
1958	2,161	6,767	638	4,900	368		1,835	3,398	953	5,378	795
1959	2,102	6,555	660	5,055	342		1,594	3,447	878	5,331	880

	2,084[a]					1,485[b]		883[c]		
1960		6,456	704	5,323	328		3,566		5,275	943
1961		6,734	728	5,442	326		3,767		5,335	1,023
1962		6,445	722	5,544	303		4,398		5,193	1,110
1963		6,289	718	5,541	329		4,290		5,175‡	1,170
1964		6,224	714	5,579	283		4,308		5,053	1,240
1965		6,175	829	5,509	236		4,187		5,022	1,275

* Figures provided by London Press Exchange Ltd.

† Audit Bureau Circulation figures from 1948 on. Before that, as provided by London Press Exchange, by individual newspaper organizations, and by the Audit Bureau. All ABC figures from 1948 onwards are for the January–June period.

‡ Changed title to "Sunday Mirror" in March 1963.

[a] Ceased publication in October, 1960. [b] Ceased publication June 1961. [c] Ceased publication in December, 1960.

TELEVISION RESEARCH: PAST AND FUTURE

[25]

Television research: past and future

In Britain, certain kinds of television research are carried out regularly and on a large scale. On the other hand, much of the research that should and could be done in the interests of broadcasting efficiency and of public welfare has for a long time been neglected. One result of this has been that quite frequently the decisions of television management and of program staff have been made on a basis of little more than guess work. Inevitably, chances have been taken and certainly mistakes have been made. Another result has been that public knowledge of the impact of television has, over the years, remained very meagre indeed so that such public judgements and such decisions as are made about television have frequently been arrived at in the absence of the relevant facts.

My main purpose in this last chapter is to outline what is not being done, to discuss what appear to be the main reasons for the omissions, and to go on to suggest some steps which might contribute to a wider use of research procedures by the television industry and by those with responsibility to viewers. First, however, let me refer to the kinds of research which *are* being done.

The Main Kinds of Television Research Being Done at Present

The most commonly used form of television research, both in Britain and elsewhere, is one which provides an estimate of the number of people watching any specified programme[a]. The results of one or another form of this measure are widely used by program planners in Britain and throughout the world and they are basic to many decisions about whether to keep a program going or to take it off the air. This measure is probably the keystone to competitive programming. At the same time it is by no means a sufficient or a complete guide, for it tells the broadcaster about his mistakes only after they have been well and truly made. The 'size

---

[a] In Britain, this type of research is carried out mainly by Television Audience Measurement Limited, and by the Audience Research Department of the BBC.

of audience' measure is basic to competitive planning but it is not in itself enough.

Another measure which has long been used, particularly by the British Broadcasting Corporation, is one which provides an assessment of people's *reactions* to programs as broadcast. It gives a comparative index of the degree to which viewers found a program interesting or liked it or thought it good, and it can also provide evidence about *what* viewers liked and disliked about that program. It is the obvious supplement to the size of audience measurement. The two measures taken together tell the producer not only how many people saw his program but what they thought of it.

Reaction reports are now available in Britain on a commercial basis as well and these will no doubt serve a very useful purpose in telling the producer about the extent of his success or his failure. Certainly they constitute a very useful step forward. However, like 'size of audience' checks, the reaction report is geared more to discovering mistakes already made than to avoiding the making of them. Furthermore the method tends to be geared to producing something about each of many programs rather than much detail about one or a few: yet detail may well be what is needed for remedying some one program's defects or for learning how to avoid similar mistakes in another program.

A third form of television research into which a lot of money and time is put is the pre-testing of television advertisements. Much of this work is done through the calculation of certain reaction indices which are regarded as predictive of an advertisement's selling power. These indices include the advertisement's memorability, its power to attract attention, its power to change a viewer's state of preference for the advertised brand. In addition, small-group discussions are frequently conducted with the aim of detecting viewer reactions at the qualitative rather than the quantitative level. Still other types of advertisement testing are carried out. Most of this work is based upon completed advertisements, but the results can be used for guidance of decisions about whether or not to use a particular advertisement in a new campaign or *which* of several to use. Clearly, valid research of this kind is vital for efficiency in television advertising. At the same time it is necessary that we see just how far valid work of this kind can take us. In the first place, the advertisements are usually in a finished form before one or another of them is chosen and this is a form of waste. It is also possible that a comparative test will leave the advertiser with the least bad of a poor bunch from which the choice was made. Nor do the techniques in more general use provide quantitatively sound information about where and how the tested advertisement went wrong or was effective — information which is most important for the development of a science of advertisement production.

My statement about the limits of these three research procedures are not intended to argue away any of the considerable contribution which they can make to broadcasting's efficiency. They can provide information which a television organization and those who buy television time cannot afford to be without. Nonetheless they are limited operations in the sense that they do not provide enough information for really safe and economic decision making. On the other hand, techniques suitable for providing quite a lot of this kind of information *are* available, but are very much under-used.

The Methods Which are Under-used

Various of the under-used techniques have been either referred to or described in detail in this book. They include the method of small-group discussion, various kinds of work with large groups, reaction analysis (using the program analyser), sample surveys, diary keeping, intensive interviewing, the use of official figures. Properly used, such methods can provide information relevant to a wide range of decisions. Thus work with large groups can be used to indicate which elements in a program are liked and which are disliked — information which would make it possible to modify and gradually to strengthen a program which viewing figures had indicated to be drawing numerically small or declining audiences. Promising and less promising artists can be identified in the same way and their individual faults and special abilities identified. The method also lends itself well to testing the comprehensibility of programs and to several aspects of advertisement testing. In addition, it can be used to study the existing knowledge and the existing attitudes of viewers with respect to some particular issue about which a program or an advertisement is yet to be prepared. Even *ideas* for programs or for advertisements can be pre-tested through the large group technique.

Group discussions and intensive interviewing methods are fitted, in their different ways, to the gathering of clues or leads which are specially relevant to viewer opinions of programs and of advertising material. Such leads may relate to what lies behind viewers' reactions to a specific program or to some broad type of program (e.g. Westerns, programs of social criticism) or even to a station's whole output. On the other hand, these leads may take the form of ideas (evoked through discussion with ordinary viewers) for modifying some aspect of an advertisement or of a program. These discussional and probing techniques are also valuable for indicating the general lines to be pursued in more formal and standardised information-gathering, itself geared to programming purposes — for example in establishing the distribution of the public's ideas about certain kinds of programs or about programs generally.

Social surveys can be used in a wide range of enquiries designed to guide both policy decisions and broad program planning. Such investigations might be designed to provide information about the nature and distribution of viewers' values, or their interests, or their availability for viewing at different times of the day. Further, such studies could be focused upon any sub-section of the population (e.g. housewives, farmers, teenagers) about which information is required. Group testing methods and survey methods can, between them, provide information about the strengths and weaknesses of opposition programs, such information to be used for the targeting of competition against them. These two methods, taken in combination with the stable correlate technique[b], have also been used to assess the long-term effects of the television medium as such, and the short-term effects of specific programs.

Between them, these and other of the available techniques can provide valuable information relevant both to the planning of program content and to the subsequent development and testing of the program. Further, they are directly relevant to the work of the student of television's social impact. *Nonetheless they tend to be under-used, some to be used hardly at all.* Programs get small audiences and are then taken off the air without anyone really finding out *why* they failed. Some programs have become great successes without any serious attempt to find out what it is that made them so. Hunch takes the place of informed decision and there is little build-up of a body of knowledge about the principles of television broadcasting. People often speculate publicly and privately about the social effects of television, but little is done to determine empirically what these really are.

The Methodological Inadequacies

There is one other aspect of television research which warrants comment in the context of what is *not* being done. This aspect relates to methodological weaknesses in at least some of the methods in major use for (i) measuring audience size and (ii) pre-testing advertisements.

A case for concern over 'size of audience' measurements springs out of the existence of differences between the results derived from different methods in common use. These methods include, among others, the meter system, the personal interview based on recall (aided or unaided), the diary method, the coincidental technique using the telephone interview, the personal coincidental interview, the telephone recall method. Meaningful differences between the results from some of these methods have been found to exist at the general level and/or for specific programs. Sometimes the differences for specific programs are large. The television industry is by no means complaisant about this situation: recommendations for research practice have been issued [4] and a certain amount of very useful methodological research has been carried out[c]. Valuable though some of this work has been, it has not yet produced all that is really needed, namely (i) information about the amount of error involved in each method and (ii) information (for each method) about the sources or causes of error. Bearing in mind that different research methods may be designed to meet different research needs, the purpose of these two items of information would be to facilitate the dropping of the too inaccurate method and to provide a basis for increasing the accuracy of the others. Nothing like this full body of in-

[b] See chapters 17 and 21.
[c] See, for example: "The Comparison of Audience Composition Techniques", Television Audience Measurement Limited, 1961.

formation has yet been developed, though the means for getting it are available. So are the research procedures for improving methods once the causes of error are known.

A similar kind of difficulty applies to the pre-testing of television advertisements. The necessary basic research for ensuring that these tests are as predictive as possible has not been carried out. This is not to say that tests currently used cannot provide valid pointers to the relative selling power of different advertisements. But it is highly probable that indices or tests of *greater* predictive power could be developed through such basic research. It may well be, too, that currently used indices/tests could be made much *more* predictive if taken in combination with other indices or tests. So much *could* be done: instead of this, most of the testing systems in use have been set up mainly on a basis of somebody's judgement and the necessary validation and development have not been carried out.

Some Reasons for the Under-Use of Television Research by the Television Industry

If the greater use of research by television management and staff is to be achieved, it is necessary that the reasons for its past (and present) under-use be understood. Accordingly, let me set out, at first briefly and then in greater detail, what I believe these reasons to be. One of them appears to be the frequent failure of the research fraternity to convince television's management and creative staff that what research has to offer is both usable and useful. There are of course two sides to this difficulty but it remains a vital one. Another important reason for the present situation is that those responsible for doing television research are often too busy doing routine things to be able to think closely about viewer reactions to their own program services, or to isolate key issues for study, or to set going research operations other than the ones heavily engaging them already. Moreover they are likely to be handicapped by the marked scarcity of properly trained research assistants to whom some of the burdens of ongoing research might be passed.

The non-acceptance of research by artists,
creative staff and management.
In writing about the attitudes of program staff to television research, it is necessary to distinguish between *size of audience figures* on the one hand and detailed program research and 'effects' research on the other. Generally speaking, size of audience figures get ready attention throughout the broadcasting industry. This is easy to understand in any society where there is competitive broadcasting and where the fate of a program is influenced by the size of the audience it draws. Even in the absence of competition, its influence is considerable, because with a mass medium of this kind there is no avoiding the implications of evidence that relatively few people are watching one's output. True, there are programs which are designed for minorities, but if the size-of-audience figures suggest that

even these are not watching, then there develops a considerable pressure for action to be taken. Obviously artists and production staff may have mixed feelings about such figures — including suspicions about their accuracy — but the figures cannot be ignored, and at management level they tend to be much awaited. It is the very importance of these figures, for production staff at the personal level and for management at the station level, which has made them an integral part of broadcasting thinking. Something of the same feeling has been generated in relation to program reaction indices of the kind produced by the BBC's Audience Research Department. Where departmental heads take note of them, it is hard for production staff to ignore them.

All of this is not to say that creative and production staff fully welcome and accept size of audience figures. Some are sceptical and some are resentful, but generally speaking the system of using such figures is accepted as part and parcel of the broadcasting scene. However, when it comes to probing and evaluative research of the kind I have described in this text, there can be a fairly marked tendency for creative and production staff to resist it or simply to ignore it when it is on offer. Anyone who has worked in research of the kind described in this book will have become aware of such attitudes. It is well that we try to understand them.

One of the more potent reasons for attitudes of this kind is that television production at its best depends upon the flair of the artist, of the producer, of the creative director. Understandably, many of these people feel that to be constrained by requirements developed by some statistically-minded researcher would stifle the creative urge and make a dull thing of output. However right or wrong creative staff may be in this belief, the fact remains that the researcher who presents a technical report which *appears* to impose requirements upon creative staff, is liable to have his work ignored. Over and above this, the artistic mind and the research mind are frequently far apart and they may on occasions be out of sympathy with each other. Where this is so, the apparent intrusion of research into the artistic domain can be sharply resented.

However, this is by no means the only kind of reason for television's under-use of research. Many an experienced and practical producer[d] is likely to take the line that he knows the business of production better than the research man whom he sees as edging into television. Even if he sees the research man in his *proper* role, namely as someone who can provide him with information relevant to the decisions he has to make, the producer is usually a very busy man who has to meet deadlines day by day. Accordingly he will not be able to give anything but the minimum of time to working out what the research man's report actually means or how to implement a suggestion made by someone not fully conversant with

[d] The term 'producer' is used here in a specially broad way, namely to denote anyone involved in decision making, large or small, in the course of a program's development — Planner, department head, Director, Producer.

television production. In the meantime, he plays his hunch — which may well be right and even brilliantly so — but which occasionally may be disastrously wrong. However experienced he may be, the decision-maker needs facts: the problem is how to present them to him in a form which he is able and willing to use in his own rather special circumstances.

As unfortunate as anything else is the remoteness of the average research man from the production scene. His basic training and his way of thought are likely to be very different from those of production staff. Yet all too often he makes no effort to bridge the gap or to familiarize himself with the problems and the realities of production. Accordingly, the scene is set against his seeing problems in production terms or reporting his results in production terms: he does not know enough about the production of television material to be of much use. This in turn means that production staff do not become favourably aware of what research might do for them.

These three are not necessarily the only reasons behind the failure of the television industry to adopt detailed program research as an integral part of its operation. Each is an important reason however, and fortunately the same course of remedial action is appropriate with respect to each of them. *This course of action is to bring the researcher into close and continuing contact with the production team.* If this is done with reasonable tact and good sense and if the researcher works at it, several things are very likely to follow. In the first place, the researcher will probably learn enough about program production to be able to discern and tackle relevant problems and to provide usable results. In all likelihood, he will come to think in production terms. Secondly, production staff will get to know him at a personal level and will learn at first hand what he can possibly do for them. If he concentrates first upon problems about which production staff are personally aware and about which they would like help, acceptance of him and his discipline will occur much more quickly than it would were he to try to impose his own ideas of what is needed. His integration into the production scene may well change his earlier views in any case. This integration will of course involve the researcher in spending a lot of time round and about the studios, and in listening to and mixing with production staff at all levels. He will have to avoid anything like mystique and jargon. These are usually the props of people who have not yet discovered the simplicity of their own craft and they can be disastrous for the acceptance of research. He will have to let production staff see how he goes about his work — not in anything remotely like lecture form, but quite informally and as opportunity permits. This involvement of production staff should include occasional attendance at group testing operations, hearing tape recordings of intensive interviews, being shown or told where the informants come from, along with the simple steps that are taken to ensure that these informants are a proper cross-section of the audience. It helps too if producers are free to look in on the analysis of viewer opinions as this analysis proceeds.

There are obvious limits to the amount of this involvement which should

be attempted and there are obvious dangers to be avoided. What the researcher has to do is to convey to producers the simple commonsense of
what he is doing and at the same time to trigger off in the producer an
awareness of the possible further uses to him of this new tool. What the
researcher must avoid at all times is any sort of blind protectiveness of
research as such. In particular, he must be willing to admit its weaknesses
and its limits and above all he must never defend bad research: there is a
real danger that such overselling and overprotectiveness will lead to his
being left alone in his importance.

With the integration of research thinking into the production department — and that is what is required — two more things should tend to
happen. Findings from program research are likely to become integrated
into creative thinking so that the lessons of this research will operate not
as controls but as a way of thinking. Secondly, when the results of some
enquiry are given to a busy producer, they will in all likelihood be results
of work which that producer initiated in order to make a particular decision. He is hardly likely to feel he is too busy to give the results his time.

For the sort of relationship outlined here, the researcher ought really
to be assigned to the production department on a continuing basis and his
office should be on production premises. In a large broadcasting organisation, his assignment would no doubt be from a central research department and his ultimate responsibility would be to the director of research.
Nonetheless his contact with the head of the production department to
which he is assigned must be a direct and working contact: anything less
than this would be too remote to achieve a real integration of program
research into production. With the *small* broadcasting station, this kind
of arrangment should be fairly easy to achieve: the research director might
possibly be the assignee himself and the latter (possibly with an assistant)
would doubtless be housed in the station and close to production personnel. His association with production heads and with station management
could easily be direct and informal. With the larger organisation, these
conditions would be somewhat harder to set up but would be by no means
impossible. However, what would have to be avoided would be the situation where the central organisation sent a researcher to the production
centre to get details of a problem, then conducted research without much
interim contact with the persons who raised and defined the problem, and
finally passed in a technical report through the director of the central
research organisation. That may sound like a neat administrative arrangement, but it will not achieve anything like the necessary integration of
program research into production thinking.

Those responsible for research are pre-occupied with routine activity
Another of the reasons for the under-use of the techniques of program
research is that those responsible for such work are often pre-occupied
with the continuing collection or analysis of specific information in some
routine way. Often enough, this preoccupation is with the collection of size-

of-audience information or with its special analysis. Obviously, these are essential activities, but they must not be allowed to distract research thinking from all other aspects of program research.

If such routines are already a necessary part of the research procedures of a large telecasting organisation, it is most important that some personnel be freed from the routine work so that they may give their attention to the appropriate use of one or another of the other research methods, according to current requirements for efficient programming. If routines such as size-of-audience measurement are not already in existence in the organisation, it will in most cases be better to contract them out, so that the station's research group stays free to concentrate upon the less routine aspects of program research.

Only if he is relatively free from the machinery of a continuous routine will the researcher have that necessary time and flexibility for detecting the changing problems of program production, and for initiating appropriate research action. Moreover, he must constantly be on his guard against being taken over by some new routine of his own making. A new routine develops all too easily. It may consist of a regularised program-testing service, of the continuing study of reaction to certain kinds of program material, of the institution of quite frequent survey work to chart relevant characteristics and attitudes of viewers. If there is a case for running such work on a continuing basis, then the routine parts of that work should be contracted out. Even for intermittent use of such procedures, it is desirable to contract out if at all possible because, once the researcher sets up the necessary machinery for carrying out a useful research operation, there is a danger that he will go on with the running of it because this is usually more settled and is easier than the exacting task of vigilant, ranging enquiry. Perhaps, too, the attractions of empire building will contribute to his hanging on to it. On the other hand, there is an obvious limit to the degree to which the researcher should stay free of routine or of the grind of detailed research. He should, for instance, go out quite often to viewer homes to conduct exploratory interviews, primarily to stay in touch with viewers, but also to pick up leads to one or another inadequacy or strength in the programming of his own station or of the opposition. He must, if such leads seem to warrant systematic investigation, give his full time and attention to the design and to the supervision of the necessary research. He must work with good speed. And no doubt he will for a time be closely occupied with the writing of the report and with its presentation.

Unavoidably, he will be involved in further detail and routine whenever group testing of programs is done. Thus he will be the one to collaborate with a producer in deciding what will be tested; he will have to plan and to organise the content analysis of viewers' reactions and to make systematic checks on the work of his analysts; he will have to do a certain amount of the content analysis himself. Then again he would be required to meet regularly (as well as in the course of day-to-day work) with producers and management and to stay closely in touch with all developments in station planning and policy. Moreover, he would have to maintain a watch over audience figures and trends passed to him in appropriate form by an assistant.

There would, then, be various things to be done on a regular basis. There would also be frequent occasions when close and sustained attention to the detail of specific enquiries would be called for. However, this situation is very different from that in which the researcher has become immersed in one or perhaps several procedures for the regular collection of specific information. Valuable as the regular provision of this information may be, the immersed researcher inevitably loses contact with the full range of the broadcasting problems of his station — and, of course, with that wider range of research methods suited to the solution of such problems.

Sometimes the contracting out of a job which is time consuming or of a routine character will be frustrated by the absence of outside facilities for doing such work. This is the more likely to be the case with a method which is fairly new. In such circumstances the researcher will have to do or to control the job himself. If for a sound reason this job was set going on a regular basis, then the researcher who intends to stay in touch with the full range of his station's research needs should make every effort to find or to train others to take over the routine of such an operation, preferably freeing himself of its operation altogether. New methods do not flourish when all our attention is being given to the maintenance of several specific research procedures. Nor, in that situation, does the station flourish. Vigilant program research requires that the researcher should know when and what and to whom to delegate and that he should know when to free himself of an established procedure altogether.

People trained for mass media research are few in number
Another reason for the undeveloped state of television research in Britain, and with it the under-use of its methods, is the scarcity of people with the necessary qualifications for doing such work. It is true that the qualifications are demanding. The efficient all rounder in television research requires, amongst other things, a sound knowledge of the different methods of social research including a working awareness of their respective weaknesses and strengths. It is essential that he be able to identify and to isolate problems and to prepare a simply worded report. Nor will he get far without a working knowledge of the television medium or without a strong sense of the practical. These are rather demanding qualifications, but there is no fundamental reason why many should not acquire them. Nonetheless, relatively few do so, and it is well to consider some of the possible reasons for this.

One reason for the shortage of people qualified to conduct television research is that very few organisations teach practical courses in the methods of social research. In the length of one's experience in research, many tricks of the trade are learnt, but there is no satisfactory substitute for basic training in what these methods are or in how to use them. A research director is likely to think very hard indeed before employing anyone who is deficient in this respect. If he does so, then almost certainly he will have the time-consuming task of putting a new employee through such a course himself. Many will baulk at this.

The necessary basic training in *methods* must include topics of the following kind, taught whenever feasible *at the practical level:* scientific method in the special setting of social research; methods of problem isolation; techniques for drawing representatives samples of the population; techniques for the selection, training and control of interviewers; the various interviewing techniqes; methods for formulating questions and for pretesting them; the construction of attitude scales and possibly of tests of some abilities; certain of the techniques of the psychological laboratory; the different techniques for analysing and systematising the information gathered; use of computer facilities; use of statistical and other indices of the meaningfulness of patterns found in the analysed information; the writing of systematic and readable reports. Obviously a general background in social psychology, particularly the psychology of perception, learning and memory, is highly desirable. In addition, the student of research methods must know not only what the different methods are, but when and why one is applicable rather than another and, most important, *how to use them.*

Requirements of this kind seem to the writer to be basic. But what does one find in practice? Whereas courses in sociology and in social psychology are widely available in Britain to those qualified to take them, the teaching of the *methods of research* is by no means common and effective courses of practical training in these methods are rare indeed.

Another reason for the shortage about which I have written seems to be that many good graduates seeking or preparing for a research career give little consideration to the mass media or to television in particular. I believe that this is partly because mass media research does not have the same prestige for these people as do various other forms of social research, and because many students and ex-students do not even consider the mass media in choosing the area of research in which they will work. At the same time, I doubt that those in media management do anything like enough to change this situation. Certainly some constructive steps are possible. For instance, with money for social research so difficult to get, even a moderate grant should be attractive to the post-graduate student. This, plus the facilities which television and broadcasting stations could so readily make available, should be sufficient to attract to television research each year a number of people with a practical orientation to research. Moreover, the basic interestingness of mass media research is such that once he practices that type of research, the post-graduate may well continue in it. The offer of facilities would be an important part of any arrangement. Automatically the arrangement should include the offer of helpful association with the station's research personnel. In addition, there should be scope, if the student wants it, for working contact with producers or other production staff, for observation of studio activity and for use, within reason, of existing films and of videotapes. This kind of relationship would have the additional advantages of setting up in the student a certain degree of familiarity with and attachment to the broadcasting organisation which provided the facilities. It would also allow that organisation to assess the potential of the student as a future employee.

A word of warning about the whole of this sort of arrangment is in order at this point. The broadcaster must not rely upon an immediate and direct payoff from the research enquiry for which he gave the grant and facilities. No doubt the student could benefit enormously from this aid but the immediate benefit would be limited to the student alone. The latter would almost certainly be a fumbling newcomer to research, and as a student for a higher degree he would in all probability feel that he must orient his research about a theoretical concept of some kind. The broadcaster's main return for helping postgraduate students in the way described lies in bringing new research talent and energy into broadcasting and possibly into his own organisation. There is the possibility too of a wider benefit in the form of extended liaison with the student's academic adviser and possibly with other teaching staff in the same department. Such liaison is almost certain to have its problems, but its potential for the teaching department and for the broadcasting organisation alike must not be underestimated. One possibility, of a very specific kind, is that the association might add to the existing stimuli for setting up suitable courses of training in research methods within the teaching organisations so involved.

Some Reasons for the Under-Use of Research for Assessing Television's Social Impact

Much of what has been written so far has been about the under-use of research as an aid to decision making by the television industry. However, research is also under-used, and markedly so, as a means for *reporting to society* about the impact of television upon those who view it. I use the term 'impact' broadly to mean such things as: the effect upon viewers of long term exposure to television; the effects of specific television programs; viewers' reactions to the different programs they view (for example, like or dislike, approve or disapprove)[e]. The very large number of viewers in Britain, the enormous amount of viewing that is done, the extent of the speculation that has gone on about the impact of television — all these constitute a very strong case indeed for carrying out research designed primarily *to tell the public* just what the impact of television really is.

---

[e] Many assessments of likes and dislikes, etc., are made for broadcasters, but *not* for general publication.

However, the fact of the matter is that apart from reaction studies conducted for the private use of broadcasters, relatively little impact research has been done. Even less has been published. The biggest deficiency concerns studies of television's long-term impact. In the period from 1950, only four major studies of this kind were carried out in Britain, a situation contrasting sharply with that in the United States of America. Moreover, these British studies have between them dealt with only a few of the many issues about which there has been speculation and evidence of public concern. Empirical studies of the effects of specific programs or series of programs have been relatively few in number, most of them carried out by the BBC's Audience Research Department[f]. Whereas the BBC has for many years conducted studies of the reaction of viewers to programs seen, the resulting reports have been for internal use. Obviously to make them public would virtually be to hand them to competitors. This tends to apply also to reports of reaction studies carried out by the ITA, some program contractors and others. The end result however is that information of this kind is not available to the general public.

Summing up this situation, we find that though the BBC, the ITA and others produce a great deal of information about audience reaction to programs, this material is not — probably cannot be — released to the general public; that relatively few studies have been made in Britain of the effects of television programs or of TV generally. In these circumstances, the public remains singularly uninformed about the impact, on them, of this pervasive medium.

One does not have to look hard or far to understand how it is that this situation came to exist. The dominant factor is that nowhere in Britain has there been an established research organisation, independent of the broadcasting industry, with a prime commitment and a sufficient capacity to carry out and to publish impact research on anything like the necessary broad front. Apart from the Television Research Unit at the University of Leeds[g], impact research designed for publication has in the past been conducted only on an occasional basis. Thus it depended on the decision of the individual student who was interested enough and commanded funds enough to conduct a single enquiry, the occasional sponsorship of a specific enquiry by a foundation or some other public spirited organisation. This uncertain 'system' produced an occasional yield of important information, but that yield was lacking in continuity and in systematic coverage.

Another important reason for the lack of published findings is that for many years it was extremely hard for the independent social scientist to get money to conduct television research even on a small scale. There were

[f] See also" Television and the Political Image" by J. Trenaman and D. McQuail [361] which had its support from the Granada Television Organisation.
[g] Much credit must be given to the Granada Television Organisation for financing this Unit.

only a few exception to this in the whole decade between 1950 and 1960[h], when the great growth of television was taking place and when so much was being said about the impact of this medium. One of these exceptions was the long term grant made by the Granada Television Organisation for the support of the Television Research Unit. Another was a grant by the Nuffield Foundation for a specific project by a single team. A third was a grant made to the writer by the London Press Exchange Limited. Welcome as these and several other contributions have been, they could not be expected to transform the situation in that decade: it was a period in which money for independent research was extremely hard to obtain.

Earlier in this chapter, I wrote at length about two other reasons for the scarcity of published reports on television's impact in Britain: the seeming lack of interest in television research on the part of university personnel; the acute scarcity of people qualified to carry out such work.

However, over and above reasons of the kind I have listed so far, there appear to be several additional factors in operation. About these, I would only speculate, but they do nonetheless seem to be important. One appears to have been a tendency simply to accept television for better or for worse. Another seems to be a predisposition, perhaps a peculiarly English one, to settle matters of social significance on the basis of argument and of armchair wisdom. Though it may have certain virtues, this is an approach which is by no means secure against the persuasive powers of 'evidence' givers who are committed emotionally, ideologically or otherwise to particular positions. The report of the Committee on Broadcasting (1960)[i] appeared to some at least to have suffered from this type of situation. It is, of course, right and proper to ask for and to study the views of people who think or maintain that certain kinds of television programs do harm or that certain other kinds are good for people. However, this process can be no substitute for finding out what these different kinds of programs *actually* do to viewers. Only research can provide information of that kind. Unfortunately, an occasional official 'enquiry' can also have the effect of distracting people from the case for setting up an empirical system for keeping continuing watch over what goes on.

One very noteworthy development in the British scene was the granting, early in 1962, of £250,000 for research into the impact of television upon society, with particular reference to the incidence of delinquency. This grant was made by the Independent Television Authority following various requests for enquiry into the causes of a rising level of delinquency[j].

[h] The Independent Television Authority's grant of £250,000 was made *after* this period. It is referred to later in this chapter.
[i] Known also as the report of the Pilkington Committee.
[j] Towards the end of 1961, the Home Secretary held a conference of representatives of the churches, educational and social service interests, the Press, broadcasters and others to discuss the present incidence of delinquency and the extent to which it arises from the general moral climate of society. Following this, and at the request of the Home Secretary, a group of

In 1963, a committee[k] was set up to initiate and co-ordinate the necessary research. This generous and substantial grant, if efficiently managed, could enlarge our understanding of the mass media. However, it is most important that we be aware of the Committee's terms of reference as set out in footnote (1). These seem to me to suggest that the grant will be used for studies of an academic kind, with some emphasis upon the psychology of communication, of attitude change and of value formation. Whether or not that is precisely the case, it is quite clear from the terms of reference that the Committee's research objectives are substantially different from those I am advocating. The Committee's 1966 progress report[m], which was largely a statement of what the Committee hopes to achieve, confirms this substantial difference in aims.

What Should be Done to Secure Greater Use of Research?

What then should be done to ensure that television research methods are properly and fully put to use? Several suggestions have already been made in the context of maximising the use of research on behalf of programme planners and of production staff. One suggestion, it will be remembered, was to bring the research man right into the production team and to keep him there. The point of this would be to help make research more useful and more acceptable to creative staff. In that close setting the researcher should learn enough about production and its problems to be able to orient his thinking and his work to its service. Such working association should also help creative staff to see research simply as a source of such information as they may want or need.

Another suggestion was to see that a station's researchers did not get tied up in some single research operation but stayed free to detect and to deal with the 'full range of the station's broadcasting problems. When it develops, continuing routine should, if at all feasible, be passed to outside agents. A third suggestion was connected with the small number of trained research personnel entering television. The suggestion was that individual

social scientists met at Sunningdale, Berkshire, in May 1962, and made recommendations as to the class of work to be carried out and recommended the formation of a committee to initiate and coordinate research[k].

[k] The Television Research Committee, under the chairmanship of Professor T.A.F. Noble. The Committee first met in July 1963.

[l] The Television Research Committee has stated its terms of reference as follows: "To initiate and co-ordinate research into the part which television plays or could play, in relation to other influences, as a medium of communication and in fostering attitudes, with particular reference to ways in which young people's moral concepts and attitudes develop and to the processes of perception through which they are influenced by television and other media of communication; and to administer any funds made available to it for such research."

[m] "*Problems of Television Research: A Progress Report*", Television Research Committee, 1966, Leicester University Press.

stations should offer facilities and small grants for postgraduate research in the field of television. That should have the effect of bringing new talent into television research, and quite possibly into the sponsor's own organisation. It should have the additional effect of furthering liaison with teaching departments and of increasing their awareness of television as a possible topic for research.

However, steps of this kind still leave unresolved the problem of how to ensure that those interested in taking up television research get the necessary training in research methods to be able to work efficiently on the full range of research problems facing the television industry. I hope that the techniques described and illustrated in this book will contribute to the solution of some of these research problems. That was the main reason for writing it. From the long term point of view, however, more is needed than the steps outlined above. In my opinion, it is most important that there be made available courses of training that will fit the newcomer to conduct television research and enable him to carry out his work in a craftsmanlike manner. This is not necessarily to suggest that teaching departments in universities or colleges of technology should at this stage provide courses of training as specific as Television Research Methodology. In present circumstances in Britain, that would be too narrow an objective. In any case, the number of persons needed for television research in Britain would not warrant it. What *is* necessary, however, is that there be made more available courses of training in the methods of *social and business research*, though such courses would have to include not only theoretical matters, but a considerable amount of *practical work* as well. Courses of the practical kind certainly *could* be set up.

Partial support, by the television industry, of promising courses in research methods would seem to be good policy, though obviously such training would call for support on a front wider than the television industry alone, or, for that matter, than the whole mass media industry taken alone. This may at first seem like setting up a large training system for the sake of some small sector of social and business research. Yet the fact of the matter is that the other branches of social and business research are as much in need of this basis training for new research personnel as is the television industry. Moreover the same sort of basic training is appropriate for all branches of social and business research. Research as an aid to decision making will be reliable only if those carrying it out have been properly trained in the techniques and the craftsmanship of their profession. Over the whole range of social and business research, there is a case for establishing practical courses in the methodology of research. If the needs of *television* research should trigger off the provision of such courses, that could only be a desirable situation.

Another important requirement of the television age is the setting up of a research institute which is independent of the television industry and which *is designed to inform the public* about the impact of television. In other words, though I strongly advocate that broadcasting organisations should make greater use of research as an aid to decision making, I advocate just as strongly that research should be carried out in order to inform the public at large about the impact, on them, of this pervasive medium. This is not meant to impute irresponsibility to the broadcaster: any society which is mindful of its own welfare needs information as much as does the broadcaster. It is quite unrealistic to leave the provision of this information to fortuitous circumstance. Society must have a continuing and freely available source of information of this kind. And in my opinion the only way to provide such a public service is to set up a special organisation, on a continuing basis, to carry out the necessary research. Otherwise that research either will not be done or will not be published.

One form of enquiry conducted by this organisation should, I think, be the assessment of the effects of exposure to specific programs. Such studies of effects could be either short-term or long-term in character, and presumably they would be based on methods of the kind described in Section III. In addition, there would be a strong case for conducting research into what people felt about different programs. This form of enquiry could provide objective evidence (in place of opinion) about what the viewers liked and what they disliked in such programs, what was found objectionable and what was approved, what was found interesting and what was found dull. No doubt the BBC, the ITA and program contractors would continue to gather information of this latter kind for their own purposes, and no doubt the Institute would at times duplicate work done by one or other of them. But some degree of duplication is an inevitable consequence of the necessity to ensure that information about the public's reactions to programs is freely available to society. Enquiry might also be focused on other aspects of programming, such as the timing of programs, their understandability, their variety. In time, regular and objective analyses of program content could be undertaken, preferably after research had established the effects of different types of content.

One other desirable function of an organisation of this kind would, I believe, be to conduct experimental work into the processes of communication and change through television, perhaps with special reference to the formation of values and interests in the young and to the development of some aspects of behaviour. Certain of this work on communication and change would almost certainly call for the consideration of other of the mass media along with television. However, this class of work would have to be kept supplementary to the impact research. It would be stimulated, guided, and given perspective by the latter. Thus evidence of major failure to understand parts of a program might well be followed by experimental work to find out more about the causes of the communication failure and to develop procedures and approaches for reducing the incidence of future failures of a similar kind. Studies of value formation would be guided by the same principle. Otherwise there would be a grave danger that the experimental work would become part of an academic excursion rather than an integral part of a service to society.

Though it would be premature at this stage to try to specify the nature of the support for and the administration of this Institute, several of its necessary basic features seem clear enough. In the first place, it would have to be a continuing organisation build around a staff of very competent research workers. Only as a permanent body could it attract and hold the most able research staff and management, or properly build upon its own experiences in research. Financial support for this sort of work might well come from the general viewing public on a subscription basis, possibly with an initiating fund from one of the country's granting foundations. Perhaps it might have government support. Obviously the Institute could not be an academic body, though it might well have a link with a university. Its administration would have to be such that contact was maintained with the realities of television broadcasting without it coming under the control of the television industry.

Obviously there could be times when some program feature (perhaps established *through research* as likely to attract and to hold a large audience) would clash with the requirements for serving society in a constructive way. It would be the function of Institute research to bring this situation to light so that appropriate action might be taken by broadcasters and public authorities alike. I think it is of the utmost importance, however, that an institute of this kind should be used not simply to inform people about television's *defects:* it should be used equally *to detect and to highlight television's achievements.* To use the Institute only to attack television would be to abuse research.

Only when broadcaster decisions and public pressures are guided by *facts* is there a reasonable chance that the constructive potential of the television medium will be approached. Moreover, it is well to remember at all times that the burden of production rests upon the broadcaster. It does not help broadcaster or society if critics bombard the broadcaster with unfounded charges about what he has done or failed to do. Something much more constructive and factual than that will be needed if he is to play his considerable but arduous part in progressively shaping television content for the greater service and benefit of society. Greater use of the available methods of research, both for television broadcasters and on behalf of viewers, can help in furthering that function of the television medium.

[26]

References and a selective bibliography

SECTION I: RESEARCH FOR PROGRAM PLANNING

1. ABRAMS, M. (1959.) *The Teenage Consumer*, London Press Exchange, Paper No. 5.
2. ADLER, M. K. (1956). *Modern Market Research*. London: Crosby Lockwood.
3. ADLER, M. K. (1965). *Lectures in Market Research*. London: Crosby Lockwood.
4. ADVERTISING RESEARCH FOUNDATION (1954). *Recommended Standards for Radio and Television Program Audience Size Measurements*. New York: A.R.F.
5. ASSOCIATED REDIFFUSION (1962). *The Londoner — A Study in Personality and Media — Explanatory Manual*. London.
6. BARTLETT, F. C. (1932). *Remembering*. Cambridge: Cambridge University Press.
7. BELSON, W. A. and DILWORTH, G. W. (1955). "A recent BBC development in the field of audience research", BBC Monograph, (Engineering Division), No. 3.
8. BELSON, W. A. (1957). "The ideas of the television public about mental illness", *Mental Health*, Vol. 16, p. 95.
9. BELSON, W. A. (1958). "New developments in audience research methods", *American Journal of Sociology*, Vol. 64, No. 2, p. 174.
10. BELSON, W. A. (1958). *Research for Programme Planning in Television*. ATV Technical Series, No. 3, London. Associated Television Series of Technical Reports, No. 3, London.
11. BELSON, W. A. (1959). "Matching and Prediction on the Principle of Biological Classification", Applied Statistics, Vol. 8, No. 2, p. 65.
12. BELSON, W. A. (1960). "Volunteer bias in test-room groups", *Public Opinion Quarterly*, Vol. 24, No. 1, p. 115.
13. BELSON, W. A. and BELL, C. R. (1960). *A Bibliography of Papers Bearing on the Adequacy of Techniques Used in Survey Research*. London: Market Research Society and The Oakwood Press.
14. BELSON, W. A. (1962). *Studies in Readership*. London: Business Publications Limited.
15. BELSON, W. A. (1963). *Respondent Memory as a Factor in Survey Research*, a paper delivered at the ESOMAR annual conference in Lucerne, Switzerland.

16. BELSON, W. A. (1963). "Group testing in market research", *Journal of Advertising Research*, Vol. 3, No. 2, p. 39.
17. BERG, I. and RAPAPORT, G. M. (1954). "Response bias in an unstructured questionnaire", *Journal of Psychology*, Vol. 38, p. 475.
18. BINGHAM, W. and MOORE, B. V. (1931). *How to Interview*. New York.
19. BLANKENSHIP, A. B. (1946). *How to Conduct Consumer and Opinion Research: The Sampling Survey in Operation*. New York: Harper.
20. BRITISH BROADCASTING CORPORATION (1952). *A Pre-Broadcast Study of the Opinions and Knowledge of the Target Audience for the Projected Television Series "Race Relations in Africa"*, VR/52/458. An unpublished report of the Audience Research Department, described in Chapter 11.
21. BRITISH BROADCASTING CORPORATION (1952). *Talking of America: A Pre-Broadcast Study of the Knowledge, Opinions and Attitudes of the Population for which a Programme on America was Being Prepared*, LR/52/1959. An unpublished report of the Audience Research Department, described in Chapter 9.
22. BRITISH BROADCASTING CORPORATION (1954). *Facts and Figures: Knowledge of Words, Concepts and Events*, VR/54/498. An unpublished report of the Audience Research Department, described in Chapter 10.
23. BRITISH BROADCASTING CORPORATION (1954). *Minors — An Enquiry Into the Interests, Listening and Viewing and Availability of the 5–20 Year Old Population of the United Kingdom*, LR/54/1688. An unpublished report of the Audience Research Department.
24. BRITISH BROADCASTING CORPORATION (1956). *Britain in Decline: A Pre-Broadcast Study of the Public's Awareness and Evaluation of Changes in Britain*, VR/56/1. An unpublished report of the Audience Research Department, described in Chapter 7.
25. BRITISH BROADCASTING CORPORATION (1958). *Evolution: A Pre-Broadcast Study of the Knowledge and Attitudes of the Viewing Public*, VR/58/120. An unpublished report of the Audience Research Department.
26. BRITISH BROADCASTING CORPORATION (1960). *The Criminal's View of Crime and Punishment*, VR/60/409. An unpublished report of the Audience Research Department.
27. BRITISH BROADCASTING CORPORATION (1963). *Music: A Study of the Musical Tastes, Interests and Behaviour of the Adult Population*, VR/63/358. An unpublished report of the Audience Research Department.
28. BRITISH BROADCASTING CORPORATION (1964). A Survey of Doctors' Attitudes Towards a Projected Medical Series on BBC-2, VR/64/535. An unpublished report of the Audience Research Department.
29. BRITISH BROADCASTING CORPORATION (1965). *The People's Activities*. Audience Research Department, 10 gns.
30. BRITISH BROADCASTING CORPORATION (1965). Audience Research: Methods and Sources. Obtainable from Audience Research Department.
31. BRUNER, J. S. and GOODMAN, C. C. (1947). "Value and need as organising factors in perception", *Journal of Abnormal and Social Psychology*, Vol. 42, p. 33.
32. BURT, C. (1949). "The psychology of listeners", *BBC Quarterly*, Vol. 4, p. 7.
33. BURTT, H. E. and GASKILL, H. V. (1932). "Suggestibility and the form of the question", *Journal of Applied Psychology*, Vol. 16, p. 358.
34. CAHALAN, D., TAMULONIS, V., and VERNER, H. W. (1947). "Interviewer bias

involved in certain types of opinion survey questions", *International Journal of opinion and Attitude Research*, Vol. 1, No. 1, p. 63.

35. CANNELL, C. F. and KAHN, R. L. (1957). *The Dynamics of Interviewing: Theory, Techniques and Cases*. New York: Wiley.

36. CANTRIL, H. (1944). *Gauging Public Opinion*. Princeton: Princeton University Press.

37. CAVAN, R. S. (1929). "Interviewing for life history material", *American Journal of Sociology*, Vol. 35, p. 100.

38. CLARK, K. B. (1940). "Some factors influencing the remembering of prose material", *Archives of Psychology*, No. 253.

39. CRISP, R. D. (1957). *Marketing Research*. New York: McGraw Hill Book Company.

40. DELIGHT, E. (1955). *Word Knowledge of the General Listening Public*. A study conducted in collaboration with the Audience Research Department of the British Broadcasting Corporation (unpublished).

41. DILCHER, H. S. (1959). *An Analysis of the Deficiencies in TV Audience Measurement*. Georgia: Emory University.

42. DOTSON, F. (1954). "Intensive interviewing in community research", *Journal of Educational Sociology*, Vol. 27, p. 225.

43. DRAYTON, L. E. (1954). "Bias arising in wording consumer questionnaires", *Journal of Marketing*, Vol. 19, p. 140.

44. DURBIN, J. (1953). "Some results in sampling theory when the units are selected with unequal probability", *Journal of the Royal Statistical Society*, Series B, Vol. 15, p. 252.

45. DURBIN, J. and STUART, A. (1954). "Callbacks and clustering in sample surveys: an experimental study", *Journal of the Royal Statistical Society*, Series A, Vol. 117, p. 387.

46. DURBIN, J. (1954). "Non-response and callbacks in surveys", *Bulletin of the International Statistical Institute*, Vol. 34, Part 2, p. 72.

47. EDWARDS, A. L. (1941). "Political frames of reference as a factor influencing recognition", *Journal of Abnormal and Social Psychology*, Vol. 36, p. 34.

48. EHRENBERG, A. S. C. (1962). *Television Audience Research: The Current Methodological Position*, paper read at the Annual Conference of the Institute of. Statisticians, 1962.

49. EVANS, R. I. (1961). "A psychological investigation of a group of demographic, personality and behavioural variables as related to viewing educational television", *Journal of Applied Psychology*, Vol. 45, p. 25.

50. FEARING, F. (1942). "The appraisal interview", in *Studies in Personality*, ed. by McNemar, Q. and Merrill, M. A. New York: McGraw Hill.

51. FENLASON, A. F. (1962). *Essentials in Interviewing*. New York: Harper and Row.

52. FESTINGER, L. and KATZ, D. (1953). *Research Methods in the Behavioral Sciences*. New York: Holt.

53. FISK, G. (1949). *Defining and Measuring Radio Audiences*. State College of Washington.

54. GALES, K. and KENDALL, M. G. (1957). "An enquiry concerning interviewer variability", *Journal of the Royal Statistical Society*, Series A, Vol. 120, Part. 2, p. 121.

55. GHISELLI, E. E. (1941). "The problem of question form in the measure of sales by consumer interviewers", *Journal of Marketing*, Vol. 6, p. 170.

56. GRACE, H. A. (1952). "The effect of different degrees of knowledge about an audience on the content of communication: the comparison of male and female audiences", *Journal of Social Psychology*, Vol. 36, p. 89.
57. HANSEN, M. H., HURWITZ, W. M. and MADOW, W. G. (1953). *Sample Survey Methods and Theory*. New York: Wiley.
58. HENRY, H. (1958). *Motivation Research: Its Practises and Uses For Advertising, Marketing and Other Business Purposes*. London: Crosby Lockwood.
59. HERZOG, H. (1944). "What do we really know about daytime serial listeners" in *Radio Research 1942-43*, ed. by Lazarsfeld, P. F. and Stanton, F. N. New York: Duell, Sloan and Pearce.
60. HIMELSTEIN, P. (1956). "Taylor scale characteristics of volunteers and nonvolunteers for psychological experiments", *Journal of Abnormal and Social Psychology*, Vol. 52, p. 138.
61. HYMAN, H. H. (1954). *Interviewing in Social Research*. Chicago: The University of Chicago Press.
62. HYMAN, H. H. (1955). *Survey Design and Analysis: Principles, Cases and Procedures*. Glencoe, Illinois: Free Press.
63. JAHODA, M., DEUTSCH, M. and COOK, S. (1951). *Research Methods in Social Relations*. New York: Dryden Press.
64. KAHN, R. L. and CANNELL, C. F. (1957). *The Dynamics of Interviewing: Theory, Techniques and Cases*. New York: Wiley.
65. KENDALL, M. G. (1952 & 1957) *The Sources and the Nature of the Statistics of the United Kingdom, Vols. I and II*. London: Oliver and Boyd.
66. KINCAID, H. V. (1957). "Interviewing the business elite", *American Journal of Sociology*, Vol. 113, p. 304.
67. LAZARSFELD, P. F. and ROSENBERG, M. (1955). *The Language of Social Research: A reader in the Methodology of the Social Sciences*. Glencoe, Illinois: Free Press.
68. LEVINE, J. M. and MURPHY, G. (1943). "The learning and forgetting of controversial material", *Journal of Abnormal and Social Psychology*, Vol. 38, p. 507.
69. MARKET RESEARCH SOCIETY (BRITAIN) (1957). *Statistical Sources for Market Research*. London: Oakwood Press.
70. MASLOW, A. H. and SAKODA, J. M. (1952). "Volunteer error in the Kinsey study", *Journal of Abnormal and Social Psychology*, Vol. 47, p. 259.
71. McNEMAR, Q. (1946). "Opinion-attitude methodology", *Psychological Bulletin*, Vol. 43, p. 289.
72. MERTON, R. K. and KENDALL, P. L. (1946). "The focused interview", *American Journal of Sociology*, Vol. 51, p. 541.
73. METZNER, H. and MANN, F. (1953). "Effects of grouping related questions in questionnaires", *Public Opinion Quarterly*, Vol. 17, No. 1, p. 136.
74. MEYERSOHN, R. B. (1957). "What do we know about audiences", *Journal of Broadcasting*, Vol. 1, No. 3, p. 220.
75. MOSER, C. A. (1950). "Social research: the diary method", *Social Service*, Vol. 24, No. 2, p. 80.
76. MOSER, C. A. (1952). "Quota sampling", *Journal of the Royal Statistical Society*, Series A, Vol. 115, p. 411.
77. MOSER, C. A. and STUART, A. (1953). "An experimental study of quota sampling", *Journal of the Royal Statistical Society*, Series A, Vol. 116, p. 349.
78. MOSER, C. A. (1955). "Recent developments in the sampling of human popu-

lations in Great Britain", *Journal of the American Statistical Association*, Vol. 50, No. 272, p. 1195.

79. MOSER, C. A. (1958). *Survey Methods in Social Investigations*. London: Heinemann.

80. MUSCIO, B. (1916). "The influence of the form of a question", *British Journal of Psychology*, Vol. 8, p. 351.

81. MYERS, L. Jr. (1958). *An Examination of Television Audience Measurement Methods and an Application of Sequential Analysis to the Telephone Interview*. Syracuse: Syracuse University Library.

82. NUCKOLS, R. C. (1953). "A note on pre-testing public opinion questions", *Journal of Applied Psychology*, Vol. 37, No. 2, p. 119.

83. PAYNE, S. (1951). *The Art of Asking Questions*. Princeton: Princeton University.

84. ROGERS, C. R. (1945). "The non-directive method as a technique for social research", *American Journal of Sociology*, Vol. 51, p. 279.

85. ROSEN, E. (1951). "Differences between volunteers and non-volunteers for psychological studies", *Journal of Applied Psychology*, Vol. 35, No. 3, p. 185.

86. ROSLOW, S., WULFECK, W. H., and CORBY, and CORBY, P. G. (1940). "Consumer and opinion research: experimental studies on the form of the questions", *Journal of Applied Psychology*, Vol. 24, p. 334.

87. RUGG, D. (1941). "Experiments in wording questions (II)", *Public Opinion Quarterly*, Vol. 5, No. 1, p. 91.

88. RUGG, D. and CANTRIL, H. (1942). "The wording of questions in public opinion polls", *Journal of Abnormal and Social Psychology*, Vol. 37, p. 469.

89. SHAPIRO, E. P. (1952). "The group interview as a tool of research", *Journal of Marketing*, Vol. 16, p. 452.

90. SHEATSLEY, P. B. (1949). "The influence of sub-questions on interviewer performance", *Public Opinion Quarterly*, Vol. 13, p. 310.

91. SHEATSLEY, P. B. (1953). "The art of interviewing and a guide to interviewer selection and training", in Jahoda, M., Deutsch, M. and Cook, S. (Eds)., *Research Methods in Social Relations*, 1953, Dryden Press, New York, p. 464.

92. STEMBER, H. and HYMAN, H. (1949–50). "How interviewer effects operate through question form", *International Journal of Opinion and Attitude Research*, Vol. 3, p. 495.

93. STEPHAN, F. F. and McCARTHY, P. J. (1958). *Sampling Opinions: An Analysis of Survey Procedure*. New York: Wiley.

94. STUART, A. (1957). "The comparison of frequencies in matched samples", *British Journal of Statistical Psychology*, Vol. 10, Part 1, p. 29.

95. TELEVISION AUDIENCE MEASUREMENT LTD. (1961). *The Comparison of Audience Composition Techniques*. London.

96. VERNIER, C. M., FAIRFAX, V. and CRISWELL, J. H. (1947). "The use of specialized interview techniques for the collection of criterion data", *American Psychologist*, Vol. 2, p. 351.

97. WALLIN, P. "Volunteer subjects as a source of sampling bias", *American Journal of Sociology*, Vol. 54, p. 539.

98. WATSON, W. S. and HARTMANN, G. W. (1949). "The rigidity of a basic attitudinal frame", *Journal of Abnormal and Social Psychology*, Vol. 34, p. 314.

99. WRIGHT, C. W. (Spring, 1961). "Television and radio program ratings and

measurements: a selected and annotated bibliography", *Journal of Broadcasting*, p. 165.
100. YOUNG, P. V. (1935). *Interviewing in Social Work: A Sociological Analysis.* New York.

SECTION II: MEASURING THE COMPREHENSIBILITY OF PROGRAMS

101. ALLEN, W. (1952). "The question of intelligibility", *BBC Quarterly*, Vol. 7, p. 147.
102. ALLEN, W. H. (1958). *Audio-Visual Communication Research.* Santa Monica, California: System Development Corporation.
103. BARROW, L. C. Jr. and WESTLEY, B. H. (1959). "Intelligence and the effectiveness of radio and television", *Audio-Visual Communication Review*, Vol. 7, No. 3, p. 193.
104. BECKER, S. L. and DALLINGER, C. A. (1960). "The effect of instructional methods upon achievement and attitudes in communication skills", *Speech Monographs*, Vol. 27, p. 70.
105. BELSON, W. A. (1952). *An Enquiry into the Comprehensibility of "Topic for Tonight"*, LR/52/1080. An unpublished report of the Audience Research Department, described in Chapter 14.
106. BERELSON, B. (1952). *Content Analysis in Communication Research.* Glencoe, Illinois: Free Press.
107. BRITISH BROADCASTING CORPORATION (1953). *A Study of Communication Through a Feature Programme*, LR/53/1006. An unpublished report of the Audience Research Department.
108. BRITISH BROADCASTING CORPORATION (1955). *Facts and Figures: The Comprehensibility of Two Programs in the "Facts and Figures" Series*, VR/55/411. An unpublished report of the Audience Research Department, described in Chapter 15.
109. BRONSON, V. and others (1963). "Determining educational communication techniques for Africa", *N. A. E. B. Journal*, Vol. 22, No. 1, p. 31.
110. BUSWELL, G. T. (1937). "How adults read", *Supplementary Educational Monographs*, No. 45, Chicago: Chicago University Press.
111. CANTRIL, H. and ALLPORT, G. W. (1935). *The Psychology of Radio.* New York: Harper Brothers (see chapter by Carver).
112. CHALL, J. S. and DIAL, H. E. (1948). "Predicting listener understanding and interest in newscasts", *Educational Research Bulletin*, Vol. 27, No. 6, p. 141.
113. DALE, E. and CHALL, J. S. (1948). "A formulae for predicting readability". *Educational Research Bulletin of the Ohio State University*, Vol. 27, p. 11,
114. DALE, E. and TYLER, R. W. (1934). "A study of the factors influencing the difficulty of reading materials for adults of limited reading ability", *Library Quarterly*, Vol. 4, p. 384.
115. DANIELSON, W. A. and BRYAN, S. D. (1964). "Readability of wire stories in eight news categories", *Journalism Quarterly*, Vol. 41, No. 1, p. 105.
116. DAVIS, F. B. (1944). "The interpretation of the frequency ratings obtained from the teachers word book", *Journal of Educational Psychology*, Vol. 35, p. 169.
117. DEUTSCHMANN, P. J., BARROW, L. C. Jr. and MACMILLAN, A. (1961). "The efficiency of different modes of communication", *Audio-Visual Communications Review*, Vol. 9, p. 263.
118. DEWEY, J. C. (1935). "The acquisition of facts as a measure of reading comprehension", *Elementary School Record*, Vol. 35, p. 346.

119. FLESCH, R. (1943). *The Marks of a Readable Style*. New York: Teachers College Contributions to Education, No. 897.
120. FLESCH, R. (1946). *The Art of Plain Talk*. New York: Harper & Brothers. London. Hamish Hamilton.
121. FLESCH, R. (1948). "A new readability yardstick", *Journal of Applied Psychology*, Vol. 32, p. 221.
122. FOULDS, G. A. and RAVEN, J. C. (1948). "Intellectual ability and occupational grade", *Occupational Psychology*, Vol. 22, p. 197.
123. GOLDSTEIN, H. (1940). "Reading and listening comprehension at various rates", *Teachers' College Contributions to Education*, No. 821. New York: Columbia University.
124. GOWER, E. A. (1948). *Plain Words: A Guide to the Use of English*. London: H. M. Stationery Office.
125. GUNNING, R. (1952). *The Technique of Clear Writing*. New York: McGraw Hill.
126. JOHNSON, G. R. (1930). "An objective method of measuring reading difficulty", *Journal of Educational Research*, Vol. 21, p. 288.
127. KIRKPATRICK, J. J. and CURETON, E. E. (1949). "Vocabulary item difficulty and word frequency", *Journal of Applied Psychology*, Vol. 33, p. 347.
128. LINGWOOD, J. (1952) "Test performances of ATS recruits from different civilian occupations", *Occupational Psychology*, Vol. 26, p. 35.
129. LORGE, I. (1941). "Reading comprehension of adults", *Teachers College Record*, Vol. 43, No. 3, p. 189.
130. LORGE, I. (1944). "Predicting readability", *Teachers College Record*, Vol. 45, p. 404.
131. LORGE, I. (1949). "Reading and readability", *Teachers College Record*, Vol. 51, p. 90.
132. LUMLEY, F. H. (1932). "An evaluation of fifteen radio talks in psychology by means of listeners' reports", *Psychological Bulletin*, Vol. 29, p. 753.
133. OJEMANN, R. H. (1934). "The reading ability of parents, and factors associated with reading difficulty of parent association materials", *University of Iowa Studies in Child Welfare*, Vol. 8, p. 11.
134. OSGOOD, C. E. (1952). "The nature and measurement of meaning", *Psychological Bulletin*, Vol. 49, p. 197.
135. McCLUSKY, H. Y. (1934). "A quantitative analysis of the difficulty of reading materials", *Journal of Educational Research*, Vol. 28, p. 276.
136. NIAS. A. H. W. and KAY, H. (1954). "Immediate memory of a broadcast feature programme", *British Journal of Educational Psychology*, Vol. 24, p. 154.
137. ROBINSON, J. H. (1923). *The Humanizing of Knowledge*. New York: George H. Doran Company.
138. ROYDS, A. (1962). "Intelligibility of schools television programmes", *British Journal of Educational Psychology*, Vol. 32, p. 159.
139. SILVEY, R. J. (1951). "The intelligibility of broadcast talks", *Public Opinion Quarterly*, Vol. 15, p. 299.
140. SPIELMAN, W. and BURT, C. (1926). "The estimation of intelligence in vocational guidance". Industrial Fatigue Research Board, Report 33.
141. TANNENBAUM, P. H. and KERRICK, J. (1954). "Effects of newscast item leads upon listener interpretation", *Journalism Quarterly*, Vol. 31, p. 33.
142. THORNDIKE, E. L. and LORGE, I. (1944). *Junior Dictionary*. New York: Teachers College, Columbia University.

143. THORNDIKE, E. L. (1931). *A Teacher's Word Book of the Twenty Thousand Words Found Most Frequently and Widely in General Reading For Children and Young People.* New York: Bureau of Publications, Teachers College, Columbia University.

144. THORNDIKE, E. L. (1948). *The Thorndike English Dictionary*, edited by Ballard, P. B. and Palmer, H. E. London: Hodder and Stoughton.

145. TRENAMAN, J. (1950). "Understanding radio talks", *Adult Education*, Vol. 23, p. 176.

146. TRENAMAN, J. (1950). "Understanding of broadcasts on science", *Proceedings of the British Association for the Advancement of Science.*

147. TRENAMAN, J. (1950). "Intelligibility of educational broadcasts", *Nature*, Vol. 166, p. 814.

148. TYLER, R. (November, 1930). "Measuring the ability to infer", *Educational Research Bulletin*, Vol. 9, p. 475.

149. VERNON, M. D. (1954). "The instruction of children by pictorial illustration", *British Journal of Educational Psychology*, Vol. 24, p. 171.

150. VERNON, M. D. (1953). "Perception and understanding of instructional television programmes", *British Journal of Psychology*, Vol. 44, p. 116.

151. VERNON, P. E. (1946). "An experiment on the value of the film and film strip in the instruction of adults", *British Journal of Educational Psychology*, Vol. 16, p. 149.

152. VERNON, P. E. (1949). "Occupational norms for the 20 minute matrix test", *Occupational Psychology*, Vol. 23, p. 58.

153. VERNON, P. E. (1950). "The estimation of difficulty of vocabulary", *British Journal of Educational Psychology*, Vol. 20, Part II, p. 77.

154. VERNON, P. E. (1950). *An Investigation into the Intelligibility of Educational Broadcasts*, LR/50/2328. London: Audience Research Department, BBC.

155. VERNON, P. E. (1952). "Intelligibility of broadcast talks", *BBC Quarterly*, Vol. 5, p. 206.

156. WALL, W. D. (1949). "Broadcasting for the backward", *Times Educational Supplement*, September 2, p. 603.

157. WESTLEY, B. H. and BARROW, L. C. (1959). "Intelligence and the effectiveness of radio and television,", *Audio-Visual Communication Review*, Vol. 7, No. 3, p. 193.

158. WOODWORTH, R. S. and SCHLOSHBERG, A. (1955). *Experimental Psychology*. London: Metheun.

159. ZUCKERMAN, J. V. (1954). "Predicting film learning by pre-release testing" *Audio-Visual Communication Review*, Vol. 2, p. 49.

SECTION III: MEASURING THE EFFECTS OF PARTICULAR PROGRAMS

160. ANDERSON, K. E., MONTGOMERY, F. S. and SMITH, S. A. (1956). "Toward a more effective use of sound motion pictures in high school biology", *Science Education*, Vol. 40, No. 1, p. 43.

161. ASH, P. (1949). "The relative effectiveness of massed vs. spaced film presentation", *Technical Report SDC 269-7-3*. Port Washington, L. I.: Special Devices Center.

162. ASHER, J. J. and EVANS, R. I. (1959). "An investigation of some aspects of the social psychological impact of an educational television program", *Journal of Applied Psychology*, Vol. 43, p. 166.

163. BARROW, L. C. Jr. and WESTLEY, B. H. (1959). "Exploring the news: an

378   *References and a selective bibliography*

experiment on the relative effectiveness of radio and TV versions of a children's news program", *Audio-Visual Communication Review*, Vol. 7, p. 14.

164. BELSON, W. A. (1956). "A technique for studying the effects of a television broadcast", *Applied Statistics*, Vol. 5, No. 3, p. 195.

165. BELSON, W. A. (1956). "Learning and attitude changes resulting from viewing a television series 'Bon Voyage' ", *British Journal of Educational Psychology*, Vol. 26, p. 31.

166. BELSON, W. A. (1958). "Selective perception in viewing a television broadcast," *Audio-Visual Communication Review*, Vol. 6, p. 23.

167. BELSON, W. A. (1961). "Communication and persuasion through broadcasting", *Business Review*, Vol. 4, No. 1, p. 1.

168. BERLO, D. K. and KUMATA, H. (1956). "The Investigator: impact of a satirical radio drama", *Journalism Quarterly*, Vol. 33, p. 287.

169. BERNINGER, L. and WATSON, D. P. (1954). "Impact of horticultural information on televiewers", *Quarterly Bulletin of the Michigan Agricultural Experimental Station, Michigan*, Vol. 37, No. 2, p. 187.

170. BRITISH BROADCASTING CORPORATION (1950). *Dick Barton and Juvenile Delinquency*, LR/50/958. An unpublished report of the Audience Research Department.

171. BRITISH BROADCASTING CORPORATION (1956). *We, the British, Are We in Decline? An Enquiry into Some of the Effects of Television Broadcasts on 'Our Attitude to Work' and 'Our Moral Standard'*, VR/56/660, An unpublished report of the Audience Research Department.

172. BRITISH BROADCASTING CORPORATION (1957). *The Hurt Mind*, VR/57/280. An unpublished report of the Audience Research Department, described in Chapter 19.

173. BRITISH BROADCASTING CORPORATION (1958). *An Enquiry into Some of the Effects of the Television Series 'Your Life in Their Hands'*, VR/59/598. An unpublished report of the Audience Research Department.

174. BRITISH BROADCASTING CORPORATION (1960). *Matters of Medicine: Studies of Reactions to, and the Effects of, the Television Programme on Immunisation and Coronary Thrombosis*, VR/60/623. An unpublished report of the Audience Research Department.

175. BRITISH BROADCASTING CORPORATION (1961). *Crime: A Report on Some Audience Research Enquiries Connected With the Television Series 'Crime'*, VR/61/1. An unpublished report of the Audience Research Department.

176. BRITISH BROADCASTING CORPORATION (1962). *'The Death Penalty': The Effect of this Broadcast Upon Viewers' Knowledge of and Attitude Towards Capital Punishment*, VR/62/74. An unpublished report of the Audience Research Department.

177. BURT, C. (1951). *BBC Further Education Experiment, Report on the Sixth Experimental Series 'Study of the Mind'*.

178. CARTWRIGHT, D. (1949). "Some principles of mass persuasion: selected findings of research on the sale of United States War Bonds", *Human Relations*, Vol. 2, p. 253.

179. CANTRIL, H., GAUDET, H. and HERTZOG, H. (1940). *The Invasion From Mars*. Princeton, N. J.: Princeton University Press.

180. EMERY, F. E. and MARTIN, D. (1957). *Psychological Effects of the 'Western' Film*. Melbourne: Department of Audio-Visual Aids, University of Melbourne.

181. EVANS, R. I. and ASHER, J. J. (1959). "An investigation of some aspects of the social psychological impact of an educational television program", *Journal of Applied Psychology*, Vol. 43, p. 166.
182. EVANS, R. I., WEILAND, B. A. and MOORE, C. W. (1961). "The effect of experience in telecourses on attitudes towards instruction by television and impact of a controversial television program", *Journal of Applied Psychology*, Vol. 45, p. 11.
183. FORER, R. (1955). "The impact of a radio program on adolescents", *Public Opinion Quarterly*, Vol. 19, p. 184.
184. FREEMAN, H. E., WEEKS, H. A. and WERTHEIMER, W. (1955). "News commentator effect: a study in knowledge and opinion change", *Public Opinion Quarterly*, Vol. 19, p. 209.
185. GARRETT, H. E. (1947). *Statistics in Psychology and Education*. New York: Longmans Green.
186. GLOCK, C. Y. (1952). "The comparative study of communications and opinion formation", *Public Opinion Quarterly*, Vol. 16, p. 512.
187. GOLDBERG, H. D. (1950). "Liking and retention of a simulcast", *Public Opinion Quarterly*, Vol. 14, p. 141.
188. HAUGH, O. M. (1952). "The relative effectiveness of reading and listening to radio drama as ways of imparting information and shifting attitudes", *Journal of Educational Research*, Vol. 45, p. 489.
189. HOVLAND, C. I., LUMSDAINE, A. A. and SHEFFIELD, F. D. (1949). *Experiments on Mass Communication*. Princeton, New Jersey: Princeton University Press.
190. HOVLAND, C. I., JANIS, I. L. and KELLY, H. H. (1953). *Communication and Persuasion*. New Haven: Yale University Press.
191. HOVLAND, C. I. (1954). "Effects of the mass media of communication" in *Handbook of Social Psychology*, ed. by Cambridge, Massachusetts:Addison-Wesley Publishing Company Inc., Vol. 2, p. 1062.
192. HYMAN, H. H. and SHEATSLEY, P. B. (1947). "Some reasons why information campaigns fail", *Public Opinion Quarterly*, Vol. 11, p. 412.
193. KATZ, E. and LAZARSFELD, P.F. (1956). *Personal Influence*, Glencoe, Illinois: The Free Press.
194. LAZARSFELD, P. F. (1947). "Some remarks on the role of the mass media in so-called tolerance propaganda", *Journal of Social Issues*, Vol. 3, No. 3, p. 17.
195. MACCOBY, E. E., LEVIN, H. and SELYA, B. M. (1956). "The effects of emotional arousal on the retention of film content: a failure to replicate", *Journal of Abnormal and Social Psychology*, Vol. 53, p. 373.
196. MERRIL, I. R. (1958). "Impact of the 'Country Agent' television series", *Quarterly Bulletin of the Michigan Agricultural Experimental Station, Michigan State University*, Vol. 40, No. 4, p. 758.
197. MINTER, P. C., ALBERT, F. A. and POWERS, R. D. (1961). "Does presentation method influence film learning?" *Audio-Visual Communications Review, Vol. 9*, 195.
198. MYERS, L. Jr. (1958). *Books and Ideas: the Impact of an Educational Television Program on its Audience*. Syracuse University.
199. MYERS, L. Jr. and GARDNER, E. F. (1960). "An inexpensive method to determine the efficiency of a television program", *Journal of Applied Psychology*, Vol. 44, No. 1, p. 39.
200. NELSON, H. E. (1948). "The effect of variation of rate on the recall by radio

380 *References and a selective bibliography*

listeners of 'straight' newscasts", *Speech Monographs*, Vol. 15, No. 2, p. 173.
201. PARKER, E. B. (1960). "Subliminal stimulation and voting behaviour", *Journalism Quarterly*, Vol. 37, p. 588.
202. ROSEN, I. C. (1948). "The effect of the motion picture 'Gentlemen's Agreement' on attitudes toward Jews", *Journal of Psychology*, Vol. 26, p. 525.
203. ROSENTHAL, S. P. (1934). "Change of socio-economic attitudes under radical motion-picture propaganda", *Archives of Psychology*, No. 166, p. 46.
204. SANDAGE, C. H. (1952). "Measuring the results", *Education on the Air*. Columbus Ohio State University.
205. SCHWERIN RESEARCH CORPORATION (1960). "When should the effects of television advertising be measured? Part 1: Recall", *Technical and Analytical Review*, No. 4.
206. SCHWERIN RESEARCH CORPORATION (1960). "When should the effects of television advertising be measured? Part 2: Changes in attitude and behaviour", *Technical and Analytical Review*, No. 5.
207. SCHRAMM, W. and CARTER, R. F. (1959). "Effectiveness of a political telethon", *Public Opinion Quarterly*, Vol. 23, p. 121.
208. SQUIRRELL, N. (1959). *Copy Research and Television Commercials*, Associated Television Series of Technical Reports, No. 4. London.
209. STANTON, F. (1962). *Great Issues Lecture: Mass Media and Mass Culture*, Columbia Broadcasting System.
210. STAUDOHAR, F. T. and SMITH, R. G. Jr. (1956). "The contribution of lecture supplements to the effectiveness of an attitudinal film", *Journal of Applied Psychology*, Vol. 40, p. 109.
211. THOMPSON, R. J. (1959). *Television Crime-Drama*. Melbourne: Department of Audio-Visual Aids, University of Melbourne.
212. WESTLEY, B. H. and BARROW, L. C. (1959). *Exploring the News: a Comparative Study of the Teaching Effectiveness of Radio and Television*, Research-Bulletin No. 12. Wisconsin: University of Wisconsin Television Laboratory.
213. WIESE, M. J. and COLE, S. G. (1946). "A study of children's attitudes and the influence of a commercial motion picture", *Journal of Psychology*, Vol. 21, p. 151.
214. WILSON, E. C. (1948). "The effectiveness of documentary broadcasts", *Public Opinion Quarterly*, Vol. 12, p. 19.
215. ZAJONC, R. (1954). "Some effects of the 'Space' serials", *Public Opinion Quarterly*, Vol. 43, No. 4, p. 367.

SECTION IV: MEASURING THE SOCIAL IMPACT OF TELEVISION

216. ABRAMS, M. (1956). "Child audiences for television in Great Britain", *Journalism Quarterly*, Vol. 33, No. 1, p. 35.
217. ABRAMS, M. (1960). "The effects of the mass media" in *Popular Culture and Personal Responsibility*. London: National Union of Teachers.
218. ABRAMS, M. (1961). "The social effects of television", *Progress*, Vol. 48, p. 163.
219. ABRAMS, M. (1961). "Who watches the commercials?" in *Financial Times*, London, September 6th.
220. ADVERTISING RESEARCH FOUNDATION. (1954). *National Survey of Radio and Television Sets Associated with U.S. Households*. New York.
221. ALBERT, R. S. (1957). "The role of mass media and the effect of aggressive

film content upon children's aggressive responses and identification choices"
Genetic Psychology Monographs, Vol. 55, p. 221.
222. ALLDREDGE, C. H. (1950). *Televisions: Its Effects on Family Habits in Washington, D. C.* Washington D. C.: Government Printing Office.
223. AUDIENCE RESEARCH, INC. (1950). *The Effects of Television on Motion Picture Attendance*. Princeton, New Jersey.
224. BAILYN, L. (1959). "Mass media and children: a study of exposure habits and cognitive effects", Psychological Monographs, Vol. 73, p. 1.
225. BANDURA, A. and others (1961). "Transmission of agression through imitation of aggressive models", *Journal of Abnormal and Social Psychology* Vol. 63, p. 575.
226. BANDURA, A. and others (1963). "Imitation of film-mediated aggressive models", *Journal of Abnormal and Social Psychology*, Vol. 66, p. 3.
227. BATTEN, BARTON, DURSTINE & OSBORN, INC. (1951). *What's Happening to Leisure Time in Television Homes?* New York.
228. BAUCHARD, P. (1952). *The Child Audience — A Report on Press, Film and Radio for Children*. Paris: UNESCO.
229. BELSON, W. A. (1958). "The effect of television on cinema going", *Audio-Visual Communication Review*, Vol. 6, p. 131.
230. BELSON, W. A. (1958). "Measuring the effects of television: a description of method", *Public Opinion Quarterly*, Vol. 22, No. 1, p. 11.
231. BELSON, W. A. (1959). *Television and The Family*. London: British Broadcasting Corporation.
232. BELSON, W. A. (1959). "The effects of television on the interests and initiative of adult viewers", *British Journal of Psychology*, Vol. 56, No. 2, p. 145.
233. BELSON, W. A. (1959). *The British Press*, Parts 1 and 2. London: unpublished research sponsored by London Press Exchange, Ltd.
234. BELSON, W. A. (1961). "The effects of television on the reading and the buying of newspapers and magazines", *Public Opinion Quarterly*, Vol. 25, p. 366.
235. BELSON, W. A. (1962). *Studies in Readership*. London: Business Publications Ltd.
236. BELSON, W. A. (1963). "A reply to Parker's note", *Public Opinion Quarterly*, Vol. 27 (2), p. 321. See also reference [315].
237. BELSON, W. A. (1963). *Respondent Memory as a Factor in Survey Research*", a paper delivered at the ESOMAR annual conference in Lucerne, Switzerland.
238. BERKOWITZ, L. and RAWLINGS, E. (1963). "Effects of film violence on inhibitions against subsequent aggression", *Journal of Abnormal and Social Psychology*, Vol. 66, p. 405.
239. BERKOWITZ, L. (1964). "The effects of observing violence", *Scientific American*, Vol. 210, No. 2, p. 35.
240. BESCO, G. S. (1952). "Television and its effects on other related interests of high school pupils", *English Journal*, Vol. 41, p. 151.
241. BOGART, L. (1956). *The Age of Television*. New York: Frederick Ungar Publishing Company.
242. BOGART, L. (1956). "Magazines since the rise of television", *Journalism Quarterly*, Vol. 33, p. 153.
243. BRIGGS, A. (1961). *The History of Broadcasting in the United Kingdom* London: Oxford University Press.
244. B. B. C. and I. T. A. JOINT COMMITTEE (1960). *Children and Television Programmes*. London: British Broadcasting Corporation.

245. BRITISH BROADCASTING CORPORATION (1951). *Television Enquiry: A Study of the Structure of the TV Public and Their Viewing Facilities.* VR/51/192. An unpublished report of the Audience Research Department.
246. BRITISH BROADCASTING CORPORATION (1955). *Viewers, Viewing and Leisure,* VR/55/300. An unpublished report of the Audience Research Department.
247. BRITISH BROADCASTING CORPORATION (1959). *The Public and The Programmes.* London: BBC.
248. BRITISH BROADCASTING CORPORATION (1961). *Facts and Figures about Viewing and Listening.* London: Audience Research Department, BBC.
249. BRITISH BROADCASTING CORPORATION (1961). *The Public and the Programmes 1958–1961,* VR/61/49. An unpublished report of the Audience Research Department.
250. BRITISH BROADCASTING CORPORATION (1961). *What Viewers Like and Dislike about BBC and ITV.* An unpublished report of the Audience Research Department.
251. CENTRAL OFFICE OF INFORMATION (1958). *The British Press,* London.
252. CLINARD, M. B. (1949). "Secondary community influence and juvenile delinquency", Annals of the American Academy of Political and Social Science, 261, p. 42.
253. COFFIN, T. E. (1948). *Television's Effect on the Family's Activities.* New York: Hofstra College.
254. COFFIN, T. E. (1948). "Television's effect on leisure-time activities", *Journal of Applied Psychology,* Vol. 32, p. 550.
255. COFFIN, T. E. (1950). *The Hofstra Study: A Measure of the Sales Effectiveness of TV Advertising.* New York: National Broadcasting Company.
256. COFFIN, T. E. (1951). *Television Today: its Impact on People and Products.* New York: National Broadcasting Company.
257. COFFIN, T. E. (1954). *How Television Changes Strangers into Customers (the "Fort Wayne Study").* New York: National Broadcasting Company.
258. COFFIN, T. W. (1954). *Why Sales Come in Curves.* New York: National Broadcasting Company.
259. COFFIN, T. E. (1955). "Television's impact on society", *The American Psychologist,* Vol. 10, No. 10, p. 630.
260. COFFIN, T. E. (1959). " 'Total effect' concept in media comparisons", *Mediascope,* February.
261. COFFIN, T. E. (1963). "A pioneering experiment in assessing advertising effectiveness", *Journal of Marketing,* Vol. 27, No. 3, p. 1.
262. COLUMBIA BROADCASTING SYSTEM (1964). "*A Review and Evaluation of Recent Studies on the Impact of Violence*", A report of the Office of Social Research.
263. CROSSLEY, INC. (1952). *National Study of Magazine Audiences.* New York.
264. CUNNINGHAM AND WALSH, INC. (1948–1953). *Videotown.* New York.
265. DEMANT, V. A. (1948). "The unintentional influences of the wireless", *BBC Quarterly,* Vol. 3, p. 135.
266. DEMANT, V. A. (1955). "The unintentional influences of TV", *Crosscurrents,* Vol. 5, p. 220.

267. DOIG, I. (1962). "Kefauver versus crime: television boosts a Senator". *Journalism Quarterly*, Vol. 39, p. 483.
268. DONNAHOE, A. S. (1955). "The impact of television on newspaper reading", *Richmond: Richmond Times — Despatch*.
269. DUGGAN, E. P. (1955). "Children at the television set", *Times Educational Supplement*, November 11th, London.
270. DUNHAM, F. (1952). "Effect of television on school achievement of children" *School Life*, Vol. 34, p. 88.
271. EAST SUFFOLK EDUCATION COMMITTEE (1959). *East Suffolk Children and Television*. Ipswich.
272. ELLIOTT, W. Y. (1956). *Television's Impact on American Culture*. East Lansing: Michigan State University Press.
273. EMMETT, B. P. (1956). "The television audience in the United Kingdom", *Journal of the Royal Statistical Society*, Series A (General), Vol. 119, Part III.
274. FINE, B. J. and MACCOBY, N. (1952). *Television and Family Life*. Boston: University School of Public Relations and Communications.
275. FINE, B. J. (1952). *Television and Family Life: a Study of Two New England Communities*. Boston, Massachusetts: School of Public Relations and Communications, Boston University.
276. FURU, T. (1962). *Television and Children's Life: A Before-After Study*. Japan Broadcasting Corporation.
277. GLYNN, E. D. (1956). "Television and the American character — a psychiatrist looks at television" in William Y. Elliot, *Television's Impact on American Culture*. East Lansing: Michigan State University Press.
278. GORDON, M. (1952). "The adolescent and television", a report on a study by a Coventry tutorial class, in *Times Educational Supplement* of October 3rd, 1952.
279. GORER, G. (1958). *Television in Our Lives*, a report by the *Sunday Times*.
280. GRANADA TV NETWORK (1960). *The effectiveness of Television Commercials*. London: Granada TV.
281. GREENSTEIN, J. (1954)." Effects of television upon elementary school grades", *Journal of Educational Research*, Vol. 48, p. 161.
282. HALLORAN, J. D. (1964). *The Effects of Mass Communication*. Leicester: Leicester University Press.
283. HAMILTON, R. V. and LAWLESS, R. H. (1956). "Television within the social matrix", *Public Opinion Quarterly*, Vol. 20, No. 2, p. 393.
284. HIMMELWEIT, H. T., OPPENHEIM, A. N. and VINCE, P. (1958). *Television and the Child*. London: Oxford University Press.
285. HIMMELWEIT, H. T. (1962). "A theoretical framework for the consideration of the effects of television — a British report", *Journal of Social Issues*, Vol. 18, No. 2, p. 16.
286. HIMMELWEIT, H. T. (1962). "Television revisited", *New Society*, No. 5, November 1st, p. 15.
287. HULL, W. D. (1952). *A Study of the Effects of Television on Communication Habits and Family Routine of Set Owners in Atlanta*, Emory University.
288. INDEPENDENT TELEVISION AUTHORITY. (1958). *Parents, Children and Television*. London: H. M. Stationery Office.
289. JORDAN, J. H. (1950). *The Long Range Effect of Television and Other Factors on Sporting Attendances*. Washington, D.C.: Radio-Television Manufacturers Association.

384   *References and a selective bibliography*

290. KLAPPER, J. T. (1948). "Mass media and the engineering of consent", *American Scholar*, Vol. 17, p. 419.
291. KLAPPER, J. T. (1954). "The comparative effects of the various media", in W. Schramm (ed.), *The Process and Effects of Mass Communication*. Urbana, Illinois: University of Illinois Press, p. 91.
292. KLAPPER, J. T. (1957–59). "What we know about the effects of mass communication: the brink of hope", *Public Opinion Quarterly*, Vol. 21, p. 458.
293. KLAPPER, J. T. (1954). *Children and Television: A Review of Socially Prevalent Concerns*. New York: Bureau of Applied Social Research, Columbia University.
294. KLAPPER, J. T. (1960). *The Effects of Mass Communication*. Glencoe, Illinois; Free Press.
295. KLINEBERG, O. and KLAPPER, J. T. (1960). *The Mass Media: Their Impact on Children and Family Life*. New York: Television Information Office.
296. LANG, K. and LANG, G. E. (1953). "The unique perspective of television and its effect: a pilot study", *American Sociological Review*, Vol. 17, p. 3.
297. LANG, K. and LANG, G. E. (1959). "The mass media and voting" in Burdick, E. and Brodback, A. J. eds. *American Votiong Behavior*. Glencoe, Illinois: The Free Press.
298. LAWTON, S. P. (1950). *When TV Moves in: A Report of a Series of Studies of Changes in Living Habits in Homes When Television Sets are Purchased*, University of Oklahoma.
299. LAZARSFELD, P. F. (1955). "Why is so little known about the effects of television on children and what can be done", *Public Opinion Quarterly*, Vol. 19, No. 3, p. 243.
300. MACCOBY, E. E. (1951). "Television: its impact on school children", *Public Opinion Quarterly*, Vol. 15, p. 421.
301. MACCOBY, E. E. (1954). "Why do children watch television?", *Public Opinion Quarterly*, Vol. 18, p. 239.
302. MAITLAND-CARTER, J. (1961). *The Relation Between Television Viewing Habits and Children's Personality and Social Background*. Unpublished M. A. Thesis, London University.
303. McDONAGH, E. C. (1950). "Television and the family", *Sociology and Social Research*, November, Vol. 35, p. 113.
304. McEVOY, P. (1959). "Media habit survey of Indiana homes", *Journalism Quarterly*, Vol. 36, p. 63.
305. McGEEHAM, J. R. and MARANVILLE, R. L. (1953). *Television: Impact and Reaction in Lexington, Kentucky*. Lexington: University of Kentucky.
306. McPHEE, W. N. (1953). *New Strategies for Research on the Mass Media*, New York: Bureau of Applied Social Research, Columbia University.
307. MEYERSOHN, R. B. (1953). "The role (of a news magazine) in the lives of its Syracuse subscribers". New York: Bureau of Applied Social Research, Columbia University.
308. MEYERSOHN, R. B. (1953). *Television Research: An Annotated Bibliography*. New York: Bureau of Applied Social Research, Columbia University.
309. MEYERSOHN, R. B. (1957). "Social research in television". In *Mass Culture: The Popular Arts in America*. Ed. by Rosenberg, B. and White, D. Glencoe, Illinois: Free Press.
310. MILLS, C. W. and ZORBAUGH, H. (1952). *Report on the Impact of Television in a Major Metropolitan Market*. New York: Plans, Research, Promotion Department, *Puck The Comic Weekly*.

311. Moss, J. L. H. (1952). "Visual aspects of television", *British Journal of Physiological Optics*, June.

312. NATIONAL OPINION RESEARCH CENTER (1950-1957). *The Effects of Television on College Football Attendance.* A series of 8 reports made for the National Collegiate Athletic Association. University of Chicago.

313. NUTTALL, C. G. F. (1962). "TV commercial audiences in the United Kingdom", *Journal of Advertising Research*, Vol. 2, No. 3, p. 19.

314. PARKER, E. B. (1961). "Television and the process of cultural change" *Journalism Quarterly*, Vol. 38, p. 537.

315. PARKER, E. B. (1963). "The effect of television on magazines and newspaper reading: A problem in methodology", *Public Opinion Quarterly*, Vol. 27(2), p. 315. See reference 236 for a reply.

316. PARKER, E. B. (1963). "The effects of television on public library circulation", *Public Opinion Quarterly*, Vol. 27, Winter, p. 578.

317. PAULU, B. (1956). *British Broadcasting.* Minneapolis: University of Minnesota Press.

318. PAULU, B. (1961). *British Broadcasting in Transition.* London: Macmillan.

319. PEARLIN, L. I. (1959). "Social and personal stress and escape television viewing", *Public Opinion Quarterly*, Vol. 23, p. 255.

320. PILKINGTON, H. (Chairman) (1962). *Report of the Committee on Broadcasting.* London: Her Majesty's Stationery Office.

321. POLITICAL AND ECONOMIC PLANNING (1958). *The British Film Industry*, Vol. 24, No. 424.

322. RAIBOURN, P. (1949). "Television and motion picture industry", *Commercial and Financial Chronicle*, Vol. 169, p. 1286.

323. RICHMOND TIMES-DISPATCH AND THE RICHMOND NEWS-LEADER (1955). *The Impact of Television on Newspaper Reading.* Virginia.

324. RILEY, J. W., CANTWELL, F. V. and RUTTIGER, K. F. (1949). "Some observations on the social effects of television", *Public Opinion Quarterly*, Vol. 13, p. 223.

325. ROODY, S. I. (1952). "Effect of radio, television and motion pictures on the development of maturity", *English Journal*, Vol. 31, p. 245.

326. ROSENTHAL, S. P. (1962). "Crime and violence in television programmes — their impact on children and adolescents", *Visual Aids Review*, December.

327. SALTER, A. (1948). "The impact of broadcasting on Great Britain's life and outlook", *BBC Quarterly*, Vol. 3, p. 1.

328. SAMUELSON, M., CARTER, R. F. and RUGGELS, L. (1963). "Education, available time and use of mass media", *Journalism Quarterly*, Vol. 40, p. 491.

329. SCHRAMM, W. (1954). *The Process and Effects of Mass Communication.* Urbana: University of Illinois Press.

330. SCHRAMM, W. (1960). *The Impact of Educational Television.* Urbana: University of Illinois Press.

331. SCHRAMM, W., LYLE, J. and PARKER, E. B. (1961). *Television in the Lives of Our Children.* Stanford: Stanford University Press.

332. SCHRAMM, W. (1963). "The audience for educational television in the United States", in *Studies of Broadcasting* (ed.) by A. Katagiri and K. MOTONO. Tokyo: NHK.

333. SCHRAMM, W. (1964). *The Effects of Television on Children: An Annotated Bibliography of Research.* Paris: UNESCO.

334. SHEATSLEY, P. B., BORSKY, P. N. (1954). *The Effect of Television on College*

Football Attendance. Chicago: National Opinion Resarch Center, University of Chicago.

335. SIEBERT, J. (1954). *The Influence of Television on the Election of 1952.* Oxford, Ohio: Department of Marketing, Miami University.

336. SIEGEL, A. E. (1958). "The influence of violence in the mass media upon children's role expectations", *Child Development*, Vol. 29, No. 1, p. 35.

337. SIEPEMAN, C. A. (1950). *Radio, Television and Society.* New York: Oxford University Press.

338. SILVEY, R. J. (1952). "Viewers, viewing and leisure", *BBC Quarterly*, Vol. 7, p. 31.

339. SILVEY, R. J. (1953). "The Third Programme and its market", *BBC Quarterly*, Vol. 8, p. 164.

340. SILVEY, R. J. (1961). "Giving the public what it wants", *Contemporary Review*, May.

341. SILVEY, R. J. (1962). "Because it's free?", *Contrast*, Vol. 1, No. 3.

342. SILVEY, R. J. (1963). *Reflections on the Impact of Broadcasting*, BBC Lunchtime Lectures.

343. SILVEY, R. J. and EMMETT, B. P. (1963). "What makes television viewers choose?", *New Society*, 14th March.

344. SIMMONS, W. R. and Associates (1952). "Reading time in TV and non-TV homes", *National Magazine Readership Survey, Report No. 2.* New York (Research Department, Crowell-Collier Publishing Co.)

345. SIMMONS, W. R. with ADVERTISING RESEARCH FOUNDATION (1962). *Profile of the Millions, 3rd Edition: At Home Viewing of Evening Television Including Station Breaks.* New York.

346. SIMON, H. A. and STERN, F. (1955). "The effect of television upon voting behavior in Iowa in the 1952 presidential election", *The American Political Science Review*, Vol. 49, No. 2, p. 470.

347. SMITH, J. A. (1947). "Children and the wireless", *BBC Quarterly*, Vol. 2, p. 162.

348. SMYTHE, D. W. (1954). "Reality as presented by television", *Public Opinion Quarterly*, Vol. 18, p. 143.

349. SPROTT, W. J. H. (1946). "The effect of broadcasting on public opinion", *BBC Quarterly*, Vol. 1, p. 110.

350. STEINER, G. A. (1963). *The People Look at Television: A Study of Audience Attitudes.* New York: Knopf.

351. STEWART, R. F. (1952). *Social Impact of Television on Atlanta Households.* Atlanta, Georgia: Division of Journalism, Emory University.

352. STOUFFER, S. A. (1940). "The effects of radio upon newspaper circulation" in P. F. Lazarsfeld's *Radio and the Printed Page*, p. 266. New York: Duell, Sloan and Pearce, Inc.

353. SUCHY, J. T. (1954). "British television and its viewers", *Journalism Quarterly*, Vol. 31, No. 4, p. 466.

354. SULZER, E. G. (1950). *The Pattern of Television's Impact in Lexington, Kentucky.* Kentucky: Dept. of Radio Arts, College of Arts and Sciences.

355. SWANSON, C. E. (1951). "Television ownership and its correlates", *Journal of Applied Psychology*, Vol. 35, p. 352.

356. SWEETSER, F. L. (1953). *School Grade Families Meet Television.* Massachusetts: Department of Sociology and Anthropology, Boston University.

357. SWEETSER, F. L. (1955). "Home television and behaviour: some tentative conclusions", *Public Opinion Quarterly*, Vol. 19, No. 1, p. 79.

358. TANNENBAUM, P. H. (1955). "What effect when TV covers a congressional hearing?", *Journalism Quarterly*, Vol. 32, No. 4, p. 434.
359. TRENAMAN, J. (1957). "Books, radio and television" in *The Book World Today* (ed. J. Hampden). London: Allen and Unwin.
360. TRENAMAN, J. (1959). "The effects of television", *Twentieth Century*, Vol. 166, p. 332.
361. TRENAMAN, J. and McQUAIL, D. (1961). *Television and the Political Image: a Study of the Impact of Television on the 1959 General Election*. London: Methuen.
362. TICKER, H. and LEWIS, R. B. (1957). "Television therapy, effectiveness of closed-circuit television as a medium for therapy in treatment of the mentally ill", *A. M. A. Archives of Neurology and Psychiatry*, Vol. 77, p. 57.
363. WARREN, H. C. (1934). *Dictionary of Psychology*. New York: Houghton Mifflin.
364. WILSON, B. (1961). "Mass media and the public attitude to crime", *Criminal Law Review*, June, p. 376.
365. WITTY, P. (1950). "Children's, parents' and teachers' reactions to television", *Elementary English*, Vol. 27, p. 349.
366. YOUNG AND RUBICAM, INC. (1951). *Effect of Television on Other Activities*. New York.
367. ZEISEL, H. (1951). *The Effect of Television on Other Media*, a talk to the New York Chapter of the American Marketing Association.
368. ZORBAUGH, H. and MILLS, C. W. (1952). *A Report on the Impact of Television in a Major Metropolitan Market*. New York: Puck The Comic Weekly.

INDEX